MW01087332

Craig James Calcaterra, Wulf Alexander Kaal
Decentralization

Craig James Calcaterra, Wulf Alexander Kaal

Decentralization

Technology's Impact on Organizational and
Societal Structure

DE GRUYTER

ISBN 978-3-11-067392-0
e-ISBN (PDF) 978-3-11-067393-7
e-ISBN (EPUB) 978-3-11-067403-3

Library of Congress Control Number: 2020951095

Bibliographic information published by the Deutsche Nationalbibliothek
The Deutsche Nationalbibliothek lists this publication in the Deutsche Nationalbibliografie;
detailed bibliographic data are available on the Internet at http://dnb.dnb.de.

© 2021 Walter de Gruyter GmbH, Berlin/Boston
Cover image: kaanates/iStock/Getty Images Plus (Broken Pig)
hidesy/iStock/Getty Images Plus (Piggybanks)
Typesetting: Integra Software Services Pvt. Ltd.
Printing and binding: CPI books GmbH, Leck

www.degruyter.com

Acknowledgments

This book calls attention to the new potential for humanity created not by the authors, but by the pioneers who have built tools and organizations for improving mankind – to foster bureaucratic transparency and social harmony, to protect personal privacy and individual freedom, to build systems based on meritocracy balanced with economic equity. The more famous people already mentioned in this book have had thousands of collaborators who brought us closer to a better future, some of whom have sacrificed everything, from Condorcet to Aaron Swartz.

People who have directly improved various sections of this book, nobly expecting no reward beyond friendship, include Prof. Vadhindran Rao, Brian Woerner, Dr. Juan Estrada, Dr. Axel Boldt, Donna Woerner, Prof. Jigang Liu, Prof. Avner Greif, and especially Jason Burrows.

I am materially and intellectually indebted to Prof. Eric Vermeulen and his wife Ingrid, Prof. Craig Parsons, Prof. Toshiyuki Kono, and Prof. Thomas Hoeren. They invited me to lecture and graciously hosted me and my family in the Universities of Tilburg, Yokohama, Fukuoka, and Muenster during the incubation of this book. My students at Metropolitan State in CSCI 690 and MATH 490 oriented my understanding of the talents of the future generations. I've learned invaluable lessons from them all that rounded out my thinking and writing.

Finally, my wife, Karen, is an uncredited co-editor. In addition to being the initial sounding board to many of the ideas, she reworked several sections and was instrumental in merging Wulf's work with my own. For many other profound reasons, whatever valuable was conveyed in this book would not be possible without her.

Craig Calcaterra

I am grateful for the support from the University of St. Thomas School of Law (Minnesota) and in particular for the School's approval of my request to write this book during my fall 2019 semester sabbatical. Without the sabbatical, it would not have been possible to find the time and peace of mind needed to accomplish this book.

This book presents not just a theoretical concept. Many of the ideas presented herein have significant practical implications for the future of decentralized computing, the common good, and the human race. Because of the very nature of decentralization, the ideas and concepts presented herein are constantly shifting and morphing depending on their context, application, and environment. I am therefore particularly grateful for the outstanding ongoing feedback and intellectual support from the computer science and developer communities who have helped shape my intellectual journey. Many friends and colleagues have volunteered their feedback, critiques, and suggestions for improvements in the shared intellectual journey toward decentralization.

Finally, I am grateful for outstanding research assistance from Nicole Kinn who was extremely helpful in finalizing the bibliography.

Wulf Kaal

https://doi.org/10.1515/9783110673937-202

About the Authors

Dr. Craig Calcaterra is Professor of Applied Mathematics at Metropolitan State University in Minneapolis. He teaches the full range of undergraduate courses in mathematics and statistics, and graduate courses on functional analysis, fractals, dynamical systems, stochastic differential equations, cryptography, and blockchain architecture. He graduated from the Montana School of Mines with a Bachelor of Science and from the University of Hawaii with a Ph.D. in pure mathematics. He was a foreign expert and visiting professor at Zhejiang Normal University in Jinhua, China, and a Fulbright Scholar at the University of Trento in Alto Adige, Italy. His technical research includes abstract dynamical systems, metric geometry, control theory, game theory, and distributed computing. His personal research interests include global history, anthropology, and religions; finance and economics; and adolescent psychology inasmuch as the research subjects in his household submit themselves to study.

Prof. Wulf Kaal, Ph.D. is a leading expert at the intersection of law, business, and emerging technology. His research focuses on innovation, emerging technology applications, digital assets, smart contracts, technology strategy, crypto-economics, institutional governance design, economic theory of regulation, dynamic regulatory methods, decentralized infrastructure products, and private investment funds. Before entering the academy, Prof. Kaal was associated with Cravath, Swain & Moore LLP, in New York, and Goldman Sachs in London, UK.

   Prof. Kaal advises international policymakers, central banks, digital asset exchanges, conglomerates, medium to large enterprises, law firms, startups, non-profits, decentralized autonomous organizations, and venture capital funds in the US, Asia, and Europe on emerging technology solutions, governance, and digital assets. As an expert witness, business consultant, adviser, and mentor, Prof. Kaal has advised leading (by market capitalization) cryptocurrency projects. Prof. Kaal has not received any form of financial incentives for writing this book.

https://doi.org/10.1515/9783110673937-203

Contents

List of Figures

https://doi.org/10.1515/9783110673937-205

Preface: Two Perspectives

Decentralization increasingly affects business and society. Despite the work that led to this book and continues beyond these pages, the authors count themselves among those who continuously learn what decentralization can offer us. We believe that the journey into decentralization requires an iterative process that questions centralized approaches to otherwise unsolvable societal problems at every level. Beginning to unlearn a lifetime of centralization is the first step into an appreciation for the power of decentralization.

The authors care deeply about the prospect and potential of decentralized systems for the future of humanity. The passion for decentralized societal solutions is motivated by distinct yet supplemental perspectives on decentralization, which have inspired this book.

As an economist and lawyer, Wulf Kaal's scholarship has been motivated by a desire to create functional institutional designs since his early Ph.D. training days as a mentee of a leading scholar on new institutional economics. Over time, Wulf's scholarly interest in institutional design and governance morphed into work on the economic theory of dynamic governance, dynamic regulatory structures, crypto economics, decentralized infrastructure products, and incentive design mechanisms in decentralized systems, including via co-authored articles with Craig Calcaterra.

Craig Calcaterra is an expert on abstract dynamical systems in mathematics who brings a unique skillset to architecture and design mechanisms in decentralized systems. Craig's Ph.D. training in mathematics and particular expertise in control theory and stochastic dynamics gives him a useful perspective for modeling and analyzing global economic and social systems with their diverse moving parts and complex inner relationships.

The authors met when Craig's wife, Karen, decided to go back to school for a law degree and took a class that Wulf was teaching. In his course, Disruptive Innovation, Professor Kaal implored his students to build relationships with more technically proficient people, like computer scientists and mathematicians, because he was witnessing and anticipating the effect of new technologies on the legal profession. Karen thought, "I know a mathematician." After an introduction in which Wulf suggested the problem of using blockchain technology to create a decentralized arbitration platform, Distributed Jurisdiction, Craig decided that his midlife crisis might as well be a swan dive from the ivory tower of math academia into the muck of real life. Four years later we've decided to write a book detailing the insights we've gleaned tackling business and social problems by collaborating with our diverse perspectives.

The journey we've taken together is being taken every day, organically, by broader society. The clean and clear, logically coherent theory of hard science and mathematics needs to reconcile itself with the messy and confusing, logically inconsistent hard realities of international issues of economics and law and social science. The precise tools of computer science are being used and abused by humans, with all their diverse

https://doi.org/10.1515/9783110673937-206

range of motivations – from idealistic generosity to malicious selfishness, from group scapegoating to individual aspiration – together on the same platforms, on social media, in international forums, and in cities around the world as diverse communities are merging in new social permutations.

In this book we hope to share some of the insights we've gleaned from computer science and graph theory, from game theory and category theory, from history and international relations, from social science and economics, applied to our chaotically churning technologically revolutionary moment in the present global business environment and social atmosphere.

What is Decentralization? A Lawyer's Perspective from Wulf Kaal

No two minds will agree on a common definition of decentralization. The word "decentralization" triggers different associations in different people, depending on the totality of their experiences, socialization, and socioeconomic upbringing. On the extreme ends, where one person will see opportunity, development, and a natural evolution, others will perceive risk, destruction, and societal doom.

Most people still see decentralization from the vantage point of centralized systems and hierarchical structures. That is very much understandable. Out of necessity, humans have engaged in centralized thinking since the emergence of tribal societies and throughout urbanization and the industrial revolution to today. Throughout history, people have been subject to the apparent chaos of natural decentralization and sought comfort in centralization. Centralization brings structure to the natural decentralized order of things. Centralization brings control, convenience, and efficiency.

Because of hierarchical structures, centrally organized entities allocate resources with minimal loss of energy and can identify and remove waste in the system. Centralized production methods efficiently reduce per unit costs. Centralized organization of society leads to efficient resource extraction, rent-seeking, and the creation of economies of scale. Yet, increasing evidence suggests that humanity's centralized economic expansion and associated natural resource extraction are unsustainable. Other indicators suggest that centralized organization of society has in many ways reached limitations: the general weakening legitimacy of the public sector; increasing economic decline; disillusionment with existing business, political, and social institutions; inadequate response to emergent geopolitical problems; and global and international pressure on countries with inefficient, undemocratic, overly centralized systems. Even centralized technologies that previously enabled more sustainable solutions encounter capacity issues. For example, the increasing connectivity of society via the internet has resulted, according to some estimates, in the need for decentralized authentication protocols.

Decentralization is saving the world. Decentralized technology and ecosystems are correcting human-created centralized destruction. Humanity's unsustainable centralized economic expansion and associated natural resource extraction are counteracted by decentralized technology solutions. For example, the disillusionment with existing political institutions' ability to address economic hardships that emerged in the aftermath of the financial crisis of 2008–2009 gave rise to a new form of technological decentralization. The Bitcoin protocol emerged in 2009 as an attempt by its founders to provide a decentralized alternative to the shortcomings of the financial system.

Bitcoin and its progeny spawned a slew of additional decentralized protocols and decentralized technology attempts and solutions that provide a gateway to future forms of technological decentralization. The evolution of decentralized protocols, ecosystems, and platforms, in turn, may provide unprecedented democratic forms of organizing business and society and coordinating human behavior. The emergence and proliferation of distributed applications (DApps) in the aftermath of the invention of the Bitcoin protocol in 2009 demonstrate that a nascent market for such applications and consumer demand already exists. Consumer preferences will continue to shape the DApps market and the solutions it may offer for commerce and society.

Unlike other societal phenomena, decentralization appears as a natural default solution for societal issues. Change in business and society is often accompanied by drastic measures and long public debates along political lines. For example, the occurrence of globalization in technology, business, politics, and society, was subject to long drawn-out public debates about the possible effects and risks. By contrast, the decentralization of business and society is mostly a quiet occurrence without much media attention that appears as a default solution based on the existing centralized network infrastructure. Decentralization is incremental and iterative and a natural default solution that is based on existing networks. Existing centralized businesses and business networks are increasingly combined with decentralized elements.

Definition?

An understanding of decentralization depends to some degree on its delineation from its centralized counterparts. In other words, a definition of what centralization in a given context, industry, or field of study means also helps define what decentralization in this context can mean. The definition of decentralization changes based on the kind of decentralization, the industry or field, application, and the overall context. What may apply in the context of political decentralization may not at all be relevant in the context of technological decentralization. Organizational decentralization, market decentralization, societal decentralization, among others, all emphasize different aspects of decentralization. Yet, each different kind of decentralization may have knock-on effects on the others. Accordingly, a definition of decentralization necessitates an inclusive scope that derives from its core characteristics.

Defining decentralization through historically formed centralized perspectives is a contradiction in terms. It undermines the true potential of decentralization. While even fully networked and decentralized systems are still subject to centralized elements, such as the agreement on certain terms and meanings in language, using a centralized understanding of a subject to explain what decentralization of that subject could mean limits the scope and scale of decentralized approaches. For example, decentralization is not just the addition of hierarchical levels in a centralized organization; decentralization is not just the redistribution of centrally organized authority or redistribution of centrally collected revenue; decentralization is not just the delegation of centralized authority to managers on all levels of an organization. Terminologically, decentralization is not just synonymous with delegation, deconcentration, disassortative, devolution, circulation, or partnership.

Even the basic societal norms instantiated in the subsidiarity principle cannot fully encapsulate the essence of emerging decentralization. The subsidiarity principle is a general principle of social organization. It suggests that social and political issues should be addressed at the most immediate level that is consistent with the resolution of the issue. Decisions should be made by the government entity that is closest to the populations affected by a given issue. The subsidiarity principle is deeply rooted in existing legal frameworks and it is a general principle of the European Union. While local government may be closer to the concerns of the people and better able to respond to the preferences of its citizens, subsidiarity alone cannot encapsulate the ontology and desirable outcomes of decentralization.

Technical Delineation

The degree of decentralization can be delineated by distinguishing several core concepts such as logical decentralization, architectural decentralization, and political decentralization. While these core concepts are distinguishable, some overlap is unavoidable.

An example from the legal system helps illustrate the overlapping concepts of logical decentralization, architectural or hardware decentralization, and political or governance decentralization. Both civil and common law are logically centralized as all decision-making power goes back to what the respective legal bodies ordained. For the most part, common law is based on legal precedents created by a diverse body of individual judges. By contrast, civil law relies mostly on a centralized parliamentary or legislative decision-making body. Architectural decentralization is disparate in civil and common law as common law has more decentralized power in the individual courts and jurisdictions that create the precedent. Governance decentralization is low in both common and civil law, as only a limited number of decision-making authorities, courts, and parliament have the ability to make changes to the body of law that apply to all of the law's subjects.

The firm – that is, a traditional corporation – provides another example to delineate logical decentralization, architectural decentralization, and governance decentralization. The firm is logically centralized as a division of the firm would typically break it apart and it would not be able to operate independently as two separate parts. This is traceable to the firm's hierarchical order that creates efficiencies and structure. The firm is also architecturally centralized as it typically is governed through one physically centralized headquarter or office. The governance of the firm is also typically centralized as only a select few can make changes that affect the totality of individuals involved with the firm.

Natural Decentralization

Nature's ecosystem provides an illustration of natural decentralization. The natural ecosystem is composed of the community of living and nonliving organisms whose interaction is facilitated by chemical, biological, and physical processes in sunlight, air, water, soil, plants, microorganisms, and animals. No central organism or system dictates when, where, and how the interactions materialize and how living and nonliving organisms proliferate and evolve.

The natural ecosystem epitomizes the characteristics of decentralized systems. The intelligent order in the natural ecosystem is distributed throughout the system without central coordination. Information on environmental factors that influence organisms' existence and development naturally, filter into the edges of the ecosystem in real time. Random genetic mutation of organisms is further enhanced through dynamic feedback effects on environmental factors that benefit a given mutation and accelerate its survivability in that environment. Mutated and adaptable organisms become more attack resistant in comparison with the original population. In turn, the ability to mutate via feedback effects for enhanced adaptability allows the adapted organism to proliferate more quickly than the original population.

Nature provides systems that create spontaneous order. Nature provides several prominent examples of spontaneous order and coordination of self-organizing behavior. Slime molds, flocks of birds, ant colonies, and schools of fish exhibit emergent and self-organizing behavior in which interactions and feedback effects between self-sufficient individuals create spontaneous order. Unrelated eukaryotic organisms, aka slime mold, are capable of existing without constraints as single cells, but can also congregate to form multicellular reproductive structures. Spontaneous order is less likely to emerge unconstrained from interactions dispersed across a system if the system has a power or information center. Distributed self-organizing systems are nimbler and able to efficiently self-repair at points of local failure through coordination without control.

The natural ecosystem evolved randomly with an inherent order and interdependent structure. Take, for example, how crops grow in nature. Crops grow best where the conditions made available by nature are most ideal. Flora and fauna quasi-randomly interact with each other to effectuate that growth. Flora, that is, plant life, develops in a particular region or time; the corresponding fauna, that is, animal life, supplements that development and grows. Birds take seeds and crops from one meadow to another area. Or, the wind blows certain seeds across vast areas of land until they find more fertile soil, and so forth.

Interoperability and interdependence characterize the development of the natural ecosystem. Flora and fauna are interdependent. Animals cannot develop in a given part of the planet if they do not have access to the right kinds of food that enable their evolution and survivability. In turn, animals enable plants to flourish in parts of the planet where they previously could not exist.

The equilibrium in the natural ecosystem is facilitated by the decentralized coordination of interdependent organisms. The equilibrium in the natural ecosystem is not created by a centralized dictator who examines the needs of nonliving and living organisms. Rather, nature's equilibrium materializes through a balancing of the interactions in chemical, biological, and physical processes. Ecological systems are usually in homeostatis, that is, in a stable equilibrium. If a given part of the ecosystem gets out of balance, the system typically naturally self-corrects. The system corrects small changes, such as the size of a particular population growing too quickly, through negative feedback. The feedback brings the changed parameter in the system back to its original equilibrium. This facilitates that the changed parameter can again correspond optimally with the rest of the system.

The process of mitosis, or cell division, provides a natural precedent and overview of the role of governance in decentralized systems. Mitosis is the process in nature whereby the nucleus of a single cell divides into two identical daughter cells, which thereafter contain the same genetic information and functionality as the original cell. After mitosis, both cells are independently fully functional. Because of apoptosis, that is programmed cell death, cell replacement via mitosis is vital. The purpose of mitosis is growth, cell regeneration, and the removal of worn out or damaged cells. Without mitosis, organisms could not be functional and would die. The cell nucleus, that is, typically a single rounded structure bounded by a double membrane, containing the genetic material, enables the process of mitosis. Similarly, in decentralized systems, information, and any functionality that depends on information, is continuously changing. As parts of system information are being outdated by the naturally changing environment, they need to be replaced to keep the entire system operational. Like mitosis, this decentralized governance process has to be autonomous and automated in the system. Decentralized governance has to be able to evolve and mutate and create new information precedent for the continuous efficient operation of the system. The nucleus of the decentralized system is the information (contained in the code) that constitutes the architecture and incentive design of the decentralized operating system. It facilitates the information exchange.

The standard model of particle physics provides perhaps the strongest argument against natural decentralized evolution. While naturally incomplete, the standard model of particle physics is the most complete model science created to describe the observable physical cosmos. It suggests that the entire physical cosmos can be traced back to a single point. Science has no answers as to what came before. If combined with the theory of natural selection, which suggests that all life on earth could be traced back to a single cell organism, the standard model of particle physics would counteract decentralized evolutionary theories. Yet, single point origin does not counteract the multiplicity of design mechanism in the following evolution.

Nature evolved through natural selection: a naturally decentralized selection mechanism. No centralized authority determines which organisms can survive when and where. Rather, the interaction of the community of living and nonliving organisms by way of chemical, biological, and physical processes and the totality of environmental factors dictates which species survive and flourish. Because natural selection is a complex process involving multiple interconnected causes with adaptation to the natural environment at its core, natural selection involves a given population with distinguishable characteristics. Variability is heritable. Random genetic mutations increase variability. No centralized order determines in what environment certain characteristics are ideally suitable for enhanced survivability. Rather, the population with the traits that are most adaptable and heritable has a natural comparative advantage. The natural selection of the most adaptable and survivable population characteristics materializes without a centralized mechanism. Even characteristics that appeared at the edges of a given ecosystem may be most ideally suited for survivability.

Technological Extension of the Decentralized Natural Order

The natural order emerged through decentralized coordination. Humans centralized parts of the decentralized natural order to enable human proliferation. In turn, increasing evidence suggests that technology enables a decentralized extension of societal organization and human achievement. Emerging decentralized technology could transform the digital universe into a complex adaptive system of the kinds found in nature.

Human utilization of nature provides a prominent example of centralized order in decentralized systems. Throughout history, humanity has been subject to the apparent chaos of nature and sought comfort in centralized control over it. The creation of property rights over the natural order of things enabled centralized efficiency for human achievements. Centralized urbanization provided protection and efficiency from the chaos of nature. Humans centralized parts of the natural order to create economies of scale that would otherwise not be possible within the natural order. For example, to control where the most beneficial conditions allow crops to flourish and result in a significant harvest, farmers try to control the environment and soil that allow their crops to grow optimally. Creating the conditions to grow most of a certain type of crop in the shortest amount of time allows farmers to more effectively control the output of their efforts and create economies of scale that would not be possible within the natural order.

The evolving decentralization of business and society is a form of a decentralized extension of the existing societal organization and human achievement. As organizational centralization reaches natural limitations, decentralized organizational elements become more prevalent. For example, internet-based platform businesses try to make organizational hierarchies flatter to increase creativity and output and instill a culture of "best idea wins." The farthest extension of these ideals is instantiated in the decentralized autonomous organization (DAO), an organization that only exists in code. Similarly, as business reaches natural frontiers, it extends its reach via decentralized structures. Companies like eBay and Amazon provide examples of centralized companies that decentralized the customer experience. These companies use the structure, control, and associated profit optimization of centralized entities and combine it with the bottom-up approach of decentralization in the form of customer reviews.

Decentralized technology is part of a natural extension of the decentralized origin of human tool-making. For example, just as language became a tool for the optimization of human outputs, decentralization can help coordinate and optimize human efforts and outputs. This is exemplified by emerging decentralized technology's ability to remove the inefficiencies and costs associated with intermediation. For example, cost free value transfer via decentralized technologies removes the cost for migrant workers. In 2019 worldwide remittance has replaced foreign direct investment in total value across borders.

Decentralized evolution is an extension of naturally decentralized development. As decentralized solutions morph and proliferate, they follow existing natural network patterns and precedents. Technology-driven decentralized systems depend on an existing infrastructure. Just as predator populations could not evolve in the natural ecosystem without prey, decentralized technology systems cannot evolve without an existing decentralized infrastructure. Generations of increasingly networked solutions enable an evolution of decentralized systems.

Basics of Decentralization

Decentralized systems depend on network effects. Network effects occur when increasing numbers of participants or users in a given network improve the value of network access for the entirety of the users. An example that illustrates network effects for an existing network is the internet. When the internet had very few users it was of limited value. As its user base increased, the totality of users benefitted from an ever-increasing use and application of internet connectivity as products and services on the internet proliferated. Similarly, eBay, the internet-based auction site, proliferated as more users offered their products for auction. The more people offer and bid, the higher the potential prices of products on eBay and the more new sellers are incentivized to join because they see that the totality of users on eBay enables them to sell their products. However, a network's infrastructure can compromise its network effects and associated user benefits.

Intelligence is widely dispersed throughout decentralized systems. Because of the lack of traditional coordination hierarchies and the lack of central intelligence, the information and intelligence in decentralized systems is more dispersed throughout the system. Information and knowledge exchange naturally occur and filter in at the edges of decentralized systems. No guarantee exists in a decentralized system that the randomly generated information is accurate. That is the case on Amazon and on the internet in general where there is no real attempt to clean the data. These are exactly the type of shortcomings future decentralized infrastructure products, such as a decentralized verification engine, need to address.

Information production is localized and subject to feedback effects in decentralized systems. Relevant information occurs randomly at the edges of decentralized systems and its relevance is determined by an initial group of users. The information is then transferred to other peers who realize the relevance of a given piece of information for their own needs. As the application of the information changes, depending on which groups and subgroups of peers in the decentralized network use it, the changed relevance of the original piece of information is then transmitted back to the original information generator who evaluates it and either applies it or further amends it. This feedback constantly updates and optimizes the quality of information.

Feedback effects enable decentralized coordination. The feedback effects in decentralized systems not only update and optimize the quality of information. They also increase the relevancy of the applications of the information. As peers in decentralized systems analyze a given set of information they receive, they also examine the application of this information for their own needs. For example, contributors in Wikipedia are engaged in the pursuit of knowledge in a constant feedback loop with other contributors pertaining to a given entry on Wikipedia. Similarly, the use of computer code as a template for a smart contract enables individual creators to benefit from the input of others. The code originates in a smaller subgroup of a peer-to-peer (P2P) network. The subgroup users examine the applicability of a given computer code template for their own uses. If the code passes muster, it may be included in a slightly changed or enhanced instantiation. The enhancement, in turn, may provide feedback to the originator group, and so forth. The feedback enables coordination of most relevant information.

The values and core belief systems of members provide cohesion and longevity in decentralized systems. For example, contributors to Wikipedia share a common belief in the power of the crowd, that decentralized collaboration for the pursuit of knowledge creates superior outputs. They collaborate because their values and core beliefs in knowledge creation unite them in a common cause.

Independent and autonomous subgroups create the backbone of decentralized structures. Subgroups are formed randomly based on individual members' ability to contribute to the common cause of the group. Members of the subgroup are typically equal and trust one another. For example, Wikipedia members are making contributions to the common cause of knowledge development in a subgroup of individuals that contribute to a particular entry. Each individual has a certain expertise pertaining to the entry. Collaboration is independent and autonomous. Some members write articles, others edit, and still others further optimize the entry. Contributors to Wikipedia trust each other to create and edit entries for the pursuit of knowledge and each is motivated to contribute to the best of their abilities. Norms of behavior evolve organically from the community, supplementing the basic set of rules provided and enforced by Wikipedia to coordinate member conduct and create and reinforce trust in the subgroup.

As decentralized DAOs emerge through decentralized technology, the value systems in DAOs are a determining factor for membership and cohesion. The desire to be connected via a DAO to like-minded individuals has two value propositions. First, individuals elect to join a DAO and thus signal their desire to cooperate in a decentralized network. Second, individuals select their particular DAO based on their values and interests. DAO members will choose to join a DAO if it corresponds with their existing expertise, inclinations, knowledge base, and beliefs.

The apparent intelligence chaos increases attack resistance in decentralized systems. Centralized coordination enables attack coordination because the hierarchical structure allows the identification of a single point of failure. The apparent intelligence chaos in decentralized systems, where information filters in at the edges of the system in real time, allows it to morph constantly. Decentralized systems can very easily mutate because the information flow is optimized through dynamic decentralized feedback effects. That ability to change without central coordination increases the attack resistance of decentralized systems.

Decentralized systems are more attack resistant, allocate information more effectively and use feedback effects for superior learning effects that optimize performance over time. Community and the efficient sharing of resources are more important in decentralized systems.

Centralization and decentralization are foundationally different approaches. Where centralization attempts to make sense of and create order in presumptive chaos, decentralization thrives in perceived chaos. Where centralization creates efficiencies via order, inefficiencies open new opportunities for participants in decentralized networks. Where centralization orders information, and presses it into a certain form, decentralization takes information from random places and utilizes it in new applications. Where centralization limits creativity through preset processes, decentralization frees the creative process. Where centralization creates hierarchies and substructures, decentralization removes hierarchies and structures and reorganizes in new ways.

What is Decentralization? A Mathematician's Perspective from Craig Calcaterra

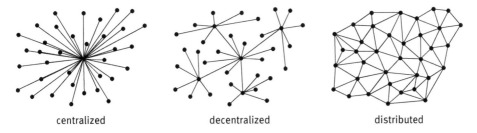

centralized   decentralized   distributed

Figure 1: Common answer to the question, "What is decentralization?"

"The above image says it all."–Rahul Behera, Content Director for Cryptosomniac. com. Top answer March 9, 2018, Quora

No, it doesn't.

Figure 1 may be a good first attempt at explaining decentralization. But it's vague and misleading. The closer you look, the more flawed it is. This figure is reproduced in many explanations of distributed computing, blockchain, or Web3. If you are going to learn anything from this book, at the least let it be how this figure is a shallow answer, and where it is wrong.[1]

Centralized means there is one person who is ultimately responsible for all decision-making – "The buck stops here." Or there is one computer in charge of how information is processed. The first graph in Figure 2 indicates how all the dots (which represent nodes, or members of the network) must answer to the central node.[2]

---

1 The word distributed is often conflated with decentralized, for good reason, because distributed means IT duties (information storage or processing or communication) are spread across many different nodes. But the concepts of distributed and decentralized shouldn't be contrasted. Decentralized networks are always distributed; distributed networks may or may not be under centralized control. So "distributed" doesn't even belong in the same image.

2 A note about nodes: Put simply, nodes are the little dots in any graph. Nodes represent the members of the network. Computer scientists often think of nodes as the different computers connected in a network. The number, variety, and connectivity of the nodes in a system impact how data is generated, the processing power needed, and the diversity of data produced. The variety and connectivity determine how much information can come from a network. Decentralization means redundantly and flatly connected. The more connections a network has, the more resilient it is, and information exchange increases.

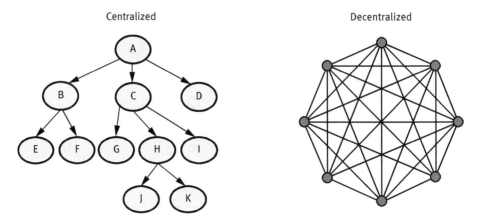

Figure 2: A better answer to the difference between centralized and decentralized. The ideal centralized configuration is a directed tree/hierarchy. The ideal decentralized configuration is a complete, undirected graph.

The ultimate centralized network is a tree graph, for example, an org chart in a company. It has a root to the tree, the leader. And it has branches that take orders from the root.

This left image of centralization in Figure 3 might represent the power structure of a god, which may be a good description of the experience of a typical app when the user is at the owner's mercy.

Figure 3: Diverse structures can display centralized organization, but they always exhibit an ultimate position of authority, the leader or root of the tree.

An org chart or a tree graph representation of a centralized organization plainly displays the advantage of a hierarchical structure. Everyone has a clear role in the organization. Their responsibilities and power are obvious from their position. The carrots and sticks can be clearly arranged, efficiently. In fact, no topology is more efficient for this purpose.[3] Decisions made by a central leader can be carried out quickly and effectively.

Therefore, the best mathematical representation of a centralized hierarchy is a *directed* tree graph. The power flows only one way. In Figure 4, power is represented by the arrows flowing from top to bottom.

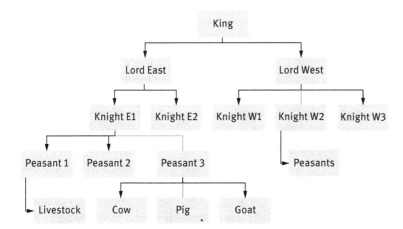

Figure 4: Feudal control centralization; part of the Great Chain of Being.

Hierarchical centralization is optimally efficient for making big decisions that affect the entire organization, and so it has historically outcompeted every other organizational structure, be it corporation or army or government. A hierarchy seems to eventually always emerge, or else the group fails.

Except that's not entirely true. Centralization comes with two major flaws that inevitably lead to its downfall.

First, every centralized organization has a single point of failure. If the leader is lacking in information, or skill, or wisdom, or charisma, the organization is bound to their poor decisions.[4] In this age of voluminous and immediate information, business and social circumstances change much faster than ever before. An organization cannot wait for its leader to make a decision on every new choice the group faces. What is the alternative?

Secondly, the very success and efficiency of a hierarchy leads its members to become dependent on it, relying unquestioningly on the institution's design. The

---

3 Topology is a fancy word for structure, or the pattern of the arrangement of a system. The mathematical meaning is difficult to pin down without more technical definitions, but it roughly means the pattern that underlies a system when you ignore irrelevant details.
4 This is a major reason monarchies have fallen within a few generations of foundation throughout history.

reliable answer to every question is "chain of command." People eventually place so much faith in the structure, it ossifies and becomes rigid. Then, while its structure may still be capable of handling some old, predictable tasks that the chain of command was originally designed to solve, the hierarchy may become too inflexible to reorganize and respond effectively to a novel crisis. (History is the record of the collapse of hierarchies. Examples include the Catholic Church in response to the Protestant Reformation and the Qing dynasty in response to Western imperialism.) What is the alternative?

Decentralized organizations thrive in both circumstances when choices multiply without bound and when novel crises arise.

Decentralized simply means "not centralized," so there is no dominant node, no leader. An example is the architecture of the internet, which was designed so that control is extremely redundant. If any local cluster goes down, the network will be able to continue functioning without a hiccup. No part of the network is crucial. No part of the network is the absolute authority. There is no president of the internet.

The notion of decentralization is captured by any graph that does not have a single node from which all power flows. The extreme form of decentralization is illustrated with a completely connected graph as in Figure 5. The goal of most decentralized networks is to achieve such interconnectivity and flatness of power distribution or complete equality of its members.

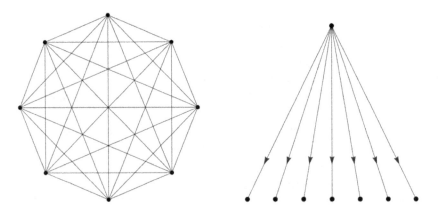

Figure 5: A complete graph with eight nodes versus simple tree with the same number of nodes but far fewer connections – stability versus efficiency.

The Spectrum between Control and Freedom

There is no clear-cut, discrete difference between centralized and decentralized. There is a spectrum between the two that any organization will fall along. The essential differentiator is the freedom of each member in the network.

In the extreme of centralization, nodes/members have no autonomy, no free-dom. Each node has a clearly defined role in the hierarchy, with explicit instruc-tions for every behavior, in how and when they can act. With recent advances in information technology, we can now build dystopias of extreme centralization to a degree that makes George Orwell's society from *1984* seem trivial.

In the extreme of decentralization, every member has complete autonomy and freedom. Each member has complete independence, choosing how and whether to participate at any given time. With the recent advances in technology, we can now build systems that give members autonomy approaching this extreme, which still allows cooperation and harmony.

The most successful organizations choose a hybrid of centralization and decen-tralization, which maximizes the strengths of each.

Dimensions of Decentralization

Networks can be decentralized along many independent dimensions.[5] For example:

1. *Location decentralization*
For example, Wikipedia's network of editors who may occupy any geographical lo-cation in any country with an internet connection. At the other extreme a classical corporation might require all employees work in the same building (see Figure 6).

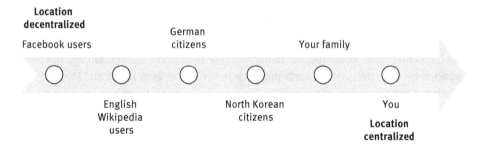

Figure 6: Spectrum of location decentralization.

2. *Control decentralization*
For example, political power, computational power, wealth, fame, etc. As of 2020, Wikipedia still has an ultimate arbiter in its founder, Jimmy Wales, and so it is not

---

5 Cf., Vitalik Buterin, "The Meaning of Decentralization," Medium.com, February 6, 2017. https://medium.com/@VitalikButerin/the-meaning-of-decentralization-a0c92b76a274 (retrieved 5/10/2020).

completely decentralized politically. The English language, on the other hand, evolves without any ultimate authority on what new words can be added. Theoretically, anyone can invent a new English word, so it is completely politically decentralized (see Figure 7).

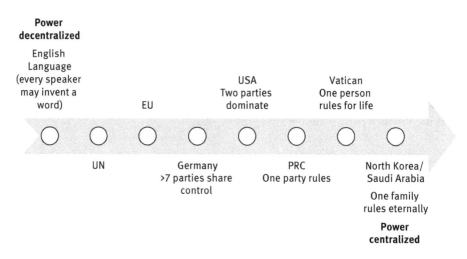

Figure 7: Spectrum of power decentralization.

3. Protocol decentralization

Is there a set of rules that everyone in the network submits to? Do all members follow the same logic and believe the same history? Almost every democracy in the West follows a set of laws more clearly specified than that of supposedly autocratic China, which has no formal constitution; its regular Five Year Plans are actually abstract aspirations for the country that each province interprets as best they can. Alternately, the French language has more rigid rules than English, so French is more protocol centralized than English. On the other hand, the French legal system is less formal than the British – French judges are less restricted by precedent and statute. Black market organizations can fall anywhere on the spectrum, but typically have much less formality in their rules than the English language does. Generally, at least some level of protocol centralization is required for group harmony and efficiency. We think of power decentralization as independent of protocol decentralization, but power determines how protocol is amended and enforced (see Figure 8).

We can further characterize most any quality along a (de)centralization spectrum. Centralized just means concentrated; decentralized means spread out. Events can be centralized or decentralized in time. Colors can be spread out along the light spectrum: a rainbow is color decentralized; a laser is color centralized. The ideals of a community can be focused or vague.

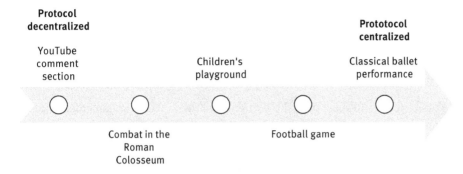

Figure 8: Spectrum of protocol decentralization.

4. Spiritual ideals decentralization

Peoples' beliefs may be more strictly focused or loose. For example, the Jewish religious belief spectrum ranges from ideologically rigid (centralized) to loose (decentralized) as illustrated in Figure 9.

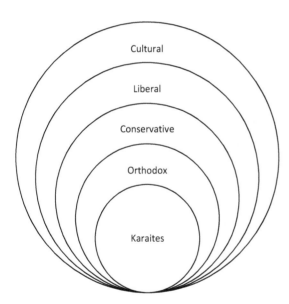

Figure 9: Spectrum of Judaic ideological adherence.

This oversimplified characterization presents the categories from more decentralized to more centralized as:

Cultural Jews – Identify with the culture and history of Jewish people, but not required to believe in any traditional religious tenet, or follow any specific strictures.

Reform/Liberal Jews – Go to synagogue occasionally; believe in the general outline of the religious tenets but allow for alternate interpretations.

Conservative Jews – "Torah was inspired by G.d." Laws strictly observed.

Orthodox Jews – "Torah was written by G.d."

Karaite Jews – Respect only the written Torah with strict fundamentalist interpretation. Reject commentary such as Midrash or Talmud.

Figure 10: Extreme location decentralization.   **Figure 11:** Extreme location centralization.

Decentralization means spread out (see Figure 10).
Abstractly, centralized means concentrated (see Figure 11).

Qualities of Decentralization: Stability, Efficiency, and Versatility

From the abstract perspective illustrated in Figure 10 and 11 we see the fundamental qualities that determine the importance of centralization versus decentralization in any application.

Decentralization is stable. Centralization is unstable. A highly concentrated object, or a structure with a great deal of complicated order, has much more potential to be destabilized. Little changes can result in major structural change. On the other hand, if you disturb something that is extremely spread out, it's still spread out. The more concentrated a structure is, the more unstable it is. The more spread out a pattern is, the more stable it is – like a stool with one central leg versus the more stable arrangement of many legs spread out.

Decentralization is versatile. Centralization is task optimized. Given a specific task, centralized organizations are more effective at the task they are designed for than decentralized organizations. Getting a centralized group to move in a single direction takes much less effort. An optimally centralized structure would have no redundancy. So centralized organizations are more efficient at solving their singular problem. Decentralization is less effective; it generally takes longer to find the right components within its network, which can solve the problem. The more decentralized an organization, the more redundant it usually is. A decentralized organization is less efficient at solving a singular task. Communicating with and convincing each autonomous member of a decentralized group is very energetically intensive – "herding cats."

However, decentralized organizations are more versatile. If you ask the BMW Motorrad company to make a new type of motorcycle, they could obviously complete the job much more efficiently and effectively than the Wikipedia community. But if you want to find a cure for a disease, invent a new type of fusion cuisine, or host a diplomatic summit between African nations, then which group would fare better? Neither Motorrad nor Wikipedia are designed to solve those problems. But the centralized Motorrad organization would waste a lot more resources and probably produce inferior results to Wikipedia's. Wikipedia could tap the potential of its diverse members, harnessing the information at the edge, to identify the appropriate talent to solve a novel problem. It is reasonable to assume BMW's members are not less talented than the average Wikipedia contributor. But the BMW hierarchy would be an obstacle to recognizing which of the many ideas the group might propose to solve the novel problem best. The hierarchy would prevent the identification of talented people if they occur at the lower rungs. And it would resist any changes needed to construct a new hierarchy for organizing the effort. Since Tesla Motors is facing dynamic challenges with inventing new technology and production processes, they have consciously chosen to decentralize many aspects of their organization in order to maximize their versatility, so they can respond rapidly and efficiently to innovations and disruptions.

From a wider perspective, **decentralization is efficient; centralization is inefficient.** In any market, centralization is dangerous. Monopolies ruin the efficiency of a market – they impair its liquidity. The most efficient markets, the most liquid markets, have high transaction rates of many goods moving between many small players. Decentralization makes truth discovery more accurate, more reliable, and more efficient. Think of the difference between 10 competing news media companies reporting on a story versus 1 news company reporting 10 times. Or a physics experiment where a single researcher measures the speed of light 10 times with the same instrument versus 10 different researchers using 10 different instruments. Averaging the results is much more accurate when there are diverse contributors. This spawns the phrase, "the wisdom of the crowd." Decentralization is both stable and efficient. Ever since the writings of 18th century Scottish philosopher Adam Smith, it has been recognized that decentralization makes the wider economy more efficient.

The goal of every organization is to be effective, efficient, and versatile. Organizations select different dimensions around which they are centralized or decentralized. Corporations tend to have centralized power, because they wish to employ a singular strategy to efficiently exploit the circumstances of the market. However, this leads to instability whenever the market swings. A brittle hierarchy may crash before it can reorganize to effectively handle a new challenge. Decentralized organizations don't suffer swings in the market. A sufficiently decentralized organization *is* the market.

Why and How?

When is decentralization preferable to centralization? Why have we recently been hearing about decentralization more and more? What has changed technologically to allow decentralization to outcompete centralization? How can we decentralize our institutions, and why would we wish to?

In this book we will discuss centralized and decentralized organization in the past, present, and future. We will see how these notions have affected society throughout history, using the examples of Ancient Egypt and China to see how stability was maintained with protocol decentralization in the justice system. We will see how the Apaches used political decentralization to withstand successive empires devoted to their downfall. We will explore how a decentralized group of Jewish traders built a business network that thrived thousands of miles along the dangerous and chaotic Silk Road a thousand years ago with rudimentary information technology tools. We will analyze how 18th century Western democratic governmental designs united nations of diverse peoples into decentralized organizations. Using these historical examples, we can understand success and failure of organizations in the present, and how these ideas can predict the course of business and culture in the future.

In particular, we will explore the power of decentralization unleashed by leaps in computational power, information storage, internet communication, and cryptographic security. Decentralized power was leveraged recently by centralized corporations like Facebook and Google and Alibaba, making them the most powerful companies in the world. P2P technologies such as blockchain and distributed hash tables are being used to decentralize power further. Smartphones are empowering individuals worldwide with equalizing computation and communication power. The open source programming movement is fostering a culture of transparency, which results in tangible technological progress through meaningful cooperation, fulfilling the promise of democracy, while increasing security.[6] Using the power of decentralization, we can create institutions that will bring harmony and stability to the new global society that is emerging. Designed wisely, such institutions will protect individual rights and empower us to cooperate for the benefit of all.

---

6 Cf., Linus' law, "Given Enough Eyeballs, All Bugs Are Shallow," named after Linus Torvalds, the inventor of the open source operating system, Linux, coined by Eric S. Raymond, *The Cathedral and the Bazaar: Musings on Linux and Open Source by an Accidental Revolutionary*, O'Reilly Media, 1999.

Overview and Introduction

The Process of Organizational Development

Human group coordination naturally progresses from the first stage, chaos (barbarians ravaging the landscape, "Raahr!"), to decentralized organization ("Let's all agree to band together to defend ourselves from the barbarians"), to centralized organization ("Long live the king").

Abstractly, the first stage is chaos, completely disorganized individualized power centers, or nodes in the network. We imagine chaos as random uncoordinated actions, the first moments after the Big Bang, the static of your television screen flooded with turbulent Brownian motion.

These individualized power centers proceed to decentralized organization when the powers become more correlated, aligned by a common principle, a transcendental goal, an ideal. The individuals may begin to partially imitate each other as they seek to progress toward this common goal. The individual nodes remain autonomous; the network does not have fixed roles for each member. But they are all responding to a higher calling as they unite in purpose. This newfound harmony makes the group more efficient than before, as they find varying ways to collaborate in more complex cooperative behaviors. "The values are the organization."

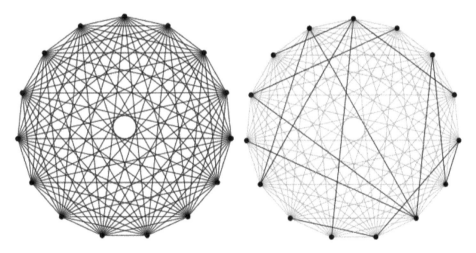

Figure 0.1: Centralized hierarchy emerges from decentralized structure by prioritizing some connections over others.

The final stage is a centralized hierarchy. The harmony and cooperation of the decentralized organization filters the group into an ever tighter and more complex hierarchical structure, raising some individuals into positions of power over others (see Figure 0.1). If successfully completed, a tree structure emerges, a hierarchy,

https://doi.org/10.1515/9783110673937-207

and the organization becomes fully centralized with a single member on top. This filtering process is usually the result of competition. Money is especially efficient in focusing the competition. Rarely, instead, a hierarchy may form from the conscious allocation of power, matching the position to the appropriate individual's talents.

If the hierarchy is successfully completed, all individuals find their positions of power statically fixed and the levers of power clear. Each member has a very limited number of formal connections to the other members of the centralized organization, instead of interacting on a relatively equal basis with all other members like they did when it was decentralized. This end stage is a completely centralized organization, with the top of the hierarchy (or the root of the tree) being the center of power (see Figure 0.2).

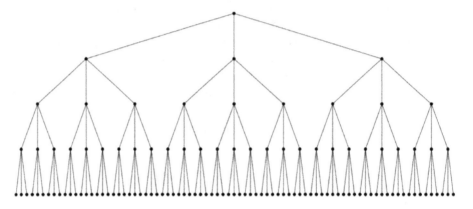

Figure 0.2: Finalized centralized organization with completed hierarchy.

Until there is a single central power at the top of the hierarchy, there is still room for more efficiency, and the organization is incomplete and in flux. Ideally, once a single central power emerges, the organization is optimally efficient and effective in addressing the challenge it was formed under. A centralized organization can rapidly change course, following the single leader at the head of the chain of command. Assumedly, the very best decision-maker is the leader who has the power to move everyone in the organization in unison to respond to those difficulties.

What comes after the hierarchy is complete? If the hierarchy is too rigid, the organization inevitably fails, and the result is a return to chaos. That's why it's called a revolution – because governmental structures have followed this cyclic pattern throughout history. The written traditions of every civilized culture include stories of how the rigid hierarchy rises from chaos, but inevitably shatters and falls back to the chaotic void.

The threats to a centralized organization can be both external and internal. External challenges that can destroy a centralized organization are novel and unexpected changes. Internally, a centralized organization can fail from corruption or friction, from ineptitude at the top or from the discontent of those at the bottom.

The organizational clarity of a centralized hierarchy makes it extremely efficient at the task for which it was originally constituted. However, any new outside challenge to the group may reveal the weakness of the structure. Tree structures of a centralized organization are optimally efficient for communicating orders from a single member. However, if too much power is held in any single office in the hierarchy, decision-making finds a bottleneck that can cripple the organization. A strongly centralized organization leaves no power of decision-making in the outer edges of the organization. "Information at the edge" is not likely to make its way from the bottom echelon (the leaves of the tree) to the highest echelon of power (the trunk of the tree). The central authority makes decisions without full information, so a centralized organization is not well designed to respond to any crisis it hasn't anticipated. If the power structure is particularly crystalline and cannot bend and rearrange its order, it cannot survive the inevitable novel challenges that arise in time when it faces a new organization that has been better formed in the crucible of the novel challenge.

The internal threat to an organization is friction. Friction is simply the inefficient allocation of power, which is an ever-present feature in any hierarchy. By inefficient allocation of power, we mean that if the distribution of power were changed, the goals of the organization could be achieved more easily. Left unchecked, friction can grind a centralized system to a halt. Typical sources of friction are communication bottlenecks, corruption, and concentration of power.

The most common type of friction comes from the natural tendency of a hierarchy to concentrate power at the top. The basic mechanism is "the rich get richer." A more powerful member can use their greater power to gain more power, in any stage, than a weaker member can. Any differentiation between members tends to separate them further as time goes on. Therefore, hierarchies tend to become centralized with a single leader on top if the process of differentiation continues long enough. This also leads to concentration of power. In the limit, if left unchecked, the most powerful member would have 100% of the resources and the others would have 0%. Clearly, getting anywhere close to this distribution is inefficient for the goals of the group. The resulting discontent is the main historical reason for revolt.

Corruption happens when a minority subgroup collects the power or wealth of an organization for its own benefit at the expense of the larger group.[7] Corruption is the type of friction that provokes our greatest moral indignation, as it offends our fundamental sense of fairness.

---

7 Compare this with the definition of rent-seeking, which is the attempt to gain wealth without reciprocally adding wealth or productivity to the group you are participating with.

The more rigid the structure, the more susceptible the organization is to corruption. There is no protocol rigidity at the chaos stage, so there is no opportunity for corruption – since there is no group goal there is no opportunity to subvert it. At the decentralized organizational stage, the group is unified by vague goals and vague protocols that roughly follow the ideals that unite the group. In this case the notion of corruption itself is vague and impermanent, open to interpretation and reevaluation. As a hierarchy begins to emerge, the original occupiers of the varied roles remember their initial motivations for organizing and remain cooperative without relying on formal rules. Their founders' zeal maintains their collaboration. At the final stage of a centralized organization, success of the group serves to fix the hierarchy. The ideals become mundane secular rules. As the hierarchy becomes stronger, the power relationships ossify, and inviolable rules naturally emerge. Once these rules are formalized, they become more important for every internal decision than the previous ideals, which held the group together at the decentralized stage.

Corruption is technically inevitable in any hierarchy, since it is impossible to create a perfectly efficient organization in practice – there is friction in every real system. Further, once the rules are set, the natural competitive impulse means its members will act creatively to intentionally corrupt the system, using the rules and protocols of the organization to one's personal advantage instead of advancing the shared goals of the organization, especially in secular institutions.

Formal secular rules are valuable for ensuring unity in a group with diverse values. Universal rules can ensure equal application to all members, which satisfies our sense of fairness. The primary problem with corruption arises with policing the rules. When the letter of the law is more important than the spirit of the law, then internal competition for power within the hierarchy reveals the best strategy is to push your behavior to the limit of what is acceptable. The easiest rules to police are clear infractions of the letter of the law, but these infractions are not the most damaging to organizational unity. As members constantly probe the edge of acceptable behavior, policing the rules becomes more expensive. The rules become divorced from the shared goals. Relationships become brittle and formal instead of warm and loose. People bristle when violators are "getting away with it." The centralized organization is destabilized.

The ultimate problem with relying on letter-of-the-law governance over spirit-of-the-law governance is that no static set of logical rules can ever succeed in preventing corruption. The Folk Theorems of Game Theory (explained in Chapter 4) prove the point that any rules that can be formally set down can be subverted. Strategies always exist, which follow the rules and yet allow a minority player to profit at the expense of the majority.

The fact that any set of rules can be corrupted illustrates two necessities for the long-term stability of any organization, but especially for decentralized organizations. First, a dynamic governance system must be designed that can adapt the rules to the circumstances. Second, the organization needs to hold to its ideals, its transcendental values. The spirit of the law must override the letter of the law. If the organization is governed by transcendental values – ideals that everyone understands yet they can never practically attain or properly instantiate concretely – then people have less motivation to probe the limits of acceptable behavior. Less policing is then required, making the organization more efficient, as time, attention, and resources can be rightfully directed toward the shared goals of the organization.

Basic Idea

Decentralized organization is a natural stage in the evolution of human cooperation. It is the step between chaos (no organization) and a completed hierarchy (a centralized organization).

A centralized hierarchy is the most efficient architecture for solving the particular limited problem it was designed to address. Centralized organizations have clear lines of power and clear membership rules, which leads to formalized rules of behavior. Power is organized rigidly and clearly, so there is little wasted effort deciding who is in charge of which task while attempting to cooperate. There is also no wasted effort from redundant actions in a perfectly centralized organization – each member would have a unique job that doesn't overlap with any other member's duties. Centralization is an optimal and natural evolutionary solution to most specific organizational problems, under static conditions. Competition is the most common driving force that leads to a centralized structure.

But centralization is not the optimal organizational structure under highly dynamic conditions. The usual strengths of centralized hierarchies become their greatest weaknesses:

1. *Ossification.* Rigid power allocation means the organization can't easily reorganize to adapt to unanticipated challenges from the outside.
2. *Corruption.* Clear rules lead to internal corruption when the letter of the law overrides the spirit of the law and members compete for power.
3. *Blindness.* New sources of information are ignored since they don't have existing lines to the decision-making authorities. Information at the edge is lost.

These three weaknesses play off and intensify each other. In the face of a changing environment, a rigid organization is blind to and ignores new information that is incompatible to the preexisting structure. But, this new information remains highly valuable. And so, an opportunity is born for an individual to exploit this opportunity for personal advantage since the organization was too rigid to take advantage of the opportunity collectively in pursuit of their shared goals. Even if corruption can be avoided in the beginning, the rigidity still leads centralized organizations to catastrophic ends, as failures naturally push members to cling even more faithfully to the rules that have saved them in the past, making the system even more rigid and brittle.[8]

Decentralized organizations, on the other hand, thrive under the types of changing circumstances that break centralized organizations. Information at the edge is naturally incorporated and communicated so the system can adapt to external threats. Decentralized organizations are more stable. They don't crash in response to new external problems like crystalline hierarchies do. Decentralizing allows an organization to adapt to change and chaos. Decentralization, while it may be seen as wastefully redundant, gives every member greater autonomous power. Centralization limits its members' powers, reducing them to mere cogs in the machine. To contrast with our previous example, if new information or a new situation arises, it is more likely to be recognized by someone at the edges (i.e., not blind), who is empowered to act on this information and take advantage of the opportunity (i.e., not rigid). But, because individuals within the organization are motivated by the spirit of the shared goals of the organization (and not by complying with the mundane rules of the organization), they seize the opportunity not for mere personal benefit, but for the collective benefit of the organization (i.e., not corrupt).

The goal of this book is to show that recent advances in technology have given decentralized systems the efficiency they have lacked in previous eras and that allowed them to be outcompeted by centralized systems. And, along with the virtues of responsiveness and resiliency, the newly realized efficiency makes decentralized systems the model for our times. But, we also want to understand whether there is anything that can destroy them. What threatens decentralized systems? And how might decentralized systems ward off these threats?

What can destroy a decentralized organization? Nothing. Decentralized organizations are invincible unless every single member loses their adherence to the values that organized it in the first place, which may happen if they transform and centralize under a different value that takes precedent. Centralization is a natural state that evolves from decentralization under competition if it is not consciously prevented by guarding members' power. It is clear how a centralized organization can be conquered – the single point of failure at the top. How can we prevent an organization from centralizing? How do we protect individual autonomy in a decentralized organization? How do we make our institutions more resilient with decentralization? Different organizations throughout history have struck upon a variety of answers. The goal of this book is to revisit these historical strategies and explain how recent advances in information technology give us new solutions to these problems.

---

8 https://en.wikipedia.org/wiki/List_of_last_stands (retrieved 8/11/20).

History

The cycle from chaos, to decentralized organization, to centralized organization is natural and attends human institutions throughout history.

Advances in information technology explain each historical leap in organizational efficiency and reach. The evolution of ever more complex human societies moves from kinship tribes to regional clans to kingdoms to corporations (religious and secular) to nation-states to empires to the emerging global society. This evolution is enabled at each stage by advances in information technology. Information storage, processing, and transmission allows larger groups of people to effectively connect and cooperate. Information technology has advanced from the spoken word (communication and storage), to complex ideas (processing and storage), to written word (communication and storage), to schools and bureaucracies (processing), to printing presses (communication and storage), to telegraphs and telephones (communication), to digital computers (processing and storage), to the internet (communication, storage, processing).

In Chapter 1 we examine the history and evolution of religion and law, politics and business, from the lens of centralization versus decentralization. We use the examples of history to illustrate how decentralization stabilizes organizations, by ensuring their members' autonomy, which makes the group more adaptable. These historical sketches show how to build decentralization into an organization, detail the natural threats to a decentralized organization, and explain how to defend against them. Ancient Egypt and China were remarkably stable for thousands of years due to the protocol decentralization fostered by their Rule of Virtue legal system. The Apache tribe used political decentralization to survive for hundreds of years against vastly better-equipped centralized empires whose goal was to eliminate their way of life. The Maghribis built a sophisticated decentralized trade network using 11th century information technology, and reputation. Eighteenth century farmers used dynamic governance designs to create the most powerful decentralized organization in history.

Present

Today, many centralized institutions are experiencing the senescence that naturally attends their rigidity, their internal corruption, and their predictable failure to respond to novel external challenges. This is provoked in obvious fashion from the massive cultural and social changes due to rapid technological advancement.

New technology for data storage (cheap hard drives), processing (computers), and communication (telephone and internet) give new tools for enabling centralized and decentralized structures of organization. These new tools make people much more powerful than ever before.

Western democracies are still using the structures developed decades or centuries ago and lack any formal interaction with this new data stream. Private, centralized companies are adapting much faster than our aging centralized legal and governmental institutions to leverage the power of the latest leaps in information technology. The most obvious ways to adapt our supposedly decentralized democracies to these new technologies of information storage, processing and transmission would be:

- Polling constituents – on past, present, and future issues. Put polls in context – reveal how many constituents from which districts voted in which way – how many didn't vote. Mandate the goal of providing intuitive user interfaces (UIs) for accessing statistical knowledge, so people can parse the data easily. (information processing)
- Stack Exchange-like websites (or Reddit or Facebook) for people to broadcast their opinions and upvote/downvote other people's posts. Require open source algorithms for how information is filtered, so analyses can be made, and everyone can understand if and how the system is being gamed by special interests. (information transmission)
- Bureaucratic transparency – Build open source websites detailing executive expenditures. Make it easy to access your representatives. Use a uniform accounting scheme of the official work all legislative representatives have done (speeches they've made, votes, meetings with lobbyists, constituents, transcripts of those meetings). A radical proposal would make it illegal to speak about public matters while a politician is in office unless they are on the record, holding politicians to the professional standards of lawyers and equity investors. Mandate the goal of making public data on justice easier to access, to expose more information on our institutions' integrity or corruption. (information storage)

These first simple steps provide some examples as to what could potentially lead to more formal interactions with decentralized democracy, such as binding referenda on basic expenditures, which could revitalize our institutions. Nineteenth century technology naturally limited our formal democratic interactions with government to biannual elections of representatives. Twenty-first century technology is completely different; society is different. And our governmental structures need to change. How do we save democracy? Simple. Make our societies more democratic.

These changes would be technologically trivial to implement, cutting and pasting existing open source projects. This is quite unlikely to happen naturally, however, without a powerful catalyst – coherent social demand. Large, decentralized networks, like national democracies, don't make fundamental changes easily. Stability is their primary quality.

Meanwhile, in a testament to the power and effectiveness of centralization, capitalist companies are rapidly innovating new uses for this torrent of decentralized information from traffic (virtual and IRL, such as Google and Baidu, and Google Maps), marketplace transactions (Amazon, Alibaba, and Airbnb), social networks (Facebook and Tencent), and economic talent (gig economy industries like Uber and UpWork). Web 2.0 has built the UIs necessary to leverage the talent of the masses with these tools.

Before advances in blockchain tech and cryptographic security, such companies needed a centralized authority for several reasons. A dictatorship was necessary for governance of the network because more sophisticated governance architectures, such as democracies, lacked the ability to govern efficiently. With 19th century technology, millions of members could only be practically polled on a yearly basis. In that case, centralized institutions were necessary, since they are far more efficient in communicating with members, storing the relevant information and history of the company, and filtering and curating the information to reward members appropriately. But information technology has changed, giving us new options for the governance of large networks of participants.

The technologies and technological trends that enabled the advances in telecommunications, internet proliferation, e-commerce, the digital transformation of society, social media, and the Internet of Things (IoT) have inaugurated unprecedented societal network capability. These advances are gateways for the deeper structural reform of society.

Decentralization tools in social media demonstrate how networked communication structures allow social groups to cooperate and co-create at an unprecedented level, transcending previous barriers due to nationality and socioeconomic status. Web3 is the vision of building tools for decentralizing our economy in a similar way.

Web3 initiatives such as Bitcoin, Ethereum, IPFS, and many others are building some of the tools necessary to allow decentralized organizations devoted to business goals. The technology is advancing to the point that fully decentralized organizations are beginning to compete with centralized organizations in profitable enterprises. And decentralized organizations have fundamentals that are superior in our rapidly changing global society. Unlike centralized organizations, decentralized organizations can give members individual autonomy and privacy, they maintain network stability under changing conditions, and they thrive under information transparency.

Future

The stated purpose of Web3 is to build the tools to empower decentralized networks to compete with traditional centralized networks, using blockchains, distributed hash tables, and more complex P2P architectures.

Bitcoin and Ethereum are building decentralized money and decentralized automated business contracts (smart contracts). These networks are worth hundreds of billions of dollars, not because people are using them, but almost entirely because of speculation. People see the future value of these tools. Their future value is the dream that people will use them to build DAOs.

DAO is the Web3 acronym for decentralized autonomous organization. "Autonomous" is to distinguish DAOs from less decentralized organizations (like Wikipedia), which still have ultimate centralized control in an owner (like Jimmy Wales, co-founder of Wikipedia) who can finalize contentious decisions among its members. The autonomous aspect of a DAO stems from its programmed governance system through smart contracts. A DAO is ultimately democratic, instead of having a benevolent dictator behind the scenes to efficiently correct course during black swan events.[9]

Marketplace DAOs can now supply level playing fields where nobody is in charge (unlike Amazon). Decentralized finance (DeFi) uses blockchain technology to provide financial tools such as banking, equity investment, and derivatives trading. DeFi promises to empower people with broader financial inclusion with new financial tools with lower transaction costs and open access across borders.

Social network DAOs and web traffic can be organized on a P2P architecture, where members opt in or out of participating in data filtering and curating. Individuals can completely control their information and share it precisely with whomever they wish (unlike Facebook or Google) and can be remunerated fairly for the effort.

Ridesharing applications and other gig economy industries can be completely managed and governed with P2P reputational systems (unlike Uber), so membership in a network gives appropriate ownership of the network, as opposed to the asymmetry of merely being a user.

The Web3 dream of the future is for DAOs to replace centralized structures with more efficient and adaptable groups throughout our society and economy.

Two important tools have been built, decentralized money (Bitcoin) and decentralized contracts (Ethereum). But it won't work until eight more decentralized institutions are built that people use to do business. Money and contracts are worthless in business with barbarians who can't be trusted to keep a bargain. To do business, we need a system where reputation means something. We have the bones of such structures, but we need to put the flesh on the animal. Then it can dance.

Let's begin.

---

9 Everyone knows there are only white swans. There is no such thing as a black swan, and there is no reason to look for one – until somebody sees one. Then everyone says their existence was obvious. A black swan event is a unique and unpredictable event, which has a major effect on the economy. The theory was developed by Nassim Taleb, who argued these events have a dominant role in human history, but that fact is not properly recognized, because humans naturally rationalize the effects afterward as predictable. Examples include the effects of World War I, the internet, or the 2020 COVID-19 pandemic in changing global economies.

Chapter 1
Historical Sketches of Centralization Versus Decentralization

Each advance in information technology has led to an improvement in humanity's ability to organize.

It is easy to observe the effect of these advances when power is centralized: you follow the choices of the central leader. Most recorded history is about centralized hierarchies. The "Great Man" version of historiography records the history of the decisions of kings and queens. It's a popular perspective for historians, because it is easier than explaining how the more important story is the litany of changes in "little people's lives." The psychological state of Henry VIII is endlessly debated, even though changes in barrel makers' techniques and their trade organization better explain why we live the way we do today. The individual is easier to recognize and relate to than abstract decentralized trends that often are unnoticed even to the people living through them.

Advances in organization mean we can cooperate more efficiently in our use of energy, making us more materially wealthy. The progress of information technology coincides with the progress of human power over their environment. The more efficient our system of communication, the larger the group that can be organized, the more powerful and efficient the group.

Groups cooperate most efficiently when there are clear rules for cooperation. Hierarchies are the most efficient pattern for creating a control structure in a group. They are used in large and small scales from an army to an emergency phone tree in an elementary school. They form naturally when power structures emerge as people differentiate themselves into more and less powerful members of a group. If competition exists, for instance, then people come to be arranged in a hierarchy. If the competition continues long enough, if there is enough organizing energy, the natural end result is a complete tree structure.[1]

---

1 This natural evolution of a complex organized structure is the basis for the confusion trapping many conspiracy theorists. We are not saying there are no conspiracies, in fact the list of genuine conspiracies includes every historical revolution (see also https://en.wikipedia.org/wiki/Contract_killing#Notable_cases retrieved 8/11/20). However, there is no need to explain events by positing the existence of extremely powerful actors who control history. Power organizes naturally to make history without guidance. "The main thing that I learned about conspiracy theory, is that conspiracy theorists believe in a conspiracy because that is more comforting. The truth of the world is that it is actually chaotic. The truth is that it is not the Iluminati, or the Jewish Banking Conspiracy, or the Gray Alien Theory. The truth is far more frightening. Nobody is in control. The world is rudderless."—Alan Moore

https://doi.org/10.1515/9783110673937-001

As a hierarchy organically arranges itself, redistributing power and wealth via competition, an exponential pattern of power centralization emerges. This is referred to as the Matthew principle, where "the rich get richer and the poor get poorer."[2] Essentially, someone who is more powerful is better able to secure more of any power available. They're more aware of whatever power is available, they have better connections and resources for accumulating power, and they're better practiced at acquiring it. As the hierarchy becomes more entrenched, this exponentially distributed power structure crushes those at the bottom, leaving minimal power and wealth for the vast majority of people. The discontent of the majority is the first destabilizing force of a centralized organization.

At the same time the very success of the hierarchy may lead its power relations to become more rigid. This rigidity can become brittle when power relations become entrenched with secular laws. Under a codified system of logic-based rules, the letter of the law tends to override the spirit of the law. Rigid hierarchies are unstable and inevitably fall, eroded from internal corruption or novel external challenges that the hierarchy is not flexible enough to adapt to. These are the second and third factors that explain why centralized organizations are unstable. Rigid competitive hierarchies with secular laws face internal corruption as members' optimal strategy is to push the rules to the limit. From the outside, any change in the problems the group faces can find the hierarchy unready to face the new challenge.

This explains the sequence of revolutions throughout history. Both the extreme power inequality and the rigidity of centralized hierarchies historically have inevitably led to collapse. Rigidly centralized organizations are seen as unstable on a historical scale, compared with decentralized organizations.

Ancient Egypt and Imperial China were relatively stable for millennia despite strong political hierarchies. What distinguished these civilizations from the many others that rose and fell around them? Their stability was due to protocol decentralization.

Humanity's ability to organize in more sophisticated networks has advanced alongside improvements in information technology. Information technology progressed from the beginnings of symbolic language (ideas and beliefs, mysticism, ideas about ideas) and proto-writing (probably before homo sapiens evolved), then written symbols (Sumeria & Egypt, ca. 5,000 years ago), then mass printing (especially in China, which used stone rubbings in 200 BC and relatively durable clay moveable type in 1100 AD; later in Germany with the improved metal moveable type

---

2 This principle is named after the passage in the New Testament Book of Matthew: "For unto every one that hath shall be given, and he shall have abundance: but from him that hath not shall be taken away even that which he hath." Matthew 25:29, King James Version. The same principle leads to Zipf's Law, Price's Law, exponential growth, unrestricted population growth, compound interest, or economies of scale.

in 1440 by the goldsmith Gutenberg). The introduction of electronic information technology with the telegraph brought humanity to the contemporary era, with global light-speed information communication (Europe, America, and Asia were connected before 1870).

In broad terms, information technology is broken into three components: information storage, information processing, and information transmission. Memory, computation, and communication. These three components are not clearly separated. For example, how you store information in memory determines how efficiently and effectively you can process and transmit information. Your means of processing determines how and what you store in memory. How information is stored determines how it can be transmitted and shared. How you store and share information determines how it can be filtered and processed.

Developments in information technology accompanied the rise and eventual downfall of empires. In Imperial China the fantastic success of the hierarchy in fostering economic cooperation gradually made its bureaucracy more rigid. China invented the printing press and used it to centralize power – politically with uniform edicts and economically with the first printed money. Eventually, the hierarchy couldn't respond to internal corruption and external threats such as Mongolian, Manchurian, and Western imperial invaders.

Europe started its own printing presses a few centuries later. Instead of using the press to centralize power like the Chinese Empire did, Europe's use of the printing press greatly decentralized knowledge. The resulting cultural transformation led to the collapse of the centralized powers. The highly hierarchical Catholic Church lost its hegemony in Europe in the face of the Protestant Reformation, which may be attributed to the dissemination of bibles to the public. Eventually the entire European aristocracy collapsed and was replaced by greater power decentralization with democracy. But the decentralized organization of scientists, which has thrived since the advent of the printing press, has been remarkably stable, unified by an adherence to the value of objectively verifiable truth.

In this chapter we explore these ideas starting with early hominids through Imperial China and the American Revolution. The primary goal is to witness the central-decentral dichotomy in its evolutionary context to understand more fully their effects on organizations. We will witness the stabilizing effect of decentralization in context and the greater temporary effectiveness of centralization. The "unstoppable power of decentralization" is threatened by unregulated competition for profits, but can be maintained in the most extreme circumstances by a secure and meaningful reputational system. Analyzing modern Western democracies, the largest DAOs ever assembled, shows networks of members with diverse values can be united with protocol centralization, and its destabilizing effect can be ameliorated by power-decentralization through dynamic design of governance. In the long run, organizations are held together by their transcendental values.

A secondary goal of the chapter is to combat our historical myopia. There is a natural inclination to accept the fallacy of uniformitarianism, the idea that the institutions and cultures we have today are natural and have always been this way, and will always be this way. History teaches us how dynamic societies have always been. Revolutions demark the regular switch between the forces of centralization and decentralization in power, different legal protocols, and different ideals. This dynamic perspective helps us better understand what freedom and power we have to reorganize our social networks.

From Hominids to Imperial China

Prehistory of Information Technology

Centralization and decentralization are two qualities of power. A simplified, cartoon model of centralized power would be a static org chart at a corporation. This hierarchical pyramid structure leads to fewer and fewer leaders at each level with an ultimate leader at the top (see Figure 1.1).

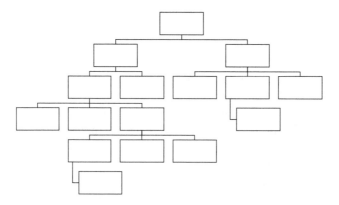

Figure 1.1: Corporate org chart illustrates centralized hierarchy.

Such powerful centralization was not universal throughout history. Anthropological theories argue the origin of kingship, but the very tentative consensus from the archaeological record indicates the type of absolute rulers attended by a bureaucracy enforcing their rule did not exist much before 5,000 years ago. The Tomb U-j at Abydos about 3320 BC identifies the first ruler of Dynasty 0 as (possibly) the pharaoh Menes who unified Upper and Lower Egypt. There were certainly smaller kingdoms before that, but we have no earlier evidence of large bureaucracies. Before Menes, local leaders exerted more or less power over tribes since before the existence of homo sapiens. Pack hierarchies are evident in many species of social animal.

Before large scale kingship, the decentralized collection of warlords exercised far less centralized power, and humanity's relatively weaker ability to organize meant we controlled measurably less energy.[3] Technological evolution in symbolic language, and later, writing, were crucial ingredients necessary for the development of the strong centralization that attends kingship. The theory of behavioral modernity posits the idea that homo sapiens made advances in information technology on the mental level with improved language 500,000 years ago, leading to sophisticated human organization around 50,000 years ago.[4] The theory claims abstract language led to improved abstract thinking, planning depth, and symbolic behavior such as art. With these new information technology tools (transmission, storage, and processing of information), people were capable of more complex cooperation, leading to more sophisticated societies, which eventually led to the first political hierarchies.

These early societies that emerged 50,000 years ago are what we would crudely refer to as cavemen. They are distinguished from earlier groups of hominids since they left a record of organized coordination that is maintained continuously throughout generations. These cavemen invented tally sticks and cave paintings. Besides words and ideas themselves, these tools are the most primitive information storage technology known. The Lebombo bone, dated to 40,000 BC, is the first known example of a tally stick. Tally sticks were used even into the 20th century in illiterate communities in Europe and Asia, to record economic transactions and ownership using notches on a piece of wood. The Chauvet cave holds the earliest picture drawings that have been found, dated to 30,000 BC. They record information on local animals and the earliest known religious objects.

Particularly important is the symbolic thought necessary for abstracting the notions of gods and sacrifice and worship that would lead to the centralization of thought and coordination of action necessary to unify large populations beyond local kinship groups. Such universal spiritual beliefs give people the harmony required to create institutional order and eventually practical secular laws.

In fact, sacralized law has been shown to generate more stable and successful institutions than secular beliefs. Sosis explains "religious communes are more likely

---

3 For an innovative perspective on the historical progress of humanity's technological ability to harness energy, see Vaclav Smil, *Energy and Civilization: A History*, The MIT Press (2017).

4 The dating is still controversial, and some researchers argue these individual behaviors may be more than 400,000 years old. Francesco D'Errico, "The Invisible Frontier: A Multiple Species Model for the Origin of Behavioral Modernity," *Evolutionary Anthropology*, 12(4), 2003, pp. 188–202. It is argued that the effects are more consistently visible in the archaeological record after a watershed moment around 50,000 years ago when people were first able to organize in stable groups of a size large enough to maintain complex traditions. Adam Powell, et al., "Late Pleistocene Demography and the Appearance of Modern Human Behavior," *Science 324*, 2009, p. 1298. Available at http://doc.rero.ch/record/210393/files/PAL_E4401.pdf (retrieved 6/22/20).

than secular communes to survive at every stage of their life course."[5] One mechanism proposed to explain the discrepancy is costly-signaling theory. The idea is that sacrificing to a religion signals commitment to the group, which solves the free-rider problem. This falls under the field of evolutionary psychology of religion, which is obviously quite contentious. There is a more basic mechanism that explains the success of spiritual values for unifying groups.

From an abstract perspective, transcendental values are more stable unifiers than formal secular rules. The Folk Theories of Game Theory (see Chapter 4) illustrate the obvious point that it is not possible to construct a perfect secular constitution, that is, a complete set of static rules that will account for all positive and negative behaviors to permanently govern a group profitably. The Folk theories demonstrate that however the rules are written, strategies exist that follow the rules yet profit the individual at the expense of the group. (See, e.g., the Nobles vs. Peasants game in Chapter 4.) When a law is written down rigorously, specifying precisely what is acceptable and not acceptable, people are obligated by competition to find the most efficient behavior possible within those rules. Such behavior is often located right on the boundary of what is permissible. This erodes stability as excessive effort is then required on policing the laws. On the other hand, a transcendental value by definition is not rigorously formalizable. When people organize around an eternally unobtainable ideal without clear boundaries, they are less likely to probe the boundaries of what is acceptable.

A more traditional spiritual tradition explains a very simple and practical method for uniting disparate members in a large stable community. An ascetic Orthodox monastery on Mount Athos in Greece has a continuous tradition from at least 800 AD. How have they managed to unite devotees from different cultures? They've maintained an open policy for new members (any Orthodox male is accepted regardless of national origin) yet they have survived for 1,200 years during numerous wars and changes in government. This cenobitic (communal but hierarchical) monastic order's solution is to pray together, work together, and eat together.[6]

We will borrow this strategy as a plan for harmonizing decentralized autonomous organizations (DAOs) using blockchain and other P2P internet technology in Chapter 4. An ideal DAO has an open membership policy for any anonymous person from any culture on the planet. How can they maintain harmony? They must share a transcendental value, work toward a common purpose (even if it's simply profit), and share fairly in the spoils of the work.

---

5 Richard Sosis, "Religion and Intragroup Cooperation: Preliminary Results of a Comparative Analysis of Utopian Communities" (PDF). *Cross-Cultural Research*, *34*(1), 2000. Available online at https://pdfs.semanticscholar.org/450a/edd9d7e55e9237ee092b0a86b3af986b46bf.pdf (retrieved 5/18/2020).

6 Graham Speake, *Mount Athos: Renewal in Paradise*, Yale University Press, 2002.

Protocol Centralization in the Law

The earliest historical evidence of law is found in Egypt. Their system was closer to our sense of holding to the spirit of the law instead of the letter of the law. The remarkable stability of Egyptian society, for more than 3,000 years, testifies to how successful prioritizing transcendental values can be, compared with a system based merely on formal rules.

The Ancient Egyptians had a strong sense of nationalism, believing that Egyptians were the best people because they had the best model of behavior deriving from the best possible spiritual ideals. (This is naturally mirrored in nearly every national identity; the Chinese and Romans are two other exemplars of such attitudes, arguably because they have had the most successful empires.) The Ancient Egyptian term Maat encompasses this collection of ideals, meaning roughly truth, balance, order, harmony, law, morality, and justice. Maat is also the goddess who upholds and polices society according to these ideals. She also regulates the stars, the seasons, and even the other gods.

Though Ancient Egypt was politically centralized in the sense that the pharaoh was the supreme hierarch, it was protocol decentralized in the sense that people were not held to explicit formal rules and a legal constitution. The application of the law was vague and applied by autonomous priest-judges who were bound by their creative interpretation of Maat, instead of precedent and formal rules. Though the Egyptians had developed writing on papyrus by 2600 BC, and therefore had the technology to implement formal permanent rules, they avoided this type of protocol centralization and enjoyed the longest period of stability of any empire in history.

Experiments with letter-of-the-law, protocol-centralized legal systems were far less stable in nearby Mesopotamia. Around 2900 BC, cuneiform writing that represented syllables was invented. This was a great leap in information storage and transmission, using abstract symbols pressed into clay (pictogram systems are about 3 centuries older).

We don't have a record of formally prescribed laws until about 600 years later when King Urukagina's code was first set down in 2300 BC, five centuries before the famous Code of Hammurabi. The stone cone on which the Urukagina code is printed is the perfect symbol of protocol centralization (see Figure 1.2). The cone begins by criticizing previous rulers "since time immemorial, since life began"[7] for undermining the original divinely decreed code. Urukagina's laws are reforms of previous failed Mesopotamian kings' style of centralized government, which led to abuses of those at the bottom of the hierarchy. The reforms revoked the centralized control of many industries: "He removed the head boatman in charge of the boats. He removed the head shepherd in charge of the asses and sheep. He removed the

---

7 Jerrold S. Cooper, *Clay Cones La 9.1 Presargonic Inscriptions,* New Haven, CT: The American Oriental Society, 1986.

Figure 1.2: Code of Urukagina. Louvre Museum AO 3278. Picture by Gary Lee Todd in public domain.

head fisherman from the fishing places. He removed the silo supervisor from control over the grain taxes of the guda-priests. . . . He removed the palace official in charge of collecting the tax." The code ends with the first legal recognition of basic equality and freedom: King Urukagina "freed the inhabitants of Lagash from usury, tax debt, hunger, theft, murder, and seizure" of their property and persons. "Widows and orphans were no longer at the mercy of the powerful." Nevertheless, Urukagina's rule lasted only eight years before he lost his brittle centralized kingdom, whose laws were set in stone.

The next evidence we have of a legal code comes 300 years later, the Code of Ur-Nammu. This gives the first evidence of a legal text containing formal logic. For example, Law #32 reads:

> 32. IF a man had let an arable field to another man for cultivation AND he did NOT cultivate it, turning it into wasteland, THEN he shall measure out 3 *kur* of barley PER *iku* of field.[8]

This law holds all the mental technology needed to build today's digital computer-programmed legal smart contracts on blockchains. The formal theoretical pattern is

---

8 Ibid. Capitalization mine.

the logical conditional IF (violation) THEN (punishment). Moreover, this law uses the logical operators, AND and NOT. By serially chaining these three functions together, the most complex business logic possible, for organizing any imaginable business arrangement, can be contained in a single legal contract. With the final addition of the mathematics of addition (3) and division (PER) at the end of the law, the people of Ur demonstrated all the logical sophistication required to use our modern smart contracts four millennia later.

These experiments in protocol centralization continued in the West with periodic revolution every century, culminating in the development of Roman law from 450 BC to 529 AD. The use of Latin phrases in contemporary courtrooms in the West attests to the influence of the system of Roman law until the present day. However, the regular changes in the languages and nations using these laws in the intervening centuries display their failure to maintain stability alone.

China and Europe

Psychological Centralization in China and Decentralization in Europe

The primary staple crops of Europe and China have influenced their respective cultural centralization. People in Europe farm primarily wheat and live in lands that couldn't support the same population density of China, where they farm primarily rice.

Wheat crops require individuals to harness animal and machine power. People work the land alone, behind an ox and plow. The basic European unit of society separated into individual family farms with large distances between neighbors, because wheat requires less than half the energy to cultivate compared with rice.

Rice farming requires intensive use of the land. Periodically through the year a large number of people are required to unite to cooperate in the planting and harvesting. As opposed to wheat, which is nourished by rainfall and sunshine, rice requires manual transplantation and regularly maintained irrigation. These major tasks are done by hand without the use of animals or machinery. It requires many people working closely together. It requires the community to come together for the job at a moment's notice, whenever the weather and the crop dictate. You need to rely on your neighbor. Communal harmony is essential for survival.[9] Value and protocol centralization attends these communal forces. Asian communities tend to be more geographically, protocol, and value centralized than European communities.

---

9 For a more nuanced assessment of the differences than the oversimplification presented here, see Shihu Hu and Zhiguo Yuan, Erratum: Commentary: Large-scale psychological differences within China explained by rice vs. wheat agriculture, *Frontiers in Psychology*, 6, 489, 2015.

Another contributor to the cultural bifurcation between East and West is language. European languages tend to be highly analytic. The many Chinese languages include some of the most synthetic languages on earth – especially Mandarin, the dominant language of China. An analytic language separates each variation on an idea into various words. For example, there are literally hundreds of different words and phrases that parse the idea of "big" in English.[10] Synthetic languages unite several ideas with the same word. For example, the Chinese word *ma* can stand for hundreds of diverse meanings for which English has completely different words, such as horse, mother, toad, hemp, wipe, scold, dragonfly, ant, grasshopper, agate, etc. Still, the English language is far more analytic and separating than that difference conveys, because each word in English can take on many different meanings depending on the tone used when speaking – anger, joy, disgust, sarcasm, etc. At the opposite end of the spectrum, Mandarin is a tonal language, meaning you must control your tone to speak the word. This means there is less possibility to inflect the meaning of the word with how you say a word. For instance, the Chinese famously do not use sarcasm. Word order in English is extremely important for generating new meanings. A common exercise for teaching adverbs in elementary school is to pick any basic sentence and insert the word "only" in different places in the sentence. Try it on the sentence, "She told him that she loved him."

The psychological ramifications are that it is easier to draw distinctions in an analytic language like English, whereas it is more natural to come to consensus using a synthetic language like Mandarin. It is natural for English speakers to have a more contentious culture, while Mandarin is more likely to evolve with a culture that encourages harmony.

Both the farming systems and the languages reflect the personal differences observed between European and Chinese societies. Europeans tend to prize individuality, while Chinese value group harmony. This is also naturally reflected in their styles of government.

Europeans have built systems that encourage an atmosphere where people can stably and predictably confront each other in debate; they set up arenas for conflict with preassigned end points, after which participants are forced to consensus, following the vote of the majority under democracy, or the will of the judge or king under monarchy.

Chinese systems of government encourage group harmony. Conflict is diffused through slower processes of group consensus through clan hierarchical judgments. Adherence to the authority of family hierarchy prevents conflicts from escalating as judgments from any level higher than the parties involved resolve the issue. The most contentious issues may move to higher levels if a judgment is deemed unfair

---

10 There are 14 pages of synonyms at https://www.thesaurus.com/browse/big/14 (retrieved 8/15/20).

at a particular level. But even unfair judgments do not cause much conflict, because their system of Rule by Virtue leaves the lessons of any particular judgment vague and doesn't create precedent. Whereas under the analytic European systems of justice, any particular conflict can create a precedent, multiplying the formal rules.

These cultural differences are reflected in some aspects of the greater power or political centralization in China and decentralization in Europe. Europeans instituted decentralized contentious democracies, first in Classical Greece and later in modern Europe and America. China's Imperial hierarchy under Confucian ideals has been the most stable centralized organization of the last 2,000 years.

Part of the reason we draw this distinction between the cultures and languages in China and Europe is to highlight how diverse global networks can be. The challenge of designing governance in networks uniting groups with broadly different sets of values requires us to consciously address these differences.

Another reason to study these differences is to be aware of the potential for different governance mechanisms when organizing a group.

Protocol Decentralization in China

Comparing Europe and China over the course of 3,000 years is an important example for the decentralized to centralized thesis. But we must be conscious that anything said about large societies over the course of millennia is plainly a contentious generalization.

Inasmuch as a society organizes itself in a rigid centralized hierarchy, it is initially very efficient and effective at addressing its problems, which leads to a temporary stability as the society adheres more to the hierarchy. At best, however, the hierarchy has always failed after a few centuries, usually much sooner, and the resulting chaos leaves fertile ground for reorganizing the old order. Successors may reorganize the conquered society completely along the conquerors' system. Or, more commonly, the succeeding power adjusts the existing hierarchy of a region slightly and partially repopulates it – especially at the top. This is **revolution**. We use a word that evokes cycles, because the hierarchy periodically collapses into chaos then naturally reemerges.

Chinese society has been much more stable in the course of the last 2,200 years, compared with Europe. Like Ancient Egypt before it, China has had many political revolutions as the heads of state succeeded each other. But the habits and culture of peasants has been much more stable in both Egypt and China than in countries with more protocol-centralized legal systems. Egypt and China had legal systems where society informally supported moral precepts more than explicitly defined, unchanging legalistic precedent. This is referred to as Rule of Virtue versus Rule of Law. Professional and social positions were clearly hierarchical, with some roles being seen as higher or lower in status, but most roles weren't organized into tightly defined power relationships. For example, judges would personally investigate a crime, getting to know a community and the principals of a case intimately. A judgment would be enforced by the community, not police. And the judgment would not be bound legally by any precedent; it held sway depending on the perceived virtue of the judge and his decision.[11] This led to the ideal man stereotype of judges, which Western audiences might recognize in Kung Fu movies, such as *Crouching Tiger, Hidden Dragon*. A judge was always a man of universal learning, typically a doctor and pharmacist, a martial arts expert, and a scholar of ancient poetry.

Even today, China is much more protocol decentralized than the West. China has a less rigid hierarchical organization with less uniform rules than the West. The People's Republic of China (PRC) does not have an enforced constitution with a clearly defined nationwide power structure.[12] Even though the Chinese Communist Party (CCP) inhabits a parallel bureaucracy in most every school, hospital, and other institution in the land, its power structure is not explicitly and formally defined. For an empire and society often seen as monolithic and autocratic, the roles in government are much more locally heterogeneous than in the West, where the roles of mayor and councilmember are duplicated much more faithfully throughout a country.

It is often claimed that China is relatively culturally homogenous. While it is true that there is a very strong impulse toward unity and harmony, the reason this has been necessary for millennia is because of China's cultural diversity. Though Han Chinese have been a culturally, economically, and politically dominant majority for roughly 3,000 years, there are many dialects of their language (Mandarin) and many other languages to go with the 56 ethnicities the CCP officially recognizes. These ethnicities display obvious diversity in their speech, clothing, traditions, and genetics. Craig lived in the Chinese province of Zhejiang, where he experienced the truth of the saying "the language of your hometown is not understood 30 km away."

---

11 In medieval China, society and the economy were largely structured by kinship-based clans. Rules were different for each clan, but it has been estimated that less than 20% of rules listed any punishment, and these were likely recommendations. See p. 11 of Avner Greif & Guido Tabellini, "The Clan and the Corporation: Sustaining Cooperation in China and Europe," *Journal of Comparative Economics*, 45(1), 2017, pp. 1–35. This is not to say that there were no rigid precepts or clearly defined rules. The Tang Code (624) was an extremely detailed, logically rigorous legal system that helped guide justice throughout the imperial period, culminating in the Qing Code of 1644.

12 "The Constitution of the People's Republic of China is nominally the supreme law of the People's Republic of China. . . . Though technically the 'supreme legal authority' and 'fundamental law of the state,' the ruling Communist Party of China has a documented history of violating many of the constitution's provisions and censoring calls for greater adherence to it. Furthermore, claims of violations of constitutional rights cannot be used in Chinese courts, and the National People's Congress Constitution and Law Committee, the legislative committee responsible for constitutional review, has never ruled a law or regulation unconstitutional." https://en.wikipedia.org/wiki/Constitution_of_the_People%27s_Republic_of_China (retrieved 5/22/2020).

The highest office in China is the president (currently Xi Jinping). This ceremonial role's only formal power is to nominate the head of the legislative body, the premier of the State Council.[13] The actual power of the president is making speeches.

Periodically, the president will make a speech about, for example, the new Five-Year Plan. This speech will be almost entirely abstract, speaking in generalities and slogans about which direction the nation should move toward. For example, the primary policy of the 2016 – 2020 Five-Year Plan was "Everyone is an entrepreneur, creativity of the masses," 大众创业，万众创新. Then the political bureaucracy interprets the speech at the local level and attempts to implement reforms or initiatives reflecting the slogans. Each locality scrambles to keep their initiatives in line with what other territories are doing, out of respect for nationwide harmony. But there are no formal rules dictating specifically how a province should implement these reforms.

This loose power structure is arguably the consequence of the revolution(s) that rocked the nation during the 20th century response to the Century of Humiliation.[14] It has been suggested that the lack of rigid hierarchy is a consequence of the relatively recent chaos of revolution. But many societies have responded to chaos with rapid adoption of stronger hierarchical organization, such as 20th century fascist governments in the West. A better explanation is that Chinese society has a very long tradition of social decentralization. This is reflected on the individual level, where mainland Chinese citizens are quite autonomous and responsible for most of their personal development and daily choices.[15] However, compared with individuals in the West, the Chinese strive more to fit in with expected normal social behavior.

Chinese history traces continuous legal thought from at least 1000 BC, with two major perspectives that have influenced China to the present. Confucius' Rule of Virtue philosophy is more protocol decentralized. Shang Yang's Rule of Law philosophy is more normative and protocol centralized.[16]

---

13 "In modern Chinese politics, the paramount leader (最高领导人, Zuìgāo Lǐngdǎorén) is an informal term for the most prominent political leader . . . [it] is not, however, a formal position nor an office unto itself. The term gained prominence during the era of Deng Xiaoping (1978–1989), when he was able to wield political power without necessarily holding any official or formally significant party or government positions at any given time." https://en.wikipedia.org/wiki/Paramount_leader (retrieved 5/22/2020).
14 "The century of humiliation (百年耻辱) is the term used in China to describe the period of intervention and perceived subjugation of the Chinese Empire by Western powers, Russia and Japan between 1839 and 1949." https://en.wikipedia.org/wiki/Century_of_humiliation (retrieved 5/22/2020).
15 On the other hand, lifelong choices that non-Chinese often judge to be personal rights are not afforded to citizens, as evidenced by the One-Child Policy.
16 Zhang Xiangming, "On Two Ancient Chinese Administrative Ideas: Rule of Virtue and Rule by Law," *Culture Mandala: The Bulletin of the Centre for East-West Cultural and Economic Studies*, 5(1), Article 7,2002. Available at: http://epublications.bond.edu.au/cm/vol5/iss1/7 (retrieved 5/22/2020).

Both Confucius and Shang Yang lived and taught during a time of chaos before the Qin and Han dynasties unified China politically (Confucius 551–479 BC; Shang Yang d. 338 BC). The political chaos of the Spring and Autumn period and the Warring States period that they lived through led both thinkers to advocate a strong politically centralized hierarchy, but they diverged in their prescriptions for less and more protocol centralization, legally. Confucius (and especially his follower, Mencius) argued people were basically good, and so administrators should rule from the spirit of the law and lead by example, displaying the highest virtues in order to bring long-term harmony. Shang Yang (and especially his follower, Han Fei) argued the Legalist school of thought, *Fajia*. *Fajia* begins with the position that people are basically evil. For them the letter of the law is therefore seen as paramount, to constrain humanity's base instincts.[17]

The Qin state would eventually unify China for the first time in 221 BC. The Qin state's decline, reorganization, subsequent triumph, precipitous fall, and rebirth is an excellent example of the strengths and weaknesses of organizing society along different points in the (de)centralization spectrum. The Stanford Encyclopedia of Philosophy archive's entry on the history of Legalism in China[18] reads as an apology for our central thesis: Centralization is a powerful mechanism for rapidly building an efficient organization for solving a specific problem (e.g., war in preunified China). The more effective and efficient the architecture is at solving the problem, the more rigid the hierarchy becomes, and the more unforgiving it is for anyone on the outside. But rigid architectures are unstable and fail when met with novel challenges. More decentralized organizations are more stable.

Thumbnail Sketch of Chinese History

After centuries of warring kingdoms in the region of what later came to be known as China, the previously chaotically unorganized people had come to be partially unified by the cultural and economic communication war unintentionally provides. They were also united in their weariness from war. This meant China was fertile ground for the centralizing effects of Qin Shi Huang's initiatives standardizing language and writing, currency, weights and measures, engineering standards for transport (roads, carts, canals) and construction, history and education (burning most books and burying scholars), etc.

Around 350 BC the weak Qin state, furthest inland from the ocean, reorganized along centralized principles. King Qin Shi Huang, following the Legalism school of

---

17 As opposed to the more philosophical *Analects of Confucius*, the *Han Feizi* Legalist text reads similar to Machiavelli's, *The Prince*, as practical advice to a ruler on how to administrate effectively. Also compare the pessimistic vision of humanity with Hobbes' philosophy.

18 https://plato.stanford.edu/archives/win2014/entries/chinese-legalism/#EpiLegChiHis (retrieved 5/31/2020).

thought, built the most powerful military China had ever seen.[19] Qin Shi Huang conquered all the other kingdoms by 221 BC, becoming the most powerful emperor in the world. Under Legalism, the Qin Empire hierarchy was extremely rigid, and equality before the law had a particularly hierarchical connotation: "The ruler creates the law; the ministers abide by the law; and subjects are punished by the law. All [. . .] are subject to law."[20]

After the Qin Emperor died, the brittle hierarchy immediately collapsed, 15 years after unification. Once unity was reestablished under the succeeding Han dynasty, their rulers quite consciously abandoned the centralizing legal policies. Valuing stability over efficiency, they adhered to the Law-of-Virtue Confucian school of thought with greater protocol decentralization.

This philosophy of protocol decentralization with clan-hierarchy-determined Chinese politics, made China the most stable empire since Ancient Egypt, with brief interruptions of protocol centralization whenever they needed to restore the state's waning economic and military power, under Zhuge Liang (181–234), Su Chuo (498–546), the Tang Code (624), Wang Anshi (1021–1086) and Zhang Juzheng (1525–1582), and the Qing Code (1644).

Finally, again under Mao Zedong in 1949, the Chinese government explicitly followed Shang Yang's philosophy of protocol centralization. In that year, after the Century of Humiliation, the Communist Revolution removed the Kuomintang government and quickly centralized their institutions following the example of the Qin success and strengthened their military to expel all foreign invaders and reunite the nation. This centralized hierarchy was extremely successful at the military goal it was designed for, but completely failed at solving other important problems once the military threat was gone. Like the Qin emperor he emulated, the supreme leader of the communist military hierarchy, Mao Zedong, ruled from the revolution until his death in 1976. During this time the hierarchy instituted reforms that resulted in catastrophic failures, such as the Cultural Revolution and the Great Leap Forward, under which more than 30 million people perished. In 1978 Deng Xiao Ping assumed power and reformed the economy, under the Boluan Fanzheng period, literally meaning "eliminating chaos and returning to normal." That is, China attempted to return to the previous, stabilizing philosophy of protocol decentralization of the Chinese Imperial period, with greater market freedoms and a Rule of Virtue justice system.

Since 1978 societies and culture have hardly been stable most anywhere on the globe. Creating a stable government in the rapidly changing economy of China during this period seems nearly impossible. Therefore, it is natural that China would swing precipitously between centralized and decentralized initiatives. The most

---

19 Preserved for posterity in Xian province. https://en.wikipedia.org/wiki/Mausoleum_of_the_First_Qin_Emperor (retrieved 8/8/20).
20 Jianfu Chen, *Chinese Law: Context and Transformation*, Martinus Nijhoff Publishers, 2008.

visible initiatives are naturally centralized. The most troubling recent examples are the Great Firewall of China and the Social Credit System, as obstacles to transparency and individual autonomy. We will return to this in Chapter 3, when we discuss the consequences of applying new IT tools to creating centralized reputational systems, in the section on Orwellian nightmares.

What lesson do we take from Imperial Chinese history for our present goal of implementing new advances in information technology? Where should we decide to draw the lines of power? Should our governance processes recognize that we are all basically evil in our hearts and that the beasts within us need to be controlled? If Shang Yang and Hobbes are right, we should give control to an impersonal hierarchy, within which we only have limited and local control. Or should we instead speak to our good side? Should we follow Confucius, believing we are all basically good at heart? Then we should tap into our better natures and encourage productive cooperation, by empowering each individual with greater freedom. Anyone who has spent an hour on a playground knows the answer is obviously both. Our governance system must prevent rapacious greed with concrete punishments. But it should also encourage and enable harmonious cooperation and individual autonomy. The lesson of Imperial China, and Pharaonic Egypt before it, is that decentralization of power, individual autonomy, gives long-term stability when there are unifying ideals that the society can believe in.

Political Centralization in China and Europe

In this section we argue that China enjoyed greater uniformity in their values than Europe did at the time. This allowed China to institute clan social organization with less legal/protocol centralization. Europe's greater value diversity required they institute corporate organization with a more rigid hierarchical structure with more legal centralization. For stability, Europe needed to relieve the pressure elsewhere.

There were great expressions of political centralization around 1100 AD with medieval aristocracy. At this time the High Middle Ages in Europe were organized around the philosophy of the "Great Chain of Being" with God at the top, served by the king, then the lords and clergy, followed by knights, then their peasants and livestock at the bottom.

Contemporaneously, Imperial China during the Song dynasty was organized around hierarchical Confucianism. From an abstract point of view, the aristocratic organization of Imperial China under the "Mandate of Heaven" was remarkably similar to medieval Europe under the "Great Chain of Being." But the civil bureaucracy of the Song dynasty controlled many times as many subjects. In 1100 AD the population of the Holy Roman Empire was roughly 10 million, while Imperial China governed 90 million.

The organizational successes of both empires can be directly attributed to advances in information technology. But the fact that the Song dynasty eclipsed Europe's

High Middle Ages is often directly attributed to China's unique adoption of transparency and meritocracy. The Chinese civil service examinations, which were open to all, regardless of social standing, led to a literate meritocratic bureaucracy as opposed to Europe's easily corruptible system of power inheritance. China's bureaucracy stored, processed, and transmitted unprecedented governmental information leading to a flourishing economy, which grew exponentially for centuries. The meritocratic system stabilized the society as its people enjoyed strong social mobility and individual autonomy.

The meritocracy also empowered generations of talented scholars and inventors who put China centuries ahead of any other country technologically. Other Song advances in information technology include woodblock and ceramic movable type printing (invented by Bi Sheng 毕升, 990–1051). Printing allowed the dissemination of rules across great distances and populations. Thanks to these innovations, the world's first banknote was seen in the Song dynasty, and paper money was first employed extensively. These advances led to much greater centralization, as the Song Imperial government dominated the right to print specie. We may assume it is natural to establish monopoly power on the right to print money. However, compare this with the history of printed banknotes that were individually issued by each bank in many times and places, especially whenever there was less centralization of power, including 19th century America.

In both Europe and Asia at this time, the centralized hierarchy expressed itself in the merchant class in the larger cities. Merchants organized into the most sophisticated guild system the world had ever seen, with clear ranking of more and less important professions, from scholars and doctors down to actors and prostitutes.[21]

As mentioned in the previous section, China was relatively decentralized in protocol through most of its history, with a Rule of Virtue legal system. This is reflected in its dominant clan structure. The major social and economic institutions of China revolved around kinship-oriented clans. You are a member of a Chinese clan if you claim to share family lineage with some common original male ancestor progenitor of the clan. Chinese clans had a less rigid system of legal enforcement, sanctions, and rewards, than their European contemporaries. Clan members were compelled to cooperate and behave well, due to moral and familial obligation, more than mere adherence to clearly stipulated laws.

In Europe there was much more protocol centralization than in China. Clans were not as dominant in personal economic life. Instead the greater focus on individuality gave a need for impersonal legal regulation and equality before the law. This led to a Rule of Law system with citywide charters and constitutions with formal rules and punishments. Instead of clans, Europe's major civic institutions were corporations,

---

21 Ebrey, Walthall, Palais, *East Asia: A Cultural, Social, and Political History*, Boston: Houghton Mifflin Company, 2006, p. 157.

with many different purposes. These corporations could be anything from religious groups to entire independent cities. "[B]etween 1143 and 1475, in Germany alone, for example, 190 cities adopted one of the twenty different law codes."[22]

China was more protocol decentralized than Europe for much of its history, but it was more politically centralized, as Imperial China ruled over a much greater population than Europe. Europe's protocol centralization was fragmented between many different kingdoms and city states, which seems natural considering the greater emphasis on individuality expressing itself in Europe than in China. So, Europe is seen as more politically decentralized compared with China during the High Medieval period, though this can also be explained by their inferior information technology, meaning they were incapable of organizing anywhere near the quantity of citizens China commanded in the same period.

Despite the differences in protocol and political centralization, the general cultural centralization that the new information technology of the time afforded led to much more sophisticated engineering projects, such as cathedrals and pagodas. Centralized economic development, especially in China, multiplied the population the regions could sustain.

However, centralization doesn't last. As leaders pass on their powers and duties, corruption sets in. As law moves from the sacred, to rituals, to institutions, people are freer to test the legal limits. No dynasty lasts more than a few centuries before it is overturned from corruption born within or by foreign invasion from without. Without a transcendental spiritual/philosophical principle to unify a society, the rules erode as exceptions to the routine are found, which improve function temporarily, yet violate the founding principles of the culture. Such violations split the population.

The very economic success that centralization affords leads societies to encounter foreign cultures, goods, and technologies. These alien experiences challenge the institutions that allowed the foreign adventure. Institutions that have been hollowed out by time and have not been revitalized by contact with the ideals from their origins are incapable of responding to exotic challenges.

Stagnant centralized institutions become irrelevant and incapable of useful response during chaotic periods, while decentralized structures thrive, such as loose labor affiliations, or black markets, or clans. Decentralized organizations naturally respond to "information at the edge." They are energized when leaders are attacked. Decentralized rebellions are strengthened by the loss of their leaders, who become martyrs. Decentralized organizations form around transcendental ideas, not on codified laws, and therefore respond well in times of chaos and remain stable in the long term.

In general, the lesson of clans versus corporations is that when a group has more unity in their values, they can have less rigidity in their legal protocols. So greater

---

22 Greif, 2017, p. 12.

value centralization allows greater protocol decentralization, which leads to greater long-term stability. But when there is more diversity in a group's values, a corporation structure emerges with more rigid legal stipulations – letter of the law becomes more important. This is because the group needs to fairly apply the law in more diverse situations to keep group cohesion. In this case a corporation is less stable in the long term. Stability needs to be sought elsewhere with other structures.

The next section explores a decentralized political organization that survived more than 300 years against adversaries with incalculably more resources. This illustrates that a decentralized organization cannot be conquered by attacking it from the outside. When you do, the group merely decentralizes further. Members become more autonomous and more devoted to the principles upon which the organization was founded. Decentralized organizations can only be destabilized by changing the entire game, by recasting the environment under which they pursue their goals to sap the power of their values.

The Apaches Versus Bitcoin

The Starfish and the Spider,[23] by Ori Brafman and Rod Beckstrom, is the most insightful book we've read on decentralized organization. Its central thesis is illustrated by the story of the Apache Native American Indian tribe.[24] Their conclusion suggests that Bitcoin won't work.

This story was relayed by Thomas Nevins, who studied and lived with the Apaches. In the late 1600s the Apaches settled into their current territory in the mountains near the border of Arizona and New Mexico. The Spanish had been continuously expanding their territory in the Americas since Christopher Columbus first explored the area in the early 1500s. The Spanish were attempting to settle the area in New Mexico, but their northward expansion failed for the first time when encountering the Apaches. (Their second northward incursion failed when they encountered the Comanches, who were also politically decentralized.)

For more than 200 years the small band of Apaches resisted succeeding empires, to remain self-sovereign. These people commanded a tiny fraction of the material wealth of their adversaries, but the Apaches were successful because of their political decentralization.

---

23 Starfish are decentralized organisms. Their nervous systems don't have a centralized hierarchical structure. This makes them slow, but practically immortal – if you chop one in half, you get two starfish. They're stable and can handle adversity. Spiders have a centralized nervous system, with a brain, so they can make decisions quickly. But you can kill them with a blow to the head.
24 Though this is not the name these tribes ever use to refer to themselves. The word *Apache* is probably derived from the Zuni word for "enemy." The Apaches themselves had different demonyms in their own dialects, including *n nee, n dee, dene, and dine.*

In the course of a few decades, the Spanish Empire, beginning with Columbus in the Caribbean, conquered tribes and empires throughout the entire Western hemisphere of the planet. Cortés conquered the Aztec empire in present-day Mexico and Central America in 1519–1521. Later the Pizarros conquered the Incan empire, which spanned extensive and diverse terrain in South America. Compared with the small Apache tribe, living in a relatively small area in the mountains of present-day Arizona and New Mexico, the Aztec and Incan empires had vast wealth and a complex effective hierarchy. Yet the Apaches succeeded for centuries where other groups, large and small, were rapidly defeated.

The crucial difference between the Apaches and other networks the Spanish Empire conquered was that the Apache's political organization was not centered around a chief. The Spanish conquistadors Cortés and Pizarro captured and killed the Aztec and Incan emperors, Moctezuma and Atahualpa. By controlling the leaders, the Spanish efficiently took control of the centralized hierarchies of the empires.

Beginning in the 1680s the Spanish built a series of *presidios* (fortified residential compounds) in the area where the Apaches lived and instituted plans for assimilating the natives of the region under their hierarchical feudal order. The Spanish plan, that was successful in many other regions, was to convert the locals religiously to Catholicism and economically to small-scale farming and bring them all under the political control of the Spanish crown. These initiatives were relatively successful with other tribes, even nomadic tribes of similar size and distribution, but failed with the Apaches, most of whom resisted the loss of their sovereignty. When the Spanish attempted to coerce the Apaches, the violence backfired. The Apaches almost casually defeated the Spanish with routine raids on their centralized holdings. After two decades of failure, the Spanish Empire had abandoned most of its presidios in Apache territory.

"Part of the reason the Spanish had such difficulty in establishing control and dominion over Apaches had to do with the dispersed, decentralized nature of Apache social organization."[25] The Apaches had no static, official rulers, which made it impossible for the Spanish to replay their strategy of killing or controlling the leader of each new territory they invaded. The Apaches had no rigid power hierarchy to manipulate. The Apache had spiritual leaders, called *nant'án*. But the *nant'án* led by example, not coercion. The members of the tribe continuously made choices whether to follow a suggestion from a *nant'án* based on his personal strength and reputation. When the Spanish would kill (or capture and coerce) a leader, the tribe would not be mollified or lose its organization. In fact, killing a *nant'án* would strengthen the cohesion of the group as they had a new example to learn from, whether the *nant'án* lived and died according to Apache ideals.

---

25 Thomas J. Nevins, Introduction to *The Apache Indians: In Search of the Missing Tribe*, by Helge Ingstad, University of Nebraska Press, 2004, p. xxiv.

Any loss would only further decentralize the Apache people. Whenever a village was raided, that encouraged the Apache to become more nomadic. The subgroups became smaller, so they were more difficult to locate and attack. They decentralized geographically across terrain large armies found difficult to negotiate.

After the Mexican Revolution in 1821 the Mexicans adopted a similar strategy to the Spanish, and so they similarly failed against the Apache. As a definitive sign of their desperation, the Mexicans put bounties on the scalps of Apache men, women, and children.

We may witness this pattern at various locations in different times throughout history. A materially superior centralized society will discover the limits of its power in conflict with politically and geographically decentralized groups. The Roman Empire's borders were in "barbarian" lands. Afghanistan is the Graveyard of Empires. The United States is only the most recent empire to find their global dominance ends when it meets decentralized territory. Before that, the Soviet invasions of Afghanistan in 1929 and 1979–1989 failed. The British failed in 1839–1842. Since the Arabs met their first major setback when they failed to conquer Afghanistan in the 8th century, no centralized authority, foreign or domestic, has been able to bring the decentralized network of Afghani tribes into uniform control.

When a superior army fails to dominate a weaker enemy, the causes invariably include the unfamiliar terrain and geographical decentralization of the enemy. But that is not the primary characteristic that determines the outcome. The U.S. policy of resettlement on reservation land can be analyzed for each of the tribes to determine how organizational style affects military success. History never simplifies down to singular causes, such as political centralization, but some trends are more evident than others. The more sedentary tribes, who relied on agriculture and were geographically more centralized around fertile locations, were more quickly conquered than the nomadic plains tribes who were widely dispersed. The nomadic plains tribes, however, were also all geographically dispersed. What distinguished the tribes who were more successful against the U.S. military? Political decentralization. Those with strong chieftains were more quickly settled on reservations. The last groups to submit to U.S. sovereignty were the most politically decentralized, the Comanche and the Apache.

With all these historical examples, what insights do we have for what stops a decentralized organization? Surprisingly, it was not until the 20th century that the United States finally succeeded in permanently converting the Apaches' way of life from nomadic to sedentary and asserting sovereignty. How did it happen?

After the Mexican American War, the United States annexed the Apache territory in 1848. The centralized U.S. military predictably copied the Spanish and Mexican strategies for negotiating with the Apaches. They built garrisons and instituted a policy of gradual but coercive acculturation and resettlement. And predictably, despite their overwhelming material superiority, the U.S. Army failed to conquer or pacify the Apache people.

Starting in 1873 the U.S. government instituted its reservation policy where the Apaches were coerced toward settling on reservation land where they were safer from reprisal, and they were promised rations. By 1878 most Western Apaches were conditionally settled, but this didn't last. Poor conditions led to revolts throughout the 1880s.

The resettlement effort was only successful with the Apaches once the U.S. military struck upon an unprecedented strategy. In 1916 the U.S. government gave the Apaches cows.

As Nevins explained, the introduction of the cattle created "a zero-sum battle over resources between lineages."[26] The valuable assets created the internal competition necessary to generate a hierarchy of power over disbursement of resources and property. Whereas formerly, the *nant'án* would only lead by example, now the *nant'án* could lead by punishing or rewarding tribal members materially. Members of the network jockeyed for power. A politically centralized hierarchy emerged in tribal councils. Bureaucratic rules were instituted in geographically centralized reservations. And the U.S. government finally had a structure they could manipulate and control.

The profit motive came to dominate the Apache incentive structure, undermining the ideology that kept the group decentralized.

Brafman and Beckstrom argue the Apache history demonstrates that decentralized organizations are unstoppable, they cannot be conquered. Three successive empires repeatedly failed in their missions to destroy Apache society. A decentralized organization cannot be controlled by a centralized authority. But you might hope to convert them to a centralized organization by finding the proper incentives; then you can manipulate the centralized power structure. As is being demonstrated again today in fighting terrorist organizations around the world, attacking a decentralized organization only makes them more decentralized and more powerful as enemies. "The values *are* the organization." A decentralized organization's power is their ideology; it keeps them together; it drives them; it inspires new recruits – unlike centralized organizations whose rigid hierarchies are maintained by universal motivations such as fear of ostracization or competition for profits.

The thesis of *The Starfish and the Spider* is that the best way to convert a decentralized organization to a centralized organization is to introduce the profit motive. They go on to suggest that the greatest danger Wikipedia faces is the potential to earn money, which would trigger the inevitable centralizing effect of internal competition. They discuss other examples, such as how book sales corrupted and undermined the power of the Alcoholics Anonymous decentralized network, sapping its energy, so that now there are numerous decentralized offshoots. Brafman and Beckstrom proclaim

---

26 *The Starfish and the Spider*, p. 148.

that decentralized organizations cannot avoid centralizing when concern for profits overrides the group's moral ideals.

The Starfish and the Spider was written in 2006, predating the first published Bitcoin block by three years. They couldn't be aware of the new advances in information technology that allowed new types of decentralized information control. We will explore these tools in Chapter 2. But despite ten years of success in Bitcoin's politically decentralized operation, there are hints that Brafman and Beckstrom are not entirely wrong. The thesis that money destroys decentralized projects by giving a focal point for internal competition is still prescient even in the face of Bitcoin. Slowly, Bitcoin hashing power has become more concentrated in mining pools, until today the majority of power resides in the single country of China. The CCP's strong economic controls could mean that Bitcoin's claim to decentralization is theoretically and perhaps even technically compromised.

In fact, almost every blockchain project we're aware of is suffering under the centralizing force of competition for equity control and profit. It's rarely possible for people to work idealistically toward the goals of the group and blithely watch the rewards be split unfairly with rent seekers at the top. Humans' sense of fairness is powerful and deep seated.[27] Good ideas will fail to be implemented unless the reward structure is balanced. Unconscious of these forces, these Web3 projects predictably move toward centralization.

Every contemporary Web3 decentralized organization we are aware of has critical flaws in its governance structure. The best run contemporary for-profit decentralized organizations, blockchains, rely on extremely primitive communication, such as informal e-mail lists (cf., BIPs and EIPs). The networks that are still progressing, such as Ethereum, rely on benevolent dictators with a cult of personality or centralized foundations with salaried members seeking profit. There are few sophisticated governance procedures that can predictably survive the deaths of the current leaders. There are very rarely any ratified statements of principles, much less an enforceable constitution that governs any such attempt at forming a genuine DAO.

How can a decentralized organization come to consensus on governance? How can a modern Web3 project agree on technology upgrades without centralizing their decision-making process? There is another architectural design, besides the new cryptographic and information technology tools, that can keep a group politically

---

27 A sense of fairness is also strong among primates and other animals, as is demonstrated by the famous cucumber experiment. Two monkeys in side-by-side cages are rewarded for performing the trivial task of returning a rock to the experimenter. One monkey receives a slice of cucumber. When it watches the other monkey receive a grape, it protests the unfairness vehemently. "Thus far, passive and active protest against unfavorable outcomes has been documented in monkeys, apes, dogs, and birds. It is thought that these species compare their outcomes with those of others so as to judge the merit of their partnerships." – Sarah F. Brosnan and Frans B. M. de Waal, "Evolution of responses to (un)fairness," *Science 346*(6207), October 17, 2014.

decentralized even when profits are on the line, in valuable blockchain networks like Bitcoin. There is a much older incentive structure that has historically proved capable of maintaining a large, decentralized network of economically self-interested autonomous group members. Brafman and Beckstrom (and perhaps also Satoshi Nakamoto and Vitalik Buterin) apparently had not considered the Maghribis.

The Maghribis were a decentralized trade organization entirely devoted to profit. These Jewish merchants from the early 11th century had none of the information technology that enables Bitcoin. Yet they remained decentralized because their organization prized something more valuable than money.

Maghribi Traders' Solution

The Maghribis were a decentralized group of Jewish traders in Northwestern Africa (in modern-day Tunisia and especially Egypt) around 1000 AD. The Maghribis traded across great distances along the Silk Road on trips that would regularly last months at a time. They managed to solve the business contract challenges of the Principal-Agent Problem,[28] asymmetric information due to time and distance separation, and limited legal contract enforceability, without any of the digital technological advantages we enjoy today.

The situation was that a merchant would send an agent out with goods and cash to trade along the dangerous Silk Road. After being gone for months and far from any control or oversight from their associates, there is a natural incentive for the agent to simply keep the profits and leave, or to return and falsely report they were stolen.

Less dramatically, it would be easy for an agent to skim without detection. The markets of the Silk Road had great volatility in their prices between distant locations and times. The little communication was highly unreliable. Even if the principal had independent communication with the distant merchant their agent was engaging, a fraction of the profits could be stolen and shared between the agent and the foreign merchant. Unforeseen costs could be invented.

Actually, records show that such embezzlement was rare. Instead, a strong sense of trust pervaded. So, what mechanism protected the principals from their agents' asymmetric information? The answer was not a strong centralized government.

---

28 In the Principal-Agent problem coordination revolves around those who delegate authority (principals) and those who are acting on behalf of others (agents). Because of natural human shortcomings, bounded rationality, incomplete foresight, and information asymmetries between principal and agent, it is impossible for principals to contract for every possible action or inaction of the agent in order to induce the agent to act in the best interest of the principal. For an overview of the relevant literature see Andrei Shleiferl & Robert W. Vishny, "A Survey of Corporate Governance," *Journal of Finance 52*(2), 1997, pp. 737–783.

The Maghribis lived under the rule of the Muslim Fatimid caliphate, who controlled Northern Africa, Sicily, and the broad fertile Eurasian plains, known as the Levant. The Fatimids had notably liberal trade policies to encourage business. Migration and the flow of goods had very low customs friction due to competitive ports. Tariffs were rare and temporary. The official legal channels for the Maghribis were slow and not to be relied upon in case a dispute arose. The Maghribis couldn't create their own politically enforced legal system. They were not capable of forming a strong centralized legal or political hierarchy, partly because any centralization of Jewish power would be seen as a threat to the primacy of the caliphate.

A system of ethics founded in their common religion helps explain the motivation for why merchants did not steal. Also, the social connection of a family-and-friend network of cooperation is undeniably important in preventing theft. However, the trading distances and durations involved, and the value of the temptations were extreme. In fact, the Maghribi network included people who lived in different countries and were part of independent Jewish communities with no family ties. The Maghribis lived throughout the Mediterranean, but they never worked with any other Jewish traders, even if the others lived and worked nearby, unless they were also part of the Maghribi professional network. Ethics and social sanctions are not enough to explain the long and powerful cooperation that sustained the Maghribis across vast distances.

The business challenges were further multiplied by the various complex tasks entrusted to the agents. The agents had to be excellent navigators, shippers, bargainers, bureaucrats, and soldiers. They had to choose the most efficient routes. They needed to hire transport caravans and boats, longshoremen to load and unload boats, and storage. The agents used their personal network of information on buyers and sellers to find the best prices, goods, and terms. These changed unpredictably, and the principals certainly didn't give precise instructions on what price to pay for what goods months before the agents arrived at their destinations. The bureaucracy of customs and tariffs and local taxes needed to be negotiated, and the agents chose their routes depending on which ports were cheaper or safer or had less traffic based on experience and rumors. Finally, they were required to deal with the hazards of travel, including weather, warlords, and bandits. If all these tasks were achieved, the agents would be entrusted with increasingly more complex jobs, including relaying market information and overseeing businesses in various locales.

How can you incentivize honesty and fair dealing under these circumstances? The agents were even officially in charge of bribing various officials along the route. Why didn't they skim for themselves?

This question is particularly relevant to today's concern with decentralizing business 1,000 years later in the 21st century. We're building economic networks that hope to incorporate anonymous members from different cultures across the globe, without being able to rely on any local legal enforcement, without constructing any centralized control structure. How did the Maghribis solve this puzzle? How did they solve their information asymmetry problems? How did they motivate long-term, good-faith cooperation?

The Maghribis' Solution was Reputation

The story we tell in this section was first detailed in Avner Greif's deep exploration of the Cairo geniza.[29] A geniza is a hidden room in a synagogue intended to temporarily hold sacred texts. It is forbidden in Orthodox Judaism to dispose carelessly of any writing holding the name of God. The genizot held worn out copies of bibles and religious commentary temporarily, before they were properly buried in a cemetery. Since business communication among the Maghribi regularly opened with religious invocations, they were often stored in a geniza. (The extensive Cairo geniza also held proof that the Maghribis used double-entry bookkeeping, predating its famous use in medieval Florence by centuries.)

Reputation gives the proper incentive to create stable, long-term business relationships where both parties act in good faith. The promise of many future contracts incentivizes an agent to honor the deal to the best of their ability. Loss of reputation would ruin a career. The entire network devoted considerable attention and energy to policing their reputation.

The Cairo geniza records show that when one particular agent, Abun ben Zedaka in Jerusalem, was merely accused of embezzlement, principals from as far away as Sicily immediately canceled their contracts with the agent. When a principal was slow to remunerate an agent because of natural fluctuations in liquidity, they would fret about the damage it would do to their reputation. In fact, records show that the reputational system was so strong that agents who were the victims of theft along the journey would regularly rise above any contractual obligations, making their principals whole from their own funds in order to protect and further their reputation.

Moreover, personal letters show the system was relied upon to the point that most deals were engaged without any formal contract. This makes sense because no instructions could detail the list of minutiae the agents were expected to perform.

Further, principals in the network would entrust their money and assets to members who had no ability to repay in case of loss. There was a type of reputation-verification system for unseasoned traders, called the *commenda*. The *commenda* relationship had reputable, older, wealthier members certifying younger agents as trustworthy and skilled – agents who were willing and able to bear the difficulties of the journey but didn't yet own the personal resources necessary to refund their principals in case of loss.

Reputation is extremely valuable for encouraging more efficient business deals. Reputation gives the purchaser the confidence to invest the money and/or assets in the venture, without spending the extra effort of investigating the agent before, during, and after the journey. Honesty would be a bad strategy for the agent if the contract was anonymous and the resolution didn't affect future contracts. In this imagined scenario, from a game theory perspective, the game would be a single-stage zero-sum game. (Game theory applied to the design of decentralized organizations will be discussed in more detail in Chapter 4.) In this case the best strategy would be for the agent to steal all the wealth entrusted to him.

By adding reputation to the game, it becomes a repeated game, and the rest of the community becomes relevant. Reputation is a future-oriented commodity, which pays off profits with the promise of future contracts. Now the game is a repeated game, which is positive sum. The best strategy changes to incentivize honesty as the promise of voluminous future business overrides the potential for a one-time payout of stealing the principal's wealth.

The positive-sum nature of the game arises, because reputation itself becomes a valuable commodity that can be created during a business deal. Reputation can be more valuable than present profits. One agent, whose writings are preserved in the Cairo geniza, sent a letter insulting his principal, "Had I listened to what people say, I never would have entered into a partnership with you . . . ."[30] Then the agent goes on to explain, nevertheless, he is giving his principal more profits than was contractually obligated. The agent had sold two loads of pepper, one for the principal when it was safe, as was instructed, and the other for himself. He gambled the price would surge if ships demanding pepper arrived before he needed to leave. The gamble paid off and the second load was sold at a much higher price. "But brother, I would not like to take the profit for myself. Therefore, I transferred the entire sale to our partnership." The agent forwent his personal profit, despite the fact he had no intention of ever doing business with that particular principal again, for the sake of protecting and building his reputation in the larger network.

Meaningful, well-policed reputation makes business dealings more efficient for two more reasons: freedom of choice of business partners within the network and contracts of short duration are preferred.

First, reputation allows business dealings with any member of the network, regardless of personal acquaintance. This requires the network to be closed, however, with a size limited by the ability to police reputation using the information technology available.

---

30 Greif, *Reputation and Coalitions*, p. 871.

In 11th century North Africa, information technology consisted of slow transmission of handwritten letters. However, we can associate one historical IT advance with the advent of the Maghribi's reputational system. The Fatimid Empire's encouragement of trade provided cheaper and more secure information transmission. There were regular shipping and caravan links between various trade centers protected by the Fatimids. The Maghribi sent letters to their business associates through other traders and through private business professional letter carriers. "The traders sent several copies of the same letter to insure that at least one would reach its destination."[31] This improvement in bandwidth (if not latency) improved broadcast security in the network, allowing a trustworthy reputational system to evolve.

With the information technology available today, we have networks on the scale of Bitcoin – open to anyone on the planet willing to join and follow the rules. The accounting necessary for policing reputation can be achieved for minute behaviors thanks to contemporary information processing. For the Maghribis, their network was limited to Jews experienced in Muslim culture, and did not accept Italian Jews, for instance, since accepting members from other cultures using other languages would have multiplied the difficulty of policing their reputational system. Today, such barriers are overcome by the universal logical structure of computer programs.

Second, reputation allows contracts of any duration. Actually, shorter contracts are preferable, since punishment against a cheating member's reputation can occur more quickly. Also, shorter contracts allow more rapid accounting and disbursement of assets. This makes business more efficient as it frees resources for further use. Contracts with quick turnaround would be dangerous to the economy, as short-term thinking would lead to more competitive and less profitable collaboration, were it not for the focus on the long-term value of reputation.

Third, maintaining a reputation system is a costly overhead for the network, but it provides a catalyst for business. When meaningful reputation is part of the system, people are willing to cooperate without performing the extra due-diligence analysis on the agent and the other circumstances of the game. The opportunity to build reputation means both the agent and the principal are incentivized to act as partners to help each other profit, for the promise of future frictionless business opportunities. The parties are willing to go above and beyond the stipulations of the contract to build and protect reputation.

Finally, a focus on reputation instead of immediately fungible cash rewards encourages decentralized organization because it disperses power, and it does so fairly. Anyone with equivalent talent is equally acceptable in an anonymous business contract, so anyone available can be given opportunities. Those who already have jobs are not available, so the exponential concentration of power from the "rich-get-richer" effect is diminished. And meritocracy is encouraged by fair accounting and rewards.

---

31 Greif, private communication, June 2020.

Reputation may be enough to keep a homogenous group like the Maghribis together, despite the differentiating effect of competition for profit. But their coordination was devoted to the singular goal of a narrow type of trade. How can we maintain the power of decentralization when competing hierarchical structures are temporarily more effective?

The U.S. Constitution's Dynamic Hybrid Solution

> The struggle between centralization and decentralization is at the core of American history.
> —Anthony Gregory

The decades leading to the foundation of the United States of America is a prime lesson in the strengths and weaknesses of centralization and decentralization. The choices of governance structures among the centralized British monarchy, the decentralized Articles of Confederation, and in the later hybrid centralized-decentralized U.S. Constitution, illustrate the power of dynamic design for making an effective and stable decentralized organization with integrated centralized elements.

The American Revolution was fought between the decentralized colonial rebels and the centralized British Empire. The British Empire itself had a long unstable history of internal revolt against its own centralized hierarchy. The British Empire had previously decentralized from its medieval feudal monarchy by dispersing power through Parliament. During the preceding centuries, the monarchy lost power in a series of revolts that redistributed power among property owners, the aristocracy (House of Lords), and the knights (House of Commons). Parliament's power rivaled and often dominated the executive monarchy. As power tends to do under the differentiating process of competition, without conscious protection, a hierarchy emerged as well in Parliament among political factions.

By the time of the American Revolution, the landowning members of the Thirteen Colonies felt the legislative branch hierarchy had become too tyrannical under the reign of King George III. The information technology of the time meant the center of the British executive hierarchy was too distant to responsively govern the hierarchy that included the American colonies. The transatlantic voyage of ink and parchment letters gave latency from 6 to 18 weeks, one way. The printing press could store a broadsheet of information within a few hours and transmission on the order of three days throughout the colonies. More importantly, the press could disseminate unlimited numbers of copies, which was a major democratizing force, decentralizing the control of information. The colonists complained they had no representatives in Parliament. Information at the edge was not making its way up the hierarchy.

Thirteen of the 23 British colonies in North America chose to break off from the hierarchy in 1776, with the ratification of the Declaration of Independence. These 13 contiguous territories had similar cultures (Christian, mostly Protestant), administrative organization, and political concerns with Britain, so it was easier for the Thirteen Colonies to communicate with each other, compared with the other nearby British territories. (One of the articles in the Articles of Confederation allowed a specific open seat for Canada to automatically become the 14th member of the rebellion, but this clause was never exercised.)

During the seven years of rebellion, the Thirteen Colonies remained decentralized. The Continental Congress was their legislative body organized under the political rules called the Articles of Confederation. These Articles were consciously authored to limit the authority of its weak central government, which had no chief executive. This made the war effort difficult because it meant the organization was very inefficient at marshalling resources. Recognizing the value of executive power during war, the colonies appointed George Washington the commander in chief of the Continental Army. However, the autonomous members of the rebellion could not be coerced to participate, to draft soldiers, to provide money or any other war materiel. Washington constantly and bitterly complained about this throughout the war.

The war produced the competitive circumstances that differentiate leaders in rank and powers, and a military hierarchy organically emerged and gained power throughout the war. Wary of the danger of centralizing power, however, the several states retained independent control of their local militias and were in charge of appointing leaders in the Continental Army up to the rank of colonel.

Nevertheless, the decentralized rebel organization, which enjoyed the support of only 40% of the population in the colonies (15% loyal to the crown, 45% neutral), eventually defeated the most powerful centralized organization in the world, the British Empire, which would soon after become the largest empire in all history.

After their success, the Rebels knew future war was inevitable. In fact, their capitol was burned to the ground by Britain in 1812. Recognizing the weakness and inefficiency of their decentralized response to the threat of war, the Thirteen Colonies renamed themselves the United States of America and redrafted their political and legal rules. This Constitution gave more power to the central government and set up a hierarchical executive branch with a central leader. Conscious of the historical instability of a centralized hierarchy, however, and desperate to preserve the individual freedoms they had fought for, the Constitution was drafted to include a dynamic design for decentralizing power.

The U.S. government has been remarkably stable. Despite many evident failings, including full civil war, the Constitution has ruled over the nation with the most diverse group of citizens ever assembled, over an enormous geography, with great success. The U.S. Constitution is the oldest protocol-centralizing document of any major contemporary country. This stability is particularly notable given its rigid, Rule-of-Law legal system (as opposed to the Rule-of-Virtue legal systems of Egypt and China).

The Constitution's success is due to the harmonious marriage of centralized and decentralized organizing principles. A separation of powers into legislative, executive, and judicial branches keeps power from concentrating in a single chief executive monarch. Yet temporary hierarchies within each branch make them efficient and effective. Dynamic system design, including predictable transfers of power by term limits and flattening of power through democratic elections, further decentralizes political power in the organization.

Democracy itself decentralizes power. However, to bring unity to a large population with diverse values, the United States has rigid protocol-centralization from a Rule-of-Law legal system. Statutory law, explicitly and formally clarifying the limits of acceptable behavior, gives a level of fairness and transparency that helps unify a large, diverse group of people, as it did 5,000 years ago to bring diverse tribes together in Mesopotamia.

However, these explicit rules lead to instability in the short-term day-to-day workings of the nation and in the long-term multigenerational history of the country. The founders consciously grappled with these problems and built several stabilizing protocols into the Constitution.

The U.S. Constitution institutes dynamic governance for long-term stability. This includes short-term and long-term protocols. An appeals process stabilizes short-term cooperation (judicial). Long-term stabilization comes from the ability to amend rules – including how the amendments themselves are made (legislative). For even longer-term stabilization, transcendental values were consciously specified to guide such higher-order legislative and judicial rulemaking. In particular, the founders highlighted the vague notions of freedom, equality, and good will (*liberté, egalité, fraternité*).

The second system that stabilizes the organization with dynamic design is the separation of powers into the triumvirate of legislative, executive, and judicial branches. Montesquieu's radical system[32] creates a dynamic design through a system of checks and balances. Power is balanced by splitting it between the three branches. Power is checked, because each branch depends on the other to act, so that each branch has cyclic power over the others. The legislative branch crafts the plans that the executive branch is tasked with carrying out. The executive branch executes the plans and pushes cases to the judicial branch for resolution. Resolution means the judicial branch dictates what has happened. Given these judicial pronouncements, the legislative branch is then tasked with developing new plans to respond to what has happened. In computer science terms, the legislative branch updates the software. Then the

---

32 Montesquieu, *The Spirit of the Law*, Book XI, 1748, building on ideas from John Locke, *Two Treatises of Government*, 1689, who took ideas from much earlier democracies. The first well-documented democracies were in Greece. In the 6th century BC, Athenian democracies split power in the same way with a legislative branch, the *ekklesia* (which is the etymological root of the word ecclesiastic), the executive branch, *boule* (a council of representatives from the ten Athenian tribes), and the judicial body, *dikasteria* (whose jurors were selected by lottery).

executive branch executes the software. The judicial branch determines the state of the system. The executive branch gives information transmission, the legislative branch provides information processing, the judicial branch gives information storage.[33]

The separation of powers was consciously designed to prevent the system from naturally devolving into a complete centralized hierarchy, despotism according to Montesquieu, or tyranny according to Madison.[34] In the cyclical system, the powers of each branch derive from the others. The natural human competitive impulse is harnessed to prevent any branch from usurping power not enumerated in the Constitution, the checks and balances to prevent centralization of power. "Ambition must be made to counteract ambition."[35] This decentralization stabilizes the effect of the rigid legal protocol centralization, and the centralized hierarchy inherent in each separate branch.

Dynamic design further stabilizes the system with the following mechanisms. First, the power hierarchy is never permanently completed, because the leaders, particularly the executive leader, are not permanently in charge. The president has term limits. Second is democracy: the means by which the new central and legislative leaders are chosen is by polling the electorate. The members at the very bottom of the hierarchy equally share ultimate authority.[36] This formally ties the top of the political hierarchy to the bottom. The power structure is therefore cyclic. This stabilizes the system by flattening the ultimate power distribution and adding dynamism to the structure, to counteract the natural impulse toward becoming a static, rigid power hierarchy. Finally, the explicit mechanisms by which the very rules we follow can be changed are again split among the three branches. The legislative branch writes the rules; the executive branch decides how to institute those rules; the judicial branch reviews those rules. Thus, decentralization further stabilizes the process.

Both power decentralization and protocol decentralization are promoted using dynamic design in these several ways. This ameliorates the destabilizing effects of

---

33 This triumvirate of control reflects the psychological experience of an animal moving through its environment. Information processing is our experience of thought (legislative), information storage is our experience of perception (judicial), information communication is our experience of action (executive). The act of these processes working harmoniously together is life. (Incidentally, this is the foundation for building strong AI.) "It may be a reflection on human nature, that such devices should be necessary to control the abuses of government. But what is government itself, but the greatest of all reflections on human nature?"–James Madison, Federalist No. 51, February 6, 1788.

34 "There would be an end of everything, were the same man, or the same body, whether of the nobles or of the people, to exercise those three powers, that of enacting laws, that of executing the public resolutions, and of trying the causes of individuals."–Montesquieu, *The Spirit of the Law*, Book XI, 1748."The accumulation of all powers, Legislative, Executive, and Judiciary, in the same hands, whether of one, a few, or many, and whether hereditary, self-appointed, or elective, may justly be pronounced the very definition of tyranny." – James Madison, Federalist No. 47, January 30, 1788.

35 James Madison, Federalist No. 51, February 6, 1788.

36 ". . . the people are the only legitimate fountain of power"–James Madison, Federalist No. 49, February 2, 1788.

formal rigorous laws with effective centralized hierarchies in each branch, particularly the complex executive branch. This gives the benefits of both centralization and decentralization in political power and legal protocol.

However, the system is obviously not without flaws, especially because it is run by humans.[37] The process described above is merely the design of the system. People are very clever. Given enough time, we will find workarounds for the rules to any game. No matter how carefully rules are designed, we can subvert the intentions of its authors, while still following the rules to the letter. That is reflected by a mathematical fact called the Folk Theorems of Game Theory (see Chapter 4). When it comes to games that really matter, games where money and property and power are at stake, people are canny and avaricious. In practice, this game was subverted on many levels before the ink on the Constitution's ratification was dry.

As an uncontentious example, consider how the executive branch predictably oversteps its bounds. In fact, this natural circumstance is why the whole system was designed, to prevent the power hierarchy from centralizing around an individual. Predictably, the executive branch has become the most powerful, commanding far more resources than the other branches combined. But the system was designed to prevent this, partly by furnishing the legislative branch with the power to set the budget.

During a crisis, the executive branch is naturally tasked with identifying the problem, for example recognizing the need to go to war. The power of the executive is limited by the requirement that the president petition the legislative branch for authorization, funding, and instructions for how to execute the war. The legislature is supposedly the only branch with the power to declare war, and it is supposedly required to be periodically repetitioned for funding the war effort. But the executive branch has periodically overstepped its powers, such as suspending *habeas corpus* or violating the 4th amendment rights with citizen surveillance. When the executive branch is given more centralizing power during a crisis, or simply takes it, the mechanism for removing that power when the threat is over has rarely been followed. Large permanent standing armies were inconceivable when the Constitution was designed.

Secondly, the system has been propped up by the external centralizing force of constantly increasing power. The United States increased in territory until 1959 and continues to advance its influence through business, foreign policy, technological

---

37 "If men were angels, no government would be necessary. . . . In framing a government which is to be administered by men over men, the great difficulty lies in this: you must first enable the government to control the governed; and in the next place oblige it to control itself. A dependence on the people is, no doubt, the primary control on the government; but experience has taught mankind the necessity of auxiliary precautions."–James Madison, Federalist No. 51, February 6, 1788. Every engineer will tell you building a machine for any task is easy, until humans are expected to use it.

development, and culture. Rapid westward expansion for more than a century to its current political territory was rationalized by the idea of Manifest Destiny. When there was a temporary time American power was seen as stagnating instead of growing in the 1970s, it was seen as a general national crisis. Today a major national concern is that a new generation is predicted to be relatively less wealthy than their parents, despite the fact that their material wealth is expanding, measured in absolute terms of energy use, due to technological advances. Not all the U.S. government's stability is due to the clever design of its rules.

The U.S. government is a decentralized organization, a DAO. Norway is a DAO – the best DAO according to the democracy index.[38] Mauritius, Uruguay, and South Korea are also DAOs. Every functioning democracy is more akin to a DAO than to a centralized corporation. To prove this, simply answer the question, "who owns the U.S."? A cynical answer might be something along the lines of "the military industrial complex" or "the corporations." The U.S. DAO has been operating continuously for more than 200 years, so naturally there is corruptive rust that builds in such an immense machine. Those answers hold more than a little truth. But the best answer to who owns the power in the United States is truly more along the lines of "the people."

There have been problems with our systems of democratic governance that were identified while they were being built (the *Federalist Papers*) and immediately after (deToqueville's *Democracy in America*) and the criticisms have multiplied ever since. Many of these criticisms are correct. Many of the flaws were unavoidable due to the nature of the culture of the people the system needs to govern. Many of the flaws were unavoidable due to the nature of the technologies that were available at the time (voting, communication, recording). So, the systems adopted were flawed. Systems are always flawed and need constant analysis and criticism. Many flaws are due to inevitable corruption in any static system – even the dynamic system of tripartite checks and balances is relatively static in the second order, since the design itself has been relatively fixed for 200 years. We see a dissolution of clarity as the branches overstep their established bounds: executives usurping legislative power with line-item vetoes and military actions without Congressional authorization; judges usurping legislative power by "legislating from the bench" and lawyers usurping executive power by using the inefficiency of the courts to coerce opponents with the threat of frivolous suits; and legislators preventing the executive from making judicial appointments.

Many of these violations are easily explained by party factionalism, which was a basic concern of the Founders, especially Madison. Duverger's Law claims a plurality voting system (whoever gets the most votes – the plurality – wins) leads inevitably to two-party factions. In Federalist 10, Madison argues the threat of factionalism (political parties) in a democracy naturally leads to a Tyranny of the Majority emerging,

---

38 https://en.wikipedia.org/wiki/Democracy_Index

and that this can only be prevented in two ways. First by giving individuals further autonomy, decentralizing interests, and breaking up majorities by encouraging the natural diversity of humanity. Second by filtering power to wiser individuals through representative democracy. Wisdom was to be measured in proportion to their devotion to encouraging individual autonomy. Twenty-first century technology can encourage both solutions using decentralized accounting for reputation.

Despite the corruption any system inevitably collects, the U.S. Constitution's design is a major reason for the success and stable governance of the nation for two centuries of unpredictable history, during which its population has grown almost 100-fold. The dynamic design of the separated powers gives it stability through power decentralization.

New systems that are emerging due to advances in information technology face even greater challenges than the fledgling 18th century republic of former colonies, the 11th century Maghribi traders, or the clans of Imperial China. Today, far larger global networks of people are forming, open to members with diverse values and backgrounds, commanding more power. Automated systems processing information at light speed can now communicate globally and store voluminous details on minute transactions. These tools are expected to be harnessed to govern ever more sophisticated business arrangements in ever more complex technological situations with ever more detailed information. How do we build governance systems that remain stable in such dynamic environments? Protocol centralization is necessary to display objective fairness, but this leads to instability. Lessons on decentralized dynamic design from the 17th century, reputational systems over distant trade routes on the Silk Road in the 11th century, and justice decentralization and transcendental value adherence in Ancient China and Egypt help us to understand how these networks are stabilized. What else made it possible to create our current global networks? What else is needed to revitalize our democratic systems and build the successful networks of the future?

Chapter 2
Contemporary Decentralization

Web 2.0 started when companies exploited the power of decentralization using the tools of personal computers and the internet. Web 2.0 began around 1999 with companies like Google, Amazon, and Wikipedia taking advantage of previously untapped talent and knowledge. Wikipedia decentralizes knowledge collection and organization; PayPal decentralizes payment services; Skype decentralizes telecommunications; Spotify decentralizes file sharing; Google Maps decentralizes data collection for knowledge about road traffic, just as the Google search engine decentralizes data collection for knowledge about website popularity by monitoring internet traffic; YouTube decentralizes video production, putting a television studio in the pocket of anyone with a smartphone. Marketplaces of all kinds were decentralized by eBay, Amazon, Craigslist, Airbnb, Upwork, and Uber. With the power of contemporary information technology and intuitive UI design, these idiot-proof applications allow children to do jobs that formerly required long training and substantial material investment to achieve.

Intuitive UIs rely on the IT advance of dynamic processing. JavaScript was a revolution that allowed intuitive and interactive functionality for Web 2.0, compared with the relatively static information storage and transmission that Web 1.0 provided with HTML and CSS programming languages. This empowers everyone to be content creators. Web 2.0 companies connect billions of these newly empowered individuals with light speed broadcasting. The resulting cooperation leads to knowledge beyond previous imagination. The decentralized interconnectivity of the web offers up this Olympian perspective to everyone on the web, further magnifying our power. By loosely curating and controlling this content with automated protocols, these companies charge fees, advertise, direct our attention, request donations, and use the knowledge of the network for market advantage. Since these profits are derived from global networks, their potential is literally titanic.

Decentralization is upon us. We are already experiencing the advantage of decentralization in most areas of our lives. The internet has given us the tools to decentralize economics, education, and entertainment. With an algorithm, YouTube automates the process of allowing anyone with a smartphone to create and share education and entertainment content with the world. PayPal allows globally networked P2P financial transactions. eBay and Amazon and Alibaba have algorithms that automate globally networked P2P trading contracts. Uber's algorithm automates the connection of riders and drivers, unlocking the working potential of anyone with a car and a smartphone. UpWork and TaskRabbit decentralize more of the gig economy, allowing anyone with any skill to match directly with customers and employers. Facebook's algorithm facilitates social connections around the globe. Google Maps and search engine utilizes the decentralized information from user traffic to feed algorithms that automate the

https://doi.org/10.1515/9783110673937-002

directions and commercial decisions of its users. Wikipedia's algorithm facilitates knowledge creation and sharing,[1] along with YouTube, which are the most important tools for learning new skills in any endeavor, from life hacks and cooking to computer programming and graduate-level physics subjects. Decentralized tools are transforming the way people behave in every level of society, in every facet of our lives.

With the launch of the iPhone in 2007, smartphone adoption rates exceeded other technological devices such as the lightbulb, telephones, TV, and the personal computer. The smartphone became the consumer technology with the fastest adoption rate, reaching 40% market saturation in just two and a half years. The role of smartphones for societal change cannot be underestimated. For the unbanked, who lack access to traditional bank accounts, but have high rates of mobile phone ownership, smartphones and mobile money are playing a critical role in financial inclusion. The smartphone provides access to stored value accounts and a growing set of financial services that can change lives. The Arab Spring of 2011 or the protests following the killing of George Floyd in 2020 sparked global changes because of the power of social media. Common citizens are now journalists and have the power of news broadcast rooms in their pockets. Average people are able to connect to more viewers than major media corporations could two decades ago thanks to social media platforms such as Facebook and Twitter.

From Social Media to Decentralized Coordination

Social media transfers knowledge from the edges of society into the mainstream. Social media allows people who hold otherwise marginalized or underappreciated views to meet kindred spirits online and form groups that broadcast and promote their shared ideas. When these newly formed social networks grow, they can increase their influence and promote their perspectives until they gain mainstream adoption. Otherwise invisible social, ethical, environmental, and political issues can thus gain traction. Increased visibility of these issues can transfer the balance of power from the few to the many. Power is diffused – decentralized.

Facebook is widely credited with beginning the Arab Spring uprisings that led to massive political protests throughout North Africa and the Middle East starting in 2011 and revolutions in Tunisia, Libya, Egypt, and Yemen.[2] How did Facebook

---

1 Intellipedia, https://en.wikipedia.org/wiki/Intellipedia (retrieved 6/6/20) is an example of decentralized knowledge creation and sharing behind a strong KYC private firewall that the U.S. intelligence community has used for more than a decade.
2 Roger P. Mellen, "Modern Arab Uprisings and Social Media: An Historical Perspective on Media and Revolution," *Explorations in Media Ecology*, 11(2), April 2013, p. 115.

know which stories were important to promote in its network? Did some nameless employee come across an important incident and spread it around the network? Not at all. The centralized company Facebook didn't know or choose to do anything directly related to the beginnings of the protest. The platform was used as a tool for protestors and revolutionaries to communicate their messages of dissatisfaction. "It allows them to circumvent state-controlled media. What we've seen in the Arab Spring in the use of Twitter, YouTube, Facebook, all of these things . . . what it allowed protestors to do was to circumvent these dictatorships, their traditional means of controlling information, which was the state television network, the state radio, the state newspapers."[3]

How do protestors use social media to organize their protests? In the subsequent global Occupy protests, in the Hong Kong protests, the George Floyd protests and many others, protests have not been centrally controlled. There is no president of the Hong Kong protests. Neither do the companies who own and run these social media platforms guide the movements. They don't know what the stories are that will spark revolution. Yet stories do go viral and change the world.

How do the owners and employees of Facebook know to tell its users the most important news stories of the day? How does Twitter know the latest cultural trends? How does Netflix know the top 10 comedy movies of the 1990s? How does Google know what the best Thai restaurant in Rome is? Quite simply, they don't. The companies don't go out and answer these questions all day every day for themselves and then share it with you. The network itself knows these answers. The network of users has the answers in their members' behavior. The social media companies simply monitor the networks' transactions and statistically analyze the information with automated algorithms.[4] Information at the edge is gleaned mathematically using the power of our new information technology.

As the broadest extension of technological decentralization, the internet era gave rise to the most significant societal decentralization. Communication and commerce were freed of geographic limitations. At the beginning of the 2020s, about one fourth of humanity engages in virtual communication on social media in some capacity. Social media created a form of social cohesion that was unprecedented in terms of geographic social interaction. Views and values could be exchanged and influenced with a global reach. Prior marginalized groups can coordinate their efforts worldwide through online groups that promote their shared ideas. Social functions that formerly belonged to local groups were increasingly being fulfilled by social media exchanges where influence is allocated to the most popular content and its creator.

---

3 CNN's Ivan Watson during a 2012 South by Southwest discussion. https://www.youtube.com/watch?v=1bSj4f9f8Eg&desktop_uri=%2Fwatch%3Fv%3D1bSj4f9f8Eg (retrieved 8/12/20).
4 The most famous algorithm is Google's PageRank, whose design is a brilliant application of linear algebra and stochastic process modeling, but beyond the scope of this book.

Societal boundaries are continuously being shifted via internet-based knowledge exchange and social media. In the preinternet era, knowledge was mostly accumulated by and exchanged with specialists. Internet-based knowledge sharing helps remove information silos and information privileges that created societal structures and privileges. With the dawn of the social media age, the level of interaction between non-specialists has increased dramatically, removing hegemony and centralized control structures over information while creating a more skilled and knowledgeable work force. For example, micro task work via Crowdflower and Amazon Mechanical Turk enable lower skilled or unemployed individuals to earn a living through micro task work over the internet. Recruitment for such work typically takes place over social media outlets, by word of mouth on social media channels.

Internet-based collective decision-making via the crowd can replace the centralized coordination functions in society. For example, in the past, product quality assessments were centrally disseminated and evaluated on consumer's behalf, by way of Consumer Reports, among others. In the social media age, collective decision-making through the power of the crowd is perhaps the most prevailing method of product evaluation and forces companies to take heed. Similarly, knowledge and views from the edges of society can be moved into societal mainstream very quickly via social media. This transfer can remove existing societal consensus, social cohesion among established groups, and order in the process. Otherwise less visible and influential social, ethical, environmental, political issues can thus gain traction rather quickly. Traditional modes of coordinating human behavior by way of political decision-making, democratic institutions, business governance, learning, among many others, become slowly less prevalent.

The increased network capability of society that is promoted by social media can change and improve the coordination of human behavior in society. Social media data and metrics can replace centralized coordination of human behavior. For example, social media posts often identify emergency information more accurately with more timely dissemination than centralized media reports. Similarly, for groups that coordinate their conduct, as for example in the Arab Spring and other reform movements, coordination via social media is not merely relegated to information exchange, but can actually coordinate protest movements. In the product context, social media conduct of groups as they relate to products becomes a very powerful placement and marketing device. Product specific or content specific conduct on social media can become a form of 'social proof' for such products or services. However, because the incentive design for social proof is suboptimal, the social media coordination function is still largely flawed and corruptible. For example, one of the first things that will happen if you open a shop on Amazon is that you will receive several messages from malicious sockpuppet wranglers offering to game the rating system to improve your company's ratings while attacking your major competitor.

Decentralized technology solutions are starting to tap into the coordination function that was inaugurated by social media, while also improving it with new tools. Social media allows the enhanced coordination of information that was previously isolated on the edges of society. Because social networks feed off interactions among people, they become exponentially more powerful as they grow, due to the network effect. But these networks are stifled by the centralized ownership and governance of the Web 2.0 companies that run them. Governing decentralized information flow necessitates decentralized incentive designs.

Societal decentralization is a byproduct of broader societal trends that derive from the combined feedback effects of decentralization of science, technological decentralization, organizational decentralization, as well as market and governmental decentralization. Such are the precursors of an ever freer and more open society. Centralized ownership and control of the Web 2.0 information filtering algorithms can be useful to prevent users from gaming the system. By keeping their algorithm opaque it is more difficult for outside interests to exploit the way these social media companies guide their users to information. The Google search engine algorithm is constantly being improved, because website developers infer the rules of the algorithm and exploit its properties to raise their site's ranking. For example, if you wanted to sell widgets on your website in 2006, you could make a blue background and type "widget" in the same blue color thousands of times. The 2006 Google search engine algorithm (PageRank) would then raise your website's relevance in any person's search for "widget." The 2007 algorithm saw through this trick and would punish any page that used it. Therefore, website developers moved on to other tricks in 2008.

But a different incentive mechanism can improve the algorithms even faster. Instead of an arms race between the outside exploiters and the centralized companies who host the network, if the P2P network were decentrally owned by the users themselves, the algorithms can be open source and still remain safe. Instead of a centralized company continually developing the opaque algorithm to punish people who try to optimize their content, P2P networks can reward members properly for improving the algorithm. By rewarding users for policing exploitation, by incentivizing the network to defend the algorithm they own, these decentralized networks leverage the power of a much larger talent pool. Instead of having few insiders and many outsiders, open access flips the ownership model, creating as many insiders as can possibly contribute. This flipping of ownership of Web 2.0 companies to a decentralized ownership model is the heart of the Web3 movement we will discuss later.

Page and Brin deserve to be lauded and rewarded for inventing the PageRank algorithm that underlied the early Google search engine. But the primitive system for recognizing only the ultimate legal winners, the Jobs's and Gates's, is being improved. The next Pages and Brins will certainly be recognized and rewarded under this new model of ownership, but the army of developers who further improve the systems will also get their due.

Sharing Economy

P2P connectivity is giving new life to the sharing economy. The sharing economy refers to the utilization of previously idle services and goods and the partial use of others' property rights in goods. For instance, you might provide your car, or your time, as part of a peer-to-peer transaction, often over a platform built to unite the interested parties. Unlike traditional centralized ways of production and selling to consumers by hiring employees, platform companies in the sharing economy typically provide the technological setup that allows individuals to share their property rights in goods or sell their services without centralized employment. Individuals who connect via platforms in the sharing economy share their property rights in, for example, cars, homes, or rent out their personal skillsets and time in a peer-to-peer form of engagement.

The sharing economy has become part of modern society's mainstream. The origins of the sharing economy can be traced back to an emphasis on sustainability, resource efficiency, and community. As the sharing economy evolved, not only did its services and industry acceptance proliferate, the sharing economy's credo of "access over ownership" became more mainstream. The public had grown accustomed to receiving services and goods on-demand via digital and mobile technologies – especially the perception of the internet as universal access to information. On-demand access to goods and services became part of modern society, it became no longer a preference and habit of millennials alone.

The sharing economy necessitates a reframing of legacy legal regimes and frameworks. The legal frameworks that regulate disrupted and associated industries are often incompatible with the emerging trends generated by the sharing economy. Cities and co-municipalities had to learn that the sharing economy requires a proactive stance to channel the sharing economy's outputs and associated new requirements into economic development while at the same time protecting the public with regulation. While some cities have joined forces to declare common commitments and principles for sharing cities[5] and many co-municipalities are developing transportation-as-a-service platforms to better meet the needs of all residents, some states in the United States have passed legislation that in some ways undermine the sharing economy.[6]

---

5 Share Barcelona, https://share.barcelona/ (retrieved 6/1/20).
6 Ballotpedia, 2017. Local Government Responses to the Sharing Economy (ridesharing/home-sharing), https://ballotpedia.org/Local_government_responses_to_the_sharing_economy_(ridesharing/homesharing) (retrieved 6/1/20). Chapman, Lizette, Eidelson, Josh, Cutler, Joyce E. & Bloomberg (September 11, 2019). Governmental requirements that Uber & Lift treat their workers as employees instead of independent contractors will certainly weaken the power the company receives from their decentralized structure. However, this may improve the industry, as it opens the space for more politically decentralized competitors. A DAO that makes each member a partial owner would not be subject to the bill since such a DAO would not have employers and employees. "New Labor Bill Passed by California Senate Would Transform the Gig Economy — And Could Cost Uber $500 Million

Yet, some countries, such as Denmark, have changed their internal regulations to better accommodate sharing economies.

The values that enabled the new flowering of the sharing economy morphed from an emphasis on connectivity for the sake of sustainability to a focus on connectivity and community as a commodity. In other words, connectivity and community building via increased connectivity became a purpose and meaning by itself. The purpose of sharing economy participants shifted from connectivity for a cause, such as a community for sustainability, toward mass consumption for convenience and transactional efficiency.

The ultimate sign of the sharing economy's success is its increasing recognition in policy, economic, and business circles, as part of the overall economy. The sharing economy has the potential to shape entire markets that are better connected and more efficient. It has started to blur the lines between industries and even former competitors.

How did we get here, and where are we going?

History of Web 1.0 and Web 2.0

In harnessing the power and talent of the masses, one of the problems that Web 2.0 companies solved was the problem of individual success under Web 1.0. Ultimately, internet users made a Faustian bargain with Web 2.0 companies to host their content.

In the early days of Web 1.0 if you wanted to post content, you would build your own webpage. Then you could buy a special router to connect your computer to the internet after obtaining special addresses (IP and AS numbers) and permissions from the King of the Internet.[7] Then you would need to keep your computer server running and your telephone lines open, so that anyone who wanted to view your webpage could contact your computer and ask it to send the information.

This was not a problem in the early days when very few people were using the internet. But the network quickly grew, so if your webpage was at all popular, this setup would create a bottleneck. The solution at the time was to hire a middleman.

---

a Year," Fortune: Tech, https://fortune.com/2019/09/11/gig-economy-california-senate-uber-law-labor-rights-union/ (retrieved 6/1/20).

7 That's an old joke about the World Wide Web. Who is the ultimate person in charge of the internet, anyway? Somebody called me a bad name. Can I talk to the manager? The web was designed to be censorship resistant with maximum autonomy among nodes. This brought about a new level of freedom of speech that is clashing with our evolutionary programming. From the beginnings of multicellular life, if one animal were to insult another, the response would be immediate and symmetric. On the internet, a troll can flame and run.

These functions could be achieved by internet service providers (ISPs)[8] who could provide the bandwidth necessary to allow your page to be seen by the world.

The idea at the time was that ISPs would compete to become powerful utilities, since they would provide essential services for the commons. They would provide as much bandwidth as possible to their users to justify their expansion. The incentive structure that would solve the problem is for originators of Transmission Control Protocol (TCP) requests[9] to pay the bill. That way ISPs who hosted more content would be paid from the ISPs who hosted more consumers.

This didn't solve the problem, as naturally the Tragedy of the Commons[10] asserted itself. Porn sites and pirated file sharing (often set up by the ISPs themselves to game the payment design[11]) quickly used up any available bandwidth. Further, negotiations between ISP providers were much more nuanced than the plan outlined above; the accounting didn't merely resolve according to TCP requests. Creators concerned with fringe issues, such as science and social issues, were not a priority and could be charged, since they cared about their causes. The ISP charged low-volume providers on a per connection basis. If your site suddenly became popular, with thousands of people constantly accessing your content, you had to pay for thousands of long-distance phone calls. Individuals with popular pages were forced to delete their content.

Web 2.0. companies provided the solution. YouTube, Facebook, and Reddit provide free hosting for your text, picture, and movie files. In exchange they have access to the information that content providers want to share. They own any personal information from viewers that can be gleaned. They control what content can and can't be shared, guiding popular opinion. And most importantly they have access to our attention.

Each of these Web 2.0 companies has disrupted their industries in dramatic ways. But these examples all use a centralized hierarchical business model for ownership

---

8 Previously, there were many independent ISPs, culminating in approximately 7,000 ISPs in the United States by 2000. Within a few years, however, the ISPs were consolidated until U.S. internet telecommunications became dominated by two companies, Comcast and AT&T. https://www.sacatech. com/2019/08/15/neverending-story-isp-market-consolidation/ Posted August 2019 (retrieved 6/3/20).
9 Transmission Control Protocol (TCP) is the primary set of rules governing the proper format for transmission of website information, e-mail, and other files through the internet. A common TCP request is to view the information at any given website address.
10 The Tragedy of the Commons refers to the reasonable and predictable situation where a shared resource is spoiled without oversight or accountability. The idea was mentioned early by the British economist William Forster Lloyd ("Two Lectures on the Checks to Population," Oxford University, 1833) who described unregulated grazing on public land – the commons – and is commonly used to explain the collapse of fisheries and other environmental problems. Here the "commons" is the shared public resource of internet bandwidth, or even the (currently) unmeasurable tone of our culture, which still has meaningful economic consequences.
11 Viktor Trón, Aron Fischer, Dániel Nagy, Zsolt Felföldi, & Nick Johnson, "Swap, Swear and Swindle: Incentive System for Swarm," *Ethersphere Orange Papers*, p. 4, draft version May 2016.

and governance of information. For example, internet-based markets – like Craigslist, eBay and Amazon – are hybrid centralized companies that decentralize the customer experience, since anyone can be a vendor and anyone can be a reviewer. Buyers and sellers are directly connected. The internet allows their platforms to scale globally. More users means exponentially more connections[12] – the network effect means the leap in connections matches customers more efficiently with vendors, increasing sales, and efficiency (see Figure 2.1).

Intuitive UIs – idiot-proof design – help maximize the size of the network. Ride-sharing businesses, like Uber, take advantage of this increased efficiency by providing free apps that anyone can use to engage business, connecting a rider with an available driver with a few clicks. The centralized owners control this software and therefore control the market and can dictate prices. They don't charge transparent fees. They adjust to real-time information about supply and demand to maximize their profits. If there are many riders demanding rides during rush hour, they can increase fees. If there are too many drivers, they can pay them less. These Web 2.0 companies use the structure, control, and profit optimization of centralized companies combined with the power of decentralization due to network effects.

Thanks to these Web 2.0 companies, which have disrupted much of the economy, consumers around the globe are becoming accustomed to the advantages of decentralized business. But improvements in P2P technology are prompting the question of whether the centralized owners of these Web 2.0 companies are necessary at all. We now have the technology to decentralize these companies completely. Bitcoin is an example of a measurably valuable network with a thoroughly decentralized ownership structure.

---

12 The exponent is 2, so a pedantic mathematician might object that it's quadratic growth. The idea is that with n nodes in a network, there are $nC2 = n(n-1)/2 \sim \frac{1}{2}n^2$ possible connections. The network effect of power scaling as the square of the number of members of the network has been in common scientific parlance since at least the 1980s and is sometimes referred to as Metcalfe's Law https://en.wikipedia.org/wiki/Metcalfe%27s_law (retrieved 8/12/20).

Compare this with the number of connections in a centralized hierarchical structure. In a tree graph with n nodes there are $n-1$ connections regardless of the number of levels in the hierarchy, the minimal number necessary to make the graph globally connected. The centralized structure is maximally efficient for sending messages to the whole group from one central leader using minimal energy. For instance, the Catholic religious hierarchy uses seven levels to create the potential to reach every person on the planet. Hypothetically, if the Pope contacted $100 = 10^2$ cardinals, who each contacted 10^2 archbishops, and so on down through bishops, priests, deacons, and lay people, then the Pope would have potential access to $10^{12} = 1$ trillion individuals requiring only six levels.

The maximally decentralized structure, on the other hand, is maximally stable in that it is maximally redundant and will not suffer any loss in connectivity when any particular connection is broken. With the contemporary advances in information technology, we live in a post-information-scarcity society and do not need to rely on the efficiency saving architectures of centralized hierarchies. Now every individual can broadcast their messages to every other individual on the planet inexpensively.

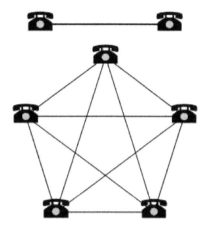 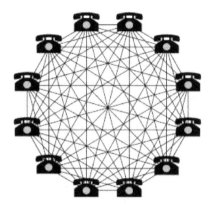

Figure 2.1: Network effects. Created by Nathan Wood.

Open Source Culture

In order to have a truly decentralized organization, the rules must be transparently available to all members. Otherwise the keepers of the knowledge have a higher status, creating a hierarchy. Further, all members must be encouraged to contribute to these rules, according to their talents. Transparency is fundamental to fostering the trust between members necessary to build a decentralized network. The functions of all software must be publicly auditable for people to trust it. If one person could own the copyright to some of the software a decentralized organization uses, then they would have de facto power over the organization, again establishing hierarchies of power within the organization. We wouldn't be talking about the decentralized organizations of the future without open source software. The open source movement has already transformed our world.

A fundamental divide exists at the heart of computer programming regarding the copyrightability of software. At the beginning of electronic computing, researchers in universities and technology companies came from a tradition of freely sharing their work in service to their field's progress. This openness in academia can be traced at least as far back as the Renaissance, but all societies' golden ages are characterized by a flourishing of innovation, which can be directly attributed to temporary open collaboration in their culture. Early computer programs were basic algorithms – they were closer to mathematics proofs than to fictional works of literature and were simply seen as elegant distillations of clear thought that anyone would come to, given sufficient time and effort. Through the 1950s–1960s most computer companies did not license their operating systems. As programs became more complex, companies began to view their software as intellectual property. In 1976 the U.S. Congress updated the Copyright Act of 1909, and based on the recommendations of the National Commission on New Technological Uses of Copyrighted Works (CONTU), wrote an amendment in 1980 clarifying software as creative art, similar to literature and copyrightable in any form.[13]

Software companies such as Microsoft, IBM, and AT&T began to enforce their copyrights with license fees and no longer distributed source code.[14] Richard Stallman is a major voice in the open source movement who decried these practices as unethical and stultifying to the field of software development, by limiting the ability to build on others' work. Advocating the use of "free" software ("free as in 'freedom,' not as in 'free beer'"[15]), Stallman created the GNU Project in 1983, which was formalized in the nonprofit Free Software Foundation in 1985. Their GNU General Public License (1989) implemented the copyleft legal mechanism, which grants users the rights to use purchased software without further charges, and the rights to modify the program's source code, but requires all future derivatives to remain under the same license.

Linus Torvalds released his Linux operating system (OS) under the GNU license in 1992, which has become the most common OS running unnoticed in most mobile phones. Linux has more than 1,500 developers.[16] The crypto community boasts anywhere from 4,000 to 200,000 developers per month. These figures are completely unreliable due to anonymity (especially due to the uncertain legal environment) and the fact that very few of these work on stable projects. Ethereum likely has the largest community with approximately 200 full-time developers.

The Apache HTTP Server software was the next major open source project, which now underlies almost every click you make on the internet. It's worth exploring the history and operation of the largest stable open source programming community, the Apache Software Foundation (ASF), with 7,800 high-level developers, called committers. Today ASF has 202 active committees working on 340 active projects.[17] They are responsible for the experience we have with the internet today, since every major software company uses many of the tools Apache has built and released for free in the last three decades. The network started in 1993 on a project that became the Apache HTTP Server, which today is the world's most popular web

---

13 Jan L. Nussbaum, "Apple Computer, Inc. v. Franklin Computer Corporation Puts the Byte Back into Copyright Protection for Computer Programs," *Golden Gate University Law Review, 14*(2), Article 3, January 1984, pp. 278–292.

14 Steven Weber, *The Success of Open Source*, Harvard University Press, 2004, pp. 38–44. More details on most of the history in this section is reviewed in https://en.wikipedia.org/wiki/History_of_free_and_open-source_software (retrieved 7/31/20).

15 Sam Williams, *Free as in Freedom: Richard Stallman's Crusade for Free Software*, O'Reilly Media, 2002.

16 https://www.linuxfoundation.org/resources/open-source-guides/participating-open-source-communities/ (retrieved 7/31/20).

17 apache.org (retrieved 7/30/20).

server software.[18] The name Apache was chosen partly to signal their affinity for the Native American tribe's indomitability and decentralized nature, and partly as a pun – their main concern in the beginning was creating Apache software *patches* for internet products.

All work released by the foundation uses the Apache license, which is an anchor of the current open source software (OSS) movement. The Apache license gives users the legal right to use the software for any purpose, to distribute it, to modify it, even to profit from it, without ever paying the Apache foundation. The Apache license differs from the GNU license in that new software deriving from work under the Apache license is not required to remain under the Apache license. New work may be patented or copyright protected by its innovators. The only constraint is that the modified ASF file must be annotated carefully with a NOTICE text file explaining the changes.

Some of the rate of technological innovation is due to the open source culture, and it is especially important in the emerging API economy. The "API economy" is a term that comes from a programming structure called an API, which stands for Application to Program Interface. In software development an API is a metaphorical bridge between two incompatible programs – the API is a third program that translates between the other two. The API economy is a recognition that the interoperability between many of the digital tools in our lives and in business is leading to great leaps in efficiency, requiring complex new legal and business negotiations due to the near continual innovation in collaboration displayed in the use of these tools.

As an example, after working on my car, my mechanic texts me the diagnosis and a bill. I choose from a list of recommended maintenance and fixes that I want them to do, and I pay through my smart phone, which stores my credit card and interacts with the mechanic's payment app to a bank account. This triggers the shipment of parts to the mechanic, automatically paying the distributor and shipping service. There are at least eight programs owned by eight different interests that are interacting in this nearly trivial transaction, but they all need APIs to interact.

APIs create the standards that allow companies to exchange data and build seamless omnichannel experiences for their customers. Interoperability strengthens networks, making them more pervasive and useful, leading to greater adoption. Interoperability thus naturally increases network effects making them more valuable to members and users.

---

18 See Netcraft, April 15, 2010. April 2010 Web Server Survey, https://news.netcraft.com/archives/ 2010/04/15/april_2010_web_server_survey.html (retrieved 6/1/20) for an external audit and more recent claims in the Apache Software Foundation Annual Report for 2020 Fiscal Year, the Apache Software Foundation Blog, July 29, 2020. Available online at: https://blogs.apache.org/foundation/ entry/the-apache-software-foundation-announces67 (retrieved 7/31/20).

As our systems become more interoperable, it will require more sophisticated APIs, which will require more access to the source code of each of the separate apps. An open source culture accelerates this development. P2P technologies provide neutral platforms for the API economy. The level playing field of decentralized technologies gives the ideal market for companies to negotiate and collaborate.

But how do we build powerful and valuable technological platforms that nobody owns? Let's first look at the Apache foundation to see how it has thrived over the last few decades.

The ASF is a decentralized organization. Because of its nonprofit status, it can survive with a very loose governance process, dominated by a do-ocracy philosophy – doing things is the primary governing force for the group. If people are interested in working on a new project and are willing to uphold the organization's values (following their code of conduct), they are usually encouraged, because a primary value of the network is to build community. Surprisingly, the major source of tension in the community is that some for-profit companies such as Facebook or Google will pay their workers to contribute to projects they need. These workers often devote far more effort to a project and sometimes push out volunteers. Then the paid workers leave once their duties are complete, leaving no one to maintain and upgrade the software in the future. The maxim "Community Over Code" is repeatedly used to promote the idea that a good community can fix code problems, but a bad community cannot maintain even the best code in the long run.

Despite the looseness of the Apache do-ocracy, such strife necessitates some foundational rules for arbitrating conflicts, such as whether a project is finished and should be released under the Apache name. In such cases, there are 781 members who may vote up +1, down – 1, or abstain 0. If the sum of the votes is positive, the proposal passes. There are three ranks of power in ASF: contributors, committers, and members. Only the members can vote. You can become a **member** if another member nominates you and the other members positively vote for your candidacy. Therefore, ASF is technically a closed organization. But the ASF is also quite open, in the sense that anyone in the world can be a **contributor** on any project, in most any capacity. However, their contributions are only suggestions until they are approved by a committer. **Committers** have the power of write access to their project repositories. Contributors with a strong record of improving projects can become committers on a project if the members in the project nominate and approve them.

How, though, can we explain the success of Apache? Why do people donate their talents and efforts to valuable projects from which they receive no remuneration? How do they maintain quality? How has the network survived for three decades? Remember, a decentralized network survives by living its values.

The members are happy to explain that their motivations include altruism, social reputation, and belonging and contributing to a community. Owen O'Malley, the VP of Apache Orc explains, "If everyone knows that I did a piece of code, then I'm a lot more careful to make it good. And if it's just something that is going into a proprietary software, then I can be a little sloppier."[19] Members simply feel good about themselves and enjoy contributing to projects that they see are helping to improve the world. Making a meaningful contribution to code that is used around the world is an impressive addition to your resume. But the most compelling argument we hear is *Funktionslust*. "When I create something, I want it to be beautiful as well as functional." The German word *Funktionslust* means the pleasure you enjoy by doing something you're good at. "We also have to work with a lot of closed-source software, and it just sucks. It's hard to debug. It's hard to reason about. With the ASF you work together with a bunch of people who chose these products to collaborate." The open source culture brings together talent from anywhere on the planet. Projects get populated with people who want to work on that product – who are good at solving those problems. Mostly, it's fun. It's fun to work together with other people who share your values, to use your talents, and improve yourself. It's fun to teach and to learn, especially on a project you care about. By acting as if they are living in a post-scarcity society, they create one.[20] Andy Shi, a developer advocate for Alibaba, explains, "Joining forces with the open source effort is rewarding. You give a little; you take back way more. So that's really what I want to share, especially with developers and companies in China. Don't be afraid to give, to share. You will get more out of it."

Eric S. Raymond wrote the article "The Cathedral and the Bazaar" and organized a committee that introduced the term open source (first suggested by Christine Peterson) in 1998.[21] The "Cathedral" refers to centralized, carefully controlled, closed-source development projects, while the "Bazaar" refers to the more chaotic, decentralized, open-source projects. Both models have advantages and disadvantages. Since before its publication, many major projects have switched repeatedly between the two models, with Apache being perhaps the most visible and enduring success of the Bazaar model.

For the last three decades, Apache HTTP has been the most popular server software in the world. Google built the Android OS on the backbone of Linux under the open source Apache 2.0 license. Android is the most popular mobile platform worldwide. The popularity of these open source platforms is largely due to the fact that independent developers have less legal confusion about what they can contribute, control, and own in the open source environment.

---

19 Quotes from the documentary feature *Trillions and Trillions Served*, the Apache Software Foundation, June 10, 2020. Available online: https://www.youtube.com/watch?v=JUt2nb0mgwg&feature=youtu.be (retrieved 7/31/20).

20 Richard Barbrook, "The High-Tech Gift Economy," *First Monday, 13*(12), 1998 with 2005 update. Available online at https://firstmonday.org/ojs/index.php/fm/article/view/631/552 (retrieved 8/3/20).

21 Michael Tiemann, "History of the OSI," *Open Source Initiative*, October 1, 2002. Available online at https://web.archive.org/web/20021001164015/http://www.opensource.org/docs/history.php (retrieved 7/31/20).

These reasons bring us partially toward understanding how the open source movement can exist. But how can they thrive? The Apache Software Foundation's near trivial governance system works in an organization whose members are not competing for power and money within the organization. The Apache foundation rightfully brags that their 227 million lines of code have given the world a value of US$20 billion.[22] Impressive for a volunteer force seeking no monetary rewards, but it's a blip in the global economy. However, not all is positive in an environment with maximal transparency. Sometimes open source projects fail to attract the necessary quality of developer that a closed-source project can reliably procure with more funding and control. Another problem is that the very success of the open source movement allows major corporations to pressure smaller projects to reveal their code, then take it and use their power to exploit the work more profitably than the startup.

How can we improve such open decentralized networks? How can we properly incentivize larger swaths of the economy to compete with for-profit centralized companies? The Apache Foundation has built a successful nonprofit software development DAO. What tools do we need to build a for-profit software development DAO? How do we build a Maghribi Foundation?

Early P2P file-sharing programs demonstrated that the untapped bandwidth available from individuals' uploading capacity was enough to compete with large ISPs. At one point, P2P networks accounted for a majority of internet traffic. The bandwidth has always been there, but the latency of past P2P projects is higher than people now demand – it took longer to receive the information from individual devices that are not optimized for broadcast speed compared with dedicated servers. New projects promise to address this problem with computation and storage sharing, not just file sharing. Let's look closer at P2P technology and see how it is being used to replace Web 2.0 companies.

P2P, Blockchains, and Web3

Technological innovation is rapidly accelerating. Hard on the heels of the computer revolution that culminated in the Web 1.0 internet, Web 2.0 disrupted major sectors of our economy by giving global networking power to any consumer. Intuitive user interfaces (UIs) transform children into gods of information, whose abilities would make Hermes blush. Using these UIs, companies are harnessing the previously untapped talent, taking advantage of new wells of decentralized information.

---

22 The Apache Software Foundation Annual Report for 2020 Fiscal Year, the Apache Software Foundation Blog, July 29, 2020. Available online at: https://blogs.apache.org/foundation/entry/the-apache-software-foundation-announces67 (retrieved 7/31/20).

Now less than two decades later, Web3 hopes to furnish the next information technology revolution.[23] This vision for the future is to fully decentralize every aspect of IT with peer-to-peer technology. The goal of the Web3 movement is to foster radical bureaucratic transparency using open source design, to further individual autonomy and privacy using cryptography, and to level the access to information and computing resources with decentralized networks.

P2P Technology

Most people are unaware of the many types of P2P technology that the internet relies on, but we are more familiar with the somewhat analogous technology of cloud computing. Cloud computing uses the internet to displace your storage and processing of information from your personal device to a more powerful distant device. Dropbox (2008), for example, is a privately owned cloud storage company that allows you to store your files (movies, pictures, documents) on their servers instead of your home device, then access the files on-demand through the internet. The advantage is that most people can trust a large company to back up their storage much more reliably than they can personally, and the files will be available regardless of how technology changes from floppy disks to CDs to flash drives, etc.

Similarly, there are cloud computing architectures for displacing information processing from your personal device to a distant computer. Chromebooks are cheap laptops which use this design approach.

Since your files are stored redundantly on many backup servers, we can say that cloud computing decentralizes the function of your personal computer. But most cloud computing is centralized in the sense that you need to rely on a centrally owned company to provide the service. The disadvantage of centralization is losing power over your personal information, paying for the privilege, and hoping the files stay secure despite the reality of their centralized point of failure (e.g., if the company goes bankrupt or is hacked). Web3 is devoted to the challenge of creating decentralized alternatives.

P2P is an alternative decentralized architecture to cloud computing. Napster was an early decentralized P2P file sharing system (1999) that revolutionized how users accessed music, completely disrupting the music distribution industry. Improving on Napster, BitTorrent (2001) protocols allow users to share files directly between each other in a more fully P2P setting, without storing file content on any centralized server. The idea is that anyone running a client (software that runs the BitTorrent

---

23 The term Web3 was first suggested by Gavin Wood, who was instrumental in the creation of Ethereum. Web 3.0 is also sometimes used to refer to Tim Berners-Lee's notion of the semantic web, which is unrelated.

algorithm) will be able to automatically share files from their computer (called seeding), making them available to anyone who wishes to view those files and download them. Large files are split into pieces and held redundantly on many different computers in the network to make them available on demand. So P2P architectures create open decentralized networks, where every user starts on an equal footing.

The point of a P2P network is to achieve distributed computing without centralized control. Distributed computing is splitting a big difficult task across many members as equally as possible. The goal is to unite a network of nodes (i.e., computers) all running the same protocol and all sharing the work. A simple example of P2P is the internet itself, where computers all over the world run the same protocol for communicating with each other and sharing data. Very roughly, the internet has a protocol for keeping track of all the website addresses (called DNS) and users' addresses (IPs, ISPs, NSPs), and a protocol for connecting computers (HTTP, TCP IP) so they can request data or computations from each other.

Other P2P services use an even simpler architecture to link a network of users, with the goal of bringing the technological requirements down to the level of the average individual's laptop, as BitTorrent demonstrates. Another example, Tor (2002) helps anonymize internet usage, protecting citizens' and reporters' access to communication under oppressive governments.[24] Each user can participate anonymously to build a cooperative network that provides greater value for all, at least theoretically.

The reason earlier centralized companies succeeded against more decentralized P2P platforms is due to the existing technology of the time and the natural incentive design that is built into our capitalist civilization. Commercial devices available to the average user were not able to provide the upload speed that industrial servers with "fat pipes" could, meaning greater latency for P2P platforms built from average individual computer enthusiasts. Centralized companies had the proper incentive design to provide better quality of experience by overseeing commercially oriented intuitive user interface upgrades. And large companies would find negotiating the central bureaucracy more worthwhile than individual computer geeks thanks to economies of scale.

One problem with most existing decentralized filesharing networks is that unpopular files (such as your personal files) are not guaranteed to be available, unlike centralized cloud computing services that guarantee availability for a fee. Centralized companies provided superior network availability and latency through centralized oversight. A centralized company's goal is to continually improve quality and has the advantage of being able to consciously analyze and control their own dataflow,

---

24 Originally developed by the U.S. Naval Research Laboratory. See Yasha Levine, "Almost everyone involved in developing Tor was (or is) funded by the US government," *Pando Daily*, July 16, 2014. https://pando.com/2014/07/16/tor-spooks/ (retrieved 8/8/20).

helping companies "get closer to their customers". The improved data allows companies to consciously personalize their services to individual customers.

However, today P2P is making inroads in the competition with private companies for internet space. The centralized client-server computing architecture is threatened by new P2P networking architectures that are being built to spread decentralized technology. Through the removal of centralized hosts and servers, the nodes that form the P2P network make computing resources, such as disk storage, network bandwidth, and processing power, directly available to each other. Network effects proliferate in P2P networks because, unlike the traditional client-server architecture that is subject to the linearly increasing per-unit costs, the P2P network costs can decrease with each added node (depending on topology).

In the last decade we've seen P2P networks flourish, the most famous of which are blockchains, which have made the first basic steps toward a proper incentive design in valuable networks by fairly remunerating their members.

Blockchains

The original and most famous blockchain is Bitcoin.[25] The Bitcoin protocol emerged in 2009 as an attempt by its founder, Satoshi Nakamoto, to provide an alternative to the shortcomings of the financial system in the aftermath of the 2008 financial crisis. A strong distrust of government and central banking is part of the political philosophy of the Bitcoin community to create an alternative to fiat currencies. The community believes cryptocurrency to be a solution immune from national governmental control.

A blockchain is a distributed ledger – it keeps track of some types of transactions from its members. For example, Bitcoin keeps track of the P2P transactions where members send digital tokens representing money (bitcoins) to each other.

---

25 Most people want to know which blockchain coins to invest in. We've read more than 100 white papers detailing the function of different blockchains and glanced at many more. We're sorry that we can't publicly recommend investment in any of them. Yet. We have faith that the technology will be a major component in the economy of the future. But the fundamentals of every one of these networks are lacking at the moment. We expect this point in history to be a more extreme version of the dot-com boom and bust, where around 1,000 to 5,000 startup internet companies failed, but the most powerful and profitable companies in history emerged. In this book we will not include our guesses for which blockchains will thrive. Instead we will explain why the Web3 boom and bust will continue, and what P2P networks must do to emerge successfully. Put simply, when you see a network that has designed secure and effective mechanisms for incentivizing development and democratically governing the deployment of those innovations, invest heavily. In 2020 the authors are not aware of a network with anything approaching such qualities. Which ones will eventually decentralize their power is impossible to predict, because it's illogical to do so until those in power are forced.

What makes this ledger valuable is a long list of qualities, some of which are unique to blockchains technology. Not all blockchains have the same qualities, but most are modeled on the basics of Bitcoin, which is immutable, immortal, open, uncensorable, transparent, and decentralized.

Blockchains such as Bitcoin are decentralized through their P2P architecture, since no central authority is completely in charge of anything, including ownership, security, or upgrades. Bitcoin is immutable, meaning the entire history of transactions is never changed – not one letter or number among the billions of records will ever change in response to the demands of any centralized authority. It's open, meaning anyone with a connection to the internet can download and run the client software to participate in the network without seeking the permission of anyone else. (Open networks are sometimes called permissionless.) Bitcoin is immortal, in the sense that as long as there is any freedom in the internet, any machine that chooses to download and run the software (even just for curiosity) will keep the blockchain alive. Further the network is perfectly transparent, allowing complete audits of every transaction, yet it protects its users' privacy through cryptography.

The Bitcoin protocol created the first decentralized P2P network that could manage valuable assets without resorting to a centralized authority. But the centralizing forces of competition led to concentration of power in the Bitcoin network, as economies of scale led to large computer farms devoted to mining for bitcoins, instead of millions of individual network members maintaining the ledger on their laptops.

Many other blockchain architectures have attempted to improve or generalize Bitcoin's functionality. They've built tools that improve on Bitcoin's protocol to inhibit Bitcoin's many problems (we'll talk about some later, such as ASIC-resistance and sharding), and they've built new tools that allow us to decentralize more of the functions of business. The most prominent blockchain besides Bitcoin is Ethereum.[26] Six years after Bitcoin published its first block, Bitcoin developers, aficionados, and critics started the Ethereum blockchain in 2015, providing a ledger with much more complicated transactions, called smart contracts.

Smart contracts are automated, computer-programmed business contracts. The smart contract program can be written in many different programming languages, the most popular being Solidity.[27] They automatically track the transfer of money and assets and labor between parties, without human oversight. They automatically adjudicate when something goes wrong (and something always goes wrong in business),

---

26 For example, it has long held the second highest market capitalization, behind Bitcoin.
27 If you have some experience with high-level programming languages such as C++ or Java, you can start programming in one of a few IDEs optimized for interacting with the Ethereum blockchain, such as Remix or Ethereum Studio (available at https://remix.ethereum.org/ and https://studio.ethereum.org/, retrieved 8/4/20). An IDE is an integrated development environment, which simplifies debugging and some command line programming, such as compiling.

again without human oversight. Thus, we say smart contracts are self-executing and self-regulating.

A smart contract allows more complex business logic than merely transferring digital coins from one user's digital wallet to another's. The idea is to be able to write sophisticated programs that dynamically control the timing and execution of any business contract, to act as automated escrow for many different types of digital business assets.

A smart contract is computer code that is executed automatically by the P2P network if it is written properly and uploaded to the network according to the transparent rules the network follows. The network of thousands, or millions, of computers create a "world computer" with a "virtual machine" using P2P distributed storage and processing, whose goal is to be fully decentralized.

The goal of decentralizing our economy doesn't end with decentralized digital money and smart contracts. More ambitiously, the crypto community blockchain developers have their sights on decentralizing every function of Web 2.0.

Web3

There are many other groups that have developed various versions of Web3 applications using P2P architecture. Below are some major decentralized applications that are currently being used and illustrate the potential for the future:

- Bitcoin (2009) decentralizes transnational currency, its production, accounting, and exchange.
- Bitmessage (2012) decentralizes messaging service for temporary information. Many others have different levels of security and interoperability. Worth noting was the Skype video and telephone P2P system before Microsoft supernodes took over in May 2011.[28]
- InterPlanetary Filing System (IPFS) (2015) provides P2P temporary file storage and computation.
- Ethereum (2015) decentralizes computation and permanent records for multiparty smart contracts.
- ZeppelinOS (2018) is a decentralized OS for smart contract developers. Built on top of Ethereum, it provides a stable evolutionary environment for developing secure smart contracts.

---

28 Dan Goodin, "Skype Replaces P2P Supernodes with Linux Boxes Hosted by Microsoft (updated)," Ars Technica May 1, 2012. Available online at https://arstechnica.com/information-technology/2012/05/skype-replaces-p2p-supernodes-with-linux-boxes-hosted-by-microsoft/ (retrieved 8/8/20).

The goal of these tools is to provide the decentralized information technology to build fully decentralized applications (DApps) for basic users. The tools listed above are already helping developers to easily build DApps to connect your cell phone to networks of other users. More ambitiously, the goal of building these P2P tools is to create DAOs. The idea is to make a single complicated set of programmed protocols that can automate the interaction between a (possibly very large, international) network of members who wish to cooperate on a business venture without requiring a central authority to make investment decisions and settle disputes.

There are three major reasons our institutions and economy will become more efficient by decentralizing with DApps and DAOs.

First, decentralization gives individuals more power and autonomy, unleashing information at the edge. It gives us autonomy over our personal information and over our economic choices, such as where and how and with whom we should collaborate. Decentralization empowers and motivates those on the edge to participate and contribute their talents, unlocking previously untapped potential. Empowering members makes the whole organization more efficient.

Second, decentralization is ideal in chaotic times, when technology and business arrangements are continually changing. The most talented members for any task are not blocked by a rigid hierarchy. Decentralized platforms can give us perfectly level playing fields for markets. Open markets find the best autonomous individuals to more efficiently solve new problems instead of relying on a large bureaucracy to organize a response using an outdated structure. This is tapping into information at the edge.

Third, the liquidity of decentralization is more efficient and stable in the long term, making regulation more dynamic and responsive. Computer processors can filter the voluminous information available through global networking to make good decisions. Information from more sources has more equal value than it does in centralized systems. Information at the edge greatly changes decision-making. Google Maps sifts through the data of millions of drivers to dynamically determine where traffic jams occur to decide how to advise on users' best routes. The opposite situation holds in more hierarchical structures, where, for instance it is very unlikely that the understandings of the lowliest employees will ever affect the decision-making of a single chief executive of a company. Decentralized information technology is needed to make regulation more dynamic. We now face unfathomably complex legal interactions governing the exponentially growing and evolving business interactions that arise with AI-enabled IoT devices (artificial intelligence enabled Internet of Things). How can we legally regulate the smart contracts that mediate between devices owned by many different companies and individuals interacting throughout the supply chain? New efficient processes lead to newer more efficient processes. Business arrangements constantly adapt to these changing circumstances giving new contracts. The choice again resolves to dictatorship versus democracy. These business problems can be solved with complete ownership by a super-trust, global monopoly firm that avoids all legal contracts. Otherwise we need decentralized markets where fair contracts can emerge.

The engineer's common perspective is to imagine that we are removing regulation with these automated processes. In fact, the purpose of smart contracts is to give much more fine-grained regulation, *more* control, not less. In order to provide a stable environment where such processes can evolve predictably, we need a decentralized organization, a level playing field for cooperation, an institution that has inertia given by a more fully transparent and democratically written history.

What distinguishes Web3 from Web 2.0 is the potential to completely decentralize valuable business networks. Bitcoin demonstrated that protocols can be designed to organize a network of P2P collaborators without the need for any centralized ownership structure, unlike the Web 2.0 companies. No single entity owns or controls Bitcoin or Ethereum. The ownership and control of these valuable networks is distributed loosely among its network members – ideally, they would be distributed according to their participation.

In Bitcoin and Ethereum, there is no formal binding governance framework declaring how the protocols for consensus might be changed in the future. This is a deep flaw that weakens these networks and will lead to instability. But their relative success in running a network with a US$100 billion market cap, the largest among all digital assets, for more than a decade – without any governance framework – demonstrates the potential of the system. Instituting a transparent democratic governance process will make the networks much more efficient and stable. We will explore some possibilities for governance in Chapter 7.

In order to grapple with the problems arising from these decentralized technologies, we need to understand the basic structures underlying these new P2P architectures.

Web3 P2P Technology

In this section we explore some of the many new P2P tools that are being actively developed for implementing the Web3 vision, making it easier for software engineers, and even students, to design tools for empowering new networks devoted to profit. We've taught several courses in law and mathematics discussing P2P technology and its impact on society. Craig taught a computer science course in the spring of 2020 entitled Introduction to Blockchain Technology. Though some students had barely heard of Bitcoin in the first class, every student had a valid idea for a novel DApp and DAO by the second class meeting. One group wanted to tweak the notion of a decentralized marketplace, like OpenBazaar.[29] Another chose a decentralized ticketing app so venues for entertainment could invent secure digital

---

29 https://openbazaar.org/

admission tokens, and attendees could participate in a transparent decentralized market for the tickets. A third chose to build a decentralized dog breed registry.

It took only a few hours for students with no previous experience with distributed computing to build a basic functioning DApp from scratch, connecting their website frontend UI to the Ethereum test blockchain with JavaScript. They simply adapted online tutorials and followed the text, *Mastering Ethereum*.[30] These tools didn't exist a few years earlier, but the technology is changing quickly, thanks to a collaborative open source community devoted to decentralization that naturally encourages widespread adoption through education.

The decentralized information technology tools available to software developers fall into 3 broad categories: processing, storage, and communication.

- Processing or distributed computing
  - Blockchain architecture, computations are performed redundantly, concurrently (e.g., Ethereum, Bitcoin)
  - Parallel processing, where computations are partitioned (e.g., IPFS, Neural network training/federated learning DCAI [2019], GIMPS [Great Internet Mersenne Prime Search, 1996], Leela@Home [chess neural network training, 2018])
- Storage
  - Temporary: distributed hashtable architectures (e.g., IPFS, Filecoin, Swarm, OpenBazaar)
  - Permanent: blockchain architectures
- Communication
  - Internet browsing: Tor, Zeronet, Freenet, dn42
  - Messaging: Bitmessage, Matrix, Whisper
  - File sharing: IPFS, Storj, BitTorrent

Software developers are rapidly improving the tools to decentralize any task provided by centralized apps. As technology and incentive structures improve, these profitable P2P tools are improving, in security and usability.

To understand how these programs achieve decentralization through distributed computing, we take a short digression into two basic math tools, hash functions and cryptography. Then we can explain in more detail how Bitcoin and Ethereum work. All of this is in service of exploring new designs for decentralized Web3 alternatives to today's centralized institutions.

We call these "new tools," despite the fact that they have been known in technical circles for decades, because the broader society has not yet absorbed the ramifications of their power. These new tools are the building blocks of our most

---

30 Andreas Antonopolous and Gavin Wood, *Mastering Ethereum*, O'Reilly Media, 2018. I recommend the tutorial at cryptozombies.io (retrieved 6/3/20).

sophisticated contemporary social media algorithms, and will be crucial for future improvements. These new tools should be common parlance for everyone interested in the future of society, but they have not yet been incorporated into the general thinking on what new organizational designs are possible.

New Tools: Hash Functions

The fundamental tool that engineers are using to decentralize the economy is pure math – especially hashing and cryptography.

Hash functions were an early computing innovation; they've been around since 1953. They have many uses, but their primary application in P2P networking is to efficiently organize the chaotic information of random messages being sent in a global network with no leader. They take any data as input and return a pseudorandom number. One of the most common hash functions used in P2P programs is SHA-256, which stands for secure hash algorithm. For example, if we input the word "decentralization" into the SHA function, we get a number that is 256 binary digits long:

SHA("decentralization") =
1011001110001110001000100111110101011101111010101100110000110101001100111011111010000-
0100111110110010110100001101110001101000111010000110111011110100100000101000111111111-
000110111101101101011000110111010101111100000011010110100011011010011000001010111111

This is a very big number, but computers can process it very quickly – combining it with other numbers – because its binary structure works naturally with binary logic circuits.

SHA quickly converts any amount of information into a 256-bit number. If we enter the first page of this book, SHA immediately outputs

1000101101000101111111110011010010100111100001010100111111111111010111100100111011100101-
110000001011111011001010000000011000111011101101000000000110101010101110011000001000-
110100111011010011111101101001011100000111100110110001011011101000100100100010110101

and if you delete the last letter SHA outputs

10110010011100111100011000100101000101000010101010011010010011011010100111101100101 0010-
1111110000110001100000100111111111101101100001111100011010110101111110011100001011110 0110-
111011000000111010111001011011110001101100110100010000001110011001100000100000110

which is different in approximately half of its digits. Notice there seems to be no pattern connecting the two numbers, even though the two inputs were almost identical, with only a tiny difference of one letter out of a page of information. We say SHA outputs a pseudorandom number, because the number appears to be randomly coming out of the function, but in fact the function is perfectly deterministic, that is, the function follows a fixed procedure. If we check the answer to SHA("decentralization") today or next week or 100 years from now we will always get the same result.

Engineers use this deterministic pseudorandomness property for error detection and proof of ownership. If someone copies a file, of any size, if there is one error anywhere in the copy, then the hash of the copy will be very different from the hash of the original, plainly exposing the error. In another application that is regularly used, if you publish the hash of your file before anyone else, then you can claim priority whenever anyone else later publishes a copy of the file. The output of the hash function is a number that is much smaller than the large data you entered, and the output is unique to that data (by any practical standard). The output is an identifier, a name, or address – an ID – for the file that is easy for computers to use.

However, the most important property for decentralized P2P applications is how hash tables organize randomly occurring data. Let's consider for a moment how the Visa credit card company keeps track of the thousands or millions of transactions that are occurring in its global network. How do they organize these transactions that are coming in randomly from different users in countries all over the world? How do they label and store them all? Now consider the problem of a decentralized payment system, like Bitcoin, which must do that without having a leader. How can the network of computers come to consensus? How do they all agree on how to name and store each new randomly occurring transaction? The hash function. If anybody in the world takes the data from a single transaction and hashes it, they will invariably come to the same output, because the hash function is deterministic. Each transaction will get a unique output for its ID, because there are so many possible outputs.

This crucial feature of hash functions, that there are *many* possible outputs to a hash function deserves to be explored for a moment. For SHA-256 there are $2^{256} \approx 1.1579 \times 10^{77}$ different outputs. The idea is that there are 2 possible outputs in a 1-digit binary number: 0 and 1. There are $2^2 = 4$ possible outputs in a 2-digit binary number: 00, 01, 10, and 11. In a SHA-256 output, there are 256 binary digits, so there are 2^{256} different outputs, which is a *very* big number. It's approximately the number of atoms in the observable universe.[31] So, since hash functions take any information input and return a statistically random output among these 10^{77} different outputs, it's almost impossible that two different inputs will get the same output.

By taking the hash output as the label for the input, we can label any sort of thing humans can ever create. Counting up every muscle twitch from every person on the planet for the next million years, would not come remotely close to 10^{77}. The different SHA output numbers naturally organize everything from biggest to smallest. In the Bitcoin blockchain, for example, in the last 10 years there have been

---

31 The number is estimated between 10^{78} and 10^{82}.

more than 500 million transactions that unpredictably entered the network from any user on the planet struck by the whim to send a coin. Thanks to the hash function, every node in the network hashes the transaction's data and independently arrives at the same answer, giving the transaction a unique ID that everyone recognizes. This mechanism drives consensus in an extremely decentralized global network thanks to the extreme protocol centralization of mathematics. This gives the technological basis for creating consensus on the creation and ownership of digital money, specifically bitcoin, without the need for a centralized authority dictating, "let it be done," which is the English translation of the Latin word *fiat*.[32]

New Tools: Blockchain Protocols

In this section we explain the architecture of the first blockchain network, Bitcoin. The point of a blockchain is to create a decentralized network that records data on the network's transactions. There are two main types of transactions the Bitcoin network needs to account for. This first transaction type is a transfer of digital tokens, called **bitcoins**, from one user to another. The second transaction that needs to be accounted for is the creation of a bitcoin. What makes these digital tokens, these bitcoins, valuable? The blockchain is the record of all these transactions – we refer to the blockchain as a distributed ledger. What makes this ledger valuable is that it is immutable, uncensorable, immortal, open, and decentralized. Further the network is perfectly transparent, allowing complete audits of every monetary transaction, yet it protects its users' privacy. We explain next how hash functions make these qualities possible.

Whenever someone sends a bitcoin digital token to another member of the network, the transaction data is hashed to give it a special identity. Everybody who is running their machine on the Bitcoin network can hear about the transaction. The hash number distinguishes it from every other transaction and orders all transactions by number. Through peer-to-peer gossiping, each machine in the network – each **node** – relays the useful information it receives to anyone else listening, and they can each independently hash the data and come to consensus with the same hash output. No central authority needs to oversee the database. Since there are so many possible output hashes, it is practically impossible for any two transactions to get the same

---

32 Fiat money is the term for national currencies that are not backed by any promise for exchange. Most of our students in math and law – and even economics – are not aware that no nation on earth still backs their paper money with gold or silver. The ability of opaque central banks to decide when to print specie, putting their fingers on the scale of the economy benefitting some over others, is argued to be the primary motivation for Bitcoin's inception. Evidence for this position includes the famous comment in the Bitcoin blockchain's genesis block: "The Times 03/Jan/2009 Chancellor on brink of second bailout for banks."

hash address (this would be called a collision). Even if every person on the planet joins the network, even if they all made thousands of transactions every second, even if the Bitcoin network lasts for thousands of years, it is extremely unlikely there will ever be a single collision.

In Bitcoin, you make a type of hash table (technically called a Merkle tree) of all the transactions that are waiting in the network cloud to be added to the Bitcoin blockchain. This is called a block. The blockchain is then the sequence of blocks (hash tables) that are created roughly every 10 minutes. If you are participating in the Bitcoin blockchain, when you win the Bitcoin lottery among all the other computers in the network, then you win about US$90,000 worth of newly minted bitcoins (block reward as of May 2020) and the right to put a new block on the chain. Your block will be the hash table of all the transactions your computer has seen in the last 10 minutes since the previous block. Then the lottery starts again to decide who will produce the next block 10 minutes later.

The way you win the Bitcoin lottery is to stick the address of the previous block into the SHA hash function. The output will be a 256-bit number, which will start with some number of zeros. If it starts with enough zeros, you win. In June 2020 you need 44 zeros out of 256, but the difficulty is adjusted automatically every 2 weeks to try to keep the average rate of block production at 1 block per 10 minutes. The first output you get is extremely unlikely to begin with 44 zeros, however. So, you can try again after adding more data to the input. This input data is called your nonce. You keep trying new nonces until you find an output with 44 zeros. On average, you will need to try 18,000,000,000,000 or 18 trillion times before you win.

Once you announce your winning nonce, everyone in the network can quickly validate that you are correct, since they only need to calculate one hash to verify for themselves. The process described above is called Bitcoin's proof of work (PoW) consensus algorithm. It's the process the network uses to come to agreement, or consensus, about how the network is going to update itself every 10 minutes, adding new transfers of bitcoins between users around the world.

The Bitcoin blockchain is open and politically decentralized, because anyone with access to the internet can participate, but no single entity is in charge – no one owns the network. Anyone can join the lottery and participate in creating the blockchain. The process is very protocol centralized, however, since everyone is supposed to use the same PoW consensus algorithm.

The blockchain is immutable, because any attempt to edit the old blocks will be immediately rejected by the network. A single number or letter changed anywhere in its entire history will result in a different hash of the information. The error-correcting property of hash functions make such attempts immediately apparent. As long as the network is following the blockchain protocol, they will automatically reject any edit, no matter how small. The blockchain grows forever and the history of all the blocks are never deleted. The hashing of the previous block built into the nonce for the next block gives security. If a single digit of information anywhere in any past block is ever changed, the hashes will not work to give a nonce with the correct number of zeros, unless the editor does the work of the entire network and finds new nonces for all the blocks after the edit, which would require them to be faster than the entire network currently while also reproducing the past work of the entire network. Anyone broadcasting false information can be quickly checked and ignored. It is therefore reasonable to assume that all information added to the blockchain is eternal, uneditable, and uncensorable.

The blockchain is uncensorable since it is open and decentralized. Anyone can publish a new block if they find a nonce. Blocks have been posted in the Bitcoin blockchain, which violate the EU's 2018 GDPR law (General Data Protection Regulation). People's private information have been included in blocks against their will. The GDPR requires the owners of the websites that post information to remove that information, however, that is certainly not going to happen.[33] The network would need to create a hard fork to remove the information. More than half of the network's nodes would be required to change their entire protocol to scrub the data and restart the blockchain. This would need to happen every time information was found on the blockchain that violated the GDPR. The only other choice the EU has is to prevent every citizen in the EU from participating in the Bitcoin network or accessing any of its information. But even that wouldn't stop the blockchain, because it is immortal.

The Bitcoin blockchain is immortal, or eternal, in the sense that the blockchain will last as long as the internet does, as long as it is in any degree free. If any one computer in any country has access to the information of the blockchain, then they can keep the blockchain running. Even if we imagine Bitcoin has no value or usefulness to society a century from now, a single hobbyist who is interested in forgotten things from the past can keep the network running.

Further, the Bitcoin blockchain embodies transparency. Every transaction is recorded eternally, and any computer that connects to the network can inspect and audit every single transaction that has ever occurred. Everyone has equal access to all the information in the blockchain. This quality is essential to allow a valuable decentralized network to function without a centralized authority to maintain the validity of the ledger.

Finally, the blockchain uses strong cryptographic tools to securely maintain its users' privacy. We discuss these tools in the next section. But first, let's consider some of the many downsides of blockchain technology.

The most common criticism of the Bitcoin network is that hashing these nonces requires a great deal of computation and energy. It's actually worse than what is

---

33 Shannon Liao, "Major Blockchain Group Says Europe Should Exempt Bitcoin from New Data Privacy Rule," *The Verge* (April 5, 2018). Available online at https://www.theverge.com/2018/4/5/17199210/blockchain-coin-center-gdpr-europe-bitcoin-data-privacy (retrieved 8/3/20).

described above. Everyone in the global network is competing to find the nonce. This means that many different computers are redundantly trying the same wrong nonces before one computer finally tries the right one. The Bitcoin network is performing about 10^{20}=100,000,000,000,000,000,000 hashes every second in June 2020. That requires as much energy as the entire country of the Czech Republic. Bitcoin has around 300,000 transactions per day, but they use much more energy than the Visa credit card network, which handles 150,000,000 transactions a day, or 500 times the volume. A more accurate name would be the Proof of Pollution consensus mechanism, since work generally strives to be useful and efficient.

That wasted energy is why most blockchain networks are attempting to find a different consensus algorithm. The leading candidate is called proof of stake (PoS), which generally involves block producers locking their money in a smart contract so they can have the chance to be picked by a pseudorandom number generator. The problem is that if someone comes up with a clever algorithm for hijacking the process, then the network will fail. We discuss this difficulty further in Chapter 4.

The second major problem with blockchain technology is that it will always be expensive, whether or not PoS is fully solved. Every bitcoin in existence originally was created as a reward for winning one of the hash lotteries when a block was built and published. The way to verify a bitcoin is valid is to check the legitimacy of the entire chain. If you want to fully participate in the network, you need to download a copy of the entire history of every transaction of every bitcoin in existence. This extreme redundancy and inefficiency means transactions will always be expensive.

This leads us to speculate that more efficient systems will emerge, which handle smaller transactions. A good idea for a DAO is a decentralized banking system built on top of the Bitcoin ledger that charges a smaller fee for temporarily storing minor transactions. These smaller transactions can then be bundled together to make a larger Bitcoin transaction reflected on the immortal blockchain. We discuss such ideas further in Chapter 8, with ZKRollups. To understand those tools, we need to understand zero-knowledge (ZK) proofs, which are explained in the next section.

The Bitcoin blockchain is a fundamental advance in decentralized organization. Before Bitcoin, there were very few examples of politically decentralized organizations that were worth money. There were decentralized religious organizations, like the Quakers. The Apache tribe was an extremely decentralized cultural organization before the 1910s. But competition for wealth centralized their organization. The Maghribi traders are the best example of an organization devoted to profit which remained decentralized. The Maghribis used secure and meaningful reputation to counteract the centralizing influence of competition for profits. But the Maghribis' 11th century system would not work in our contemporary globally connected networks. We want to go much further than the Maghribis and build economic networks that allow the autonomous members to protect their privacy by remaining anonymous. We are doing this with the second major advance in information technology: modern cryptography.

New Tools: Public-Key Cryptography and Zero-Knowledge Proofs

Cryptography is the art of writing secret codes. The word lends its prefix to the words "cryptocurrencies" (like Bitcoin) and "crypto-economy," alluding to the fact that the technologies are built from a profound devotion to providing user privacy in a decentralized and pseudonymous setting.

Public key cryptography allows secrets to be passed securely within a public network, despite the fact that every message is shared with everyone else. This is essential to providing privacy in a decentralized network, as you don't need to rely on a centralized authority to maintain security and keep your secrets safe from others. Public key cryptography was first presented in 1976 and has been used for decades to secure internet messages, such as making purchases on websites.

For example, when you make a purchase on Amazon or Alibaba, you enter your credit card number into your computer and send it off to their company through the internet. The internet relays the information around various nodes, and these messages are available to thieves around the world. So, of course your credit card information is encrypted.

But how does it get encrypted? Amazon sends your computer the instructions for how to encrypt the message. You use their public key to scramble the information. But the thief is also listening to these instructions. The thief knows how you encrypted the information – the thief has Amazon's public key – and the thief has your encrypted information. Why can't the thief unscramble your information if they have your scrambled message and they know how you scrambled it?

The trick involves just a little bit of elementary school arithmetic, divisors and remainders, but more math than we want to drag our readers through. Basically, Amazon has another key, called a private key, that makes it easy to unscramble the information. But if you don't have their secret private key, then it takes an enormous amount of computation to unscramble the message by brute force – more computation than all the computers on earth working in parallel for the next billion years.[34] This mismatch between the sender and the receiver's power is called asymmetric encryption.

Public key cryptography's most useful feature in P2P systems is called a digital signature. The idea is that you can invert the process described above. The owner of the secret private key can encrypt their message with the private key, then anyone in the network can use the public key to unencrypt the message with the public key.

---

[34] This is considered sufficient standard for security in the present, but it ignores the possibility of radical future improvements to information technology. However, as long as there is not a centralized monopoly on computational power, then these P2P tools will be safe in the foreseeable future. Even threats such as theoretical future quantum computers have already been resolved with open source cryptographic algorithms, which are hardened against quantum computing. https://en.wikipedia.org/wiki/Post-quantum_cryptography (retrieved 8/22/20).

That way anyone can verify that the sender of the message must have the private key, without requiring the owner to reveal the actual private key. That digital signature trick is how you can prove you own a bitcoin or any other digital asset without losing it, and so underlies any P2P system involving valuable tokens. You need to keep the private key secret, or else anyone who finds it immediately gains control of your assets. (Billions of USD worth of bitcoin have been lost in this way.[35])

The digital signature trick is the simplest example of a zero knowledge proof. The idea is that the private key owner can prove they are the owner without revealing the private key. The other members have proof of ownership, while the owner reveals zero knowledge of the specific key string. More complicated zero knowledge proofs (ZK proofs) are giving P2P application users the power to privately interact despite being in a public and decentralized network. For example, a DAO devoted to healthcare insurance can give members a synthesized health score from 0 to 100. The protocol for synthesizing your complex health history is public, but your particular health history stays private while you reveal only your final health score to the insurance DAO. Even that number could be secured, by mixing it with other information, such as parts of your property to be insured, or other members from your company.

Anonymity: Pros and Cons

A major advantage of anonymity in a large network is that it can encourage justice by eliminating many sources of discrimination. In a DAO whose members are anonymous, discrimination based on superficial identifiers such as race, ethnicity, sex, gender, sexuality, age, and social class is eliminated to the first order. At the second order, when people infer those qualities from behavior, anonymity doesn't protect a group from discrimination. It also doesn't protect a group from third-order effects of systemic discrimination. In fact, anonymity can exacerbate second and third-order effects, as it makes it more difficult to detect. To combat such effects, different mechanisms in the governance of a decentralized organization must be employed.

---

35 An early and famous case is the Mt. Gox theft, in which 850,000 bitcoins belonging to customers and the company were stolen in 2014. At the time, those coins were worth about $US500 million. In 2020 they would be worth $8 billion. Bitcoin.com has estimated that more than US$3 billion worth of cryptocurrency was stolen in 2018 alone. https://news.bitcoin.com/9-million-day-lost-cryptocurrency-scams/ (retrieved 7/20/20). It's important to note that all of this theft comes from centralized institutions, especially centralized currency exchanges, like Mt. Gox was. The Bitcoin network itself has never made a single mistake; not a single bitcoin has ever been stolen from the blockchain by a hack directly on the network, even though its entire source code is publicly available for analysis. Its decentralization architecture provides remarkable stability and security, even under complete transparency and globally open access to participation.

The most basic economic effect of anonymity is to provide safety for its members. Safety gives people confidence to engage in business deals, to participate in larger networks of collaborators. Safety is an institutional overhead burden, like insurance and appeals processes. But it's used because it gives business a catalyst to make deals. This makes the entire economy more liquid and efficient, so the investment is worthwhile. Anonymity provides safety through privacy, which is especially important in a global network. Anonymity encourages more contributions, making the network stronger. The network effect gives an advantage to any strategy that makes a network larger.

If the globe has access to your data, it can be used against you. Reporters, political dissidents under oppressive governments, and whistleblowers all have obvious enemies they need to protect themselves from. In many such cases, they cannot work without anonymity. In a world with 7 billion potential actors, people get attacked online without any apparent reason. Wikipedia editors who simply curate generic articles regularly get attacked. If you want to create an environment where people can contribute to controversial pages on either side of an issue, expect to be targeted by enemies with an agenda. Participation will crater if contributors are afraid every nugget of information they share will be available for the rest of their career for analysis by superiors.[36]

However, anonymity can give people too much safety in a decentralized network. With anonymity you get many more trolls – anonymous participants might feel safe enough to attack other members without fear of retribution. Therefore, anonymity should be balanced. Your power to broadcast your voice should be tempered by having that voice tied with a pseudonymous[37] account with meaningful and valuable reputation. If you abuse your broadcasting power, then you should lose your reputation.

Is it possible to allow anonymous participants to broadcast their messages, to participate in a network, especially when money is on the line, and expect anything but a series of catastrophes? The Tragedy of the Commons is a natural consequence of allowing anonymous participation. Anyone who has spent a few hours delving past the top filtered contributions on platforms such as Twitter, YouTube comments,

---

36 "Respondents raised concerns about what it could do to their reputation if current and future employers or coworkers knew what information they were contributing to Wikipedia." Cited from Drexel University, "Just give me some privacy: Anonymous Wikipedia editors explain why they don't want you to know who they are," https://phys.org/news/2016-10-privacy-anonymous-wikipedia-editors-dont.html October 12, 2016, which cites Andrea Forte, Nazanin Andalibi, Rachel Greenstadt, "Privacy, Anonymity, and Perceived Risk in Open Collaboration: A Study of Tor Users and Wikipedians," Proceedings of Computer-Supported Cooperative Work and Social Computing, Portland Oregon. http://andreaforte.net/ForteCSCW17-Anonymity.pdf (retrieved 8/20/20).
37 Pseudonymous means using a false name. Anonymous means you do not reveal your name. This subject is important to the cryptocommunity and some get bogged down arguing the small semantic difference.

or Reddit can observe the toxic results of anonymity. Occasionally graffiti is interesting, but most anonymous comments are worthless bile that randomly express people's dissatisfaction with their condition, without communicating any lasting connections that can improve society.

An excellent experiment to test this question, of whether anonymous groups can create productive collaborations was Reddit's Place,[38] which started on April Fool's Day, 2017. The commons, in this case, was a blank canvas of internet space – one million pixels, 1000×1000. Once every 10 minutes, any registered Reddit member could change any pixel's color. The idea was to get subreddit communities to collaborate and compete to create art in a limited space for a limited but unspecified time.

Communities promoting their bases with symbols such as national flags and pixelated works of classical art (The Starry Night and the Mona Lisa) competed with subversive groups such as r/theblackvoid, which coordinated attacks to desolate established territories. Anything was possible, and Reddit's editorial board was nervous about the message the final image would convey about their site and their users, as inevitably, thanks to the freedom from repercussions that anonymity provided, hate symbols emerged, such as swastikas.

In the end, however, each time a hate symbol cropped up, it was replaced with something more positive. In the end, r/place was a success because even though their anonymous members had the ability to destroy, they also had the power to defend their own creations. This effect is regularly observable throughout history. For example, the first Chinese dynasty, the Chin empire, quickly collapsed after following the Hobbesian perspective that humanity is fundamentally evil. For most of the subsequent 2,000 years of Chinese history, stability prevailed under the more generous Confucian perspective of empowering and encouraging the good side of humanity.

We need to build a decentralized auditing system to keep track of pseudonymous reputation. To do that we need sophisticated distributed programming that automatically updates a member's reputation based on communally accepted protocols. This is solved with decentralized smart contracts, first extensively implemented by the Ethereum blockchain network.

New Tools: Decentralized Smart Contracts

The blockchain technology that allows decentralized execution of unlimitedly complicated business contracts between millions of members across the planet is quite complex. The math and logic that it's all built on, however, is not deep at all.

---

38 Josh Wardle & Justin Bassett (u/powerlanguage & u/Drunken_Economist), "Looking Back at r/Place," April 18, 2017. Available at https://redditblog.com/2017/04/18/place-part-two/ (retrieved 7/16/20).

The operations of NOT and AND are **functionally complete**, meaning any program imaginable can be built by chaining them together. Specifically, any program with finite inputs, which results in TRUE or FALSE at the end of the program, can be written with chains of these operations. For example, if you study symbolic logic for a week,[39] then you will learn DeMorgan's law:

$$NOT(x \text{ AND } y) \Leftrightarrow (NOT\, x) \text{ OR } (NOT\, y)$$

So we can write OR as a chain of NOTs and ANDs as follows:

$$NOT\,((NOT\, x) \text{ AND } (NOT\, y)) \Leftrightarrow (NOT\,(NOTx)) \text{ OR } (NOT\,(NOT\, y)) \Leftrightarrow x \text{ OR } y$$

Remember the code of Ur-Nammu (ca. 2100 BC) discussed in Chapter 1. Law #32 reads:

> 32. IF a man had let an arable field to another man for cultivation AND he did NOT cultivate it, turning it into wasteland, THEN he shall measure out THREE kur of barley PER iku of field. [Ed.: capitalization mine.]

IF (x) THEN (y) is equivalent to y OR (NOT x). So we can chain NOTs and ANDs together to write

$$IF(x)THEN(y) \Leftrightarrow (NOT\, x) \text{ OR } y \Leftrightarrow NOT\,(x \text{ AND } (NOT\, y))$$

This symbolic logic is not simple; it can get incredibly complicated by chaining these operators together in unlimited arrangements. But it's not deep. We're just using NOTs and ANDs. So we only need to use two logic circuits to build the most sophisticated legal contracts imaginable to organize a global economic network in a DAO. The power comes from the fact that these operations can be performed reliably, at the speed of light, millions of times per second.

Similarly, Ethereum's ability to use these logic operations, and basic arithmetic, and storing and reading information, makes it **Turing complete**, meaning it can theoretically approximate any mathematical model that exists.[40] However, Ethereum is not practically capable of mimicking the power of even the cheapest smartphone with its virtual machine. The storage limit is currently extremely small, because anything stored in the blockchain needs to be stored redundantly on thousands of nodes for all time in the future. Any message passed through the network

---

39 That knowledge is necessary to understand this paragraph, but not necessary to understand the rest of this book. Symbolic logic is also not that difficult, and many resentful children master the skills every day, despite lacking the motivation of understanding why it might be useful. Our education system is in dire need of repair. http://intrologic.stanford.edu/public/home.php (retrieved 8/8/20).

40 Alan Turing is one of the most interesting people in history. It is well worth a Wikipedia dive into his past.

is repeated millions of times. So Ethereum decentralizes computation of smart contract computer programs, but they are necessarily extremely primitive, compared with the functions of centralized Web 2.0 companies, like the services Google offers.

Therefore, we have built many systems to adapt to these limitations. The InterPlanetary Filing System (IPFS) is a P2P file-sharing system that temporarily stores files on some of the nodes in the network, based on how popular or important the files are. IPFS was launched at around the same time as Ethereum, independently, and interacts well with smart contracts. As an upgrade to BitTorrent, IPFS incorporates a nascent incentive design with its own native token to motivate users to maintain the availability of less popular information. We'll discuss other architectures for improving the function and efficiency of blockchains, such as sharding and ZKRollups, in Chapter 8.

With these extensions to blockchain functionality, many new groups are developing decentralized alternatives to centralized applications. These decentralized apps are called DApps. DApps are intended to compete with centralized apps, in the hope that decentralization will give users more power, making them more competitive than centralized systems. For example, there are several initiatives developing ride sharing alternatives to Uber, which hope to give greater transparency to customers and drivers.

The idea is that users will download a DApp from a cryptographically verified decentralized P2P service like IPFS, then run the DApp on their own computer, instead of using the blockchain to redundantly perform all calculations. The development layers are detailed in the Figure 2.2.

When software designers refer to themselves as "full stack engineers," they mean they can negotiate the APIs (application to program interfaces) between each of these layers.[41] An API allows the different computers running the different layers to communicate. The most common APIs for Ethereum are integrated in the Truffle framework, which helps developers connect (migrate) the functionality on one layer with another, and organize the interfacing programs.

Development tools such as the Truffle framework and ZeppelinOS (2018) are making the process of developing DApps for DAOs easier every year. OpenZeppelin library has a curated collection of carefully tested smart contracts that developers can copy to build their projects. ZeppelinOS is an interface of smart contracts that are independently deployed on the blockchain and are actively running for anyone to use, so developers don't need to redeploy them (or pay to deploy them in the first place).

With the open source atmosphere of Web3, every success is quickly replicated and extended in new applications. Truly successful DAOs don't exist, yet. Once the

---

[41] Though very few of these people are telling the truth on their resumes, since it is a rare programmer who ever engineers machine code. In practice a full stack engineer knows how to use JavaScript on a UI, together with a high-level programming language, interfacing directly with the hardware.

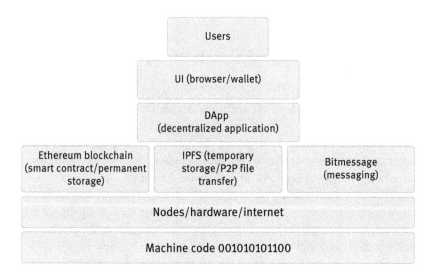

Figure 2.2: Ethereum DApp stack. A DAO would consist of a network of users who are all running the same DApp on their personal devices, using IPFS and Bitmessage to communicate less securely, and the blockchain to securely finalize transactions.

architecture of a single DAO is successful, however, it will be quickly cloned and adapted to every imaginable economic and social organization. In the next chapter, we discuss what is holding them back. What is wrong with the open source movement that has produced these remarkable tools, and how can it be fixed? What is needed before Web3's DApp-enabled DAOs can unleash humanity's economic potential?

Chapter 3
Future Decentralization

The goal of decentralization is to give most individuals more power, improving the entire group. But it does not remove all walls and regulations. With this new individual power, we will make more walls and more cryptographic security. But the new powers of information technology give us the power to make regulation more complex, more dynamic and responsive. IT helps people to make doors, empowering us to move between spaces securely, anywhere on the planet.

IT advances secure your spaces by walling off those who don't want to make positive contributions, protecting material and ideal spaces from Tragedy of the Commons degradation, free riders, and rent-seeking. Cloning successful open source DAO governance structures will allow people to collaborate on any projects they wish, opening other doors for those not interested or capable of contributing to the spaces they are walled off from. Digital doors and walls can be much more powerful than material walls and doors have ever been.

Vision of Human-Centered, AI-Enabled Internet of Things

> It is remarkable how closely the history of the apple tree is connected with that of man.
> —Henry David Thoreau, "Wild Apples: The History of the Apple-Tree"
> *The Atlantic*, November 1862

The Internet of Things (IoT), organized by a decentralized platform with many collaborating DAOs, is an example of how decentralization can add significant efficiency to the economy. IoT is the idea that in the future, all our devices will communicate through wireless internet technology and share information so they can work together more efficiently. Since the 1960s there have been futuristic designs for our refrigerators to monitor our pantry and automatically send orders to the grocer for deliveries. With cheap processors and WiFi, IoT promises to unite every device in our society. This provokes privacy concerns and the question of who owns and controls the data.

To achieve the promise of IoT, several ingredients are required. A system of device identification is needed, as well as a coherent system for communication between many different devices with different broadcasting and memory capabilities. Neutral business territory – a decentralized marketplace – is needed to contractually agree on the protocols of automated collaboration between devices owned and controlled by independent businesses. And the entire structure must be transparent, so that audits of the system can be performed to maintain integrity as it continually evolves.

Web3 P2P technologies embody these properties of decentralization, autonomy, efficiency, personal privacy, and bureaucratic transparency. Web3 is being built to

https://doi.org/10.1515/9783110673937-003

develop the smart contracting environment for providing precisely these solutions. But an evolutionary structure that encourages continual systemic improvement for business collaboration is needed.

Consider the market orbit of an apple, its supply chain: all the organizations and resources involved in bringing the apple to a consumer. The apple's entire history is full of valuable market information, from before the origin of the seed of its tree, until after its core has been composted. If each step along its history can be reliably recorded and verified by a host of independent companies, we can regulate its quality, and objectively verify its value. This will improve efficiency and ensure satisfaction for all parties involved – from producers, handlers, shippers, holders, vendors, and customers, to all the ancillary parties that supply each of these parties with products or services. In point of fact, the strong interconnectivity of contemporary markets means the supply chain of an apple is ultimately linked with every actor in the entire economy – a violin lesson in Vietnam is three degrees of separation from an Austrian *Apfelstrudel*.

When the apple seeds are sold to the farmer, their provenance can be verified. When the seeds are planted, the planting can be verified. When the tree is watered, the sprinkler can verify the position, the weather, and the amount and quality of water used. The consumer scans the tag on the apple, which verifies the exact moment the apple was harvested, processed, shipped, delivered to the vendor, and placed on the shelf. Then a program will analyze how the apple's history indicates its quality and nutrition according to a scientific algorithm. If its shipment was delayed at the warehouse, it's not as fresh as it could be and not as valuable. If the apple was handled optimally at every step along the way, it's worth more.

At this point the apple's market orbit is only half finished. Who buys it, how long it's stored, where it's stored, how it is used or wasted, whether it's composted, what procedures the composter uses, what products that compost fertilizes, what happens to those products, are all part of the apple's supply chain. If each step can be reliably and economically recorded, each actor can be fairly rewarded, giving all parties the confidence to do business while minimizing corruption and rent-seeking. Big data generated by mobile telecommunication and all the devices in the IoT allows researchers to understand new correlations, which allows better decision-making and improves efficiency at every level. Contrary to the criticisms that have been lobbed against blockchains as being designed to dodge regulation, the actual goal is to ensure effective, efficient, adaptive regulation in a truly decentralized manner, ultimately exceeding the current level of oversight. (Their adherence to transparency means their understandable disdain for slow and unresponsive centralized regulation often leaks beyond their development circle.)

In order to create a sustainable infrastructure for IoT, we need an endlessly expandable platform that properly incentivizes productive collaboration. The endless expansion includes countless smart contracts that need to be continually developed, maintained, policed, and improved, to intercommunicate at every step of the market orbit of every material item in our lives. Smart contracts will provide immediate business negotiation and resolution in dynamic AI-enabled interchanges. For this we need a diverse list of DAOs for each of the business interests along the supply chain, with the relevant background expertise. We need a system that incentivizes productive collaboration between numerous independent DAOs and individual actors. The system must negotiate fair valuations of each fine-grained contribution.

P2P collaboration provides the neutral territory where independent companies or organizations can do business. Smart contracts provide cheap and efficient automated regulatory mechanisms, linking the processes of the supply chain.

There are two major structures from our contemporary economy, however, that are still missing in the Web3 environment.

First, we need an incentive mechanism for productive collaboration. Like the Maghribi traders, Web3 needs a secure and meaningful reputation system to maintain their decentralized structure of collaboration in the face of the centralizing tendency of competition for profits. Reputation enables the self-policing that is necessary to maintain a DAO's integrity.

Second, the decentralized economy needs effective governance structures. It must adapt to rapid technological and organizational innovation in a network of diverse parties with diverse goals. The decentralized economy needs many different DAOs with rigid governance protocols, to harmonize the diverse groups, yet allow them to adjust to market changes. Like the architecture of 19th century democracies, these DAOs need a dynamic system to maintain their integrity and protect individual autonomy.

It is conceivable that the IoT infrastructure will be governed by ever evolving DAOs. A DAO that has mastered decentralization internally can thus help IoT infrastructure products utilize such decentralized governance structures for their own governance and interoperability. We believe that effective decentralized DAO governance necessitates reputation verification systems. DAOs that are internally well-governed by a reputation verification engine allow other IoT infrastructure entities to simply clone the DAO governance for their own purposes and run a DAO with the same governance metrics. As we will explain further below, this system of transplanting governance has several beneficial aspects.

Each process in the supply chain must self-police in separate DAOs. For example, orchard farmers will be part of a DAO that verifies their particular reputation for growing apples. They will choose protocols for watering their orchard when the conditions require it, and will record that they have performed the task with GPS devices attached to their sprinklers. The orchard farmers themselves have the best knowledge for protecting the value of their own reputation. If some of their members are not following protocol – if someone attempts to game the system and provide inferior products by cutting corners – the farmers themselves are best able to anticipate and respond to the attack, developing the most efficient protocols to police bad-faith actors and support those with good faith. The power of decentralization is individual autonomy. Self-policing their own members is more effective when the members have the power, unlike a centralized hierarchy that is more prone to structural corruption when each member holds distinct powers and responsibilities. Each DAO is motivated to continually improve their own processes and protect their own reputation, in order to attract business from the other systems in the supply chain.

The GPS-enabled sprinkler-monitoring device will be installed by members of a separate DAO whose expertise is to police their own industry. They will cooperate with the orchard farmer DAO in order to attract their business, so the orchard farmer DAO will rely on the device DAO's reputation and smart contracts to police the farmers' growing operations. Working together, each of the DAOs' reputations become more valuable in the larger economy when they help each other provide a superior product.

This dynamic IoT object-automated economy will be integrated with the human-experienced economy. Each person's contributions can be fairly valuated for their present and future value to the decentralized economy with smart contract protocols. Rights within and between numerous DAOs can be parsed and negotiated, automatically and immediately, according to the protocols of each DAO. Contributions that previously were ignored as too insignificant to be efficiently accounted for, can now be fairly evaluated, thanks to improved processing and transmission power. This will encourage greater participation and a culture of meritocracy that will incentivize authentic collaboration.

For the whole supply chain to work in harmony, numerous DAOs must cooperate. Countless protocols will vary among the various expertises. On-demand products and services will be automatically negotiated and engaged through dynamic programming. Unanticipated legal contracts will regularly be invented through micro-second AI calculations to optimize business outcomes in a dynamic environment that moves too quickly to wait for human corroboration.

The system that hosts such a complex network of DAOs with such a variety of business behaviors must be general enough to adapt to the endless protocol innovations required, but expressive enough to rigorously capture the specific protocols needed for each individual expertise. The core structure must be designed to generate any type of DAO and provide the choices needed to make effective governance structures. In Chapter 7 we detail the necessities for secure and effective decentralized governance. Before that, in Chapter 6, we detail the construction of secure and meaningful decentralized reputation, which gives the proper incentive mechanism for gluing the whole decentralized collaboration together.

The Internet of Things is a complicated structure to wrap our heads around. But more complicated systems are already guiding our daily decisions. Before we discuss the details of DAO governance, we should delve deeper into our understanding of the technology we rely on today.

Algorithmically Automated Control

Automation is responsible for the majority of material advances humanity has enjoyed since World War II. Since before Watts's steam engine, ideas from control theory have been making humanity ever more materially powerful.[1] Improvements in computer processors have made increasingly sophisticated algorithms for automating systems that are controlling more functions in every aspect of our lives. The list of instructions that automated machines can now be given is seemingly unlimited, since an algorithm can now be as long as the memory the computer controller can hold – and with Wi-Fi controllers, that expands to include the entire internet.[2] Artificial intelligence – especially in the form of neural networks and evolutionary programming – is making another technological leap past the most complicated human-designed algorithms.

Algorithmic automation optimizes human outputs, performance, and interactions, elevating every material function in society. At the same time, the conveniences and benefits bring with them risks to humanity that cannot be fully quantified. As we use new technologies, we come to rely on them, until we can no longer survive without them. This has been true since humans first invented spears and shoes. Our societies grew to a size that could not be supported without technology. Without the Haber process, a technology that creates fertilizer from the air, the earth would not be able to support its 7 billion people.

Algorithmic automation is affecting society at a large scale. Since the early 2010s, algorithmic functionalities and algorithms that utilize big data from sensors, IoT devices, GIS systems,[3] and other big datasets, have begun dominating social and business

---

1 For example, Christiaan Huygens invented flyball governors in the 1600s. Huygens's governors were used to regulate the speed of windmills by automatically adjusting the angle of its vanes when the flyball spun quicker, without requiring a human to intervene. The physicist Maxwell did careful research explaining their function, which was used in 1788 by Watt in his steam engine.

Enrique Fernández Cara & Enrique Zuazua Iriondo, "Control Theory: History, Mathematical Achievements and Perspectives," *Boletín de la Sociedad Española de Matemática Aplicada*, 26, 2003, pp. 79–140.

2 According to the IDC the internet held more than 18 zettabytes in 2018. That's more than 18,000,000,000,000,000,000,000 bytes of data – a number too big to be intuitively comprehended by humans. https://www.seagate.com/files/www-content/our-story/trends/files/idc-seagate-dataage-whitepaper.pdf (retrieved 8/6/20).

3 GIS, which stands for Geographic Information System, is a framework for integrating numerous types of global geographic data. There are layers that map the location, quantity, and type of minerals in the ground; a layer describing the location and quality of groundwater; layers describing the types and distribution of biological organisms from bacteria to mammals; a layer describing every detail of civil engineering projects, such as streets, buildings, sewage, and electricity; a layer describing social patterns, such as traffic, crime, and monetary flow. Algorithms built for analyzing this public data can be used to make more accurate valuations of property, so that using GIS, McDonald's knows whether a location will give a successful franchise before they invest. Neal Ungerleider, "How Fast Food Chains Pick Their Next Location," *Fast Company*, August 25, 14.

decisions. As internet-based applications are becoming increasingly prevalent and used by humans, such as Google, Facebook, and Amazon, such applications not only provide conveniences in humans' daily lives, but the algorithms themselves are accumulating more power due to their usefulness in society. We are becoming conscious of the fact that we spend a lot of our time devoted to doing tasks that serve the computers, instead of the computers serving us. As a single example, the Google search engine already dictates many mundane decisions we make in our daily lives, such as what to buy and where to buy it; it settles arguments and tells us what is true and important by guiding us to authoritative information. Algorithmic automation guides societal outcomes and therefore it benefits some groups over others – whether or not its owners and developers intentionally manipulate these outcomes. Centralized ownership and control of algorithmic automation is an important issue for society. Decentralized systems can counteract the downsides and threats of algorithmic automation, thereby enhancing the long-term benefits of technological solutions for humanity.

Algorithmic functions can transcend bounded human rationality. Human actions and outcomes are increasingly optimized with big data and its analysis. The quantification of human thought, feeling, and action and their algorithmic optimization can improve social behaviors in ways that are too complex for humans to understand without the data-driven algorithmic aids. For example, the increasing availability of health data and analytics improves human health-related choices, especially if reinforced with algorithmic applications that interact with humans. Health data through sensors, wearables, and internet monitoring gives us recommendations on how to improve our lives and treat and prevent disease.

Given the analytical and predictive skills of algorithmic applications, data and algorithmic oracles can improve individual behavior, experiences, and achievement. But they can also improve the achievement of large networks of people, even larger society. For example, algorithmic applications can incrementally upgrade democratic processes in society. Big data and algorithmic data analytics today enable centralized algorithmically automated systems (such as Google, Facebook, and Amazon in the early 2020s) to discover individuals' political preferences better than the individuals can themselves.[4] Algorithmic data analytics-driven human choice transcends humans' bounded rationality.[5] As algorithmic analytics and predictions of human

---

Available online at https://www.fastcompany.com/3034792/how-fast-food-chains-pick-their-next-location (retrieved 8/6/20).

4 Daniel Kahneman, Barbara L. Fredrickson, Charles A. Schreiber, & Donald A. Redelmeier, "When More Pain Is Preferred to Less: Adding a Better End." *Psychological Science, 4*(6), November 1993, pp. 401–405.

5 Kahneman's cold water experiments suggest that humans listen to a narrating self in political decision-making, follow a peak-end rule, forget the vast majority of political events during a given legislation period, focus exclusively on a few extreme outlier events, and give largely disproportionate weight in political decision-making to the most recent events. Ibid.

preferences and choice become increasingly accepted, exercising human political will by proxy through algorithmic interpretations may become increasingly common.

Taken to the extreme, centralized control of algorithmic automation could negate human input in data systems if the systems are designed to ignore individual choice, in preference to the goals of the platforms' owners. Humans' bounded rationality creates inefficiencies that can be improved upon. Human consciousness is more limited on many matters than networked computer systems.

However, decentralized systems can preserve human power and control, while providing superior outcomes by objective standards. Decentralized systems can outcompete centralized systems. Centralized algorithmic automation uses centrally collected data to enhance decision-making and outcomes with opaque algorithms to further the goals of the few owners. Decentralized systems are guided by the wisdom of the crowd, from humans and machines. Where centralized algorithmic automation would systematically remove the human presence in an effort to optimize efficiency and outcomes, decentralized systems use the power of algorithmic applications to enhance its features and outcomes with an omnipresent human backstop. Where centralized algorithmic automation would create an autocracy powered by centralized algorithmic human predictors, decentralized systems would create a meritocracy powered by optimized human decisions that increase diversity of choice for all.[6] Decentralized organizations give their members more power and autonomy. A decentrally controlled and owned algorithmically automated control system puts ultimate choices (such as design) back in the hands of people.

How can complicated algorithmic systems that are beyond individual human comprehension be built with foundational human backstops? How can we build systems that profitably exploit the wisdom of the crowd? Decentralization is the key. For example, in the early 2020s, cryptocurrency startups have started to experiment with more sophisticated upgrades to democratic systems. Complex voting schemes are being explored with a focus on incentive designs. These evolving technologies with human voting inputs can, over time, become automated to regulate the most minute decisions with decentralized consensus. The voting structure can be abstracted to scale decentralized power: mundane choices like "which self-driving car gets to pass" can be automated, while sophisticated choices such as "which social programs deserve more funding" or "how to design the automated voting systems" can be consciously and manually controlled by humans. We will explore how these systems are being designed in Chapter 7 and the consequences of such a microdemocracy.

---

6 As Karl Popper put it, "The growth of knowledge depends entirely on disagreement." Karl R. Popper, *The Myth of the Framework: In Defense of Science and Rationality*. Routledge: London, 1994.

Decentralized Commerce

Decentralized technology solutions create disruptions for existing legacy commerce. The emergence and proliferation of distributed blockchain applications (DApps) in the aftermath of the invention of the Bitcoin protocol in 2009 demonstrate that a nascent market for such applications and consumer demand already exists at the beginning of the 2020s. Consumer preferences continue to shape the DApps market and the solutions it may offer for commerce and society. Significant markets for blockchain applications will be the corporate marketplace, banks, legal, realty, and insurance. These markets will all be impacted significantly. DApps create solutions for business and society that are subject to far fewer and rather different transaction costs compared with centralized legacy businesses in the same industries. Through code-based solutions, DApps can help increase the overall trust of consumers and market participants at an unprecedented scale. Despite many cybersecurity issues associated with cryptocurrencies, among others, code-based trust can help lower transaction costs, but it can also increase consumer and overall market confidence and certainty, which facilitate economies of scale that are only occasionally and temporarily possible in centralized structures. Through the lower cost structure, decentralized platforms have the ability to remove consumer fees that are an integral part of their centralized competitor businesses. Removing such centralized fees also allows for the removal of downward pressure on the platforms' worker compensation as costs are less likely to increase and be passed on to workers and consumers. The lack of fees can help create a more efficient marketplace through the removal of the rent-seeking intermediators.

Decentralized technologies' ability to lower transaction costs by removing otherwise needed intermediaries disrupts existing business models. For example, in the early 2020s, blockchain technology provided numerous examples of evolving decentralized technologies that create an independent and transparent platform for establishing truth and building trust. Intermediaries, bureaucracy, and old-fashioned procedures are replaced by code, connectivity, crowds, and collaboration. An example here is the decentralized finance (DeFi) market, where financial products are increasingly offered on top of digital assets to facilitate disintermediation of legacy systems such as underwriting, banking, and trading – the middlemen are removed. The technology increases transparency, openness, and speed, while at the same time significantly reducing costs by automating the functions of traditional intermediaries.

The many applications of evolving blockchain technology have the potential to change business models. Because of its implicit code-based guarantees, the technology allows a qualitatively different solution for agency, a foundational element of capitalism. Blockchain technology can replace agency constructs for many business relationships. The guarantees ensure that participants cannot circumvent the rules embedded in the code, contracts execute only if and when all contract parameters are fulfilled by both parties and verified by a majority of miners/nodes in the system. Blockchain-based guarantees remove agency costs because principals are less essential for monitoring agents, which addresses the inherent agency problems in modern finance and corporate governance.

Similarly, decentralized technologies reform business, administrative, and legal processes that rely on intermediaries. Any such processes may be updated and improved with decentralized technologies. For example, corporate processes that have ledger functionality but rely on legal intermediaries could be streamlined very quickly by implementing blockchain technology. When blockchain technology becomes more widely accepted and applications further spread into consumer-facing markets, legacy business processes and structures will likely be among the first to be amended. The combination of blockchain technology startups with platforms and machine learning present enormous opportunities to improve business and society. These technologies used in combination with big data and machine learning are becoming increasingly profitable and efficient. These tools, in turn, creates a surge of new and innovative platforms with disruptive effects for many industries.

Decentralized payment systems' ability to rely entirely on cryptocurrencies creates comparative advantages over centralized systems. Centralized legacy fiat payment systems and platforms typically require some form of an existing banking relationship in order for consumers to utilize their services. Holding and storing cryptocurrencies does not require a banking relationship. While many legacy banks are cognizant of their limitations and are ready to embrace cryptocurrencies, centralized legacy fiat payment systems remain subject to payment processing issues and slow processing times for payments. Intermediaries such as banks and PayPal also require high fees. The fees make it only economically viable for higher volumes of transactions, creating barriers to entry in the process. Decentralized payment systems are not subject to these limitations, as anyone connected with the internet can create a free digital wallet and participate on decentralized platforms. Finally, while money laundering has traditionally been a problem in these markets, anonymity of market participants in cryptocurrency networks can also increase participation in certain markets and economies. As the technology and its uses evolve, traditional markets are increasingly encapsulated by it.

Legacy payment systems, cash, and bank notes are gradually losing ground to other payment systems.[7] At the beginning of the 2020s, in Northern Europe, as few as one in every five transactions is made in cash.[8] Cash usage in the United States, the United Kingdom, the Netherlands, Sweden, Finland, Canada, France, among

---

7 Kenneth S. Rogoff (2016). *The Curse of Cash.* Princeton: Princeton University Press: Princeton; Brugge, Jonathan, Denecker, Olivier, Jawaid, Hamza, Kovacs, Andras, & Shami, Ibrahim, "Attacking the Cost of Cash." *McKinsey & Company: Our Insights,* https://www.mckinsey.com/industries/financial-services/our-insights/attacking-the-cost-of-cash (retrieved 6/1/20).
8 Ibid.

other industrialized nations, has fallen well below 50% of total transaction volume.[9] In the United States, transacting in cash costs the consumer around 200 billion dollars annually – about $637 per person annually, which is a result of the cost of production, storage, and transportation, among other factors.[10]

The end of technological life cycles of legacy systems in the early 2020s and associated emerging trends in payment systems necessitate central banks' enhanced examination of alternative payment systems.[11] Central banks and governments around the world have been experimenting with government-sponsored digital and cryptocurrencies since 2015.[12] In the case of central banks, such experimentation was already close to launch[13] or fully operational in the early 2020s.[14] Most major tech companies in the private sector have been experimenting with cryptocurrency projects since 2017. Several governments have issued their own

---

9 Ibid.

10 Ibid. The cost of cash is primarily associated with counting, managing, storing, transporting, guarding, and accounting for bank notes. Aleksander Berensten & Fabian Schar. "The Case for Central Bank Electronic Money and the Noncase for Central Bank Cryptocurrencies." *Federal Reserve Bank of St. Louis Review, 100*(2), 2018, pp. 97–106; The theft of cash alone costs U.S. retail businesses losses around $40 billion annually. Will Yakowicz, September 20, 2013. Cash Costs U.S. Businesses $40 Billion a Year. Inc., https://www.inc.com/will-yakowicz/dealing-with-cash-costs-american-businesses-55-billion.html (retrieved 6/1/20).

11 Morent Bech & Rodney Garratt, Central Bank Cryptocurrencies. *BIS Quarterly Review,* 2017.

12 Garrick Hileman & Michel Rauchs (2017). Global Cryptocurrency Benchmarking Study. *Cambridge Centre for Alternative Finance,* https://www.jbs.cam.ac.uk/fileadmin/user_upload/research/centres/alternative-finance/downloads/2017-04-20-global-cryptocurrency-benchmarking-study.pdf (retrieved 6/1/20); Yves Mersch (July 24, 2017). Central Bank Speech at the Cent. Bank of Malaysia Monetary Policy Conference [transcript available at https://www.bis.org/review/r170807c.htm]; Digital Currency Initiative, MIT Media Lab, https://dci.mit.edu; Monetary Authority of Singapore, *Financial Stability Review,* November 2017, https://www.mas.gov.sg/-/media/MAS/resource/publications/fsr/FSR-2017.pdf; Jack Meaning, Ben Dyson, James Barker, & Emily Clayton (May 2018). Broadening Narrow Money: Monetary Policy with a Central Bank Digital Currency. *Bank of England* [Staff Working Paper No. 724]; J.P. Koning (2016). Fedcoin: A Central Bank-Issued Cryptocurrency, R3 Report, 15; Motamedi, Sina (July 21, 2014). Will Bitcoins Ever Become Money? A Path to Decentralized Central Banking, *TannuTuva.org,* https://tannutuva.org/2014/will-bitcoins-ever-become-money-a-path-to-decentralized-central-banking.

13 The Bank of Canada and Bank of England announced in 2016 that the technology was not ready for a central bank-sponsored cryptocurrency. Yet other central banks, such as in Singapore and Sweden, have already launched their e-currency projects.

14 Usman W. Chohan (February 7, 2018). Cryptocurrencies as Asset-Backed Instruments: The Venezuelan Petro [unpublished paper], https://papers.ssrn.com/sol3/papers.cfm?abstract_id=3119606; Zagaris, Bruce. U.S. Bans Venezuela's New Cryptocurrency and Adds 3 Officials to Sanctions List. *International Enforcement Law Reporter, 34* (3), 2018, pp. 157–161; Julie Hirschfeld Davis & Nathanial Popper. White House Bans Venezuela's Digital Currency and Imposes Further Sanctions, *New York Times*, March 20, 2018, p. A1.

digital currencies. Examples include Tunisia (eDinar),[15] Senegal (eCFA),[16] Sweden (eKrona),[17] Dubai (EmCash),[18] Japan (Jcoin),[19] Estonia (Estcoin),[20] and Ecuador,[21] among others.[22]

Reputation Systems and Orwellian Nightmares

In order to build politically decentralized networks devoted to profit, we argue that it is necessary to follow the Maghribis' example. In order to keep a decentralized organization aligned in the pursuit of their goals, you must provide something more valuable than money: reputation. With our new information technology, we can build global networks of billions of people united with a single set of protocols. We can track their reputation with digitally accurate computer processing and storage.

Fiction has already furnished many cautionary tales about developing a reputational system to monitor citizens in a society. The fear is in our collective unconscious, as demonstrated by the many recent novels, television shows, and movies devoted to portraying dystopias of injustice generated by poorly designed automated reputation systems.[23]

---

15 Ricard Kastelein (December 28, 2015). Tunisia to Replace Its National Digital Currency, eDinar, with Blockchain-Driven Monetas Currency. *Blockchain News*, https://www.the-blockchain.com/2015/12/28/tunisia-to-replace-its-national-digital-currency-edinar-with-blockchain-driven-monetas-currency/ (retrieved 6/1/20).
16 Samburaj Das (November 28, 2016). Senegal Will Introduce a Blockchain-Based National Digital Currency. *CCN*, https://www.ccn.com/senegal-will-introduce-blockchain-based-national-digital-currency/
17 Afraid of a few commercial entities controlling cash supply in Sweden, the Swedish central bank has kicked off its digital currency project e-krona. Amanda Billner (October 26, 2018). Now There are Plans for 'e-Krona' in Cash-Shy Sweden. *Bloomberg: Economics*, https://www.bloomberg.com/news/articles/2018-10-26/riksbank-to-develop-pilot-electronic-currency-amid-cash-decline
18 Jon Buck (October 1, 2017). Dubai Will Issue First Ever State Cryptocurrency. *Cointelegraph*, https://cointelegraph.com/news/dubai-will-issue-first-ever-state-cryptocurrency
19 Arjun Kharpal (September 27, 2017). Japanese Banks Are Thinking of Making Their Own Cryptocurrency Called the J-Coin. *CNBC: Tech Transformers*, https://www.cnbc.com/2017/09/27/japanese-banks-cryptocurrency-j-coin.html
20 Kaspar Korjus (December 18, 2017). We're Planning to Launch estcoin – and That's Only the Start. *Medium*, https://medium.com/e-residency-blog/were-planning-to-launch-estcoin-and-that-s-only-the-start-310aba7f3790
21 Rosenfeld, Everett (February 9, 2015). Exuador Becomes the First Country to Roll Out Its Own Digital Cash. *CNBC.com*, https://www.cnbc.com/2015/02/06/ecuador-becomes-the-first-country-to-roll-out-its-own-digital-durrency.html
22 Thomson Reuters (October 25, 2017). Cryptocurrencies by Country, https://blogs.thomsonreuters.com/answerson/world-cryptocurrencies-country/
23 Cf., MeowMeowBeenz from the television show Community, Season5, Episode 8 "App Development and Condiments," March 6, 2014. Black Mirror, Season 3 "Nosedive." The Orville, Season 1, Episode 7

But the tools of information technology are too powerful to deny. Back in 2013, publisher Tim O'Reilly (who was instrumental a decade earlier in promoting the term Web 2.0) explained its inevitability.[24] Using the example of the Uber ride-sharing app, he argued how decentralized feedback loops are more efficient for self-policing and regulating social behavior than top-down hierarchical governance. The scandals that have pestered Uber in the intervening decade have almost always derived from centralized decision-making.

Centralized reputational systems are already functioning and guiding peoples' behavior. eBay has had a feedback reputational system for customers and vendors since its inception in 1995, with an updated Seller Rating system in 2008. Insurance companies are employing apps to monitor and reward or punish customers based on their behavior. Most major automobile insurance companies have smartphone apps to monitor their customers' driving habits. Most major health insurance companies have apps to monitor their customers' exercise and dietary habits, tracking their movements and purchases. Currently these are opt-in, given traditional Western attitudes on privacy, but it is easily foreseeable that the information could be valuable enough to make it too punishing for members to opt-out, *de facto* mandatory.

Temporary gig workers in the platform economy are subject to reputational systems, such as TaskRabbit and Upwork. All major centralized social media platforms have opaque reputational systems for monitoring their users. Since 2018, to combat the spread of fake news on their platform, "Facebook has begun to assign its users a reputation score, predicting their trustworthiness on a scale from zero to 1."[25] Throughout civilized history governments have instituted surveillance programs, judging their citizens for trustworthiness. Singapore, Estonia, and Israel have especially sophisticated contemporary programs.

The most ambitious and pervasive reputational system for controlling peoples' behavior is easily the Chinese Communist Party's Social Credit System (SCS). The Social Credit System[26] gathers information on minute behaviors, such as jaywalking, littering, and helping your neighbors. The SCS then uses computer algorithms, including artificial intelligence, to analyze the data and give you a Social Credit Score. This score is then used to determine whether you are eligible for a particular

"Majority Rule." https://en.wikipedia.org/wiki/App_Development_and_Condiments (retrieved 8/8/20).

24 Tim O'Reilly, "Open Data and Algorithmic Regulation," 2013, in B. Goldstein (ed.), pp. 289–300, *Beyond Transparency*, Code for America Press, San Francisco.

25 Elizabeth Dwoskin, "Facebook is rating the trustworthiness of its users on a scale from zero to 1," *Washington Post*, August 21, 2018.

26 The article https://en.wikipedia.org/wiki/Social_Credit_System (retrieved 8/8/20) uses 150 references attempting to explain the extremely complicated system. Any paragraph-sized distillation misses important aspects. For instance, there are many different Social Credit Systems in different regions in China as they experiment with what systems will be most effective.

job, whether your children can attend better schools, even whether you can travel to other provinces.

The Social Credit System evokes reflexive fear in the average Westerner, but it is received much more positively in mainland China. The mainlanders[27] have a very different culture than Western societies, due to a very different experience from their recent history. "The result of decades of control . . . is that Chinese society suffers from a lack of trust, says veteran sociologist Zhang Lifan. People often expect to be cheated or to get in trouble without having done anything. This anxiety, Zhang says, stems from the Cultural Revolution (1966–1976), when friends and family members were pitted against one another and millions of Chinese were killed in political struggles. 'It's a problem the ruling party itself has created,' Zhang says, 'and now it wants to solve it.' The stated purpose of the social credit system is to help Chinese people trust each other again."[28]

The fact that people were starving in the streets in the 1960s, the fact that most people have family members in living memory who starved to death, means the entire society past a certain age were severely traumatized. Everyone else was raised by people who were traumatized. Many social ills derive from this experience.

Mainland Chinese often mistrust the people in their own society. They have a dim view of human nature. So, they follow Han Fei's Hobbesian philosophy of Legalism and rigid centralization. They don't believe in democracy – people should not be trusted to rule. The West's attitude is not currently quite as cynical. More often Westerners believe people are good at heart, despite all the evidence to the contrary, since every human society appears to be founded on traditions and laws reflecting historical violence.

Second, the Chinese have had a tradition of formal social policing on a much more pervasive scale than the West. *Baojia* is a formal system of communal self-policing that had been in place continually for the last thousand years with only occasional interruptions during major revolutions.[29] Roughly, a *Bao* is a basic watch group consisting of 10 families who rotate their policing duties. A *jia* is a collection of 10 *Bao*, or 100 families whose representatives meet to report and unify their standards. Since the last major revolution in 1949 policing became much more

---

27 It is easy to argue Chinese people have a greater diversity of attitudes than Europeans. The Chinese who live in Hong Kong, Singapore, Taiwan, Mongolia, Xinjiang, Tibet, and elsewhere, in every country around the world, obviously have extremely diverse history and experiences. Within mainland China the perspectives vary widely. A Chinese attitude toward any subject is impossible to pin down, yet we persist in speaking as if the Chinese are a monolith. Simplifying and generalizing in this way is necessary, however, in order to say anything about cultural and historical trends.
28 Simina Mistreanu, "Life Inside China's Social Credit Laboratory," *Foreign Policy*, April 3, 2018. Available online https://docs.house.gov/meetings/FA/FA18/20180711/108531/HHRG-115-FA18-20180711-SD001.pdf (retrieved 6/18/20).
29 Sui-wai Cheung, "Baojia System," in *Encyclopedia of Modern China, Gale Cengage Learning*, 2009, pp. 136–137.

personally invasive as speech and thought were carefully controlled by the CCP, for example, with *danwei*, *hukou*, Golden Shield, and modern grid policing.

Third, mainland Chinese naturally feel like other countries in capitalistic systems are adversaries; they feel that other countries are trying to exploit them (cf., the Century of Humiliation); that they are still in an economic crisis and need a system that can efficiently and rapidly respond. So, they naturally choose a centralized solution to outcompete their enemies.

For all these reasons and others, the existence, nature, and current popularity of the SCS system should not be particularly surprising, though its obvious Orwellian overtones provoke an automatic negative reaction in the West.

There are many good reasons to implement the SCS. (But its likely use to oppress minorities, such as Uighurs and Tibetans, makes it uncomfortable to discuss any positive aspects.) It is a powerful tool that is being used to improve many social conditions, especially corruption, on a personal level, at the corporate level, and in public institutions.[30] The SCS uses the new tools of information technology in a formal manner with respect to their government. That can be incredibly powerful and valuable for improving society.

A similar type of social monitoring was implemented in 2020 in response to the COVID-19 pandemic. The Alipay Health Code is an app created by the local Hangzhou government with the help of Ant Financial, a sister company of the e-commerce giant Alibaba. People in China sign up through Alipay. On any given day the app assigns its users a color green, yellow, or red to judge their health. Then users display their color to guards before they are allowed into markets or on subways. Within weeks of the outbreak, the system was already in use in 200 cities and is being rolled out nationwide.[31] The opaque algorithm monitors its users' locations and assigns a score based on how close the users were in contact with known outbreaks of the virus. The *New York Times* studied the algorithm and "found that as soon as a user grants the software access to personal data, a piece of the program labeled 'reportInfoAndLocationToPolice' sends the person's location, city name and an identifying code number to a server."[32]

Many in the West are afraid the success of the SCS in furthering social harmony, efficiency, and productivity will force other countries to adopt a version, to remain competitive. However, the West doesn't have the same fundamental factors

---

30 Official purposes are described in the document "State Council Guiding Opinions concerning Establishing and Perfecting Incentives for Promise-keeping and Joint Punishment Systems for Trust-Breaking, and Accelerating the Construction of Social Sincerity," *GF* No. 33, State Council, May 30, 2016, posted on China Copyright and Media, October 18, 2016, available at https://chinaco pyrightandmedia.wordpress.com/ (retrieved 6/18/20).
31 Paul Mozur, Raymond Zhong, & Aaron Krolik, "In Coronavirus Fight, China Gives Citizens a Color Code, with Red Flags," *New York Times,* March 1, 2020. Available online at https://www.nytimes.com/ 2020/03/01/business/china-coronavirus-surveillance.html (retrieved 8/8/20).
32 Ibid.

motivating its implementation. If they do implement such a system, in a centralized form, it will be from fear of social unrest or due to an abdication of individual responsibility. Just as the Snowden leaks in 2013[33] revealed the U.S. governments abuses of its citizens privacy has led to no meaningful reform, centralized authorities have a long record of using crises to justify the introduction of monitoring tools that outlast their original purpose. The COVID-19 pandemic led to centralized nationwide monitoring of citizens with contact tracing apps in many countries, and the expansion to reputational systems would be a simple modification.

But implementing any centralized nationwide reputational system would be a major mistake since a decentralized system would be far superior in most every way.

Centralized and opaque systems like the SCS are unstable in the long run. They are particularly dangerous because their computerized bureaucracy makes them inherently rigid. Their early successes will make them more and more brittle. The SCS will certainly be successful in the beginning, and it will justify the strengthening of the centralized government of the PRC. However, within a few years it will lose its relevance and efficiency because society will change faster than the centralized governing bureaucracy can adapt – its effectiveness will not help, since that will only accelerate the social change. Suggestions that AI will solve these problems are misguided and will fail for the same reason. Neural networks are merely a complex mathematical architecture for performing statistical regression, which is always extremely unreliable when applied to novel situations. Successful new business arrangements lead to successful new business arrangements. There will always be new social situations to monitor. Any success achieved by automating the SCS will only make it more brittle, and more dangerous.

Until the Chinese people trust each other, they will not choose transparency and decentralization of power. Assuming the CCP continues to use the SCS for propaganda, showing violations on the nightly news, they can maintain the Hobbesian view of the world, and prop up the SCS and the opaque power centralization of the CCP, no matter how poorly it eventually functions, until the only solution is violent revolution.

The SCS is the opposite of the reputation system we suggest. Without being able to look at the actual design of the CCP Social Credit System, we infer it has the following design properties:

– Synthesizes all types of reputation into one type of token. The reputation token tells you whether you are a good or a bad citizen.
– Completely closed membership. You cannot opt in or out.
– No privacy. You are not anonymous in the system. You have one account with strict identity control. You have no power over your own information.
– Centralized with opaque governance. Complete lack of transparency in the operation and protocol updates.

---

33 https://en.wikipedia.org/wiki/Global_surveillance_disclosures (retrieved 8/8/20).

The Web3 reputation systems that will be detailed in Chapter 6 make precisely the opposite design choices:

- Many types of reputation tokens. 1 for each type of DAO. DAOs should be split into many different types with many different DAOs for each type of expertise.
- Open membership with anonymous accounts gives you complete freedom to join or leave.
- Privacy enabled by public key cryptography. Digital signature technology and other ZK proofs allow you to use your information without revealing it.
- Decentralized governance. Total transparency in operation and protocol up-dates. An open source design is necessary to run any program in a P2P environ-ment, because decentralization means the source code needs to be shared by all if it isn't controlled centrally.

As Karl Popper argued in 1945, an open society can outcompete closed societies.[34]

> It was Popper's great insight that where knowledge is subjected to competitive evaluation and peer review by autonomous communities of scholars, theories that genuinely advance human progress can be tested and improved. The unseen advantage of open societies over authoritarian ones lies here, in their capacity to innovate, to unleash creative minds, and to turn their knowl-edge into insights, products, techniques, and systems that reduce human suffering and improve our life together. . . . Single party states have made a very different bet: they are gambling that they can reconcile innovation and progress with political control and single party domination. The key unanswered question about how the twenty-first century turns out is which kind . . . of institutional form – open societies or single party states – will turn out to be the more success-ful, which society will best fulfill the needs and aspirations of their people.[35]

The Old Versus the New

Engineers are rapidly building the tools to decentralize our economic institutions. There are many well-funded proposals for dispute resolution for smart contracts that bypass our centralized justice system. Our traditional institutions are failing to respond to these alternatives. The correct response in a democracy is not to fight against progress, but to adopt these new tools – to decentralize power and make bureaucratic information more transparent.

But these institutions are old. Their original legal constitutions were drafted with goose feather pens on sheepskin parchment, bound together and stored in a single library, placed at the center of town. The technology of the time did not

---

34 Karl Popper, *The Open Society and Its Enemies, Vol. I: The Spell of Plato*, London: Routledge, 1945.

35 Michael Ignatieff, *Rethinking Open Society*, pp. 15–16, Central European University Press, 2018.

permit a conception of information processing that gives these new tools for decentralized governance and transparency.

The amount of democracy and transparency the founders of our current system did achieve has been subverted in the intervening decades by the natural concentration of power that evolves under competition. The hierarchies have ossified. They are likely too brittle now, to adopt processes that come from such radically different information technologies. Changes are likely to be seen as a threat to power and resisted. If that is the case, engineers will continue to build systems that sidestep them as irrelevant obstacles to efficiency.

On the other hand, changes can be a threat to the order and efficiency we have already achieved. The new is not always better, and ignorant engineers can be more dangerous than obstinate bureaucrats.

The Fallacy of Uniformitarianism and Chesterton's Fence

> In the matter of reforming things, as distinct from deforming them, there is one plain and simple principle; a principle which will probably be called a paradox. There exists in such a case a certain institution or law; let us say, for the sake of simplicity, a fence or gate erected across a road. The more modern type of reformer goes gaily up to it and says, "I don't see the use of this; let us clear it away." To which the more intelligent type of reformer will do well to answer: "If you don't see the use of it, I certainly won't let you clear it away. Go away and think. Then, when you can come back and tell me that you do see the use of it, I may allow you to destroy it."
> —G. K. Chesterton, The Thing (1929)

People tend to believe that the experience they have today has been the same throughout history. That contemporary attitudes and opinions are natural and have never changed and will never change.

We assume the peace we live under today emerges automatically, perhaps because of human nature. The social harmony we enjoy is taken for granted. The paved streets and water and power lines maintained with taxes collected peacefully and efficiently are not perceived as any miracle of social engineering. Somehow this wealth of peaceful cooperation seems natural to me, despite the fact that I reflexively curse the idiot who always seems to be driving in front of me.

The fallacy of uniformitarianism is to believe that the social harmony we enjoy today, especially in economically advanced nations, is natural and automatic. We falsely believe that if we dismantle our cultural and public institutions, we will still enjoy our current level of social cooperation and its resulting wealth. Some even believe that our cultural and civic institutions have always been the primary obstacles to greater material prosperity and social harmony.

Ignorant of history, our software engineers are building technological workarounds to fight corruption and inefficiency by eliminating escrow lawyers, and police, and insurance salesmen with Web3 solutions. Engineers see the improvements they can make by removing the cost of these middlemen without always understanding the original reason for their existence.

Engineers see the corruption, the business friction, and they build systems to eliminate it. But you shouldn't mistake the catalyst for the friction. Friction in a system is inevitable. So, in order to overcome the friction and achieve motion – achieve liquidity in an economy – you need catalysts. Catalysts provide activation energy.

When synthesizing a chemical, in the lab or in our living cells, we often use a chemical catalyst to start the reaction. Every cell in every living thing devotes much of their activity to building chemical catalysts, like the ATP catalyst constructed in the mitochondrion. The mitochondrion adds three phosphate ions to adenosine to build ATP, adenosine-triphosphate. The third phosphate ion gives ATP an abundance of energy. ATP then jiggles around in the cell until it meets up with a protein with a phosphate receptor. The ATP bonds with the protein, dropping off its third phosphate ion, giving the protein an energy kick. This gives the protein the activation energy to do its protein-y job. Remove the ATP catalysts from a cell and it will suddenly stop moving and die. Catalysts are the key to temporarily avoiding the inevitable deterioration the Second Law of Thermodynamics promises – ordered systems degenerate toward disorder. We need to provide energy to catalysts so that our systems don't stop.

Middlemen are the catalysts that exist to overcome the friction of economic corruption. Police, lawyers, and insurance salesmen eliminate threats to business activity from different angles. These middlemen are paid to overcome these corruptions and frictions. Unfortunately, they have an incentive to not entirely eliminate the corruption. Whether these overhead industries become corrupt themselves, or if they are merely falsely identified with the corruption itself because of their close association, we sometimes think that the middlemen are responsible for the business friction. We often miss the original reason for their existence. "No greater mistake can be made than to think that our institutions are fixed or may not be changed for the worse."[36]

Remove the middlemen business catalysts and the economy will soon die. Liquidity will dry up. A few people will unfairly lose on business deals, then no one will take the risk to initiate a business deal. The goal should not be to eliminate these middlemen. The goal is to make these industries more efficient. The goal is to automate them, to eliminate their own corruption and friction.

Automating these middlemen functions makes them more efficient, like the chemical catalysts in a cell. Unlike human middlemen, automated middlemen can be designed so that they don't contribute to the corruption they were designed to fight. If we automate these processes, then we have the power to maintain these

---

36 Charles Evans Hughes, *Conditions of Progress in Democratic Government* (1909), published by Forgotten Books, 2019.

functions for ourselves. Individuals become more autonomous and powerful. We can choose the level of catalyst protection that we need.

Carelessly dismantling these institutions could be catastrophic. Sociocultural advances from the past are necessary for successful business.

But ignoring the inefficiency and corruption of these institutions to protect entrenched hierarchical power will also lead to catastrophe. Decentralization and transparency can save these institutions, making them more relevant and efficient.

Both sides are wrong when they fail to understand each other. We need to transform our institutions to match the new technological advances, without losing the value they currently provide.

Obstacles to Decentralization

For 10 years the Bitcoin network has been running without any centralized oversight. No authority has ever stepped in to refund a single transaction. Many billions of USD worth of bitcoin has been stolen and embezzled from centralized organizations, which provide service to customers using bitcoin. But the network itself has never made a single mistake. No network transaction has ever sent the wrong quantity of bitcoin or mistakenly sent anything to the wrong account. No digital token has ever disappeared or was mistakenly duplicated. Not a single bug has been found to create any type of accounting error in a system worth hundreds of billions of dollars, despite the fact that no single authority is in charge.

This is a spectacular success. Bitcoin illustrates the power of decentralized cooperation and transparency.

Nevertheless, there has been no significant adoption and use of bitcoin currency in the economy in the last decade. Neither has there been any serious use of Ethereum smart contracts, or the InterPlanetary Filing System, or any of a host of other decentralized P2P services that have been promised. These radically decentralized tools have not pervaded the mainstream economy despite billions of dollars in investment. Why not? What is missing?

In short, almost everything. We are still waiting for a single application, a killer app for Web3. What will be the killer app for the decentralized economy? The answer is a DAO.[37]

The idea of a profitable DAO is to make a company, which is governed autonomously by smart contracts and organized in a decentralized way, without any single permanent governing authority, no concentrated ownership. Decentralized companies would give fair distributions of power to its workers, according to how they

---

37 This language is influenced by a 2017 speech by Andreas Antonopolous, https://www.youtube. com/watch?v=OWI5-AVndgk (retrieved 8/6/20).

benefit the group. The existence of diverse types of DAOs would drive the economic output of the large-scale decentralized economy, justifying the existence of the other decentralized overhead tools – like cryptocurrencies, smart-contract escrow, decentralized insurance, and justice.

But there aren't any DAOs, yet. The crypto economy is hollow. Why? Well, partly because the crypto community's psyche was scarred when the first DAO failed spectacularly.

The 2016 DAO

In 2016, within the first year that Ethereum created programmable contracts that could autonomously govern the behavior of a decentralized organization, the first DAO was built, called confusingly enough, the DAO. This 2016 DAO was to be a decentralized venture fund, set up as an organization based purely on code and smart contracts. It did not have a conventional corporate structure, no incorporation, and had no physical address or headquarters. All traditional control mechanisms employed by principals in agency relationships had been entirely removed. People who worked for the 2016 DAO had a different kind of agency relationship. Workers were engaged in a dynamic set of relationships that continuously self-organized around projects and outcomes, not corporate hierarchies with implicit hierarchical biases.

The 2016 DAO instantly attracted thousands of members and US$150 million in investment, 14% of Ethereum's total value. It failed almost as quickly. Within two weeks, 30% of the money, $45 million, was stolen, causing the nascent Ethereum network to collapse and reboot its network. The 2016 DAO had a programming bug called re-entrancy, where two lines of code were in the wrong order.[38] But that technical design flaw was not its most serious problem. The system would have eventually failed more spectacularly because it was designed poorly on other levels. For example, if someone ever gained 51% power in the system, they could have taken the money by outvoting the rest of the members to invest the group's money in their own worthless pet project. Voting power could be purchased, so we know precisely how much money it would cost to destroy the 2016 DAO. If it were more successful, and lasted longer than a month, someone would have eventually amassed the money to arbitrage the trivial governance structure.

Since the failure of the original DAO, the community has been scrambling to provide new DAO alternatives. Major new DAO proposals appear almost quarterly in the 2020s. Most fail because of a lack of decentralized governance solutions.

---

38 Andreas Antonopolous and Gavin Wood, *Mastering Ethereum*, p. 326, O'Reilley Publishing, 2018.

Most organizations that use P2P technology are not decentralized and they are not autonomous. They are governed by a centralized group of developers and owners. The desire to invest in DAOs was not quelled by the failure of the 2016 DAO. For example, Aragon collected US$25 million within 26 minutes in a capped ICO[39] one year later in 2017. Since then, the Aragon group switched focus a few times, and developed one of the most sophisticated general DAO governance protocols in the blockchain space. That is a backhanded compliment, though: their reputation system and legislative and judicial governance protocols are trivial.[40] In 2020, Aragon declined to use their own protocol to arbitrate an internal dispute, which is testimony to the lack of trust of their system designers in their own system capabilities.

The 2016 DAO has a lasting impact on emerging DAO designs. It creates core commonalities and associated path dependencies in future generations of DAOs.[41] The common denominator for all DAO token members is the unifying desire to optimize the DAO token value. Accordingly, performance assessment in the DAO structure is based on value optimization, not on hierarchical or political processes. On the upside, token holders and contractors work toward a common goal of optimizing the DAO and the token value. Nonperformance reputational penalties can minimize racial or cultural biases inasmuch as anonymity is maintained. Yet, the focus on the value enhancement of fungible tokens can lead to short-termism and may ignore ethical and governance issues.

---

39 An initial coin offering (ICO) is a decentralized version of an initial public offering (IPO), which allows anyone with access to the internet to pseudonymously participate in the equity sale of a smart-contract-enabled company or asset. The coins may be programmed with autonomous power in the company.

40 https://github.com/aragon/whitepaper (retrieved 7/6/2020).

41 The idea of a path dependency is that a technology or a process may become entrenched and continue to be used even after more efficient or effective technologies emerge because of institutional inertia, or the short-term costs of switching to the alternative. An example is the QWERTY keyboard vs. the DVORAK set up. Standard computer keyboards use the QWERTY setup because the first commercially successful typewriters used them. The design is measurably slower for typing in English, because more words have characters off of the home row and more words are typed with one hand than DVORAK. It is argued this was designed intentionally, to eliminate key sticking in the original mechanical typewriters. Such issues are not a concern with electronic typewriters and computer keyboards, but the standard was stuck. Now QWERTY is so established that there is little chance of switching, because further innovations have incorporated the QWERTY style, such as keyboard shortcuts like CTRL-Z, X, C, & V for copy-pasting. In QWERTY these letters are all close together, but using them is more awkward in DVORAK. As technological development moves down its path, processes become more standardized depending on their history, leading to entrenchment and behavioral inertia. The larger the institution, the more likely it will display path dependencies beyond what is rationally expected, which constrains advancement.

Martin Stack & Myles Gartland, "Path Creation, Path Dependency, and Alternative Theories of the Firm," *Journal of Economic Issues, 37*(2), 2003, p. 487.

Creating a true DAO, one that is successful and stable, is a lot more difficult than it sounds. Even a centralized company is difficult to create, though we have plenty of successful centralized examples to copy. In recent history, the only long-term successful examples of politically decentralized companies devoted to profit have been Bitcoin and its permutations. We're all holding our breaths wondering how long they can defy gravity. We're not impressed by how little agility they've demonstrated. The Bitcoin network has not had much of a record of innovation, which is not surprising considering its complete lack of formal governance, and the fact that its inventor has remained anonymous.

Path Dependencies

Path dependencies create a major obstacle to decentralizing our institutions and businesses. Humans have psychological inertia, and cling to any familiar system, but especially those that have given them comfort in the past. Groups have lived in hierarchies since before civilization began. Our human history is one of organizing in centralized networks. We understand hierarchies on a deep, animal level. It is reasonable to fear the chaos that naturally follows the cataclysm from the collapse of a hierarchy. The conscious intervention necessary to prevent the chaos is not as certain to occur as the revolution and change of power.

Similarly, decentralized organizations that take advantage of our contemporary advances in information technology allow global participation, blithely trading across borders. This violates basic principles of territorial integrity in nations, which is a foundational principle of international law.[42] Forced imposition of a border change is an act that traditionally justifies war. However, as society increasingly adopts powerful new technologies, such as the cell phone or internet that cross borders with new forms of collaboration and value creation, these traditional notions of protecting territorial integrity by controlling the natural resources, products, services, and behavior of its citizens become obstacles to improved efficiency in business.

In the early 2020s, government-controlled regulation of the evolving digital asset space is perhaps the leading obstacle to decentralization. The Securities and Exchange Commission, among other regulatory agencies in the United States, is attempting to fit decentralized technology solutions and their digital assets into the existing regulatory infrastructure. Carve-outs and safe harbors were discussed but not seriously considered. The emphasis of regulatory initiatives in the 2020s was on securities tokens and legal ways to trade such tokens in the then existing securities

---

42 It is enshrined in Article 2(4) of the UN Charter and has been recognized as customary international law.

law infrastructure. Government control of the industry was an indispensable aspect of the legal initiatives. Yet, decentralized technology solutions, at their core, negate external control, censorship, and oversight. Accordingly, the then-proposed approaches largely undermined the evolution of decentralized technology. Without the ability to experiment in a legally protected environment, decentralized products and technology cannot evolve, and consumer protection rightly trumps decentralized product experimentation. Switzerland in the 2020s has been at the forefront of legal experimentation with decentralized infrastructure products and DAOs.

The regulatory infrastructure solutions for decentralized products and technology of the early 2020s is largely following the characteristics of the product issuers. Tokens issued by government entities (government coins) are compliant with and followed the legal environment established by the issuing government. Similarly, tokens issued by corporations in a given jurisdiction (corporate coins), are designed to be compliant with the legal guidance available at the time of their issuance in the given jurisdiction. More decentralized products and technology solutions (people coins) typically do not fit into such regulatory solutions in a given jurisdiction. As a result, the more decentralized products that are more censorship resistant, autonomous, and cannot be controlled by regulatory agencies, are largely left in a regulatory vacuum. The associated legal uncertainty limits their expansion, reach, and evolution.

The regulation of government coins versus corporate coins versus people coins bifurcates the established regulatory infrastructure for decentralized technologies. Government coins and corporate coins can develop and evolve with regulatory oversight. Governments, such as the PRC, can promote the use of the technology through the tokens they sponsor and force users and merchants in their jurisdiction to embrace the technology. The government sponsored use of the technology, through government coins and corporate coins, also enable a flourishing ecosystem that evolves around the government-sponsored decentralized technology solutions. In the case of corporate coins, just as in other industries like the oil and gas industry, corporate influences support and enable regulatory approaches and solutions they could comply with, support, and control. Such corporate-driven legal solutions operate at the expense of more decentralized products and technology that are not always as compliant with the centralized legal infrastructure for the cryptocurrency and blockchain industry. People coins and the innovations they create are largely subject to regulatory uncertainty and evolve much more slowly or not at all. As a result, evolving government coins and corporate coins create their own path dependencies and engrained product deficiencies with suboptimal levels of decentralization.

These are some of the external and internal obstacles to building the decentralized economy. But there is an even larger problem. We're simply not ready to build a DAO that can compete with centralized corporations. When someone tries to form a centralized company, they are supported by an enormous infrastructure devoted to helping them succeed. That infrastructure is called "all of civilization." All our civilized institutions have evolved over the centuries and millennia to make centralized business a little easier and a little more efficient. The entire environment of the decentralized economy needs to be built before it can support its first truly successful DAO.

Overhead Institutions are Catalysts for the Economy

> Environments are not just containers, but are processes that change the content totally.
> —Marshall McLuhan, *American Scholar*, Volume 35, p. 200 (1965)

The modern legal system promises no one will steal from us in any stage of our business. It regulates markets to create an efficient and level playing field without a warlord tipping the scales. In developed countries, we don't need to bribe anyone to begin a new business arrangement – the licenses and certifications are publicly known and transparently reported and audited. The invention of the modern police force centralized personal defense. Instead of every individual constantly expending the energy to display our personal imperviousness to predation, we've concentrated the effort into a centralized institution that protects everyone, by outsourcing revenge.

The contemporary legal system needs to incorporate the new advances in information technology. Or the Web3 vision of the future needs to build the efficiency of our current legal system into its vision of the future economy. In the early 2020s, decentralized legal infrastructure solutions are almost entirely missing. The incompatibility of decentralized technologies with the existing regulatory frameworks suggest that decentralized legal infrastructure solutions should flourish. While some startups are experimenting with ERC-20 tokens and forms of decentralized arbitration, such solutions lack sufficient scale, decentralization, anonymity, and autonomy.

Cyber security attacks erode the trust that people might build from the sophisticated cryptographic tools that are available. The open access of cryptocurrency-based tools makes it nearly impossible to police cyber criminals in varied national jurisdictions. Global trust in internet security is in steady decline, with the United States being significantly more suspicious than average.[43] This lack of trust is exacerbated by majority ownership of traffic control in a few geographical monopolies. These monopolies create information silos and constrain knowledge exchange. The resulting lack of competition and cooperation impedes innovation, including at the protocol level and diminished consumer protection and rights. Skype video-messaging and teleconferencing service started with a decentralized P2P backbone (based on the decentralized music sharing app, Kazaa). This P2P service distributed more than

---

43 Edelman (January 21, 2018). 2018 Edelman Trust Barometer: Global Report, https://www.edel man.com/research/2018-edelman-trust-barometer (retrieved 6/1/20).

660 million worldwide users by the end of 2010.[44] Skype was sold to Microsoft the next year. In 2013 the Snowden files revealed that Microsoft shared American and international users' information with U.S. security agencies.[45] Whenever decentralized organizations pose a threat of disruption to any established centralized industry, they will naturally face competition and resistance.

The strong libertarian focus of some of the most influential Web3 developers means the crypto community is extremely reticent to cooperate with mainstream institutions and corporations. This ornery streak extends to the lack of cooperation within the crypto community on different projects. Many projects are attempting to build the "Bitcoin killer" or the "Ethereum killer." Instead of building compatible technologies in the service of interoperability, most are competing with each other, contradicting the open source culture that should pervade the space if it has any hope of thriving. But collaboration would require an environment with clear ground rules – an overarching governance process that everyone could agree upon. Without such basics, the fraud and regulatory uncertainty that currently characterize the crypto community – which are certainly exaggerated by establishment media but are still based in reality – will inevitably continue. However, any such scheme of broad governance over multiple P2P platforms seems unlikely to emerge in the current climate, even though that system is exactly what their mainstream centralized corporate competitors enjoy.

The current political system provides the material infrastructure so that our centralized businesses can run efficiently – taxes are peacefully collected to build roads to help deliver our supplies, to provide electricity, water, and sewers. It marshals a military, to give us confidence our investments will not crumble in March each year when armies feel like pillaging. Our religious and educational institutions are designed to make customers, workers, and partners who will behave well in all their dealings.

The contemporary political system should incorporate the new advances in information technology. Otherwise the Web3 vision of the future needs to build at least the features and social advantages of our current political system into its vision of the economy. Otherwise the decentralized economy will merely be a parasite

---

44 Statista. https://www.statista.com/statistics/272014/global-social-networks-ranked-by-number-of-users/ (retrieved 8/8/20).

45 "[N]ine months after Microsoft bought Skype, the NSA boasted that a new capability had tripled the amount of Skype video calls being collected through Prism. Material collected through Prism is routinely shared with the FBI and CIA, with one NSA document describing the program as a 'team sport'. . . . In June [2013], the Guardian revealed that the NSA claimed to have 'direct access' through the Prism program to the systems of many major internet companies, including Microsoft, Skype, Apple, Google, Facebook and Yahoo."

Glenn Greenwald, Spencer Ackerman, Laura Poitras, Ewen MacAskill, & Dominic Rushe, "How Microsoft Handed the NSA Access to Encrypted Messages," *The Guardian,* London, July 11, 2013.

on the dying host that is the traditional mainstream economy; in that case, once the host is dead, the social advantages we enjoy today will be lost.

News media and other communication infrastructures have been influenced throughout history to serve business. Early adoption by business has always driven advances in electronic information technology. Some of the first financially success-ful ventures in telegraph technology were commercial stock tickers for businesses. They remained in use until the 1960s when businesses became early adopters of per-sonal computers for telex transmissions. In the 1860s transatlantic telegraph cables were laid with the express purpose of providing London with market information from New York exchanges to improve trade and reduce prices. The efficiency gains are estimated to have been "equivalent to 8 percent of export value."[46] A large percentage of early radio broadcasts throughout the world were market reports, especially through telex technology, which adapted telegraphy to wireless radio transmissions for business. Early adoption of telephones and later cellphones and smartphones, Blackberries for texting and apps, etc., was driven by business uses.

In the decentralized economy, trusted news sources become even more important, as business contracts become more automated. Automated news services in P2P sys-tems are called oracles. Many oracles exist today, but most are centralized. To make a DAO secure, many different trusted decentralized oracles need to be developed. (We'll come back to this in Chapter 9.)

Still more institutions have evolved over the centuries to subtly improve cen-tralized business, including banking and underwriting. Most people have no sense of how important underwriting and insurance is to business. Nothing happens in any business transaction, in any market, without underwriting to improve its effi-ciency. Every transaction is a gamble on the future, and insurance gives people the confidence to take the risk, which provides the liquidity to make the markets more efficient (see Chapter 8).

When these overhead institutions work well, they are extremely efficient, be-cause business then uses them less. When the legal institutions work well, business is less corrupt, so there is less need to appeal for justice. The better the system runs, the more these institutions fade into the background.

The natural hope of most Web3 engineers is that these institutions can be auto-mated away until they vanish. The hope is that self-regulating smart contracts will never require an appeal to justice. Decentralized oracles will eliminate the need for any original investigation from independent media. Automated systems will elimi-nate the middleman. These hopes are somewhat misplaced.

The middleman provides an essential service. Business contracts are not getting simpler as our technology becomes more sophisticated. Each successful business

---

46 Claudia Steinwender, "Real Effects of Information Frictions: When the States and the Kingdom Became United," *American Economic Review, 108*(3), 2018, pp. 657–696.

agreement leads to more complex arrangements for more sophisticated systems of cooperation. If the services these middlemen provide can be automated away, they most certainly will be. Many functions in society have been automated away in the past, especially manual labor. But many types of middlemen have persisted. Why? There are certain junctures in business where novel problems regularly arise whenever circumstances change. These problems require creative solutions, and people step in to capitalize. These persistent junctures become business institutions.

The imagined future decentralized economy is missing almost all the functions these institutions provide. Without decentralized versions of these services, DAOs will not be able to compete with centralized companies.

Summary

What's missing from the decentralized economy? Almost everything.

What are the obstacles to decentralization? Most of the economy – most of the world – is centralized and sees any newly emerging structure as a threat to power. Many people can't imagine an alternative to centralization.

Is resistance futile? Certainly not. Decentralized organizations are as natural as centralized organizations. In many situations they are superior and will outcompete centralized institutions without the need for direct conflict.

Interoperability, the API economy, is most efficiently achieved, in the long run, on decentralized platforms. Negotiations made on a level playing field are fairer, resolve quicker, and encourage more business. When a centralized corporation owns the playing field there is less incentive to participate, knowing they will always take a piece of the action – as much as the market will bear. Monopolies are bad for the economy. Centralized companies are already trying to build platforms according to decentralized principles, like Google's Play Store, and open-source design, such as TensorFlow.

As our experiences and decisions move online, our privacy is being diminished. Our behaviors are monitored by computers, and our decisions are guided algorithmically. Auto insurance apps monitor our driving. Health insurance apps monitor our exercise and diet. Credit card companies monitor our purchases. With the COVID-19 pandemic, contact tracing apps are being instituted with continuous global monitoring of peoples' locations.[47] Centralized companies are building the tools faster than decentralized organizations, but people are resisting the threats to their privacy,

---

47 Apple Newsroom announcement, April 10, 2020, "Apple and Google partner on COVID-19 contact tracing technology" https://www.apple.com/newsroom/2020/04/apple-and-google-partner-on-covid-19-contact-tracing-technology/ (retrieved 8/9/20). Since 2019 Apple and Google have held 99% share of the global smartphone mobile OS market. https://www.statista.com/statistics/272698/global-market-share-held-by-mobile-operating-systems-since-2009/ (retrieved 8/8/20).

making the apps less effective.[48] People more willingly participate with decentralized apps, if their information remains under their personal control. ZK proofs allow people to do exactly that, sharing complex information for the purposes of social improvement, while maintaining control of their personal information.

The 2020 COVID-19 pandemic was the first 21st century global crisis demanding global coordination of peoples' information, and we failed miserably. There was no sophisticated coordination that allowed national governments to guide their citizens in nuanced ways. In the U.S., states dictated quarantine protocols without regard to whether the business was in a sparsely populated rural area or a dense urban locale. Based on the latest information, a successful contact tracing algorithm would have been able to dynamically advise each person on the safety of movement, and the changing needs for precaution.

Government by algorithm is already here.[49] Reared in a centralized world, we reflexively turn to centralized solutions. But a decentralized approach is more effective for such global problems. Decentralized networks encourage interoperability through bureaucratic transparency. This allows us to integrate data (on human movement, medical information, and more variables we haven't anticipated) more effectively than if one source attempts to dictate the development. With the privacy controls of decentralized technologies, with open source culture allowing public audits to guarantee security, we promote an atmosphere of participation.[50]

Decentralized developers are moving remarkably fast, but they still have much to improve. Bitcoin and Ethereum have provided primitive decentralized versions of currency and business contracts. How do we build decentralized versions of all the rest of the institutions that business and society rely on? What should we expect to see before we can confidently participate in the decentralized economy? The rest of this book analyzes these questions and provides a guide for navigating the future decades as we experiment and fail with decentralized structures, as we filter out the centralized impurities that our flawed understanding of decentralization will inevitably expose.

---

48 Charlotte Jee, "8 Million People, 14 Alerts: Why Some COVID-19 Apps Are Staying Silent," *MIT Technology Review,* July 10, 2020, https://www.technologyreview.com/2020/07/10/1005027/8-million-people-14-alerts-why-some-covid-19-apps-are-staying-silent/ (retrieved 8/8/20).

49 https://en.wikipedia.org/wiki/Government_by_algorithm (retrieved 8/8/20).

50 "We should have a global, decentralized system for collecting medical, movement, interaction and lifestyle data from everyone on the planet–and methods to analyze it in a secure, anonymous way. Statistical and AI analysis should be guided democratically by everyone contributing data [. . .] without sacrificing privacy."–AI researcher Ben Goertzel in "Decentralized Tech Will Be Ready for Humanity's Next Crisis," *Coindesk,* August 8, 2020, https://www.coindesk.com/decentralized-tech-will-be-ready-for-humanitys-next-crisis (retrieved 8/8/20).

Chapter 4
Technical Perspective

Before we explain how to build the major institutions that are lacking in the decentralized economy, we need the technical perspective to explain why these particular solutions are even necessary. Setting up the rewards and punishments in a DAO to ensure productive collaboration is not easy without a central authority to umpire disagreements and maintain harmony. Impossibility results illustrate the right perspective for developers to understand the logical limits of democratic collaboration. Game theory is necessary to properly justify incentive design.

Since this is not a technical book, we assume our readers have a variety of backgrounds. However, authors don't truly understand a subject if they can't explain it simply, without technical jargon, to an intelligent and interested audience. Nevertheless, this is a technology subject, so we need to make a short excursion and explore some technical ideas, to put the leading-edge solutions that programmers are developing in perspective.

Our goal is to build a DAO, which has open membership to anonymous individuals from around the globe. In this chapter we argue that building effective and efficient DAOs requires a secure and meaningful reputation system, maximum bureaucratic transparency through a dynamic governance structure, and coherent transcendental values for long-term stability.

Building such large, decentralized networks is a new challenge in history. Previously, groups were unified by local identifiers. At the very beginning, people would share close family. Then religions unified many different families. Then notions of patriotism, culture, and philosophy bonded people who shared cultural similarities such as languages. Geographical closeness could unite people into kingdoms by their similar experiences and lifestyles. Ancient Mesopotamia and China were able to unify many diverse cultures and geographies thanks to the advances in information technology of writing and increasingly complex ideas (bureaucracy and laws). When the laws were strict – Rule by Law – then the hierarchy formed rigidly and was very efficient temporarily, before its rigidity led to its instability and eventual collapse. This is protocol centralization. When the laws were loose – Rule by Virtue (throughout most of Ancient Egyptian and Chinese history) – then the organization was more stable. This is protocol decentralization.

Later, modern Western democracies with diverse populations required the unifying force of rigid protocol centralization. These letter-of-the-law legal systems were required to achieve political decentralization, since equality demands impartial and universal application of the law. To maintain stability under this rigid protocol

https://doi.org/10.1515/9783110673937-004

centralization, the founders instituted a dynamic political system. Its concrete rules for shifting power periodically and building checks and balances into the rigid protocol relieves the tension of the impersonal bureaucracy and rigid power hierarchy.

Our contemporary challenge is to bring together people of every background who wish to contribute toward an economic goal. Ideally, members could participate anonymously, to maximize the size of the network and encourage contributions. With these obstacles, how can we possibly create a system that stays coherent?

The new tools of information technology allow rules with perfect logical rigidity – rules that are rigorously and immediately enforced by smart contracts. Their application may be completely transparent for everyone in the global network to witness. This allows unprecedented protocol centralization, which will help keep such diverse groups organized and coherent as they strive to cooperate toward their economic goals, while remaining politically decentralized.

Despite the challenges exposed by rigid smart-contract-executed protocols that govern DAOs, we also have the tools to address these challenges. Contemporary information technology allows us to decentralize power by polling every member nearly instantaneously. Our processing ability allows any regulating instructions to be securely computed nearly instantaneously, without a central executive power. Our decentralized information storage and processing tools allow us to keep track of contributions and to reward and punish behaviors fairly without any ultimate, centralized arbiter to resolve disputes.

However, protocol centralization leads to instability if it is not implemented wisely. The point of this technical chapter is to illustrate two things:

1. No static set of rules can ever perfectly reflect the will of the group without leaving loopholes for adversaries to profit at the expense of the majority. There will always be an arms race between policing and those who will push strict rules to the limit. Therefore, to achieve stability a DAO must institute a dynamic governance system with a clear and accessible process for amending the rules and appealing the automated conclusion of smart contracts. Since decentralized organizations don't have leaders or a hierarchy of control, any governance process must be instituted from the very beginning.
2. Proper incentives are crucial for harmonious collaboration.
    a. Short-term business deals require a secure and meaningful reputation system.
    b. Long-term stability is determined by transcendental values.

To illustrate the logical necessity of these stipulations, in this chapter we briefly summarize some mathematical results from economics and social science: Condorcet's Paradox, Arrow's Impossibility Theorem, and the Folk Theorems of Game Theory.

Impossibility Results

There is a cultural difference between mathematicians and engineers, which meets at the boundary in computer science. Engineers are trained to believe that for any problem in any situation, we can find a solution. Given any gorge, we can design a bridge that can safely span the distance.

Mathematicians, on the other hand, are trained to categorize and completely understand the set of all possibilities related to a problem, and outline what is possible and impossible given a strictly delimited set of rules. This leads them to anticipate that there are questions that have no solutions. Math is filled with impossibility results. Some very basic examples are as follows:

1. $\pi = 3.14159\ldots$ is irrational, meaning it is impossible to write the number as a fraction with two integers.
2. It is impossible to trisect some angles with a straightedge and a compass.
3. It is impossible to find an algebraic formula for solving general 5th order polynomial equations.
4. There is no elementary antiderivative for the Gaussian distribution.
5. There are literally hundreds of impossibility results in the computer science field of distributed computing.[1]

This does not mean these problems cannot be solved. These results just show you cannot solve the problems within the limitations of a fixed set of tools. The engineering attitude that anything can be solved may be valid if you look at the problem from a new angle and invent a new strategy.

The intuition we are trying to convey in this chapter is that there are logical limits to what can be built. If you don't respect them, you will bang your head against an unsolvable problem. The impossibility results show we can never design a static set of rules, which will eternally sustain a DAO. But that just means we need to set up DAOs to run from the beginning with a dynamic set of rules.

Condorcet's Paradox

Marquis de Condorcet was a philosopher and mathematician who embodied the ideals of Enlightenment rationalism during the French Revolution in the 18th century. Condorcet promoted free and equal public instruction and equal rights for women and people of all races. As the main author of the Girondin constitutional

---

1 Hagit Attiya and Faith Ellen, *Impossibility Results for Distributed Computing*, Morgan & Claypool, 2014.

project, he built these ideas explicitly into the primary rules of his political party's proposed French Constitution.[2]

However, Condorcet's constitution was never put to a vote. The Montagnards asserted their own rules, which became the French Constitution of 1793, after they gained control of the convention. Condorcet criticized their proposal and was named a traitor. The Montagnards were the most radical group in the Assembly. They were responsible for the Reign of Terror under their leader, Robespierre. In the course of one year 16,594 official death sentences were carried out and an additional 10,000 died in prison without trial, including Condorcet himself.[3]

Before he was imprisoned, Condorcet continued to promote Enlightenment ideals while in hiding, by writing what has been described as the final word on the Enlightenment.[4] *Sketch for a Historical Picture of the Progress of the Human Spirit* (1795) argues that progress in the history of civilization is measured by improvements in justice, which are achieved in step with our advances in scientific understanding of the world.

While he believed the goal of humanity was to strive toward ever more just and productive societies, which increase our individual potentials, Condorcet was not a naive utopian scientific rationalist. Condorcet was a subtle thinker. His impossibility result, discussed next, illustrates how no ideal mathematical/mechanical process can ever be practically implemented. Condorcet subsequently focused on promoting the incongruous qualities of diverse individuality as the best means for improving the morality and justice in our social structures. Diverse humanity is Condorcet's foundation for objectively superior values. Universal and eternal principles are impossible for humanity to apprehend. Individual liberty is therefore crucial for a society to improve their path through history.

Condorcet's Paradox[5] demonstrates it is impossible to construct any method that will faithfully discover the will of a group, with any type of democratic voting system. Whenever there are three or more candidates, there can be circularities of preference, similar to the paper-rock-scissors cycle, with no clear winner. This simple observation proves it is not possible to design a perfect democratic governance system.

---

2 *Plan de Constitution présenté à la Convention nationale les 15 et 16 février 1793, l'an II de la République (Constitution Girondine)* is an elegant work that contains designs which are still relevant to building DAO constitutions today. For example, the plan was to cycle the presidency of the executive council between 7 ministers every 15 days. Elections would occur in two stages. Candidates consist of the members with the most votes in the first stage, so that any candidate in the population has the opportunity to be chosen. Three times as many candidates as the number of open seats then run during the second stage of voting.

3 Condorcet was in prison at the same time as the American revolutionary Thomas Paine, who also coauthored the Girondin constitution.

4 David Williams, *Condorcet and Modernity*, Cambridge University Press, 2004.

5 William Gehrlein, "Condorcet's Paradox and the Likelihood of its Occurrence: Different Perspectives on Balanced Preferences," *Theory and Decision, 52*(2), 2002, pp. 171–199.

Here three different majorities within the group might prefer A over B, B over C, and C over A. For example, see Table 4.1 for three voters:

Table 4.1: Voter preferences.

Voter 1	Voter 2	Voter 3
A	B	C
B	C	A
C	A	B

The result is:
2 voters prefer A to B.
2 voters prefer B to C.
2 voters prefer C to A.

Even though each individual has a clear personal ranking of the candidates, the group itself may have no clear ranking of what is best.

We may think that the situation fabricated in Table 4.1 is rare, but in fact the probability of a cycle occurring when there are three candidates is higher than 8% when there are more than 10 voters. As the candidate options grow, the chances of a cycle occurring somewhere among the options quickly rises to 100%.

One of the dangerous consequences of this situation is in primary voting. Consider the situation where A and B are paired in a primary before the winner runs against C in the general election. Under the preferences chosen in Table 4.1 we see A beats B in the primary, then A loses to C in the general election. Candidate C wins overall. But rearranging who runs first in the primary can force any of the candidates to win. Therefore, in this situation, those who have power over arranging the order of the contest, have the ability to determine the result. This is especially an issue with sports tournaments, as the organizers have some power in determining the outcome based on their choice of initial matchups.

Application to Network Forking

These Condorcet cycles are the simplest demonstration that no rules can be created to consistently discover the will of the group. But the astute reader may object, that in this situation, the group doesn't really have a preference, so we can't expect any process to conclude otherwise. First, that is a major problem for democracy. Sometimes there is no consensus to be had. This leads to the second conclusion that sometimes network forking is inevitable.

A network fork happens when two or more subgroups of the network split into separate networks. The profusion of religious sects provides voluminous historical examples. The most famous example in blockchain was when the Ethereum network experienced an irreconcilable philosophical difference early in its history with the original 2016 DAO.

In 2016, a decentralized venture capital fund, the DAO, was crowdfunded with a US$120 million token sale. One month later a third of its funds were siphoned off with an unexpected programming exploit. The split in the Ethereum community came down to two opinions. The majority of members chose to refund the money to the investors in the young network by changing the software that the members employ to communicate with each other. A sizeable minority refused to switch to the new software, continuing as before, changing the name of their fork of the network to Ethereum Classic.

In general, forking is bad, and forking is good. When a network splits in half, from an abstract perspective, we consider that each side is worth one quarter of its previous value or power. That's bad. The idea is that a network is valuable because of its connections. A general rule of thumb is to calculate the power of a network by squaring the number of members. A network with twice as many members has four times as much power.[6] This is the primary quality referred to with the term "network effects."

However, forking is probably good in the long term. Persistent, profound differences in goals and talents can arise within a group. This signals the need for specialization of domains of power. To be able to achieve that specialization without splitting irrevocably in a hard fork is sometimes more efficient as it keeps the strength added by more members and connections, but not always if the member-multiplier is outweighed by the strife involved with forcibly maintaining a bond between members with irreconcilable approaches to solving a problem.

The general problem of coming to democratic consensus is much worse than the mere existence of cyclic voting preferences. Even if we ignore these cyclic situations, there are still more elementary logical obstacles to deciding issues fairly. Another basic voting result to be concerned about is Duverger's Law, which applies to the current American system for deciding the president. The official ranking system is called plurality voting: whoever gains the most votes (the plurality) wins. This has long been understood to lead to our current two-party system. Third parties are unstable, since people naturally want their vote to matter if they bother to vote. Therefore, under plurality voting, people are naturally incentivized to game the system by

---

6 Is this theoretical claim backed up by data? In this example we come to no conclusion. In general, it is no surprise that Ethereum lost some value in its market cap in the months after the DAO event. But there are many variables in play. The price of this very young network was (and continues to be) extremely noisy. So, it's not even definitively clear the event affected its market cap in any particular direction, in the long term. The failure of the network could account for more of the drop than the split. Or the quick and decisive response could account for the fact that it didn't collapse. Or that same response is interpreted by some (including those who split) as reason for the drop.

voting for their preference of the perceived top two candidates, instead of "wasting their vote" on someone who has less chance – even if a third person is their authentically preferred candidate. Small parties never win, so there tends to be only two viable parties in the long run. These two parties must distinguish themselves from each other. So, plurality voting predictably leads to a system that swings between two polarized parties who are less acceptable to the majority, but strongly preferred by interested minorities – Duverger's Law.

Such obstacles to democracy are part of the reason it can be more efficient to rely on dictatorships and centralization, for example, in private companies. We will advance through more complex results in the next sections.

Arrow's Impossibility Theorem

In 1951 Kenneth Arrow proved that there is no voting system that decides the winner of an election according to the will of the voters in all situations. Arrow makes some simple, reasonable assumptions, then proves they cannot all be met under one system.

Stated briefly, Arrow's Impossibility Theorem proves it is not possible to design any system, within specific strict static assumptions, which a decentralized organization (a group without a dictator) can follow to come to consensus on a question with 3 or more options in a fair way. "Fair" is defined according to the technical, but reasonable, requirements of Unrestricted Domain, Pareto Efficiency, and Independence of Irrelevant Alternatives.

Unrestricted Domain means each individual voter has the freedom to choose any ordered ranking of the candidates from first to last.

Pareto Efficiency means if every member of the group prefers candidate A to B, then the system cannot choose candidate B as the winner.

Independence of Irrelevant Alternatives means that if the system would choose A as the winner, the system should not change the winner just because a single voter who prefers A > B > C might change their vote to preferring A > C > B. In this case, B and C are the "irrelevant alternatives."

Arrow's Impossibility Theorem proves you can't have all three assumptions in one system. This shows that if you want a democratic system with very basic standards for fairness (Unrestricted Domain and Pareto Efficiency), there will always still be an opportunity for voters to disrupt the election with strategic voting (manipulating their irrelevant alternatives). A sufficiently patient and clever minority power can always corrupt the process and profit at the expense of the majority, assuming your process has static rules and finite, discrete execution. There is no perfect voting system. All processes can be manipulated and corrupted while following the rules.

No voting method can be constructed to decide the winner of an election that properly reveals the preferences of two or more voters on three or more candidates, which satisfies these basic and obviously desirable assumptions. For instance, the most complicated axiom, independence of irrelevant alternatives, requires the winner should not change if a voter changes their opinion about the relative ranking of two losers.

Similarly, our much more complex goal of finding a single, automated system that correctly rewards all contributors to a collaboration can never hope to be perfect. Instead such results encourage us to widen our perspective. We analyze families of different systems to determine which motivations are incentivized by which reward systems. Then we ensure the system is motivated to dynamically respond to the inevitable gaming and attacks that will occur, from within and without, whenever money can be won, with an evolutionary protocol for continual improvement.

The natural question is whether we can use some other polling method to prevent the strategic subversion of the intentions of the majority with good will. Can we police strategic voting, punishing false reports? We have new tools for voting now – new technologies for communication and recording. We can weight our preferences continuously, splitting our vote into percentages between candidates. We can know the state of the election and change our vote continuously up to the last minute. We can coordinate with other voters while monitoring the poll. Does that help or hurt discovery of the will of the group?

Many alternatives have been explored in the literature. In all the methods discussed, the answer has always been that changes both help and hurt. New approaches solve old problems, but they create new opportunities for manipulation. In computing this is called "increasing the attack surface." To give us a better intuition for the theoretical limits of our modeling abilities, infinitely many more alternative solutions – and problems – are illustrated in the next section.

Folk Theorems of Game Theory

The Folk Theorems of Game Theory are important for designing decentralized organizations, because they rigorously illustrate two ancient dictates of common wisdom.

1. **Delayed gratification is crucial for success.** The incentive structure is radically changed between short-term and long-term perspectives. A secure system for tracking meaningful reputation is crucial for creating long-term stability when designing a DAO. "A good reputation is more valuable than money."[7]
2. **The spirit of the law is more important than the letter of the law.** It is impossible to set up formal rules for a group to keep them behaving in a cooperative manner in the long run, even if the rules are policed perfectly. Evolution must be built

---

7 Publilius Syrus (85 – 43 BC), Sententiae, Maxim 108. Cf., 大器晚成 Large vessels take longer to complete. Common Chinese idiom/chengyu.

into the design of any temporary rules. To keep these dynamic rules coherent in the long run, a decentralized organization must commit to transcendental values as primary. "Transcendental" means these values cannot be specified precisely, logically, and completely with formal rules.[8]

The Folk Theorems give a rigorous justification of these two aphorisms, so that technological constructions such as digital DAO constitutions can be engineered carefully for long-term stability.

The goal of this section is to explain the Folk Theorems of Game Theory and how they apply to network situations, as clearly as possible to a general audience who is not interested in examining the minutiae of every mathematical detail.[9]

Prisoner's Dilemma

To illustrate the Folk Theorems, let us go through the most famous basic example of a strategic game called the Prisoner's Dilemma (PD). Two people get together to exchange closed bags, with the understanding that one of them contains money, and the other contains diamonds. Either player can choose to cooperate by putting their assets into their bag, or they can defect by handing over an empty bag[10] (see Figures 4.1 and 4.2).

Playing this game once gives only one stable and successful strategy: both players' best choice is to independently defect, handing over empty bags. This leads them to suffering the loss of opportunity of a good business deal, but not as much as if they lost their property. The strategy of defecting is best possible under the assumption that your adversary is brilliant (they can anticipate your strategy[11]) and ruthless (they will hurt you if it benefits them). This assumption is called rational self-interest in economics and game theory. The pair both defecting is what is called a Nash equilibrium, because any deviation from this strategy would lead to a worse outcome for one of the players, so eventually everyone will agree and settle at the equilibrium as the best strategy for the game.

---

8 "When mores are sufficient, laws are unnecessary; when mores are insufficient, laws are unenforceable."—Émile Durkheim "Look, that's why there's rules, understand? So that you think before you break 'em."—Terry Pratchett, *Thief of Time*, 2001.

9 For these details, see, for example, George J. Mailath and Larry Samuelson, Repeated Games and Reputations: Long-Run Relationships, Oxford University Press, 2006. This text is recommended because it highlights the case of repeated games with reputation.

10 Paraphrased from Douglas Hofstadter, "Ch.29 The Prisoner's Dilemma Computer Tournaments and the Evolution of Cooperation," *Metamagical Themas*, Bantam Dell Pub Group, 1985.

11 It is often assumed that your adversary has mystical insight into your psychology. Axel Boldt (private communication) has another interpretation: Imagine both players have spies that can report back the strategies of their adversaries. Before you finalize a strategy and play the game, the spies report and so the players can change their strategies. But then the spies report on the new strategies. This can happen infinitely often before the game is finally played.

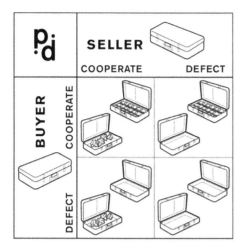

Figure 4.1: Prisoner's Dilemma strategy combinations. Image by Chris Jensen and Greg Riestenberg.

SELLER BUYER	COOPERATE	DEFECT
COOPERATE	1 1	2 -1
DEFECT	-1 2	0 0

Figure 4.2: Reward matrix for basic Prisoner's Dilemma game.

It is worth developing a rigorous intuition for this situation. When we first encounter this game, our natural human instinct is to think of the defection strategy as cheating. It's bad. And we think of the cooperation strategy as self-evidently good, on a moral level. Why then do the game theorists insist the best strategy is to defect? Are game theorists morally bankrupt? Not exactly. They are looking at the game from a coldly calculating perspective of ignoring morality and merely accounting for what is the most efficient strategy. This perspective is useful for explaining why certain behaviors are observed in business and society, as the most efficient strategies tend to win out in the long run, despite moral misgivings.

If you are like most people, that will not assuage you. But the good news is, we can prove that cooperation is the optimal strategy if you allow people to play the game repeatedly – the moral perspective is the right and rational one if you have to live with the consequences of your behavior tomorrow. However, the Folk Theorems show that nothing is ever simple and introduce a nagging wrinkle into any complex game.

Repeated Prisoner's Dilemma

Next, if we change the setup to assume the business deal is repeated day after day, the best strategy Nash equilibrium changes dramatically. The opportunity to repeatedly make a good business deal means both players would greatly improve their outcomes if they can find a strategy of long-term cooperation.

The first strategy is called **grim trigger**: you will cooperate as long as your adversary cooperates. If the adversary ever defects, then you promise to defect ever after, punishing your adversary forever.

Under the grim trigger strategy, your adversary's best option is to always cooperate. Any deviation from cooperation leads to a worse outcome, so eternal cooperation is a Nash equilibrium under the circumstances.

Grim trigger illustrates that the Nash equilibrium for a single stage of PD (both players defecting) changes to a radically less efficient outcome if you are in a repeated game. Being stuck in the grim trigger trap is significantly worse, so the better strategy is to cooperate. Switching your perspective from a single point in time, to viewing all eternity in the future, we achieve a completely different perspective in our incentives. When we inhabit infinity, we realize our reputation for cooperation overrules our immediate impulses of fear and greed.

This new leap in efficiency as the players cooperate can only be achieved if there is the possibility of creating a policeable reputational system. The players must have a history, and that history must be available to the other players. Therefore, transparency and communication are essential for making policing effective and efficient.

Repeated Prisoner's Dilemma with Precommitments

Another important insight that arises from repeated games is that there are infinitely many other strategies in this scenario, which are also Nash equilibria. It is wrong to assume that there is some ideal strategy in any realistic scenario. This is a basic example of what is called a Folk Theorem in repeated games.

To illustrate this point, consider a new situation where we assume a competitor can **precommit** to a strategy. An example of a precommitment would be if you sign a smart contract that will automatically execute your orders in the future in a way that you cannot stop. Specifically, in the **Noble vs. Peasant** repeated PD game set up, let's say the noble signals their precommitment to the strategy of cooperating 9 times out of 10 but deviating on the 10th time. The noble also precommits to the grim trigger strategy of defecting for all eternity if the peasant ever defects even once. Given this signal from the noble, the peasant now has the choice of defecting forever and gaining nothing, or cooperating forever and being betrayed 1 in 10 times, but profiting 9 in 10 times. The second option is more profitable for the peasant. So even though it is not fair (the noble gains +12 every 10 stages and the peasant gains +8), it is the rational choice for the peasant (+8 > 0).

The Folk Theorem for this situation shows there are infinitely many different possible payout profiles the noble can force with different precommitment strategies. The noble can defect 4 times out of 10 to force a payout of $(noble, peasant) = (+14, +2)$. The peasant still is better off with a payoff of +2 every 10 rounds instead of +0 for all eternity. Or the noble can defect 49 times out of 100, or 499 times out of 1,000. In this abstract theoretical setup, the noble defecting anything less than 50% of the games still makes it profitable for the peasant to participate instead of suffering the consequence of the grim trigger for all eternity.[12]

Similar game setups with reputation policing explain the situation where a business will rationally tolerate a small level of theft when policing is more expensive, such as when a grocer will ignore a street urchin who nabs an apple once per day. This helps us understand the rationality of some exploitative long-term relationships such as parasites and bullying, and the need for careful protocol design to prevent that type of corruption/inefficiency.

This leads to the intuition that however rules are formalized in a realistic situation, there are strategies that follow the rules, but still subvert the intentions of the framers. There are legal strategies that profit the individual adversary at the expense of the group.

Infinite Variations of Prisoner's Dilemma

The many folk theorems of game theory show there are many new strategies possible with each new assumption about the game. We showed this above with the change to repeated games and again with the change to allow precommitments. Each new change in assumptions leads to new strategies. This suggests there is no way to create a static protocol, which can guarantee consensus behavior from all members of a group playing a complicated and realistic repeated game.

For example, there are new equilibria strategies when there are different levels of patience in the players (technically called discounting). Then old equilibria fail, and

---

12 Technically, for simplicity, we are assuming a discount factor of $\delta = 1$ so we can speak freely without extra qualifications. We can make this more complicated by modeling how patient the peasant is, $0 \leq \delta \leq 1$ but the wider conclusion stands.

new equilibria arise when you change the game to assume players have imperfect information. With each change of assumption in the game, old successful strategies fail to be Nash equilibria, and new successful strategies arise.

Or if you allow periodic opportunities for renegotiation, then you might be able to get out of a grim trigger trap. This sounds like it would improve outcomes, but in fact it gives new opportunities for defecting/cheating. If you know there is a chance to renegotiate, it might be to your advantage to defect and gain the reward, and gamble that you can talk your way out of the punishment of grim trigger later. Again, the Folk Theorem in this case reveals infinite successful strategies.

Further PD alternatives that give new successful strategies include:
- partial or periodic opportunities for player communication (e.g., to punish shirkers, or collude, or reward players at retirement)
- accounting for the cost of policing deviations
- accounting for a player's history or reputation
- stochastic variations, including
  - results are not perfectly reported
  - memory of the past is not perfect
  - strategies not implemented perfectly, "trembling hand"
- new players allowed to enter or leave at various times, "long- or short-lived players"
  - tournaments
  - tournaments with history/reputation
- changing assumptions about the population/market (e.g., how cooperative or ruthless)
- evolutionary concepts added to incentives (e.g., accounting for a large population through time)
- continuous strategies (variable amounts of cooperation or betrayal)
- asymmetric rewards (one party stands to lose or gain more than the other)
- asymmetric timing (one party plays before the other)

All these basic assumptions listed above apply to many different models of realistic situations. None of those models come close to completely encapsulating the set of all behaviors that can occur in any natural setting.

We further argue this important point with the following meta-theorem[13] due to the instability of Nash equilibrium strategies with respect to changing assumptions:
1. No matter what game you are playing, you can add a new assumption to make a more complicated generalization of the game, so that the previous winning strategy becomes a losing strategy, and a new winning strategy arises.

---

13 We call this a meta-theorem because it cannot be formalized. To make it mathematically rigorous, you would need to explicitly state the context or domain in which each successive subset is the domain of a subgame. For example, if the action space was in R^n then we could imagine generalizing the game to R^{n+1}. But the point of the meta-theorem is that whatever universe you specify

2. Life is not constrained within any given game's assumptions. You can always come up with a new strategy that takes advantage of the previous myopia under a static set of rules.[14]

Game theory gives us the intuition that in any slightly sophisticated repeated game (such as Prisoner's Dilemma), there is not one optimal strategy, but many possible successful strategies. Further, these successful strategies are unstable when new assumptions are made. Whenever we add a new twist to the formal description of a game, new successful strategies arise and old strategies become unsuccessful. Any realistic situation has innumerable assumptions. In fact, you can always change the assumptions by behaving in a new way as you play any realistic game according to a new desire. If you design a network to improve its members' circumstance by cooperation, then if it succeeds, it will change their circumstance, and their desire. It is not possible to design a game in real life with a unique and perfect optimal strategy. In any realistic situation, people always discover new strategies or merely arrive at alternative successful behaviors, which subvert the intentions of the designers.

Any set process or set of rules that we can ever design will ultimately fail to secure a network for all time. Especially a decentralized network. Especially if we want to allow anyone on the globe to join. Especially if we want to allow anonymity. Any set of rules that can ever be designed will always need to be amended in the future as the environment changes, to keep the network running healthily. We cannot rely eternally on a static set of rules, or else the system will inevitably become corrupt or irrelevant.

The point of the Folk Theorems is that it is necessary to design our systems with an evolutionary mindset. A dynamic governance process is crucial. We need

---

as the domain, you can easily make a natural assumption that runs out of that category, for example, from R^n to a probability space, and from there to a much more general metric space. And there are no limits to generalizing categories beyond that. (Basic paradoxes, such as Russell's paradox, demonstrate the logical futility of posing the existence of "the set of all sets" as your universe.)

14 This is the sort of perspective that Byzantine Fault Tolerance algorithm testers display. Byzantine behavior means breaking the stated rules. "(i) Byzantine behavior is unconstrained, hence, one can only implement a subset of such behaviors; and (ii) the subset of Byzantine behaviors to be tested are chosen by system developers, who are naturally tainted by having designed the system with certain limited Byzantine behaviors in mind."—Shehar Bano, Alberto Sonnino, Andrey Chursin, Dmitri Perelman, Dahlia Malkhi, "Twins: White-Glove Approach for BFT Testing" April 22, 2020 https://arxiv.org/pdf/2004.10617.pdf (retrieved 5/6/20).

The point is that life cannot be entirely contained in any mathematical model, no matter how complicated. We have infinite-dimensional spaces that contain only a tiny fraction of a model. For example, if you try to model something as simple as a child's bouncy ball, you will need infinite dimensions to model its vibrational modes as an elastic sphere. But that is a hopelessly simplistic representation of an actual ball, as no actual ball is a perfect sphere. Every imperfection is ultimately important, but even if we started to include a few of the infinitely many imperfections, the model would quickly become incalculably difficult to render in a computer. So, we simplify all scientific models drastically, so we can achieve computable results in a reasonable time.

always keep in mind the spirit of the law is more important than the letter of the law. To maintain a decentralized network's integrity, we must firmly hold to our transcendental values as our eternal goal, instead of focusing on any formalizable set of rules of behavior.

Zero-sum Games and Code-is-Law Smart Contracts

In the DAO hard fork, which split the Ethereum network as described above, the minority fork's principled objection was to maintain their ideal of Code is Law.

The Code is Law Principle holds that however a smart contract executes in following the logical steps of its program, that result is legal, regardless of the intent of the author of the smart contract. In the environment of Ethereum Classic minority, there is no such thing, legally, as a bug in a program. "The network does what the network does," is the whole of the law.

The Ethereum Classic fork consists of the members of the original Ethereum network who refused to adopt the new software that "fixed" the bug in the original DAO smart contract costing users in the early network more than US$50 million. The Code is Law Principle divided the community from those who were afraid the hard line would scare away investment because of the insecurity of living with every unintentional error.

Despite how alluring the simplicity of the Code-is-Law credo is, that extreme puritanical line is not an efficient solution for business.[15] In the wider context of the future of business in a decentralized world, we must consider some practicalities. Unintended consequences of contracts arise in almost every business arrangement. We are not able to predict the weather one week in advance, much less the future of any complex human scenario. It is not strategically sound to make business decisions based on gambling. For mutually beneficial, long-term cooperation to thrive, it is necessary to allow review of contracts assuming good faith from both parties when unintended consequences arise.

A zero-sum game is one in which the total rewards of the game are fixed beforehand and at the end of the game the rewards end up split between the players. If the economic system we construct in the Web3-enabled decentralized economy is merely a zero-sum game, then cooperation is not possible as the only feasible long-term strategy is the pirate code: take anything not nailed down and leave nothing for your opponent. Then people are incentivized to play the most ruthless strategies available to hurt the other parties of a contract. Especially when anonymous parties are involved, this leads

---

15 But we are still sympathetic with the Ethereum Classic community. Especially if their motivation was to send a message to programmers and investors that messy thinking will be punished. Especially because a Code is Law environment is more efficient.

to an extremely degenerate situation. Adversaries are right to spend some extra energy to determine the minimum effort needed to satisfy the Code-is-Law smart contract.

However, the principle behind Code is Law is still an ideal to strive for. The efficiency and clarity that can be achieved in the long run by using the absolute mathematical logic and electronic speed of computer programmed and executed smart contracts is an indispensable opportunity for business. Relying on the smart contract regardless of outcome is extremely efficient. A Code-is-Law assumption is needed to deal with the unbelievably complex legal interactions governing the exponentially evolving business interactions that arise with AI-enabled IoT devices. How can we legally regulate the smart contracts that mediate between devices owned by many different companies and individuals interacting throughout the supply chain? New efficient processes lead to newer, more efficient processes. Business arrangements constantly adapt to these changing circumstances giving new contracts. The multiplicity of options in a dynamically changing market demands instantaneous legal enforcement without waiting for a centralized response of human interjection.

How do we choose between the efficiency of Code is Law and the business necessity of continuing an arrangement after the contract is technically broken? The ability of the network to review decisions is necessary. Then, "the network does what the network does" approach to Code is Law is not broken. This is one of the many reasons there is not a robust decentralized economy using blockchain technology, yet. The decentralized solution to reviewing cases without enabling the Tyranny of the Majority still needs to be built.

A thousand years ago, the Maghribis found their solution. And 200 years ago, modern democracies found theirs. A secure and meaningful reputational system and dynamic governance are two of the building blocks. We will explore contemporary applications of these ideas using recent advances in information technology in chapters 6 and 7.

As smart contracts become more sophisticated, they may include many of the eventualities that most commonly happen in business situations. But as contracts become more complicated, that allows more complicated business arrangements, which means more complicated unintended consequences and disputes. This is an eternal race as we develop more solutions that breed more problems. We can never design the ultimate program to solve all business problems or solve all human relations. Instead we need to wisely build a properly incentivized, evolutionary environment for generating more efficient contracts that encourage better cooperation.

Application to PoS Consensus Algorithms

The goal of all existing proof of stake (PoS) algorithms (mentioned previously in Chapter 2) is to create a protocol that incentivizes everyone in the blockchain network to behave the same way. We want everyone to run a single canonical program that eventually synchronizes everyone's perspective about the global state of the network, even though at any one time we each see only part of the state, because we share messages in the cloud by forwarding messages we receive from nearby nodes to other nodes near us. We want the protocol to make it very unprofitable for anyone to try to run a hacked program to gain any advantage – by doing less work, for example (shirking), or ignoring messages that don't benefit us (censoring), or by sending false messages that break consensus (Byzantine faults), etc. PoS must punish anyone who violates the protocol strongly enough so that the vast majority of the network (at the very least 67%) will not copy their behavior.

Ethereum announced their intention to eventually implement a PoS algorithm since its inception in its original yellow paper. Despite the intense pressure they are under to perform, they have been looking in the wrong place, for years. A major component of their plan is to develop an algorithm that is "correct by construction (CBC)."[16] That is, an algorithm that is rigorously provably correct: given a specific set of realistic assumptions about the nature of the network, they wish to prove that Byzantine behavior is impossible, or at least highly disincentivized. In the first place, this is simply false advertising. Most people don't understand that CBC doesn't mean it's mathematically proven to be perfectly resistant to all attacks; it's only resistant to the attacks the theorists consider reasonable at the time. Secondly, this is too ambitious to wait on for years as the network is wasting energy on PoW. Further, there is a better strategy that will be more secure and more efficient in the long run.

Finding a correct by construction algorithm that incorporates all possible, or even practical, assumptions of possible network statuses, is not possible. Given any set of assumptions about how the network will behave, you can always break those assumptions by valuing some other result.

Given the impossibility of creating an algorithm that will be perfectly secure in all circumstances, we should instead focus on developing a governance process that allows us to update our algorithm to adapt to the changing network circumstances to the security level required – an evolutionary algorithm that encourages improvements to the system with balanced rewards. Simply incentivize people to develop protocol improvements instead of unleashing attacks, by giving meaningful reputation.

Similarly, any DAO will need to adapt to changing circumstances in their user base to maintain security and keep incentives aligned in service to their goals. We are always fated to engage in a technological arms race to maintain security in any realistic setting.

From the perspective of game theory, we think of a PoS consensus algorithm as a repeated game. The game is played each time a block is manufactured and accepted

---

16 "Guide to Ethereum Proof of Stake and Casper," Online Introductory Resources: https://ethstaking.io/correct-by-construction-cbc-casper/ (retrieved 8/8/20).

by the network. The goal is to design the game in such a way that the only profitable strategy is to follow the canonical protocol. Technically, we might think of PoS as a game design that makes the canonical protocol the unique subgame perfect Nash equilibrium.

This is the most challenging problem in decentralized computing, and the best minds in the area have been devoted to solving the problem since before Bitcoin was invented. Bitcoin's proof of work algorithm (PoW) is the first major implementation of a practical protocol to solve this problem. PoW has been successful enough to guarantee consensus for more than a decade in a network of millions of users, worth about US$100 billion. Despite the fact that anyone can run any hacked version of the algorithm at any time from an anonymous account, there has not been a single protocol violation – meaning no message has been incorporated in the finalized blockchain that breaks the rules of the algorithm.

However, we suspect that the Bitcoin PoW algorithm is ultimately flawed. In fact, we believe that every consensus algorithm is flawed. Further we are confident it is not possible to create an algorithm that is not flawed. Impossibility results from mathematics abound. The vague goal of finding a perfect protocol for guaranteeing eternal universal consensus in the messy situation of real life, with constantly changing market environments, with arbitrary anonymous actors, is certainly too ambitious. The Folk Theorems of Game Theory display the vanity of that goal.

Application to Reputation Tokens

Game theory can prove several insights are valid with DAO design. To create the proper incentives these design choices should be considered.[17] In this section we consider some traditional applications of game theory to explaining economics and the theory of the firm that DAO architects may consider in the future.

First, we can disincentivize defection/betrayal by charging admission to the DAO. With the sunk cost of joining, it is more expensive to cheat, since then it would be expensive to rejoin even if members could be anonymous. This is described as costly signaling. It is more effective when the environment contains more cheaters, then people are incentivized to join the group that has differentiated themselves. (This can give some justification for the Denial of Service (DoS) fees that we use in the design given below.)

On the other side, blacklisting accounts can incentivize cooperation, especially with KYC[18] protocols.

---

17 See Avner Greif, *Institutions and the Path to the Modern Economy: Lessons from Medieval Trade*, Cambridge University Press, 2006, pp. 428–452.
18 KYC is the acronym for "Know Your Customer," which refers to identity verification protocols used especially in banking and insurance. KYC protocols are generally antithetical to the Web3 movement,

Another issue with repeated games to discuss is the end period. When is it better to choose the strategy of cooperating for long-term gain versus the motivation to choose short-term gain by betraying the opponent with defection? Short-term gain is the better choice if you are impatient, that is, if the reward today is much more important than a reward tomorrow. In finance and game theory this is measured by the future *discount factor*. A guarantee of $10 in the future is rarely as valuable as $10 today. Natural economies have inflation because goods spoil in time, so it's better to invest your $10 today and get more than $10 in the future. Alternatively, you may be desperate for the $10 today and don't anticipate the need tomorrow. The fraction between the future and present value of the reward is the discount factor for each stage of the game. If the discount factor is too low, then it is better to defect. Or the dual problem is, if you know the game will end soon, then the future reward is too low, so you should again defect.

Therefore, the promise of future profits must outweigh the present value to ensure cooperation. The advantage of a large or global network in building a reputational system is that the reputation will have a more stable and predictable value. Though they are not as fungible as currency tokens, reputation tokens in P2P systems can be correlated with expected future salary, appraised (with hedging if they are tied to auditable past behavior), and sold. In this way, reputation tokens derived from smart contracts makes them more valuable and efficient than the vague notions of reputation from the past.

Another advantage to digital tokens in open global networks is that the loss of opportunity from having your reputation slashed grows as the size of the network increases. Further, given the incomplete information due to anonymity, the value of the information from reputation tokens increases. When potential business partners have less knowledge of your identity, the knowledge from the number of reputation tokens you hold becomes more important. Moreover, the lack of personal knowledge encourages the members to devote more effort to fairly policing reputation tokens, so meritocracy is encouraged.

Next, a DAO design that allows anonymity must guard against various sockpuppet attacks. One strategy is to have one account that acts honestly and one that cheats. If the cheating account can funnel the gains to the honest account, without detection or punishment, this sets the system up for failure.

Another situation where DAOs with smart contracts have an advantage is with compliance. Algorithms can be written that exclude members who cheat from having access to their market. Punishment for cheating becomes automated and therefore credible. Free riding in policing can at least partly be eliminated by

---

which has a preoccupation with privacy and user control of their own information – especially because nothing is ever deleted on the internet: "Experts: Deleted Online Information Never Actually Goes Away," *Chicago Tribune*, August 21, 2015 https://www.chicagotribune.com/business/blue-sky/chi-deleted-online-information-never-goes-away-20150821-story.html (retrieved 8/8/20).

automation. In traditional business, members would police cheaters by withholding their business. But to make the threat credible, you would need to police the other members and punish them if they did business with cheaters. And so on, to make the threats credible, you would need to police those who did not police those who did not police. Algorithms can be written proactively to only supply contracts to those who have sufficient reputation. If your reputation is slashed, you will not be chosen by the algorithm.

Another motivation for transparency is that the value of reputation is directly related to how well punishment can be distributed in response to cheating. The more transparent the system, the more accurate and efficient policing can be.

How to Build a DAO

If, out of the present chaos, there is ever to come a world where free people live together peacefully . . . we shall have to furnish the pattern. It is not enough to restore people to an old and outworn pattern. People must be given the chance to see the possibilities of a new world and to work for it.

—Eleanor Roosevelt, *The Eleanor Roosevelt Papers, My Day,* December 16, 1941

Now we're ready to design a basic DAO. (This is an example of what is called a toy model in science and engineering, because it neglects much of the details needed to make a full blueprint.) For specificity, we'll draft a DAO devoted to reviewing software for money. However, the basic design will apply to autonomously organizing any decentralized group for any purpose. In this case our group of software experts will be focused on judging new software products to determine how safe or useful they are. The group will be called the Software Review DAO, or SRDAO.[19]

Fully describing how to organize a company from scratch is necessarily complicated and tedious. Describing how to organize a decentralized company, where members can be anonymous and geographically separated but still need to share power and profits, is necessarily extremely complicated and tedious. Readers should assume all design choices are options. Stringent requirements will be instituted in any specific instantiation of an actual DAO.

The SRDAO is a collaboration between anonymous software experts. They hash their reviews and post the hashes to the blockchain. The validated software can be hashed and recorded along with the reviews. Users can check whether the software they are downloading is also valid if it has the same hash. The power of the review is

---

19 The idea for the SRDAO was inspired by Clemens Cap and Benjamin Leiding, "Ensuring Resource Trust and Integrity in Web Browsers Using Blockchain Technology," *Advanced Information Systems Engineering Workshops* – CAiSE 2018 International Workshops, Tallinn, Estonia, 2018.

checked by how many DAO experts staked their reputation to vote for it. Invalidated software will have pools where experts stake a lot of reputation to vote against it.

The fees will eventually come from the fact that your peer reviewer platform is valuable. The public would unconsciously use the SRDAO's work because their UI would only recommend software that had a sufficiently high review. Companies that want to prove their products are safe will eventually pay fees to have their software reviewed quickly (especially patches, for example).

Ultimately, we want to show how the members can be paid for their work. The challenge is to organize a group with no leader and no hierarchical structure. All members have the same roles. The members do only one job for one type of customer. (Different roles should have separate DAOs with separate types of reputation tokens. With interoperability being a main concern of developers with the goal of increasing network effects, separate DAOs will interact by subcontracting to cooperate.)

How do we set up the reward structure so that nobody can game the system? From the Folk Theorems, we know we cannot set up a perfect system. The best we can hope for, is to design a system that makes it easier to help the group than to hurt it. We need to set up a system so that the members themselves will be encouraged to police the bad actors, to protect their own profits.

For maximal applicability to general DAOs that have different goals, we will assume the worst-case scenario: Members from any location can join. Members could therefore be located in any jurisdiction and cannot be tracked or punished for any bad behavior by appealing to outside authorities – the only punishment available is to take away their potential future profits in the DAO. Members are all anonymous. Members might have multiple anonymous accounts (sockpuppet accounts). The only way to discourage malicious actors from joining is to charge money to join, which hampers recruitment efforts. Finally, we assume there are a significant number of bad actors who would harm the DAO if there was any opportunity to do so, whether or not it was profitable. Therefore, a nominal fee to join will be charged as resistance to basic DoS attacks.[20] This fee merely needs to be high enough so that the effort to police the bad actors is profitable, but not so high that it prevents people of good will from joining. This number depends on the market environment. Automation should make this feasible.

The only levers of power the DAO can wield over their members is to reward them by sharing DAO profits or punish them by withholding those profits. The DAO will therefore institute a reputation token system to push these profits as far as possible into the future, to give time to review the members' actions and encourage good behavior. For specificity, we assume the reputation tokens will be created and tracked using a blockchain such as Ethereum. Alternative P2P approaches

---

20 Denial of Service (DoS) attacks happen when anonymous adversaries flood the system with automated requests for superfluous tasks, thus preventing the network from engaging in productive work.

are available, such as a distributed hash table, which would be more efficient (especially for voting) and less secure.

A periodic reputation-weighted salary will distribute all fees the DAO earns to all members. Individuals who perform tasks that bring fees to the DAO will be rewarded with reputation tokens, not the fees. Members who own more reputation tokens share in a larger percentage of the fees. This solves the sockpuppet attack: if you have 10 accounts with 1 reputation token each, it's the same as 1 account with 10 reputation tokens.

So, there are two types of tokens to keep track of, reputation tokens and fees. The fees come entirely from customers who engage the SRDAO to review their software. These fees are fungible currency such as bitcoin or USD.

The basic function of the SRDAO is as follows:

1. A customer uses the SRDAO smart contract (SC) to engage a reviewer by encumbering the fee in the SC and uploading the software to be reviewed.
2. The SC randomly picks a reviewer/member from those members available. (The only other smart contract in use will be an availability smart contract, which members engage by encumbering their reputation tokens.)
3. The reviewer evaluates the software according to the principles the SRDAO has previously collectively agreed upon.
4. The reviewer posts their review.
5. The review triggers a validation pool – a voting pool where any member can stake their reputation by voting to approve or disapprove of the review.
   a. The SC mints new reputation tokens in proportion to the size of the fee.
   b. The new reputation tokens are staked half in favor of the review in the reviewer's name; half are staked against and left unassigned.
   c. Majority wins and the reputation tokens are split proportionally among the winners.
6. Results are posted displaying how the software was received by the reviewer and whether the SRDAO community agreed.
7. The fee is split among the entire SRDAO in proportion to their reputation holdings (reputation-weighted salary).

See Figure 4.3.

We are assuming that every stage of this process is automated. The most energetically intensive step is 4, where the reviewer reviews the software, but even this is imagined to be largely automated once the SRDAO is fully operational. The idea is that members use a uniform preapproved protocol for doing everything. That way, participating in the validation pool is also typically automated.

In a well-functioning DAO every validation pool will result in nearly unanimous votes – the only contrary votes should be against those shirking their duty, who will lose their reputation tokens for coming to the nonstandard conclusion. The validation pool is simply for policing the group and maintaining unity. It is not for gambling.

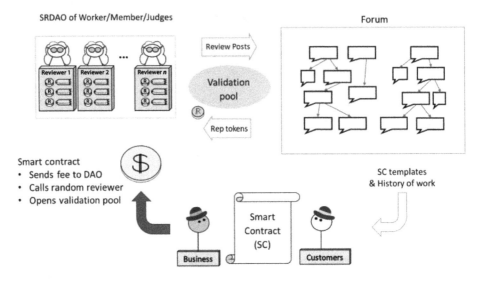

Figure 4.3: SRDAO process governed by smart contract designed by DAO members, called by customers, who find the SC in the forum.

Reviewers don't get fees directly for their work. Instead they get more reputation tokens, if they are successful in the validation pool, because of Step 5b. The rest of the members share some of the newly minted reputation tokens for participating in the policing of the DAO.

In the beginning, this Software Review DAO will review software for free. In this beginning stage the SRDAO is building value, until the collection of reviews becomes useful.[21] The reviewers/members will gain reputation tokens for their work. Once the SRDAO attracts fees, members' early seemingly altruistic efforts pay off with the reputation-weighted salaries. Since all fees are shared with all members, this eliminates the incentive to positively review software just because a company sends a big fee. Basically, a single expert reviewer cannot be bribed as easily if the fees are shared with everyone.

The creation of every step of the DAO from the very beginning follows this same 7-step procedure.

– **New member review.** A new member submits an application smart contract as if they were a customer. The fee would go to the DAO, new reputation tokens would be minted and staked in the applicant's name in Step 5b. The rest of the DAO members would validate the application, or not, to police the DAO.The

---

21 Insights from past OSS projects are essential for initiating effective DAOs. A useful guide to the values that encourage the success of these groups is given by Katherine J. Stewart and Sanjay Gosain, "The Impact of Ideology on Effectiveness in Open Source Software Development Teams," *MIS Quarterly, 30*(2), 2006, pp. 291–314.

first member of the DAO would follow the same procedure to receive the first newly minted reputation, since there would be no one to vote against them.

The second member would need to convince the first member to vote for them, because the new tokens are staked half in favor, half against – so the first member would have complete control of whether or not the validation pool resolved in their favor.

- **Proposals for new protocols.** Suggestions for updating how the DAO should run can be submitted for review by staking reputation as a fee. The process would mint new reputation tokens, and if the protocols are accepted, the proposer would gain half of them, the rest would be shared with the group for participating in policing.

The system is evolutionary in structure. The SRDAO continually rewards work on new software reviews and it encourages the creation of more sophisticated protocols for how to run the DAO. They should continually create more sophisticated protocols for reviewing the reviewers' reviews.

The idea is that for most software reviews, a reviewer does several standard statistical tests, explaining which ones were done in their review. The SRDAO will have developed a common reviewing program, which if run faithfully, will always give the same result. Then when the other experts validate the review, they merely need to run the tests themselves and upvote the reviewer. The idea is that a faithful reviewer who is following SRDAO protocol will win every single validation pool, and never lose a single reputation token. Those who shirk will eventually be discovered and lose their reputation.

How does a reviewer review a new piece of software that requires new techniques that aren't spelled out in canonical SRDAO protocol precedent? Propose a new protocol.

How does the DAO set the fees? How does the DAO decide how much to reward protocol creation compared with day-to-day work of reviewing a standard software product? Much more complicated procedures can be developed since smart contracts are technically capable of any type of business logic. We will explore more options for DAO governance in Chapter 7 when we explore how different choices of reward and punishment rules (particularly at Step 5 a, b, and c) encourage behavior to reflect different values at different points in the life cycle of a company.

However, we mostly rely on the market for many of our answers. This is not a cop out. The market is well understood to be the most efficient mechanism for price discovery. Secondarily the market determines how many members the DAO can support in its network, and how much work they should do. The market's answers find the right equilibrium between all the industries and companies to determine how much of each work and good is required to keep civilization running efficiently. Decentralization improves the market in its efficiency at price discovery and liquidity.

The liquidity of a market is its momentum. Liquidity is measured by its velocity (dynamism, motion, rate of transactions), but also by its mass (how valuable are the total goods or assets). When there is too much mass in a market and not enough velocity, it can gunk up the engine. When there is too little mass in the market, it can be cleared too quickly, resulting in vapor lock. One of the problems with centralization is that the power accumulates, which is bad for market efficiency, for liquidity. Monopolies are a threat to market liquidity as they can have too much mass or too much velocity. Decentralization is better, as it means the mass and velocity are uncorrelated meaning more stable and predictable liquidity and therefore more market efficiency.

This exact process of steps 1–7 can be cloned to build a news story review DAO. Reviewers could judge stories' veracity according to the standards the DAO chooses. As before, reputation in the Review DAO becomes valuable once News DApps steer viewership to stories based on your DAO's reviews. Then media sites will pay fees to get their stories reviewed more quickly. Reviewers will be incentivized to give honest reviews despite fees, because the reputational system rewards members mostly based on future fees. As members have all power of policing, they are naturally incentivized to encourage reviewers to maintain the integrity of the system.

Notably, the transparency and openly reviewable nature of a DAO greatly adds to the trustworthiness of the system. Being eternally open to audits and reviews from anyone on the planet greatly improves the integrity of the system. Such improvements to transparency and accountability in the institutions of media and education have the opportunity for improving many aspects of society.

Consider also how this process can be cloned with little variation to initiate a decentralized organization devoted to most any goal.

We'll discuss further details of reputation token creation and governance in chapters 6 and 7.

Chapter 5
Eight Institutions

Before the vision of a radically decentralized economy can be achieved, engineers and architects need to solve eight big problems that business solved centuries ago. All eight problems need to be solved simultaneously, and the solutions need to be integrated with each other.

This is similar to the electrical revolution that took more than a century to come to fruition, because of the need to develop uniform standards for production, transmission, storage, and utilization. But in the 1880s the electrification of cities made the revolution seem to miraculously appear from nowhere. The Web3 vision of revolutionizing the entire global economy makes the electrical revolution seem trivial.

Engineers have managed to prototype two of the solutions: decentralized currency (Bitcoin) and the distributed computing needed to make smart contracts (Ethereum). We're still missing most of them. The legal system, the political system, the media, banking, and other services are all needed before the first DAO will be a genuinely profitable addition to our economy.

All these institutions will be improved, in effectiveness and efficiency, due to the benefits of transparency and liquidity provided by decentralizing their power structures. These eight institutions are necessary for business. Business grinds to a halt without them, but they require a tiny fraction of the resources in the economy when they are running well. It is only corruption that leads them to be perceived as leaching from the economy. Well-designed systems minimize those economic frictions.

A dynamic design with checks and balances and the incentive design insights of game theory are necessary to keep these networks running productively. The architecture guiding one institution can be reasonably ported to many other DAOs with superficial changes.

The dream of full decentralization is an extreme democracy with autonomous individuals contributing the resources necessary to maintain the organization of the community. Powerful and truly decentralized organizations are now possible, thanks to advances in:

1. Digital information storage, which allows each person to be the authoritative holders of the entire organization's history. No centralized authority is needed to oversee the record.
2. Data processing (computation) allows each person to equally participate in filtering and curating the information.
3. Networked communication from the internet allows each member of the organization to immediately connect with every other member on the globe. Complete bureaucratic transparency is possible as global communication is speedy and affordable.

https://doi.org/10.1515/9783110673937-005

4. Cryptographic tools guarantee security, privacy, and power over personal information.
5. Distributed computing architectures give security and transparency in establishing network uniformity.

Whenever a healthy decentralized organization in the past began to earn money, it quickly devolved to a centralized institution. Their ideals shifted from the transcendental value which originally united them to a desire for money. Without the previous equalizing ideal to moderate, the competition generated by the profit motive led inevitably to the organization centralizing with rigid rules for who has power and wealth. The largest and most decentralized organizations of the present are nonprofit (e.g., Wikipedia). This leads us to wonder whether decentralized organizations can ever survive economic success.

The answer is yes. The five tools listed above give us new power in designing and implementing decentralized organizations. They allow secure and efficient accounting of voluminous transactions that happen in a decentralized network, so that money can be shared appropriately in an organization without resorting to centralized dictators arbitrating the dispersal of funds. If, however, the goal of the organization is to maintain decentralization (assuming that is preferable), then these tools must be used wisely to prevent the natural concentration of power that occurs when inefficiencies in the economy allow pockets of corruption to accumulate rent-seeking actors.

Finally, no decentralized organization devoted to profit can be successful in the contemporary marketplace against centralized organizations until eight big problems are solved, all at once.

A decentralized economy requires:

1. *Money. Coinage.*
   Bitcoin proved it was possible to create a decentralized digital representation of value. Because this proof of concept technology doesn't have the rest of a decentralized economic environment to exist in, it is not efficient enough to use widely.

2. *Processing/smart contracts.*
   The executive policing functions of our business and government should be automated to prevent corruption. Ethereum proved this was possible, to process secure and valuable business contracts in a decentralized network. Like Bitcoin, it won't be efficient until it lives in a robust decentralized economy. It won't last unless its governance is fixed.

   Still missing are six more essential facets of the economy that all need to work together. Each one needs the others to exist in a working economy fit for the average consumer. (Organized in roughly the chronological order of what needs to be built first.)

3. *Reputation.*

   This is the proper goal, instead of money, for motivating good behavior in business and governance. Properly accounting for reputation switches the incentives from short-term zero-sum thinking to long-term positive-sum motivation. Without building a secure and meaningful reputational system, none of the other aspects of the decentralized economy can be effective in the long run.

4. *Governance.*

   Decentralized power regulation has been a conscious goal since the 18th century. Today the technology has improved, so that it is possible to account for good and bad behavior on a near infinitesimal scale and reward and punish fairly. A sophisticated system of governance is required to effectively adjust to market changes and to maintain stability. Executive (automated policing), legislative (nonautomated protocol development), and judicial (both automated and nonautomated dispute resolution) governance must be considered.

Reputation and governance are the two most important institutions that are lacking in the decentralized economy. They occupy the majority of our concern for the remainder of the book. Once they are solved, the rest of the missing pieces are relatively easy to supply. Including:

5. *Finance.*

   Stablecoin: This is a currency that doesn't fluctuate wildly in price. The artificially scarce bitcoin currency is deflationary as long as its market expands. Like gold, its fluctuation makes it unsuitable for daily commerce. Without stability, typical consumers will never hold their checking account in the currency. No one will make a long-term contract for an essential service in such a currency. Gambling with your contracts is inefficient, economically. Renegotiating contracts whenever the currency changes is expensive, and continually and randomly punishes at least one of the parties. We need a robust decentralized economy (#6, below) before the stablecoin can be efficient – another chicken and egg problem.

   Decentralized Marketplaces: Neutral platforms for trades in properties and services are needed for thriving business with various rules for participation.

   Banking: provides a necessary service to absorb the risk of less secure but more efficient small transactions. These are then bundled before a more expensive but secure transaction happens with the central bank. In P2P, the redundant and eternal storage of the blockchain takes the place of the central bank.

   Underwriting: We need trust that the transactions in the marketplaces will go through, or that otherwise the contract will be made whole by the platform running the marketplace. Underwriting is essential for every type of business transaction, every type of property, every type of worker/service you hire. Every type of economic action is made more efficient when decisions are hedged, so we can confidently change our investments, keeping the market liquid. Lending and insurance are essential catalysts for business, that require someone to underwrite the risk. Like policing, underwriting can be decentralized and automated, giving each member the power to control the level of security they require.

6. *Services.*

A diverse DAO ecosystem is crucial. Consumers require many services our current economy provides, which all need to be decentralized, such as commerce and trade jobs. The gig economy is rife with horror stories, but a fully decentralized structure with proper governance could solve many of its problems.

7. *History.*

A marketplace must be trustworthy, with momentum. How is attention focused, on which details, with which narrative? What is the internet search engine for the decentralized economy? How do you tell the story of what the data means? How trustworthy is each DAO, compared with other DAOs? We need ratings for everything. Who controls the information? News services (oracles) and information repositories need to be decentralized.

8. *Transcendental Values.*

DAOs derive unity from their ideals, their common goals and aspirations beyond the protocols. This final requirement is the most important for long-term stability and will require eternal reevaluation. Decentralized institutions require strong unifying values to remain coherent.

For the remainder of the book, we will explore these categories, which have mostly been neglected by P2P engineers. The new tools of information technology can make major efficiency improvements in these traditional institutions.

Chapter 6
Reputation

Reputation is the proper incentive, instead of money, for motivating the most efficient cooperation and long-term stability in business.

Markets are a necessarily chaotic environment that must permit an enormous variety of behaviors, where all parties need the freedom to invent new strategies for cooperation. Such freedom also creates limitless opportunities for preying on anyone with less information. Such information asymmetries create endless arbitrage opportunities: renegotiating, leveraging an opponent's sunken costs, pushing the limits of the law, or breaking it outright. Markets lose their ability to create value and profit when the efficiency of cooperation is sapped by opportunistic behavior. When the environment becomes too adversarial, when trust is diminished, collaboration is no longer profitable. The market collapses.

How do you prevent the chain reaction of opportunistic behavior provoking worse behavior until the market collapses? Relying entirely on strict legal enforcement is not practical since it limits the opportunities for creativity in business arrangements. Strict legal enforcement is not efficient, because all energies devoted to policing are energies that could be used to cooperate productively. Strict legal enforcement is not possible when the market becomes sufficiently complex and dynamic – laws cannot keep up with the creative contracts that arise when leading experts are continually improving business arrangements.

To prevent people from devoting all available energy to taking advantage of their business associates, you need to change the relationship from adversary to partner. Reputation does this with the promise of future business opportunities. This changes the transaction from a single-stage zero-sum game to a repeated positive-sum game. The value that is created in the transaction is that the reputation of both parties is improved in a harmonious profitable transaction.

In this chapter we discuss what reputation does for an organization, how to build a secure reputational system and what to avoid, and the consequences of a secure and meaningful decentralized reputation for society and the economy.

The failure of many DAOs, so far, has been their reliance on the good will of the members of the network. A designer will often imagine the members are incentivized to help the network so they can have business in the future. As the network grows, however, the members become more anonymous. Individually they become less important, so cheating is more locally enticing and less noticeable globally. Eventually (or immediately) the system will collapse when it becomes obvious cheating is the best individual strategy.

Many recent DAOs do recognize how important reputation is, and so, there have been many flawed instantiations of reputational tokens. The system most commonly used is called the Web of Trust. After explaining this natural but flawed idea, we

https://doi.org/10.1515/9783110673937-006

introduce a system that uses the power of decentralization to solve the problem of secure reputation by putting the power to democratically police reputation in the hands of the members of the network.

We now have the technological tools to create a transparently auditable reputation on the global scale of Bitcoin. Light speed digital internet communication has eliminated the information asymmetries that attended the Maghribi traders. Instead the modern challenge is to foster productive collaboration between anonymous actors from diverse backgrounds in globally large groups.

The tools of P2P technologies upgrade our ability to create a valuable reputation. More accurate automated accounting is available through smart contracts. A transparent history of past bureaucratic transactions enables decentralized governance and regulation. With the proper design, a cyclic relationship between customers, the DAO member workers, and the platform's protocols and history, gives feedback loops, which engender continual evolutionary improvements. The transparency and open governance procedures create a fair environment that enables a DAO to evolve in healthy and productive ways.

The new technology of decentralized consensus with "triple-entry bookkeeping" that Bitcoin introduced allows decentralized networks to collaborate on profit-motivated projects, while maintaining individual privacy with zero knowledge proofs. But they must be organized properly, with the proper incentives and governance.

We will explore what is required to build a secure and meaningful reputation system and suggest a basic architecture. First, we discuss a commonly used reputational architecture that is *not* secure.

Web of Trust

Most every DApp developer becomes aware a reputational system is necessary to keep their DAO together. Ideally a reputational system will run in the background without needing any conscious user input. As long as a member is behaving properly – following the stipulated protocols of the DAO – their reputation should improve automatically. Those who violate the protocols should lose reputation, so they lose power in the network and cannot cause as much harm. Most every developer comes up with a solution to automating reputation based on the Web of Trust. Every implementation we've seen stumbles into some minor variation on this same basic trap, so it's worth dwelling on what goes wrong before explaining an alternative solution.

The Web of Trust was first used in giving decentralized security to e-mail and other internet data transmission technologies in a scheme called PGP (pretty good privacy) encryption, published by Phil Zimmerman in 1992. The idea is to design a system for growing a network of trusted public keys specifying the correct owners of addresses. Then message senders can look up the addresses and be sure they are sending the message to the correct owner. The fear is that a malicious user can falsely claim ownership of an address in the directory in order to intercept messages. How does the decentralized network add new members?

A third party, who has a previous reputation in the network as trustworthy, verifies that the new member is who they say they are. As more parties verify addresses, eventually within the whole system, the subnetwork of people you trust will include a chain of trust between members indirectly connected to the address you are requesting. The more people in your trust network who verify an address, the closer the connection, the more trustworthy the information is.

The basic design that incorporates the basic Web-of-Trust scheme in an abstract reputational system is as follows. Imagine a network of people who participate in business transactions. Each transaction is recorded by each member along with a rating for how satisfactory it was. If Alice and Bob have a first transaction, Alice rates Bob and Bob rates Alice. The value of the transaction is multiplied by their rating from – 100% to 100% to determine the reputation the transaction generates. The entire history of self-reports can be stored, decentralized in the blockchain, available for anyone to read. Alice's reputation is now calculated by one of many possible schemes for summing up the reputation contained in each transaction. Generally, the reputation generated by a more reputable person has greater effect on the sum than a less reputable person's transactions. And more transactions with higher value will create more reputation.

Unfortunately, the sockpuppet attack will suck all value from the network. Setting up fake accounts, an attacker can build their reputation by making transactions between their own accounts. Once their reputation is sufficiently large to trick a member, they can use it to cheat the system.

In response to the sockpuppet attack, a developer may choose to handicap the system by charging fees to make transactions (similar to DoS defenses) or imposing identity protocols – referred to in banking as KYC, know your customer protocols – to solve the problem. Then it would be too expensive to mount a sockpuppet attack, since you would need to pay for each transaction. This doesn't help. Such defenses push the cost of defending the network onto the users. The cost to defend it is exactly as much as it is worth to break the defense, except it's multiplied on every transaction with every member in the system. If the reputation is worth $1,000, and it takes $900 to fake the reputation, the attacker has an incentive to do it.

Further, lessening the anonymity of your members weakens the power of the decentralized network. Personal privacy protects your members, so it's more secure. Members can be more transparent in their business dealings without fear of being victimized, so the decentralized network is more efficient.

These problems with the Web of Trust, incidentally, are part of why it's called "pretty good privacy" instead of "good privacy." It works well for low-value information transmission, but it should not be used for transactions involving larger wealth in the general economy. Those transmissions incorporate stronger cryptographic security.

The proper solution is to give your members more power over their reputation. Give the members themselves the power to police their own reputation. The leading experts, themselves, are the people who are best equipped to invent the regulations for policing their own industry. They are best incentivized to defend their own reputation and future profits. The best way to encourage continual long-term improvement, is to reward them properly for policing and legislation and development.

Inductive Argument for Reputation Architecture

We want to build a reputational system that is mostly automated, like Bitcoin, or the Web of Trust. So, it should maintain decentralized consensus as long as the majority is running the automated program honestly, that is, they haven't hacked the program. However, we need to make a system that is not susceptible to the type of gaming that the Web of Trust is prey to.

In order to make a secure and meaningful reputational system, in a decentralized network, several requirements need to be met. Once these are articulated, the most basic elements of the architecture are revealed. This justifies the elementary design described in Chapter 4. We assume the most successful DAOs will be open to any anonymous applicant in the world for its members. Open membership and anonymity are not necessary to build a secure and meaningful reputational system, however, and therefore are not included among the following necessities:

Necessity #1: Forum
To remain decentralized, all members are assumed to be relatively equal. Therefore, evidence of all bureaucratic work needs to be posted in a universally accessible location for eternal review. Similar to blockchain digital currency creation, without a central verifying authority, every reputation token in a DAO needs an openly verifiable history. (*Transparency*)

Necessity #2: Validation pool
In a decentralized environment, consisting of potentially anonymous actors, the only fair way to assign reputational power is to allow all members to judge the value of contributions, democratically. To avoid the Tragedy of the Commons (the nothing-at-stake problem, "skin in the game"), reputation must be staked and risked with votes on work evidence. This ensures all experts are motivated to police every reputation-staked action, to protect the value of their investment.

Members who fail to participate (liveness fault) will be stably punished because reputation tokens are deflationary: if they don't participate they will not gain any portion of the newly minted reputation tokens, therefore, their own unused reputation holdings will represent a smaller percentage of the total, so they will receive a smaller percentage of future reputational salaries.

To avoid sockpuppet attacks and the Tyranny of the Majority, each user is capable of staking any portion of their reputation token holdings, creating a proportional democratic governance process.

The vast majority of validation pools should be completed automatically, by running the reputation program, with no conscious decision necessary from any user. When things are running well, the only exceptions should be when the members are debating new rules, as we discuss in Chapter 7 on governance. All other votes should resolve unanimously, with the only dissent due to people who are not running the consensus program, or otherwise not following the rules. This is seemingly enormous redundant calculation overhead. But compare it to the calculations Bitcoin or Ethereum use to maintain consensus. It is the price to pay for decentralized consensus. It wasn't possible before the recent advances in information technology. (*Democratic investment*)

Necessity #3: All the new reputation tokens are minted in proportion to fees
Whenever a new reputation token is minted, to be meaningful it must be grounded in something real. In any DAO devoted to profit, the foundational object is money. So, all reputation tokens need to be tied to the fees the DAO earns. (*Foundational meaning*)

Necessity #4: All new reputation tokens are initially staked 50/50 in a validation pool, for and against the post that brought the fees into the DAO
For security, when a reputation token enters the system, it should be neutral, so that one faction is not favored over another. Validation pools should begin fairly. Newly minted reputation tokens should be staked half in favor, half against. This ensures that all actions can be fairly judged by existing token holders, who will not be swayed by an unbalanced validation pool from a large fee. (*Fairness*)

Necessity #5: Reputational salary
All fees should be shared with the entire network of reputation holders relative to their holdings. This is the key to making reputation tokens valuable and future oriented. The importance of reputation is its ability to motivate members to cooperate, to harness their own selfish interests in service to the future well-being of the group. The incentive that makes this possible is the promise of future rewards. Delayed gratification is the key to group harmony and long-term stability.

The active member who performed the work that attracted the customer fee is not paid directly; instead the fee is split in the reputational salary. The direct reward for the worker is that 50% of the newly minted tokens are staked as an upvote in the validation pool in their name, so they can win these new reputation tokens if they performed the work properly, according to the protocols of the DAO. This prevents many short-term arbitrage opportunities.

Further, the salary needs to be reputation-weighted, that is, people with more reputation get more money for two reasons. First, to satisfy individual selfish interests. Second, to prevent sockpuppet attacks. If salary is distributed more equitably, say equally to all members, then the obvious strategy for gaming the system is to create multiple accounts and distribute your work between the accounts. (*Meritocracy and future orientation*)

Necessity #6: Review through references
Each new post can reference older posts. If the new post is validated, its value can affect the value of past posts positively or negatively. Old posts can have their reputational value change, depending on how important users perceive the precedent for the system. This further stabilizes the system by magnifying the power of reputation for motivating people to behave in ways that help the group in the long term. It also encourages innovation.

This gives members the ability to review past actions, allowing a more careful analysis of patterns of behavior, encouraging actions that make lasting contributions (such as protocol development) and punishing actions which are judged to harm the long-term health of the platform. (*Valuing the past*)

Necessity #7: Multiplicity of token types
Reputation tokens need to have power limited to their proper domain, meaning that for each different expertise there is a separate type of noninterchangeable reputation token. Each type of reputation token is only powerful within the DAO containing the members with a skill specific to that token. So, there may be different reputation tokens for developing smart contracts, or for advertising products, or for making governance decisions in each DAO. Each user will likely own several different types of tokens related to their individual expertises. (*Domain-specific expertise*)

Consequences of the Architecture

Many types of DAOs with diverse reward structures can be created to address the variety of business needs.

The meritocratic incentive structure of the architecture ensures stability and security by motivating self-policing of a DAO.

Fair reward structures introduce proper incentives to ensure continual improvements instead of degeneration from rent-seeking.

Adopting the seven principles creates a balanced, meritocratic, incentive-driven positive feedback loop. The elements of the system that cyclically drive and change each other are:
1. The outside *customers* (analogous to information transmission)
2. The *members* inside the DAO, that is, the workers (information processing)
3. The *forum* (information storage)

The feedback loop is as follows: The *customers'* fees encourage the *members* to work and to develop improved protocols for work. The *members* post to the *forum* their evidence of work, the results of validation pools, and new protocols for how they do business. The *forum* makes the DAOs history available for *customers* to evaluate which services seem useful and which smart contracts they should engage.

The feedback loop exists within the rigorous code-is-law system of smart contracts that allows efficient self-execution and self-regulation. But its dynamic nature gives the system the slack needed to redress failings with appeals (as smart contracts improve to include the logic that enables them) and with reviews through references.

This feedback loop creates an evolutionary platform, which continually improves the DAO. New posts reinforce or reverse precedent. Code-is-law smart contracts are continually improved for usability and to better reflect the authors' intentions.

The word "evolutionary" is key. DAOs have the freedom to organize any way they choose. If they fail to find the right incentives for productive behavior, they will certainly go extinct. The feedback loop that includes customers outside the DAO naturally punishes any unproductive DAOs, by loss of fees.

The impossibility of creating eternally perfect protocols, as illustrated by Arrow's Impossibility Theorem and the Folk Theorems of Game Theory, is addressed by a system which continually improves protocols and smart contracts to react to changes in the market. This way the system is more stable and better reflects the spirit of the law as it evolves in the long run.

The 6th necessary structure, review through references, is crucial for moving the members' motivation to the future. First, references that decrease old posts' values allow us to punish behaviors that are later found to harm the platform. This discourages gaming the system, and helps address the problem posed by the Folk Theorems, of not being able to create a perfect static system. We can create a system that improves over time by reviewing its past. Second, references that increase the value of an old post enable a DAO to create an incentive system, which encourages a culture of development. But the DAO must actively create the culture that encourages development, using protocols with substantial rewards for productive development. This requires effective governance (which will be discussed in the next chapter) to ensure the DAO participates in following a protocol, which regularly recognizes the value of old posts with references.

This helps create a decentralized history for the DAO, which gives us momentum. History gives clarity on where we are and where we are going. History is the basis for making governance (which etymologically means "steering") more effective. History allows members to judge whether they are properly promoting their unifying transcendental values. History brings stability (see Chapter 9).

Reputation dilates time. It allows us to slow down immediate transfers of wealth, allowing us to consider the future and the past. Future-oriented incentives come from reputation-based salaries. Past-oriented incentives come from the editability of reputation. We can slash reputation, through references, based on actions from any time in the past that are later seen to be harmful. Or we can augment reputation for actions later seen to be helpful to the network.

In any market, as technology improves, services improve, and the service providers themselves are best capable of assessing the service. In this case, regulations should be created by service providers. In a hierarchical structure, where members are siloed and have few formal connections with those immediately above and below their tier in the hierarchy, this leads to the moral hazard problem that the service provider has an incentive to weaken the standards and regulations. In centralized systems, this means the regulators and service providers need to be separated. In a decentralized system the whole group consists of equal-powered service providers, and they have an incentive to regulate each other, to protect their own reputation.

A variety of values can be effectively encouraged by manipulating parameters in the reward and punishment structure of reputation distribution, as will be analyzed in Chapter 7 when we discuss decentralized governance.

Security

The seven requirements listed above are borne out of the necessities of security.

Sockpuppet attacks are inevitable if you want the membership to be open and to allow anonymous members. These properties are essential for fostering the individual autonomy that makes a global decentralized organization efficient and powerful. Therefore, every time reputation is used, it must be weighted, so that 10 accounts with 1 token each have the same power as 1 account with 10 tokens.

Second, most reputational systems fail from the sockpuppet attack on the Web-of-Trust model. As mentioned above, the idea is that an attacker will set up sockpuppet accounts to follow the reputational system faithfully, but only add reputation to their own sockpuppet accounts, building their own power, until they can exploit the network with false reputation.[1] This is prevented by committing to a reputation system that follows Necessity #3, that all the new reputation tokens are minted in proportion to fees, working in concert with Necessity #5 that all fees are shared proportionally

---

1 This is the flaw in every single reputational implementation we've audited in the blockchain DAO space. For example, an active project we particularly respect, SingularityNet, also falls into this trap. Their reputation system essentially boils down to tracking and accounting for the self-reported quality of transaction (our #6), the quantity of value of the transaction (our #3), the length of time of satisfaction (our #6), and the weight of the previous reputations of those involved in the transaction (our #2). Without implementing the other necessities, the sockpuppet attack will eventually erode their value, once it becomes valuable enough to merit the attack. See the details of their system, which implement some of the necessities, in "A Reputation System for Artificial Societies," by Anton Kolonin, Ben Goertzel, Deborah Duong, and Matt Ikle. Available online at https://arxiv.org/ftp/arxiv/papers/1806/1806.07342.pdf (retrieved 8/8/20).

with the entire group. Then the cost of corrupting the system with the sockpuppet attack becomes impractical. Without stipulating Necessity #5, the sockpuppet accounts can pay themselves, so the attacker doesn't lose much money (just DoS prevention fees, like Ethereum gas). With #4 and #5 implemented, the cost of faking your reputation is (at an absolute minimum) double the value of the reputation.[2] This is the essence of how you make reputation more valuable than money and focus the group on the goal of improving the reputation for its future value. With a dynamic governance model (next chapter), such attacks can be monitored and policed in a profitable manner that completely eliminates the threat.

Concentration of power is the greatest threat to any decentralized organization. Especially one that is devoted to profit, which is inherently competitive. This is known in distributed computing and blockchain as the 51% attack. The idea is that if a single member, or even a sub-coalition, gains 51% of the power in an inherently democratic organization, they will eventually control it, no matter what the safeguards are. A stable 51% power becomes a dictator, and the organization is no longer decentralized.

Improved information technology, itself, promotes decentralization. When everyone has access to the same technology for broadcasting and processing information, monopolies on communication are harder to form. One person cannot take all the jobs and exponentially accumulate concentrated reputation.

Fair accounting and transparency in reputation promotes decentralization. When customers can reliably compare reputation, they are able to harness the available talent, instead of waiting for the most talented to become available. The differences in reputation do not accumulate as much when weaker members are given the opportunity to exercise their talent.

Anonymity promotes decentralization. The cult of personality is less likely to develop around one member who has comparable talent to others.

The nonfungibility of reputation tokens naturally promote decentralization. Each reputation token has a separate history that can be slashed or augmented in the future. So, every different token has a different value. While every token may theoretically be sold at auction, it will be more difficult to sell a token for full value at auction, because of the devaluation due to risk. A reputation token is inherently more valuable for a person who deserves it, than for someone who merely bought it, because of its secondary use in making future earnings. Compared with cash coinage, reputation is more difficult to accumulate. So, economies of scale are weakened. Reputation tokens are earned (not bought) when they are created, and so they are not as transferrable between enterprises. For all these reasons, the market for reputation will be much less liquid than for more fungible tokens representing cash.

---

2 This calculation is performed in Craig Calcaterra, Wulf A. Kaal, Vlad Andrei, "Blockchain Infrastructure for Measuring Domain Specific Reputation in Autonomous Decentralized and Anonymous Systems," University of St. Thomas (Minnesota) Legal Studies Research Paper No. 18–11, February 18, 2018.

The economy of reputation tokens is inflationary, since they are constantly being created with each business transaction. Therefore, reputation naturally promotes decentralization of power. People earn new reputation with every productive act. Therefore, the total quantity of reputation grows continually, so the value of a single token decreases (assuming steady state, and not, e.g., exponential growth of customers). This also makes reputation tokens more difficult to trade, because their variable inflation makes it difficult to value precisely. If one member happens to have a very high reputation, they need to do proportionally more work to maintain the disparity, making reputation less likely to concentrate when people have comparable talent. This promotes equality and decentralization of power as a natural counterbalance to the accumulation of individual power. When we discuss governance in Chapter 7, we will see how an organization may choose to manipulate the parameters determining how inflationary the token is, thereby promoting different values.

Decisions made by weighted reputational power also protect the tokens' value from the Tyranny of the Majority. Under a one-person-one-vote system, half of the members have less than average expertise, but equal power. This incentivizes experts to gain power by catering to the prejudices of nonexperts, instead of following the most effective decisions. Under reputation-weighted voting, the incentive changes to follow the majority of expertise, which changes weight, based on the success of actions.

Decisions made by weighted reputational power also protect the tokens' value from various Tragedy of the Commons problems. Tragedy of the Commons occurs when members are not properly incentivized to police the evolution of the organization. For example, if complicated technical smart contract improvements are put to a vote by a large organization, very few people will have the ability or interest to participate in the debate. When they vote, they will not have the expertise to make a sound judgment and so experts would again be incentivized to manipulate nonexperts with sophistry. Therefore, many different types of reputation tokens are needed for the many types of expertise. Then, the validation pools that oversee every action in the DAO incentivize experts to participate or else they risk losing the opportunity to gain more reputation tokens and maintain or increase their relative power. Sharing the newly minted tokens with those who police the action inhibits this free-rider problem of nonparticipation.

Dynamic Design Example

We repeat the basic process of generating reputation, generalizing from the example of the Software Review DAO given in Chapter 4. Imagine a generic DAO consisting of worker/members devoted to a task and customers willing to pay a fee to engage a worker and pay a preassigned fee for that task:

1. A customer uses the DAO smart contract (SC) to engage a worker by encumbering the fee in the SC and specifying the task.

2. The SC randomly picks a worker/member from those members available. (The only other smart contract in use will be an availability smart contract, which members engage by encumbering their reputation tokens.)
3. The worker completes the task according to the principles the DAO has previously collectively agreed upon.
4. The worker posts evidence of their work.
5. The work evidence post (with customer comments) triggers the SC to open a validation pool – a voting pool where any member can stake their reputation by voting to approve the work or disapprove:
    a. The SC mints new reputation tokens in proportion to the size of the fee.
    b. The new reputation tokens are staked half in favor of the work evidence in the worker's name (this is the worker's reward); half are staked against and left unassigned (they are burned if opposition wins, so there is no bias in policing).
    c. Majority wins and the reputation tokens are split among the winners. Ties favor the worker.
6. Finalized results are posted for review.
7. The fee is split among the entire DAO in proportion to their reputation holdings (reputation-weighted salary).

See Figure 6.1.

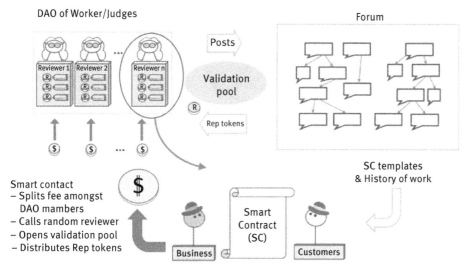

Figure 6.1: Reputation is created when fees are collected, distributed according to work, and determines each member's share of the fees.

A slightly more complicated scheme could borrow from the dynamic design of U.S. Constitution, to create a cyclic system of checks and balances. The Workers, the Judges, and the Customers could each have three separate types of reputation tokens. The Customers would use their reputation tokens (along with a fee) to request work from the Judges. The Judges assign jobs to Workers with contracts, encumbering the fees. The Workers actively complete the jobs for the Customers according to the contract to release the fees.

The separate Judge DAO, Worker DAO, and Customer DAO would each separately maintain their own forum for storing their history and protocols, including standards for work and fees they've negotiated to accept. The Judges would mediate between the smart contracts the Workers and Customers found acceptable and handle appeals when Customers or Workers are not satisfied with the completion of a contract. Presumably, the best Judges would be Workers, who would know best how to regulate their industry; the best Workers would be Customers, who would know best what is desired; the best Customers would be Judges who would best understand the most effective work to engage.

The checks and balances feedback loop is:
- Customers motivate Judges with fees
- Judges motivate Workers with contracts
- Workers motivate Customers with work

See Figure 6.2.

Figure 6.2: Feedback loop driving improved business. Judges develop and protect good business practices with continually improving smart contracts.

How will the fees and work standards be determined? The market. This answer is not a cop out. It is well understood that the market provides the most effective mechanism for price discovery (see Chapter 8). Secondarily the market determines how many members the DAO can support in its network, and how much work they should do. The market's answers find the right equilibrium between all the industries and companies to determine how much of each service and commodity is required to keep civilization running efficiently.

Will the market find the right levels for these rewards? It hasn't been perfect in the past. Monopolies and centralized companies are built to prevent the market from discovering the right price. Liquidity is how a market achieves price discovery. Liquidity is given by decentralization, so decentralized markets will perform more efficiently, once the overhead institutions are deployed providing the proper catalysts for business.

Criticisms

The P2P architectures that have been most successful, so far, in organizing large and valuable networks have been blockchains, such as Bitcoin. The Ethereum blockchain has the ability to organize DAOs with reputation tokens and smart contracts that can poll their members. Unfortunately, the technology today is too slow and expensive to poll its members on every transaction that a member takes. The number of messages required to make sure all nodes are aware of all votes by all members on each action a member takes, quickly multiplies into an unmanageable number, even for light-speed computers, partly because of deliberately added latency required for decentralized consensus in redundant distributed computing. Voting is not efficient on contemporary blockchains.

This is another chicken and egg problem. Voting will be more efficient with valuable reputation. Reputation can't be valuable without meaningful voting. Part of the reason you need a large number of nodes is because we shouldn't trust individuals, so we decentralize control by making it redundant. But if we had a meaningful reputational system with the potential for review, we could rely on fewer nodes. This mechanism is one reason PoS is more efficient than proof of work. We could randomly select fewer nodes who are staking their reputation to do the work of polling the group. Then we can review their work in the future. As discussed above, the consensus necessary to build reputation is expected to be near unanimous nearly all of the time, as you build reputation by following the preapproved protocols. So, it will be easy to detect any Byzantine behavior from the randomly selected nodes, and punish them appropriately. We discuss how the efficiency improvement of randomly delegated consensus can be implemented securely later, in Chapter 8, when we explore banking and ZKRollups.

As will be discussed in the section on governance, in Chapter 7, when a DAO is developing their protocols, the votes to poll consensus will not be near unanimous. Such contentious debate should not use strict validation pools anyway. You should not stake your reputation tokens in order to register your opinion on a contentious topic. Only once the debate has settled, should members risk their reputation to verify consensus with validation pools. So, debates should be held on platforms hosted by DAOs, which use more efficient P2P technology than blockchains, such as distributed hash tables.

Summary

Reputation has lost much of its meaning during the disruption that we are experiencing as the global society is emerging. As old institutions fall, there is a fire sale mentality among people in dying fields where they cash in on the reputations that were built over previous generations. As our political systems fail, politicians behave avariciously, playing any dirty trick available for short-term gain that in previous stable times would have been unthinkable. As print newspapers fail, they publish false and libelous stories in order to gain popularity or clicks. Everywhere, standards of behavior that protected reputation in the past are eroding. Reputation itself is becoming a suspect concept as people use it and value it less and less.

Long-term thinking is necessary to guarantee cooperation. Reputation is the mechanism for incentivizing long-term thinking in business and government. Fungible cash rewards are short-term, immediate rewards. Reputation rewards people in the future. Designing the incentive structure of your organization with a focus on reputation is necessary for stability.

Reputation is not merely an option for any DAO that has power or value. It is absolutely essential. For a DAO that is devoted to an altruistic ideal – a religious organization like the Quakers, or an educational organization like Wikipedia – the unifying force is the ideology. Members won't squabble and jockey for power if the organization is not devoted to power. For DAOs that are built to make money, ideology is important to maintain the long-term stability of the organization, but ideology is not enough.

The ideal DAO relies on the power of decentralization. It needs to give its members maximum autonomy. This means the DAO must be open. The members are free to participate or not, they can come or go as they please without being excluded. For privacy they need anonymity.[3] The members of the DAO may come from any location or culture on the planet, and hide their true location behind VPNs. How do you maintain integrity and cohesion for the group with such extreme decentralization?

A thousand years ago, the Maghribi traders solved a similarly difficult problem with far less tools than we have. Using only handwritten letters, the Jewish merchants set up a reputational system in a decentralized network that spanned the Silk Road. A reputational system that built trust in contracts that would take months to execute. With complete control of the assets, there would be nothing to prevent agents from vanishing or skimming or burying the profits and claiming bandits stole the merchandise. Nothing prevented the agents from cheating, except the promise of building better reputation.

---

3 Or pseudo-anonymity where they have an invented code name – or many invented code names – since the system must track them somehow.

Reputation was the key to maintaining the internalized firm efficiencies of free trade of information and free business contracts between members, despite enormous technical challenges including extremely limited communication (latency on the order of months) that created strong information asymmetries and the attendant adverse selection and moral hazards in the principal-agent problem.

When reputation in your DAO credibly promises future business, your members are incentivized to go above and beyond the stipulations of the smart contract. Without the promise of improving your reputation, a zero-sum mentality dominates the arrangement. Both parties' best strategy becomes exerting the absolute minimum of effort while still technically fulfilling the stipulations of the contract. That degenerate system will destroy the business atmosphere. Self-executing, self-regulating smart contracts between anonymous parties in an open system, create a near perfect zero-sum situation – unless your DAO also includes reputation.

With a meaningful and secure reputational system, the situation becomes a positive-sum game. When there is a chance for each party to build reputation at the conclusion of a smart contract, they are incentivized to fulfill the stipulations to the best of their ability. In fact, they should go above and beyond the stipulations to satisfy the other party. This is amplified with the modern tools of information technology. When the record of your behavior can be eternally stored for review, when anyone on the planet may scrutinize the details of how the transparent bureaucratic details of the contract were fulfilled, when the accounting process for reputation tokens is publicly auditable and digitally secure, reputation's value is magnified.

How do we incorporate reputation into a decentralized organization? If there is no ultimate centralized leader to be the arbiter of what is right or wrong, how do we know what is a good or bad reputation? Democratic systems can solve this problem without a centralized dictator. With the new advances in information technology we can efficiently keep track of much more complicated reputation-building behaviors with digital tokens. With advances in cryptography and distributed computing algorithms we can keep our reputations private and decentralized and secure against subversion by those who would game the system.

By giving all people more power, we create a system where leaders are continually rediscovered immediately where and when they are needed – we create a liquid meritocracy. With secure and meaningful reputation, our liquid meritocracy has momentum and history.

To make the system effective in the long run, we need decentralized mechanisms for guiding the group. To make it efficient, it needs stability, so these steering mechanisms need to be subtle. Before any of this Web3 vision of the future has a chance of success, we need a revolutionary new system of decentralized governance.

Chapter 7
Governance

> Many people believe that decentralization means loss of control. That's simply not true. You can improve control if you look at control as the control of events and not people. Then, the more people you have controlling events – the more people you have that care about controlling the events, the more people you have proactively working to create favorable events – the more control you have within the organization, by definition.
>
> —Wilbur L. Creech, *The Five Pillars of TQM*, 1995

Governance is a fundamental human concern, which has been continually debated since humans learned to speak. Governance is a primary subject of study within philosophy, ethics, economics, political science, law, sociology, social psychology, cybernetics, control theory, etc. Choices of governance structures for DAOs must consciously grapple with these theories and examples that have arisen throughout history. Throughout history, however, people have repeatedly failed to organize effectively, and corruption has arisen in every circumstance, even without anonymity, in the less extreme situation involving identified members of the same culture under face-to-face circumstances with deep community ties. What chance do we have of eliminating corruption and perfecting our governmental institutions? None, of course. In his *Dictionary of Philosophy*, Voltaire highlighted the Italian proverb, *Il meglio è l'inimico del bene*. The perfect is the enemy of the good. But we can improve our institutions if we use the advances of technology wisely. Today we have new tools at our disposal for improving governance.

Governance is the set of protocols that determine what behaviors are acceptable or unacceptable and how they are rewarded or punished. Governance determines how an organization is organized. Governance *is* the organization. Governing a decentralized organization, however, is much more difficult than governing a centralized hierarchical organization.

This book probably seems obsessed with stability. In order to achieve the goals of a decentralized organization, some measure of control is required. The organization must be organized. Decentralized organizations are naturally more difficult to control or guide than centralized organizations. They are more difficult to govern. The word "govern" comes from the Greek word *kubernos* meaning to steer. *Kubernos* is the origin of the term cybernetics, which is the mathematical subject of control theory, which helps us steer rocket ships to the moon and underseas robots through the Mariana Trench. Control theory gives us the design to keep controlled explosions running stably for decades in nuclear reactors, and it keeps our global supply chain running efficiently with less redundancy and downtime thanks to dynamic programming.

Steering a decentralized organization, guiding it without centralized control, is a delicate procedure. Governance is the process of keeping the organization stable and on track to achieve its goals, without letting it devolve into a centralized

https://doi.org/10.1515/9783110673937-007

organization, which is a natural progression once clear goals are identified and competition emerges.

There are flaws with every governance process that has ever been implemented. In fact, it seems clear no perfect governance system is possible under very minimal assumptions, such as nondictatorship (cf., Chapter 4). Nevertheless, it is our goal to find practical and effective governance structures for the most challenging groups that exist: DAOs.

Part of the challenge of governance is that most members should never notice its existence – when they do, something has probably gone wrong. The best governance will require only the subtlest changes in the reward mechanism to keep the organization healthy, as changes happen in the DAO and in the marketplace. Ideally, even these subtle changes would be automated, so that only changes to the changes need be debated (third-order governance).

Decentralized power has been a conscious goal since the 18th century.[1] In the long term, or when the situation is dynamic and unpredictable, decentralized organizations can be more efficient than hierarchical organizations. We gain greater flexibility and more options for efficiency using the decentralized power structure of interacting domains of expertise. Now the technology of accounting has caught up, so that it is possible to account for good and bad behavior on a seemingly infinitesimal scale without resorting to a centralized system for recording, processing, and transmitting information. Advances in digital electronic data storage make it possible for the first time in history to record every member's contributions to an organization. P2P technology gives actors and organizations the environment to collaborate on neutral territory, where each member has equal power in creating the environment where everyone can broadcast to and receive from an unlimited network of members. We have arrived at a historically novel situation technologically. We now have the power to create far more decentralized and democratic institutions than ever before.

---

1 Of course, there are many precursors, which are also worthy of study. Quaker governance, since the 17th century, has put special emphasis on nurturing member communication with strict protocols. No decisions are ever made except unanimously (which may account for their doctrinal fragmentation into various sects). There are no votes. Debates are not permitted, nor even direct responses to others' contributions. The idea is not to have your personal argument win, but to discover God's will.

Ancient Greek society hosted a particularly direct democracy, which governed the highest decisions to the lowest, from deciding whether to wage war down to where the next street will be built. Greek direct democracy relied on a clever process of sortition. Sortition is the random selection of representatives. They used a *kleroterion*, which was a device somewhat analogous to a complicated bean board or pachinko machine, to select their temporary delegates.

In a testament to the power of logic to withstand millennia of change, Aristotle's *Ethics* and *Politics* (4th century BC) are still remarkably cogent expositions categorizing and analyzing the different possible governance structures, whose insights are required reading for 21st century digital architects.

Decentralized organizations can be more productive because they can distribute the proper amount of power to the proper talent at the proper time, eliminating system frictions such as corruption. To ensure such dynamic power organization is successfully implemented, the governance structure of a DAO must incentivize members to collaborate productively, by fairly rewarding development, work, and the policing of any diminishments.

Many issues arise when attempting to implement a governance system, which incorporates these qualities yet is also effective and efficient. Benevolent dictators are much more efficient and effective than messy democracies, but the long-term stability of a powerful public P2P network is threatened by such centralized governance. So, there is naturally debate (in the blockchain community, e.g.) about the best way to find consensus on protocol changes.

There is not a single P2P project in existence today which has anything close to a sophisticated governance process. Most are grounded with a strong anarchic or libertarian attitude. These revolutionary projects are responses to failings in our current system. Therefore, the very mention of a constitution for a P2P platform has invoked a reaction of disgust in the past. Developers have naturally been suspicious of any attempt to build old systems of control into their revolutionary platforms. The old systems are failing, and new architectures are necessary to properly exploit the technological innovations of this new age.

All P2P networks need to organize soft forks for protocol upgrades, because there can never be a perfectly designed system, as the Folk Theorems attest. More practically, every network must continually improve to survive. To attract members and users, user interfaces need to be intuitive; the programming interfaces must keep up to date with the latest changes in software design to keep and attract developers; the technology must use the latest engineering advances for hardware. How do you motivate all this work?

Blockchains that have instituted (or intend to institute) on-chain governance to a greater extent include Dash, Bitshares, Lisk, MemoryCoin, Tendermint, Tezos, Aragon, Cardano, Maker, and NuShares. To a lesser degree, the Ethereum carbon vote represents on-chain governance. Examples of off-chain democratized blockchain governance have included Bitcoin Improvement Proposals (BIPs), Ethereum Improvement Proposals (EIPs), mailing lists, and nonbinding suggestion pages on the internet such as GitHub trees. At the moment, however, no major blockchain is entirely decentralized, because they all lack pure binding coded P2P anonymous governance.

Choosing no explicit or formal rules is still a governance choice. That choice defaults to the prehistoric rule of might makes right. Since might is defined by wealth, they've chosen oligarchy. In 2020, all the major valuable platforms are naked oligarchies, where rule changes are determined by whoever has the most fungible platform currency or concentrated computing power.

The entire history of civilization has shown us how dangerous that is. It leaves itself open to many arbitrage opportunities, such as Soros' Break-the-Bank attack on the British pound. (We'll discuss that example in Chapter 8 for stablecoins.) This is especially insecure in a system that strives for anonymity and places itself beyond the protection of any national jurisdiction. Currently, there are not many useful institutions such as banking in the decentralized economy, which would allow adversaries to take advantage of their governance weaknesses. With only a few US$100 billion in capitalization driven entirely by speculation that the platforms may be useful in the future, the crypto economy is not yet a significant factor in international commerce. Competing platforms have an incentive to keep the peace until these P2P platforms prove the economy needs them. However, we can witness these realities developing quickly. When they do materialize, the decentralized economy will be rocked by catastrophes, which expose these weaknesses.

The lack of governance is especially dangerous for these P2P platforms, because it is extremely difficult for decentralized organizations to change their rules. The United States built a system into its Constitution for amending the rules, but in 230 tumultuous years of operation there have only been 14 changes. This despite yearly crises, including a civil war that split the country across the middle. This despite changes in information technology that started with writing the original rules with goose feathers on sheepskin. Hundreds of millions of new network members follow those old rules, but now the rules are shared by bouncing them off satellites in space between citizens' pockets.

When a large, decentralized organization needs a fundamental rule change, it often happens because a large minority subgroup is being treated unfairly. That typically means the majority is advantaged by the rules and are therefore not incentivized to change the rules. Then the only way to make foundational changes is revolution. When Ethereum chose to make a minor change to fix a single bug exploited by a single member (the 2016 DAO attack) a minority revolted, splitting the network. Distributing power in a valuable network creates major path dependencies. Getting the governance system right from the beginning is absolutely crucial.[2]

Currently, the vast majority of Web3 projects rely on their founders to do a good job at the beginning and hope there never needs to be an important structural update after the first roadmap is complete. Since the field is in massive flux, the lack of governance is pretty well hidden. No important roadmaps have been completed, yet. The fact that the reliance on founders represents *de facto* centralization isn't too glaring, yet. At the moment, since new companies come and go, new problems can be addressed by cloning older open-source architectures with superficial changes.

---

2 "You will never get right until you start right." – Voltairine de Cleyre, "The Economic Tendency of Freethought," *Liberty*, XI(25), 1890.

Since no major P2P organization has anything resembling effective decentralized governance, none of them are viable in the long term. They will all eventually be disrupted with superior clones. This doesn't mean they won't be useful in the short term, so predicting when they will become irrelevant is impossible.

It is perhaps understandable that these immature systems don't have sophisticated governance mechanisms. Designing a single consensus algorithm is infinitely easier than designing a consensus algorithm that will incorporate all future updates to the consensus algorithm. Before the decentralized economy can actually emerge to improve our current institutions, though, this must be achieved for long-term stability. Many developers are beginning to understand this, and the hard line against constitutions is softening.

How do we achieve governance in a decentralized organization without imposing a centralized hierarchy to make decisions? Fortunately, we've been addressing this impossible necessity and developing governments based on decentralized principles throughout history. Egypt practiced decentralized judicial governance for 3000 years. Every democratic government since Ancient Greece has been an experiment in decentralized executive governance. The most powerful DAO in history was the United States. All governments have been flawed, but we can learn from their mistakes.

In this chapter we explore what is needed to design an effective governance process for a decentralized network or DAO without any central hierarchy to make decisions or drive innovation. Essentially, we need a constitution for a radically democratic organization. An incorruptible governance process, one which has never been achieved before, sounds unlikely – especially as we witness old and established democratic institutions failing.

But there are new information technology tools that give us more power to democratically govern decentralized organizations. We can poll every member of the group almost instantly. We can keep track of every member's contributions. We can judge them according to programmed processing of unlimited complexity. All these information technology tasks can now also be achieved redundantly, by each member of the group, so each member is autonomous and doesn't rely on some central overseer or repository.

The only requirement for decentralized governance is to design this third governance processing protocol by which the entire organization can agree to judge each other by. The first goal of this chapter is to identify such a governance process that keeps the organization decentralized and stable.

Secondly, once this governance process is established, we need to make design choices that reflect the goals of the group. The goals are literally what the group values. For instance, if the group values long-term stability, they should encourage investment and tokens of power, which pay annuities in the long term. If they value immediate innovation, they should reward development more than maintenance.

Decentralized Governance with New IT Tools

The purpose of a pure DAO is to allow any users on the planet to join anonymously (or pseudonymously). Such users have a natural incentive to exploit any opportunity to profit personally, even if it comes at the expense of the group. At the same time, DAOs have no centralized authority empowered to police or guide behavior. A program for solving all these problems under these extreme circumstances is forbiddingly ambitious. What hope do we have of finding an effective governance structure when users are likely to be pseudonymous and occupy uncertain locations in various jurisdictions?

How do we create a system that can update itself in a peaceful, stable, and predictable way, in response to unpredictable future changes in the market? We need a constitution that outlines the powers of the legislative, executive, and judicial systems of the decentralized network. The legislative system updates the constitution itself. The executive system enforces the constitution. The judicial system handles inevitable disputes. All of this needs to be built into a code-is-law smart contract small enough to be easily parsed and audited by humans and run efficiently in a redundant peer to peer setting.

Contemporary P2P technology allows us, for the first time in history, to coordinate communication without a centralized authority in a secure and redundant fashion, to keep track of every important contribution, and to store those records eternally for future review. This review gives us the chance to analyze the consequences of every action and fairly reward the positive contributions to the group and punish the negative. One of the major efficiencies of a decentralized organization is that all rewards can be shared with the people who contribute to the success of the group, fairly, according to their merit.

We broadly define corruption in an organization as any action that benefits a minority at the greater expense of the group. Corruption arises when power is distributed inappropriately as measured by efficiency. Corruption arises in the dark when people or institutions have the power to act without review. Broadcasting technology provides us the opportunity to transparently share evidence of all actions so they can be reviewed. Processing technology gives each person the power to independently judge these actions' value. This inhibits corruption, by distributing power efficiently to those who can use it best to improve the group.

Just because we can cite every action from a company on a blockchain, however, does not mean we have conquered corruption. More information does not ensure more productive collaboration. How do we discern the signal through the noise? Members must be properly motivated to behave correctly and to police corrupt behavior when it happens. This is the goal of governance.

Cash profits are a bad immediate incentive for business and government. The cartoon scenario of a DAO consisting of anonymous members who stake their currency on rigid smart contracts gives the worst imaginable motivations for collaboration. If the entire proximal goal of a transaction is currency, all participants will naturally behave in the most selfish manner possible, exploiting any opportunity for individual profit at the expense of the group.

Further, rigid "code is law" smart contracts involving fungible currency exchanges are designed to guarantee irreversible, unreviewable, programmed self-execution. Very rarely does any business venture proceed exactly as imagined from the beginning. To enter any business arrangement, parties need to have confidence that fair resolution will occur when transactions do not go according to plan. They need to know whether to continue business after an unforeseen event.

Moreover, rigid "code is law" smart contracts will need to be extremely complex to account for the many possible eventualities of practical business situations. The insurmountable reality is that bugs or hacks can never be certainly precluded in any programmable contract.[3] Beyond this, long-term attacks will always be possible for any complicated and rigid set of rules, as the infinitude of strategies generated by the Folk Theorems demonstrates. If the entire reward is short-term currency profit, all parties are naturally motivated to push the contract as far as possible in their favor, and they will naturally exploit any weakness in the contract design to their advantage.

The typical engineering attitude is that such problems can be entirely avoided with perfect system design. This is naïve. Exceptions will always exist. Business competition always seeks optimal solutions, which occur at the limits of the rules of behavior. Good system design is possible, but requires dealing with the exceptions. Once the process is in place for dealing with exceptions and improving the process to handle exceptions, exceptions become more and more rare, and the system becomes more efficient. As much as possible, we must automate such constitutional functions for efficiency. This requires explicit formal rules for as many behaviors as possible, which multiplies the protocols without limit. In tension with this requirement, we must limit the rules to make them as simple as possible and allow maximum freedom for innovation. The ideal rules never need to be enforced as they are naturally incentivized by productive cooperation that achieves the goals of the group.

The motivation for all parties to behave as selfishly as possible creates instability for any business transaction. More harmonious collaboration is motivated when improved reputation is the proximal goal. The situation is no longer a zero-sum game when either or both parties can create valuable long-term reputation from the transaction.

---

3 Despite the laudable efforts toward secure purely functional programming languages such as Haskell.

Instability from Profit Motive and Rigid Rules

The major characteristics of the network that dictate design choices are 1) whether the group is devoted primarily to profit, and 2) the values of the group.

The two ends of the spectrum are nonprofit organizations with uniform values, and for-profit companies with diverse values. Ideologically centralized (uniform values) nonprofit organizations are extremely stable and work well without explicit rigorous rules. Historical examples include much of the history of Imperial China, the Apache's nomadic period, and Wikipedia. DAO examples would include non-profits devoted to charity, local community social organizations (like YMCAs), and local governance subcouncils devoted to improving the community of a nondiverse population. The less explicit the rules are, the more they should not strictly adhere to precedent – spirit of the law must supersede the letter of the law. If the system has less explicit rules, the unifying force is transcendental values – values that cannot be explicitly written down, dictating what is acceptable or not. An example of a transcendental value is the Golden Rule, "Treat others like you would be treated." An example of an explicit rule is, "Murder is punished with 10 years in jail."

Ideologically decentralized (diverse values) for profit organizations are the decentralized organizations we are concerned with in this book. They are on the other end of the spectrum from value centralized nonprofit organizations, and so they are naturally very unstable. We assume these DAOs want to maximize the network effect, and therefore, they are trying to build the largest, most inclusive group of members possible. They are open to anonymous members with a diverse set of values from a globally diverse set of cultural backgrounds, who can join or leave at will. These characteristics make such DAOs extremely unstable, so they need powerful stabilizing structures.

The internal competition for profit creates the natural tendency to centralize power as the members differentiate themselves with wins and losses. This centralizing tendency is another force further destabilizing the organizations.

Diverse (decentralized) values require protocol centralization (explicit, enforceable rules), because stability requires impartial application of laws to display fairness. Explicit rules can unite a larger group of more diverse members. In other words, the governance system must follow rigid Rule of Law, instead of loose Rule of Virtue.

Explicit rigid rules are also more efficient. Members waste less energy making choices.

However, these unifying rules further destabilize the group in the long-term, because of internal corruption and external changes that make the rule structure ineffective or inefficient.

This situation of for-profit, open, diverse-valued, rigid Rule of Law run decentralized organizations is maximally unstable. Therefore, you must add powerful stabilizing forces to their governance.

Reputation Counters Instability from Profit Motive

The main problem with all current P2P governance structures (such as they are) is the lack of proper incentivization. In business or in government, all participants need to be motivated to improve the whole organization over the long term. Otherwise, when short-term fungible rewards are available, the natural response is to always attempt to game the system for maximal personal profit and to ignore how your actions may damage the group.

A reputational system that is formally linked to profits makes the members forward-thinking and cooperative, to combat the natural tendency of competition to separate members. It also motivates members to self-police their past investments. Reputation changes the incentive structure from a single-stage, zero-sum game to a repeated positive-sum game.

Reputation gives the promise of future rewards. Reputation can be objectively valued, by estimating the probability of future business deals, taking the expected value of that probability, and calculating the present value of those business deals. Yet this value can seemingly be created from nothing, in a place it didn't exist before, based solely on whether the participants choose to display good will toward each other. This makes reputation a positive-sum property from the game-theory perspective.[4]

No centralized platform, such as Amazon or eBay, has been able to create meaningful and secure online reputation. Because they are centrally owned and controlled they cannot give members the power and incentives they need to police their own reputation, protecting it from the infinite strategies available to adversaries for subverting the intentions of the designers (which the Folk Theorems of Game Theory illustrate). With the new opportunities that P2P technology creates, decentralizing and distributing reputation fairly, and tying it to the profits of the organization, the members can be properly incentivized and empowered to police all actions. Giving DAO members the ability to fairly apportion power in a variety of domains lessens the danger of the principal-agent problem and combats several Tragedy of the Commons problems, such as nonrepresentativeness and free riding.

A platform that vests users with secure and valuable reputation gives us the opportunity to effectively filter the voluminous information that contemporary technology produces. People with higher reputation will have greater voice.

---

4 Arguably the source of good will would be the promise of profit from rational choices in long-term cooperation in an expanding market. Like physics experiments where energy is added to a subsystem, Conservation of Energy is not actually violated from the wider, universal perspective. The positive-sum situation holds from the near-sighted perspective of specific subgroups over a limited time period. From the eternal perspective, reputation allows the system to achieve a subgame perfect Nash equilibrium with a higher profit level, so the reputation is not value created from nowhere.

Power is diffused by reputation, as discussed in Chapter 6. Thus, reputation stabilizes the organization by decentralizing it. One of the major sources of instability from unequal power distribution is the ever-present possibility of a majority oppressing a minority. De Tocqueville criticized American democracy as being particularly susceptible to this Tyranny of the Majority and argued it could ruin any democratic organization. De Tocqueville and Madison[5] and others claimed the best safeguard against this is by diversifying interests. Giving individuals more autonomy naturally diversifies the expressed interests of a group. Encouraging individual autonomy by decentralizing power creates more minorities, which is the best way to protect minorities.

Any such reputation system must address the many problems, such as sock-puppet attacks, Tyranny of the Majority, Tragedy of the Commons, 51% attacks, and free riding, that have undermined the meaning and value of digital reputation on all previous platforms, centralized or decentralized. Further, it needs to be a dynamic and evolutionary system, able to anticipate and react to gaming that will inevitably result from whatever rules are in place. Review Chapter 6, to see how to address such problems.

Alternatives to reputational systems for countering the instability generated by profit competition include external stabilizing forces (such as governmental fiat) or rapidly expanding profit opportunities (which will only stabilize a group until the expansion stops). Colonialism gives historical examples, such as the Spanish Empire in the Americas or the Dutch East India Company.

Trying to institute dynamic rules to attenuate the instability due to a for-profit motive is a mismatch. Similarly instituting a reputational system is not an efficient method for attenuating the instability due to a group's diverse values.

Once reviewable reputation is the focus instead of more fungible currency rewards, damaging arbitrage opportunities are minimized. The next major concern

---

5 "It is of great importance in a republic, not only to guard the society against the oppression of its rulers, but to guard one part of the society against the injustice of the other part. Different interests necessarily exist in different classes of citizens. If a majority be united by a common interest, the rights of the minority will be insecure. There are but two methods of providing against this evil: the one by creating a will in the community independent of the majority, that is, of the society itself; the other, by comprehending in the society so many separate descriptions of citizens as will render an unjust combination of a majority of the whole very improbable, if not impracticable."-- Federalist No. 51, February 6, 1788.

"In a free Government, the security for civil rights must be the same as that for religious rights. It consists in the one case in the multiplicity of interests, and in the other in the multiplicity of sects. The degree of security in both cases, will depend on the number of interests and sects; and this may be presumed to depend on the extent of country and number of People comprehended under the same Government." – Federalist No. 51, February 6, 1788.

"The essence of Government is power; and power, lodged as it must be in human hands, will ever be liable to abuse." – Speech in the Virginia Constitutional Convention, December 2, 1829, *The Writings of James Madison: 1819–1836*, ed. Galliard Hunt, 1910, p. 361.

for creating a healthy governance process is to decide how to reach consensus on protocols for behavior. What process do we use to enforce laws?

Dynamic Design Counters Instability from Rigid Rules

The instability generated by the rigidity of the rules is solved by making the rules dynamic. Dynamic governance includes short-term and long-term protocols. An appeals process stabilizes short-term cooperation (day-to-day business, single contract). Long-term stabilization (year to year, group to group, part of one generation) comes from legislation, the ability to amend rules – including how the amendments themselves are made. For even longer-term stabilization (generation to generation), adherence to transcendental values guides higher-order rulemaking.

Like the dynamic design of the U.S. Constitution discussed at the end of Chapter 1, which stabilized and decentralized the federal hierarchy, we can add dynamic design to DAO governance to encourage decentralization (or equity or meritocracy or any other value your organization holds). Larger changes are effectuated by legislative governance. Subtle changes in reward parameters can be automated to steer the DAO toward the goals of the group.

Executive Short-Term Governance Automated with Hard Protocols

Short-term cooperation is regulated by executive governance. This is single-contract policing. Executive governance is regulatory governance – policing. Such regulation should be governed by hard protocols. In other words, in a decentralized organization, the entire executive branch's function should be automated.

Hard protocols are programmed rules for how the organization performs its functions. For instance, each DAO will automatically share profits with its members, where the core program will automatically calculate each member's salary in proportion to their reputation token holdings relative to the entire group. As a second hard protocol example, each DAO will determine how reputation creation, distribution, and policing are handled – for instance, the level of approval required before reputation tokens are granted. As a third example, references to past work-evidence posts will re-valuate member reputation. Precisely how does a reference reward the author? The many possible options provide many diverse choices of incentives with which to motivate DAO members, as will be examined throughout the book. Such hard protocols determine the programmed reward/punishment structure of each DAO.

In a radically democratic system where power is truly decentralized, every member of the organization oversees all executive governance, all the time. With the new tools of information technology, this is now possible.

As described above in the system that generates reputation, each member is capable of participating in the validation pools. In this way, when the system is working properly, the executive system is completely automated. Every validation pool on executive governance should be completely uncontentious, with every vote resolving unanimously. The only time a member should use their executive power consciously is when they decide whether to join, that is, whether they want to run the program that polices the members or not. After that choice, the hard protocols are entirely algorithmic, in the sense that anyone honestly following them will automatically choose the correct vote, which drives the system to unanimous consensus. The most efficient applications should be automated, so that honesty is defined as running the algorithm the organization has agreed upon, unedited.

The only time the members should make a conscious choice when using their reputation tokens for governance, is if they are interested in participating in the legislative governance process of debating updates to the hard protocols.

Policing is an overhead institution in our traditional economy that centralized personal defense. Policing as we know it, with permanent, professional, centralized police bureaucracies funded by taxes, is only about 200 years old. Throughout history there were decentralized militias and posses, that were based on communal spirit in democracies or family-oriented clans (e.g., Imperial China and feudal Italy[6]). Governments always employed specialized military units for policing their citizens, but before the modern era, there were rarely any standing armies, so policing was intermittent. Aside from this, marshals and constables were typically paid by courts or individuals with bounties or retainers.

Starting in 1800 in London, public taxes first funded the Thames River Police to prevent crime near merchant import properties, following a royal French system that predated it. Motivated by this success, the 1829 Metropolitan Police Act created the first modern police force, that is, the first public police bureaucracy for maintaining social order by investigating general crimes. London passed the act to address the social upheaval engendered by the industrial revolution. The United States later copied this British innovation in Boston in 1838 and New York City in 1845. The point we are stressing, is that the systems we take for granted as natural are by no means universal or eternal. Policing in major cities was not well established until the 1880s, and towns with less than 100,000 residents didn't institute salaried police until well into the 20th century.

From a wider, nationwide perspective, outsourcing personal revenge to a publicly sanctioned, centralized police force led to a leap in efficiency. But this centralized institution is an obvious vector for corruption. Police exist to fight corruption. They understand corruption better than others and are the only group sanctioned to directly

---

6 The Towers of Bologna (https://en.wikipedia.org/wiki/Towers_of_Bologna) are a testament to the function of clan policing. Each clan had a tower from which they could monitor the town and defend themselves.

address it, so they generally police themselves. Because the centralized bureaucracy is hierarchical, there is less transparency than there would be in a decentralized organization, since only a few people observe what each other person is doing, because of the limited and static power relations within the org chart. With the advances of information technology, we can achieve another leap in efficiency and security, by decentralizing and automating policing, giving every member of a network the power to check every other member on specific behaviors. Bitcoin does this, for example, by using error correcting codes and public key cryptography. Whenever a message is sent in the Bitcoin network, each node in the P2P network checks the message to see that it is properly formatted following Bitcoin protocol before passing it along in the gossip network. Then each block is hashed many times, and the nonce is checked to police the claim that the hash lottery winner is the correct block producer. Finally, each Bitcoin money transfer is cryptographically checked by every node in the network to verify the transaction sender and recipient accounts are the correct owners of the private key through digital signature technology.

Advances in information technology, especially processing and transmission of data, enables the decentralization of policing of many other DAO functions, giving each individual in the network the power to check everyone else is following protocol, through the weighted democratic system of validation pools. We will discuss how these can be automated in Chapter 8, when we discuss banking.

Legislative Long-Term Governance with Deliberative Soft Protocols

In order to adapt to changing market threats and opportunities, DAOs need legislative governance to update their hard protocols. How can we develop new rules or protocols in a completely decentralized system with anonymous members? We need to use reputation tokens if we want to achieve complete decentralization, anonymity, and autonomy. Protocol development is contentious, however. If unanimous consensus is strongly incentivized by every validation pool, our DAOs will degenerate quickly, as alternative options will not be raised by members with minority opinions for fear they will lose all reputation tokens. So, the basic functioning of validation pools described above is inadequate. One more tweak is needed – loosely coupled votes.

The legislative system in a DAO is the process for updating the system – essentially rolling out new versions of the software all members of the P2P network use. This legislative process can be broken down into the steps of identifying problems, proposing solutions, deciding between solutions, and deciding how to implement those solutions. The goal is to ensure a stable but active legislative process that responds to inevitable market changes. The goal is to drive group consensus toward improvements in the system.

The design should use the reputation system to democratically come to consensus on each of these steps. There are two basic processes: filtering attention to ideas and then debating the ideas.

First the network needs to harness the power from decentralized networks to access information at the edge by filtering their attention to focus on good ideas. New advances in information technology allow anyone in the network to propose an idea and to use an upvote-type system, like Reddit or Stack Exchange (but with secure and meaningful reputation), to make good ideas more visible to the group.

Once an idea meets a certain threshold of attention, how do we decide on whether to implement the idea? How do we guarantee consensus on the protocol change? This second process is a series of votes before the larger group. This will involve contentious debates on how to develop new regulatory/executive protocols. Such debates can be held in P2P distributed hash table forums and subjected to a validation pool with **loosely coupled votes**. "Loosely coupled" means reputation tokens cannot be lost during such validation pools, but can still be staked on contentious posts to register each owner's opinion. Loosely coupled validation pools poll the opinion of the group. These polls allow a DAO to gauge member body opinion without upsetting the balance of power with disruptive token transfers. Such debates encourage authentic deliberation on protocol development, in order to 1) efficiently explore the most effective modes of behavior for the organization, and 2) ensure genuine and thorough consensus on all protocols.

In order to encourage development actually happening, that is, to force consensus in a timely manner, the debate can gradually move to **tightly coupled votes**, where part or all of the reputation tokens staked on a losing bet will be redistributed to the winners. When a protocol development debate finally moves to a perfectly tightly coupled vote (where all reputation tokens staked on a minority position in a validation pool are lost), proof is given that the outcome has become precedence, the protocol becomes noncontentious, and unanimity is ensured. Updates to the consensus algorithm can be made and it will be ensured that everyone in the DAO will download the new algorithm and run it, or else risk losing reputation tokens when the new protocol is engaged.

Loosely coupled voting encourages dissenting opinions. Tightly coupled voting guarantees consensus. The process moving from one to the other can be slow or fast depending on the importance of the debate versus the need to solve the problem rapidly.

In order to enforce a limit on the time of a debate, the DAO may choose to include a mechanism where validation pools transition gradually from loosely coupled voting to tightly coupled voting. This transition allows authentic deliberation to take place during the loosely coupled voting phase, since divergent views are not punished. When the debate transitions to the tightly coupled voting phase, the Tragedy of the Commons problems of meaningless votes (the "nothing-at-stake problem") and nonparticipation (i.e., free riding) are avoided, fairly and stably, because members who do not participate effectively will lose reputation or at least lose opportunities to gain reputation tokens, whose future value will greatly increase if the protocol improvement successfully attracts fees to the platform.

Figure 7.1 categorizes the difference between contentious and noncontentious posts.[7] Noncontentious posts, such as work-evidence posts, will be rigidly policed and binding in the allocation of tokens. Protocols will start as flexible and nonbinding when they are validated as contentious posts. Flexible means members will not be required to follow initial contentious post protocols subjected to loosely coupled votes. Nonbinding means no reputation tokens are sacrificed for violating the content of such posts. As consensus is gradually achieved and protocol suggestions become validated in tightly coupled validation pools, the protocols become rigid and binding, so that violating them results in loss of reputation tokens.

	Binding	Nonbinding
Rigid	Noncontentious post & tightly coupled (e.g., work-evidence post, mandatory plebiscite)	Noncontentious post & loosely coupled (e.g., poll of consensus on established precedent)
Flexible	Contentious post & tightly coupled (e.g., forcing consensus on protocol development)	Contentious post & loosely coupled (e.g., protocol development poll, advisory referendum)

Figure 7.1: The types of posts split according to whether the issues are contentious and whether the consequences are binding.

This process of moving protocol development posts from contentious to noncontentious is meant to address wicked problems,[8] which are generally intractable, yet

---

7 adapted from the EU governance study by Oliver Treib, Holger Bähr, Gerda Falkner, Andreas Follesdal, & Simon Hix, "Modes of Governance: A Note Towards Conceptual Clarification," No. N-05-02. Available online https://www.ihs.ac.at/publications/lib/ep6.pdf (retrieved 6/23/20).
8 Jeffrey Conklin's defining characteristics of a wicked problem are:
1. The problem is not understood until after the formulation of a solution.
2. Wicked problems have no stopping rule.
3. Solutions to wicked problems are not right or wrong.
4. Every wicked problem is essentially novel and unique.
5. Every solution to a wicked problem is a "one shot operation."
6. Wicked problems have no given alternative solutions.

consensus must still be reached in a timely fashion. Therefore, a well-designed method for encouraging careful deliberation is crucial. Approaches from operations research (e.g., problem structuring methods[9]) to social and political science and history (e.g., Quaker governance, managing a commons[10]) will help organize the process, depending on the particular application and DAO.

The means by which members come to consensus on protocol development is by following soft protocols. The soft protocols form a socially developed system of rules that guide members in their conscious decisions – as opposed to hard protocols that are automatically, algorithmically followed by DAO members to police the value of work-evidence posts. Such soft protocols are intended to guide members to complete their deliberations following the commonly agreed upon transcendental values of the DAO. A healthy DAO will have an effective set of soft protocols for expressing their common values with regular innovative rule improvements that keep the DAO on an efficient path toward achieving their goals.

These soft protocols move the DAO from loosely to tightly coupled votes, from legislative governance to executive governance with hard protocols.

The collection of currently validated hard and soft protocols comprise the legal constitution of a DAO. Similar to nation-states, most members of a DAO will never exhaustively analyze every legal facet of the constitution. So, the UI design is as important as the constitution to the success of a DAO.

Minority interests are passively protected by decentralizing power as discussed in Chapter 6. To further protect minority interests and ensure stability, DAOs often will choose to institute certain initial charter rules that are hard coded to require near unanimous consensus to change, similar to a nation-state's foundational constitution. By protecting minorities from the inevitable transient interests of the majority, this would encourage recruitment of a diverse population of members, increasing the DAO's power from the network effect.

Judicial Short-Term Governance with Hard and Soft Protocols

The necessity for appeals is crucial in any business deal. Business contracts are designed to bring confidence and clarity to the future. While code-is-law smart contracts give a technological leap in efficiency and clarity, with efficient digital self-execution, their supposed self-regulation will always be ultimately lacking.

Cf., also, a super wicked problem, which is also relevant. Jeffrey Conklin, *Dialogue Mapping: Building Shared Understanding of Wicked Problems,* Wiley Publishing, 2006.

9 Jonathan Rosenhead, "Problem Structuring Methods," in *Encyclopedia of Operations Research and Management Science,* 3rd ed., Springer Verlag, 2013, pp. 1162–1172.

10 Ostrom, Elinor, *Governing the Commons*, Cambridge University Press, 1990.

The smallest problem is programming bugs. These will always be inevitable, even with logical advances such as strong, statically typed, purely functional programming languages such as Haskell, which prevent many of the accidental logical loopholes of more popular languages. Such problems can be solved with an evolutionary platform, which has a history and good incentive design to encourage continual improvement in the smart contracts. But business arrangements are becoming more complex. Each successful modification leads to more opportunities for modifications. With each increase in complexity, the "attack surface" of the business arrangement grows. Mistakes will always surface.

Far more importantly, a business contract is a plan for the future. Even if all the business parties are well-intentioned, plans fail. When you buy wood to build a shed, a few pieces from the delivery may be too twisted or knotty to your liking. Do you terminate the smart contract? Do we build more complex clauses into the contract handling any eventuality? Perhaps we stipulate how many knots the wood can have, and measure precisely how twisted the wood is allowed to be. How do we build a smart contract that can judge whether the seller or the buyer is pushing the boundaries?

It doesn't matter whether the other party is well-intentioned or not. Sometimes (often) business parties genuinely disagree. For efficiency, disputed contracts need to be able to be resolved in more sophisticated ways than simply terminating them early. An impartial third party might be able to resolve the dispute in a more efficient manner. The existence of an efficient and fair appeals process helps give parties the confidence to enter a contract in the first place. A fair and efficient judicial system, like insurance, is a catalyst for business that makes the wider economy more liquid and ultimately, more efficient.

To maintain the efficiency of the self-executing code-is-law smart contract, the appeals process must be built into the code. In the same way the executive functions of the DAO are automated with smart-contract-enabled hard protocols, the appeals process is also automated with hard protocols. Triggers are built into smart contracts that either party can engage when a dispute arises. The idea is that the assets encumbered in the smart contract from the beginning (digital properties including currencies, tokenized assets, and reputation tokens) would be frozen and partial powers of disbursement would be transferred to a third-party arbiter. This judge would stake their reputation for expert knowledge in the DAO's protocols and experience with resolving the most common disputes. Then a predetermined appeals process is enacted. The cost of such a process needs to be transparent and negotiated by the DAO, which hosts the smart contract before it is recommended to its customers. A long history of successful and efficient dispute resolution is necessary before customers would gain the faith needed to guarantee the system is worth using from the beginning.

However, soft protocols are also necessary. Beyond the limits of the typical transaction, there will be new events that the DAO must be able to handle. Ideally, these situations would be vanishingly rare, but even then, it is necessary for the DAO to have a system in place to give users confidence. The third-party arbiter must sometimes make a creative decision based on the unique evidence of a novel dispute. In that case, the arbiter should rely on soft protocols that cleave to the spirit of the law, similar to how new protocols are created during legislative debate. These soft protocols would be founded on precedent and guidelines developed over time to steer the DAO toward its transcendental values. Without such unifying ideals, liminal cases will fragment the network. Ultimately, transcendental values are always necessary to maintain the stability of a network, so they are the first thing the DAO should establish.

Network Forks and Black Swans

Finally, there is no way to design a system that can anticipate every future eventuality. Conditions change. The group can develop persistent irreconcilable differences in talents or philosophy or goals. Sometimes the group will be more efficient if competing minorities have the freedom to pursue their own values.

A mechanism for forking needs to be implemented so the value created by the previous history is not erased. Otherwise the group will arbitrarily downvote the minority, creating resentment and unnecessary strife. However, forking should always be discouraged, until the split becomes obvious and detrimental, because of the value lost in any fork due to the network effect.

The mechanism of forking is illustrated by the Ethereum Classic blockchain fork. Members who disagree with a new protocol or vote that results in unfair loss of reputation tokens, can create a new protocol and start their network consensus algorithm from any point in the past, ignoring any new messages sent according to the old protocol.

Eight Qualities of Effective Decentralized Governance and Authentic Deliberation

Eight general qualities have been identified in modern democratic institutions as useful for evaluating how effective a governance system is. Upholding the ideals of decentralization, security, and anonymity while remaining stable in the long run is difficult and requires the governance structure of the DAO to encourage a deliberative democracy. A deliberative democracy by definition values authentic deliberation for legitimating consensus on the rules, over the mere act of achieving a majority vote. The eternally reviewable history of any debate in the forum may provide an ideal mechanism for achieving the transparency required for authentic consensus, if the deliberation process satisfies the following eight qualities: 1) open, 2) balanced, 3) conscientious, 4) dynamic, 5) informed, 6) binding, 7) reviewable, and 8) escapable.

Open. An ideal governance process should allow access and power to anyone with the ability and desire to make positive contributions.

Balanced. Power and profit must be shared fairly. Productive contributions must be properly rewarded based on the improvement they make to the group. Negative contributions must be properly punished based on the damage they do to the group. Arguments should be considered from contrary perspectives. Every member has the opportunity to post any contentious opinion without fear of reprisals, especially if they are given the opportunity for anonymity.

Conscientious. Participants should sincerely consider the merits of arguments and act in the interest of improving the DAO. This cannot be ensured without proper security and incentivization.

Dynamic. The governance process must be very flexible if it is to adapt to the inevitable gaming that will occur in any complex group. In this sense, the ideal is to create an evolutionary system where rules are able to change continually to avoid threats and seize opportunities (micro soft forks). The ability to review past actions and revalue their worth is necessary. Participants must accept that policies and protocols will eventually change, and therefore should have a perspective that is open to influence.

Informed. Authentic deliberation is required for the development of the protocols that will guide the behavior of group members toward productive collaboration. Three properties are necessary to authentic deliberation: i) as much information as possible on any subject must be available to all participants, ii) contrary points of view must be considered, iii) the weight of an opinion should be partially measured by expertise.

Binding. If a rule is broken through incompetence or maliciousness, punishment through loss of reputation tokens is necessary. Unanimous agreement is therefore the goal of validation pools for work-evidence posts. In contrast with the desire for the ability to review past actions, clarity on the finality of decisions is required for stability. Arguments have the goal of ending in policy.

Reviewable. Governance is a human institution and therefore flawed. The inevitability of mistakes demands a system to redress them. Unaddressed injustice undermines stability.

Escapable. Network effects show that forking is often damaging to the total value of any collaboration. So, forking should naturally be discouraged. However, persistent, valid, minority opinions will arise in any collaboration between members with different talents. In this case a fork can increase the total value of the individual groups when they are given the freedom to pursue their separate goals yet still receive the recognition they deserve from past achievements. For the health of the system there needs to be a mechanism whereby a carefully considered fork may be stably effectuated. Ideally a symmetric mechanism would be available allowing branches to merge, perhaps when the larger DAO agrees to recognize the smaller group's reputation.

Secondly, individual members should have a stable way to exit the system by selling their reputation tokens for a fair market valuation of the future expected value of their reputational salary. This is more problematic for reputation than for most other cryptocurrency tokens, since reputation is less fungible because a to-ken's value is tied to the post in which the reputation was created and subject to separate review. But in principle it could be algorithmically valuated.

In a competitive environment, a governance process for 1) an open and 8) escapable system must be 3) conscientious, 5) informed, and 6) binding in order to promote the system's legitimacy. Legitimacy is achieved when members have confidence the gov-ernance process is 6) binding and that the process will persist. Legitimacy is at odds with a 4) dynamic structure, since members recognize the process will inevitably change. In the presence of this tension, stability requires the system to be 2) balanced.

The bulk of this chapter is concerned with analyzing how to best ensure the governance process is 2) balanced and 5) informed. The most challenging aspect of good governance in this context is creating a process that properly rewards partici-pants for their contributions and encourages authentic and thorough deliberation on protocols.

The value of deliberation is at odds with time-efficiency and finality. That is, a 4) dynamic, 7) reviewable, 2) balanced, and 5) informed process is at odds with a timely and 6) binding process. The values and needs of any particular DAO will change between these two extremes throughout its lifetime. The parameters that de-termine which extreme is preferred include the length of validation pool timeout, the percentage of reputation tokens risked when moving from loosely to tightly cou-pled validation pools, and the reference weight standards.

Design Choices Match Values

By subtly manipulating the reward structure in a DAO, it changes the incentives in the group, which drives different values. So, if you want to encourage a particular value, you need to design the governance structure with this in mind. The parame-ters determining how power is distributed in the DAO determine the reward struc-ture. The parameters determine how reputation tokens are created and distributed (in validation pools) and how their values are reviewed (references and appeals). In this section, we analyze how manipulating these parameters affects DAO security, stability, protocol development, recruitment of members and outside business, and retention.

The goal of good governance design is to engineer the proper incentives so that independent and self-interested actors will discover that their optimal strategy is to collaborate productively toward the goals that serve the DAO's values. Without knowing the architects' intentions beforehand, we should be able to observe the functioning of a system at steady state and guess the original intentions of the ar-chitects. Put another way, it doesn't matter what the architects' intentions are, the resulting rules of the game tell the players what to value. So, if you don't value what a DAO encourages you to achieve, you shouldn't join. Put another way, if you know what your values are, you should design the DAO so that it rewards actions that achieve goals reflecting those values, and punishes actions that hinder such achievements.

In this section we will identify a few choices in DAO governance design and match them to some basic values that DAOs may choose.[11]

Connecting Values with Protocols

We specify several desirable qualities for a DAO and identify several protocols that encourage each quality.

A general point of view from game theory is that even if a particular behavior is only slightly favored in each round of a repeated game, it is strongly favored in the long run and so dominates behavior and outcomes. For example, the house has less than a 1% advantage in blackjack gambling in typical casinos, yet the game is an enormous source of predictable profit, as demonstrated by the ostentatious display of wealth in Macau or Monte Carlo or Las Vegas. Therefore, changing governance parameters, only slightly, should be enough to steer long-term member behavior toward the goals of the DAO.

The basic protocols that determine how power is distributed comes from four stages:
1. How workers are chosen for a task.
2. How members can judge a task and how reputation is distributed according to the judgment.
3. How the profits are distributed to the members.
4. How reputation is reviewed.

First, we explain how different types of distributive norms (i.e., standards for how power is shared and apportioned and adjusted in a group) may be encouraged with particular choices of parameters. Next, we discuss how parameters may be set and how they might evolve for a toy model of a basic company's life cycle.

Distributive Norms

To encourage harmony, careful attention must be paid to the manner in which power and wealth are distributed in any DAO. Subtle changes in the governance structure of different DAOs can encourage many types of distributive norms.

---

11 For a more thorough technical introduction, see Craig Calcaterra, "On-Chain Governance of Decentralized Autonomous Organizations," May 2018, available at https://ssrn.com/abstract= 3188374 (retrieved 6/1/20).

A distributive norm is a standard for sharing wealth and power within the organization. Typically, for small, newly founded DAOs, the standard will be equity to encourage members to join, but this would change to favor meritocracy, as the DAO matures and wants to encourage improvement. Other norms that encourage different behaviors can also be incentivized with the appropriate choice of protocols. We explore the effects of parameter manipulation on six categories of distributive norms.[12] These separate norms conflict or overlap with each other, but a complex network will typically merge several different norms to balance the needs of its members.

Distribution Proportional to Input (similar to Legal Equity):[13]

Under this distributive norm, members' outcomes should be based on their inputs. Under this norm an individual who has invested a large amount of input (e.g., time, money, energy) should receive more from the group than someone who has contributed little.

This distributive norm will be typical for early DAOs focused on business enterprises. This is encouraged with the basic default setup described previously in chapters 4.3 and 6.3:

1. Reputation-weighted random selection of workers.
2. Reputation-weighted voting and rewards in validation pools.
3. Reputation-weighted salaries.

Distribution Proportional to Result (Pure Meritocracy): instead of measuring how much energy the individuals contribute, you measure how their efforts have improved the organization, and reward them proportionately.

This is encouraged with the basic default setup described above, with the addition of

4. Reviewing previous contributions according to analysis of results. Reputation is augmented or reduced appropriately. (See Chapter 9 for further discussion of the details of how reviewing can be automated in a DAO.)

Equal Distribution of Output: Regardless of their inputs, all group members should be given an equal share of the rewards/costs. This requires that someone who

---

12 These categories closely follow those described in Donelson Forsyth, *Group Dynamics*, 5th ed., 2006, pp. 388–389, Cengage Learning.

13 The term equity has different interpretations in different contexts. Social equity can mean historical issues are accounted for and so those who were given less in the past are given more in the present. This overlaps largely, but not entirely, with equity in economics. The goal might be to give members the power that most allows them to contribute to individual and group welfare, or the goal may be to level all power. Legal equity can mean many things, including that past powers should be protected, since different properties or assets are never perfectly fairly interchangeable. Throughout this book we have used equity in the sense from economic theory, where those with less are given more.

contributes 20% of the group's resources should receive as much as someone who contributes 60%.

This can be incentivized by
1. Random selection of workers according to membership, not reputational holdings
2. Equal votes and rewards in validation pools according to membership, not reputational holdings
3. Equal salaries for each member

This is impossible to maintain under the current technology with open access and privacy, since sockpuppet accounts would be abused. Improvements in ZK proofs and identity protocols, however, are making it possible to combat efficiently and securely such sockpuppet attacks.

Distribution to the Powerful: Those with more authority, status, or control over the group should receive more than those in lower level positions.

This norm may be achieved by maintaining early users' majority power by skewing reputation-weighted power to further advantage those with more reputation in 1) random selection of workers, 2) voting and rewards, and 3) salaries. Reputation can be treated as an artificially scarce resource, continually decreasing how much is minted, making it more difficult to earn and more valuable as time goes by. This makes the economy of reputation tokens deflationary.

Distribution from the Powerful (Responsibility): Group members who have the most should share their resources with those who have less.

Reversing the previous distributed norm may be promoted by instituting several possible hard protocols, which periodically redistribute power by
i. Actively transferring tokens
ii. Passively redistributing tokens by
    a. Destroying all reputation tokens as they age (deflates the reputation economy)
    b. Increasing the rate of reputation minting as time progresses (inflates the reputation economy)

Distribution According to Need (Equity in economic theory): Those in greatest need should be provided with resources to meet those needs. Such individuals should be given more resources than those in possession, regardless of their input. The goal is to equalize the power of all members.

This norm is promoted using the methods described in Equal Distribution of Output, and Distribution from the Powerful. Again, such a system can obviously be abused in an open distributed setting through sockpuppet attacks if complicated policing is not instituted.

A more sophisticated governance structure will switch between norms as the DAO matures, or in response to market changes, as discussed next.

Company Life Cycle

Now we illustrate the effect of adjusting three parameters of reward distribution for encouraging different behaviors in the course of a company's life cycle. This illustrates an implementation of dynamic governance in a decentralized organization thanks to decentralized information processing.

We use the toy model of the Software Review DAO described in Chapter 4. The three parameters control

1. How quickly new reputation tokens are minted
2. How much the new reputation tokens reward work versus paying for policing
3. Speed of debate, as the voting moves from loosely coupled to tightly coupled

The life cycle of this toy model DAO is split into five stages. It starts with *protocol development* from the founders. The next stages are *member recruitment, collecting evidence of expertise, attracting fees*, and finally *policing work* in the equilibrium stage where the DAO collects the most fees. In practice, there would be more stages that would repeat and overlap. Further, each division of a company (each expertise) will not experience the same stages contemporaneously with other divisions.

Stage 1: Protocol Development

The DAO first must decide how the group is organized, how power will be shared, what regulatory and legislative governance process will be used. Second, the DAO specifies how to perform software analysis – what logical and statistical tests are used on what types of software. Third, protocols for validating another expert's work are specified. Such protocol development is encouraged by setting the three parameters as follows:

1. Highest. The DAO is not attracting public fees until Stage 4, so reputation tokens are minted in proportion to minimal DoS fees paid entirely by the poster. Therefore, the ratio of newly minted reputation tokens is set to the highest value for these posts, to encourage protocol development and reward the founders.
2. Highest. The percentage of newly minted tokens is shared more with workers proposing new protocols than those policing the new protocols.
3. Longest. The small founding group is expected to be highly collaborative so contentious debate posts should move quickly to noncontentious posts, establishing precedent. However, this is the stage that should require the longest period of time to settle differences. That is, these should be the longest periods of time between loosely coupled votes to tightly coupled votes, as the protocols move from soft to hard.

Stage 2: Member Recruitment

Once the founding members have established satisfactory reputation holdings, the DAO will recruit more software evaluator experts, requesting applications to be posted to their forum for validation. The parameters are set as follows:

1. Third highest. The proportion of reputation tokens minted from the minimal DoS fees paid by the recruit will be set to determine a recruit's initial reputation holdings will be high.
2. The percentage given to policing is 50%. Policing is important at this stage, and new members shouldn't overwhelm founders' reputation.
3. Short. Debate on the recruit's application will move quickly from loosely coupled to tightly coupled to force consensus in a reasonable time period.

Stage 3: Collecting Evidence of Expertise

Experts advertise their credentials and produce work-evidence posts without collecting public fees – evaluating software for free. They will be posting with minimal DoS fees, so the parameters are set as follows:

1. Second highest. Members are doing work for free, so newly minted reputation should be much higher than the DoS fees they pay to participate in the group.
2. The percentage given for policing is 50%. New contributions are important at this stage, but so is policing. New contributions of evidence of expertise shouldn't overwhelm founders' reputation for protocol development.
3. Third shortest. Debate is rare and short. Most cases should have been settled by the protocols developed in Stage 1. These posts should move quickly to tightly coupled and noncontentious votes.

Stage 4: Attracting Fees

Once a body of work is established, this stage requires a new effort to attract customers, both general public and software companies that send fees. The parameters are set as follows:

1. Fourth highest. Newly minted reputation is minted in higher proportion to the fees, to encourage enterprising effort.
2. The percentage given for policing can be higher than 50% if protecting the expertise is more important, or lower than 50% if the DAO is more interested in attracting customers.
3. Second shortest. Debate should be almost nonexistent, with the only doubt being whether the fees are corrupting the DAO.

Stage 5: Policing Work

This is the desired equilibrium stage of the company. Members are attracting fees from off-chain work for software companies and posting work-evidence to the forum for validation. The protocol is that a company downloads a template request for work (RFW) smart contract that the DAO has written and posted to their forum and chooses several parameters that the DAO has suggested, including the amount of work requested and the fee they are willing to pay. This RFW smart contract selects a random DAO member for off-chain analysis of their product. This random selection requires DAO members to have already posted availability stakes using their own availability smart contract, which encumbers part of their reputation holdings to be engaged for off-chain work. The randomly selected availability-stake smart contract engages with the RFW smart contract to allow the selected reviewer to post their review to the forum for validation, with the fee sent in their name, so that half of the newly minted reputation tokens are staked in the reviewer's name. The fee from the software company is distributed to the DAO in the reputation-weighted salary. The parameters are set as follows:

1. Lowest. Newly minted reputation is minted in proportion to the fees. This is the stage where reputation gets its meaning.
2. The percentage given for policing is 50%. This is the standard for maintaining the value of the reputation. This can be adjusted to respond to market changes to encourage policing or working.
3. Shortest. Debate should be nonexistent, with protocols followed algorithmically.

After Stage 5, the life cycle of the DAO will repeat as innovation research requires new protocol development to keep the organization relevant to the changing market.

Deciding how and when to move between the stages is a matter of debate. Legislative governance (previous section) is required to develop a system for making those executive decisions in response to changes in the DAO and the market, but it could be automated and change from Stages 3, 4, and 5 according to the fees the DAO collects

Microdemocracy

Representative democracies in the 21st century are revealing weaknesses as they age. Delegating one's vote to a third party without solid information about their ethics or belief system is unwise. Delegating too much power to an individual or a party naturally leads to corruption as smaller groups advantage themselves above the greater good. The system worked better in the 18th century because social life was much more uniform and enmeshed on a local geographical level. People spent much more time and energy communing and monitoring their neighbors. In developed countries today, it is less likely you will know your neighbors' names, much less their detailed moral stances and political views. Without the ability to hold them to account, representatives are not incentivized to vote for outcomes that reflect the presumptive wishes and needs of their larger constituency, but for promoting the agendas that benefit their personal interests and maintaining their own power.

When we delegate power, it should be given to people or groups that we know and respect, communities we have spent time building without being limited to geographical proximity or ethnic identity. These issues with representative democracy are eliminated with direct democracy.

Voting incentives and outcomes are different under direct democracy. In Ancient Athens, for example, citizens voted on any public issues directly, in the town square. Public issues as significant as whether to go to war or as mundane as where to build the next road would be decided by oral acclamation. Incentives, voting outcomes, and democratic legitimacy are aligned. Democracy is increasingly under threat and needs upgrades. However, information technology determines the limits of effectiveness and scope of any system that uses it.

Ancient Greek direct democracy, using the primitive information technology of the spoken word, was limited to the size of a village. And direct democracy led to significant problems. The loudest and most persuasive people held the most sway. This led to schools devoted to training aristocratic children in manipulative rhetoric, sophistry. To combat such manipulation, competing schools trained children in logical tools for identifying and deconstructing sophistry. And so the Greeks invented analysis and philosophy, to defend their civilization, and themselves, from lies.[14]

---

14 Like any historical story, this one is also a simultaneous simplification and exaggeration. Aristotle referred to other experiments, but the first detailed records of Greek democracy are from Athens, which technically had a representative democracy, though representatives were probably selected randomly using the *kleroterion* (see footnote 162).

Though the word "analysis" is etymologically Greek, the idea is certainly as old as civilization, but probably much older. One of the oldest stories in history is the Babylonian creation myth, *The Enuma Elish*. Committed to writing some 1,500 years before Athenian democracy, the story faithfully recounts the process of modeling, analysis, and synthesis.

The Babylonian god-king Marduk has an array of weapons he uses to confront the threat of chaos, particularly magic words (spells), a magic net, and a magic sword. The chaos monster, Tiamat, is initially represented as the world-circling ocean. Marduk uses his magic words to force Tiamat into the definite form of a dragon that can be grappled with. His magic net then captures the dragon, he chops the captured monster into pieces, and uses those pieces to build the very structure of society and tools for its use.

The magic words that cohere the ocean of chaos into the definite form of a dragon is the first step of the modeling process, that is, choosing the right context. Capturing the dragon with the magic net is the process of establishing the mathematical existence, uniqueness, and stability of solutions to the model. Analysis is the process of dividing or cutting apart the model into its basic elements. Synthesis is the process of forming new structures from these constituent pieces, to gain new forms of control. Finally, the point of repeatedly telling this story is to give us an example to follow, making us confident we can reenact its stages at any time in the future when the chaos monster comes back in a new form. This is extensibility of the model. Cf., Erich Neumann, "The Origins and History of Consciousness," 1954. One of Marduk's many names was "He Who Makes Ingenious Things from Combat with Tiamat."

With the success of direct democracy, groups grew in power and size, beyond the capacity for people to govern by shouting at the *agora*, beyond the limit of how many can fill an amphitheater. As villages grew to cities, direct democracy failed to reflect the will of the group. There is a limit to how many people can speak, even at an amphitheater, because there is a limit to peoples' patience and endurance. To overcome the technological limits of information transmission through shouting, democratic societies devised a system of representative democracy, where a select group of representatives – as many as could convene together physically and communicate – would make decisions on behalf of their larger constituency. People were quite aware of the natural downsides of democratic delegation, such as corruption, bribery, and biases before representative democracy started, but the advantages of the network effects of a larger population were well worth the overhead cost of policing such frictions.

Decentralization disperses concentrated power, delegated power, returning it to the individual members of the network. Contemporary decentralized information technology enables direct democracy at scales larger than our modern national representative democracies. Contemporary technology no longer limits our ability to communicate to the number of people who can fit in a room and patiently wait for their turn to speak. With the advances in information transmission, storage, and especially information processing we can now register our opinions on the smallest matters, store them for asynchronous consideration, and broadcast our responses globally. The power of our individually owned computers, with millions of cycles per second, allows us to process this information using complicated algorithms without relying on a centralized bureaucracy to analyze the information. The limits of our perception make it seem as though our devices can continually post our votes on the most minute concerns. They continually signal where we are, what we are buying, and what our heartrate is. Our devices can signal our will on the most minute matters, creating a new level of direct democracy: *microdemocracy*.

Microdemocracy and proper incentive design can reverse decreasing voter participation that undermines representative democracies. Experimentation with electronic forms of voting allows new forms of allocating votes to prioritize societal issues for each voter.[15] The more important a given societal issue is for a given

---

15 Quadratic voting, for example, allows a first glimpse of the innovations that are possible with microdemocratic systems. In this scenario each voter is periodically allocated a limited number of vote tokens. These tokens may be spent to vote on any issue the voter is concerned with during the period. If you allocate more vote tokens, you have a bigger influence in the outcome than someone who allocates less, signifying the priority you place on the issue. Lalley and Weyl argue the ideal way to count the votes is quadratically. That is, you can spend 1 token for one vote, but 4 of your tokens are needed to register 2 votes, 9 tokens for 3 votes, and so on. They argue this inhibits negative effects that harm other systems. Tyranny of the Majority results from one-person-one-vote schemes, but this is inhibited if one person can register their greater concern by devoting more of their voice on one subject. In this way minorities can override majorities on issues they are most

voter, the more effort or power the voter will allocate to the issue. For example, as more and more people become aware of the climate crisis faced by humanity, they will increasingly allocate their votes on issues that reflect their increasing awareness. Change is realized as people allocate their votes prioritized by their preferences and awareness. Moreover, part of the power of this microdemocratic approach derives from the higher levels of knowledge a given voter has on a particular issue that is evidenced by the voters' proportional attention. It is less likely that voters will engage with issues they know relatively little about. The discovery of the will of the electorate is improved, and previously disenfranchised constituencies are empowered.

Microdemocracies must address the problem of the Tragedy of the Commons. In microdemocratic systems, individual voters act independent of the totality of voters according to their self-interest. Acting for their own self-interest may be contrary to the common good of the group of all voters. Without controls, some self-interested voters may be depleting or spoiling resources they share with the rest of society, such as the environment or public goods. Similarly, majority rule may mean discrimination against the minority. As discussed above, the Tyranny of the Majority happens naturally, and must be policed consciously in a microdemocracy. Perhaps the best way to protect minorities is to make more of them, by promoting the natural diversity of interests in humanity by empowering individuals. To prevent the Tyranny of the Majority, rights protecting minorities must be enshrined in any overarching rules, and protected by nurturing values that respect diversity and individuality.

A key advantage of a microdemocracy is the speed with which it can enact change. In the early 2020s, representative democracies are largely slow and inflexible because their constitutional and legal infrastructure were designed decades or centuries before contemporary information technology was invented. Large-scale political change usually depends on the election of a new government after, typically, around four years. By contrast, microdemocratic voting would provide a more immediate feedback system between voters and their representatives. Because decentralized technology enables the transparent and incorruptible tallying of votes, nearly instantaneously, voting can be more dynamic and incremental and political will can be exercised more directly.

Decentralized technology can improve voting technology in representative democracies. Voting technologies in existing representative democracies were woefully outdated at the beginning of the 21st century. Since the 2000 U.S. presidential

---

concerned with. At the same time, quadratic voting inhibits the Tyranny of the Interested Party, as it limits those with the greater concern on subject from dominating the group, because their megaphone is muffled by the requirement of expending more and more vote tokens to register each new vote.

Steven Lalley & Glen Weyl, "Quadratic Voting: How Mechanism Design Can Radicalize Democracy," *American Economic Association Papers and Proceedings*, 1(1), 2018.

election,[16] which necessitated reexamination of punch holes in paper voting cards, existing voting systems with analog or paper technology have been proven suboptimal. But the problems with existing voting systems do not end with technology. Redistricting or gerrymandering, that is, manipulating the boundaries of a voting district to affect voting outcomes, and other issues such as election financing show that voting and the democratic institutions built to facilitate basic tenets of representative democracies have been under attack and require updates. Decentralized technologies have technological features that can provide solutions. But, such solutions also require political will. For example, voting on a public blockchain that overcomes the trilemma of blockchains (decentralization, scaling, security) may become a core application of the technology. Decentralized technologies have the capacity to change the incentive design for voting, which helps address some of the dangers presented by existing internet voting. And computer security is strong enough to maintain privacy, yet allow transparent, publicly auditable records through ZK proofs, as demonstrated by Bitcoin's $100 billion decentralized protocols.

Decentralized technologies provide inherent microdemocratic features that can help instantiate microdemocratic principles and processes in society. Decentralized technology enables smaller scale democratic decisions for global communities. In the early 21st century, internet platform businesses and social media companies inaugurated new forms of voting. The "Like" button, while deeply flawed in its incentive design and voting-related outcomes, inaugurated a new form of voting on social outcomes and, at the same time, trained the voting public to engage more directly with voting-governed systems. Decentralized technologies create extensions of these forms of more direct democratic votes. Unlike their centralized predecessors, decentralized technologies, for the first time in history, enable improved incentive designs that help overcome the insufficiencies in voting outcomes of representative democracies. As voting pools in decentralized systems increase, deepen, and diversify, they can become supplemental voting systems that help overcome the lack of legitimacy and improve representative democracies.

The printing press taught the people how to read. The internet is teaching people how to write. Decentralized technology will teach people how to vote.

Of course, such upgrades to existing representative democracies will require establishment governmental support – the existing representatives must vote to change the structure that brought them to power – which is dubious. Again, large, decentralized organizations are very stable. It's more likely that organic advances in decentralized networks will make the established institutions irrelevant until they are bypassed and ignored. This is not a problem if we build all the hard-earned social protections into the new decentralized networks. That can only happen if we

---

16 Bush v. Gore, 531 U.S. 98 (2000).

consciously work to protect these historical advances of civilization while promoting the diversity of humanity by empowering individuals.

Summary

The goal of this chapter was to introduce governance design and analyze the consequences of different protocols for promoting the chosen values and goals in any particular DAO. The goal of these solutions is to make it easy to participate for the maximal number and types of users throughout the greatest variation of DAO goals. Users should not need to be technological authorities to navigate the system and add value. In the vast majority of cases, for the vast majority of users, the user interface (UI) will hide all of the details discussed. An intuitive UI can recommend posts and allow users to quickly evaluate post after post, staking varied amounts of their limited reputation in varied degrees of tightly and loosely coupled votes. How the system actually counts the votes and determines the reward structure for references will determine what values and goals are promoted in any particular DAO. Though the reward structures will be openly available for any DAO, the members will soon become experts on how to effectively navigate the system without poring over the technical details, merely from repeated use.

Weighted democracy is crucial for solving the Tragedy of the Commons and Tyranny of the Majority problems. For example, Dr. Craig should have more weight than the average person in the decision on which new math classes to run in the fall at Metropolitan State University. Craig's vote is not equal to your vote, Dear Reader. Similarly, the average Metro State student should have more weight than the average Minnesotan on this issue, but less weight than a math major's vote. Finally, the average American should have more weight than the average South American. In our imagined perfect system, the average South American would still be able to register their opinion about what classes should be offered in Minnesota, as long as they are interested in the subject and willing to stake their reputation to influence the vote in a positive way. But their opinion would have much less power than a professor who works at the school. One-person-one-vote is not the right way to govern on every issue.

This may seem like fantasy, where a global weighted democracy could register such disparate opinions on globally trivial details and filter that information down to meaningful governance, but the technology is already in place. People already curate valuable information on supranational platforms with their reputation. With more than 10 million global users, Stack Overflow is a centralized Web 2.0 company that leverages the power of decentralization through the internet to build knowledge bases for many subjects including computer science and other technical disciplines that is relied on by many practicing experts. Similar to Reddit's reputational system, users' reputation grows in proportion to their contributions through questions, answers, and comments in proportion to others' upvotes and downvotes.

The only thing missing is that the system doesn't share power with their users. Since Stack Overflow and Reddit and Facebook and Twitter and all the other successful social media sites are privately, centrally owned, their governance processes – their algorithms for distributing reputation – are necessarily opaque. This is because the incentives are not properly aligned for their users to police their own reputation against gaming. Some of the idealistic users would certainly try to police the site from sockpuppet accounts and malevolent groups if they were given more power in a transparent system. But the millions who are not financially invested in the system would not have the proper motivation to fight against the few hackers who could exploit the system for profit using the same information technology processing abilities we propose to empower all users with. When it's more profitable to game the system than protect it, the centralized organization needs to keep the underlying protocols opaque to maintain the system's integrity. But that type of centralized regulation is not as dynamic and responsive as a decentralized governance process would be if it empowered its users to develop protocols to fight gaming.

We have the power, now, to track and audit such seemingly trivial choices as what a pseudonymous Bolivian thinks about the class offerings in the math department of a university on another continent. We have the processing power to weight those opinions based on their earned reputation, and to control how they affect the ultimate decisions. We have the computational power to institute sophisticated weighted-democratic governance protocols on a global scale for trivial matters, to fairly and efficiently adjust reputational power to encourage productive cooperation.

Eric Raymond famously said, "Love doesn't scale." He was arguing that capitalism, not socialism, is necessary for giving people the proper economic incentives to keep business working together to supply larger society with the resources necessary to survive. He was referring to how we may behave altruistically toward our family and friends, but when it comes to economic decisions on the global stage, you can't count on a democracy to make decisions that benefit all when local individuals could profit at their expense. One-person-one-vote loses coherence as it scales up to a global democracy.

Love doesn't scale, but reputation does. Weighted democracy, properly measured and aggregated, can scale from valuating expertise on a local level to expertise on global issues. If you find the right balance, if the valuations of reputation tokens between distinct DAOs find the proper equilibrium through market freedom, the various reputations can achieve coherent meaning for making decisions at the global level. The math required is basic arithmetic. The elementary logic is more than 4,000 years old. Contemporary information technology can handle the demands of global decentralized governance. We simply need sufficient investment in transparency and democracy and individual autonomy – in decentralization – to pull it off.

Chapter 8
Finance

Finance is not merely about making money. It's about achieving our deep goals and protecting the fruits of our labor. It's about stewardship and, therefore, about achieving the good society.
–Robert J. Shiller

Decentralized finance (DeFi) has been the goal of blockchains since their inception with Bitcoin. The goal of Web3 is to provide intuitive UIs for complex financial tools, unleashing the economic potential of humanity – similar to how Web 2.0 tapped into the power of decentralized information. The major financial tools that the Web3 crowd is currently developing include payment, investment, trading, lending, and insurance via P2P technology. Ethereum is leading the way in 2020 due to their support of innovative smart contracts, with approximately 3% of their ether tokens (market cap US$26 billion) locked in DeFi smart contracts.

The obvious concern with Web3 enabled DeFi is that the average customer will not be protected without a centralized bureaucracy to maintain order. Since the decentralized economy is currently lacking in many of the protective civil institutions that we enjoy in the larger economy, the average person should not invest anything in the crypto economy. In this chapter we discuss what is emerging and what is missing and what can be done to include more people in the decentralized economy.

Bitcoin transactions proved digital payment could be decentralized. Ethereum proved investment could be decentralized with initial coin offerings (ICOs). These ICOs are analogous to initial public offerings (IPOs), but are open to anyone on the planet who has access to the internet. In other words, ICOs allow anyone to participate in business investment.

The ICO is run by a smart contract that can create any type of business logic. The ICO smart contract creates digital tokens – the coins of the ICO – which represent equity ownership in a DAO. These tokens may be programmed to confer voting power to their owners or any other rights imaginable in the DAO, such as automated profit sharing or control of functions within the company. The ICO smart contract specifies how many tokens can be created and sold, for what price, at what time. Anyone with a public key address in the Ethereum blockchain who satisfies the contract by transferring the required assets at the right time will be given ownership of the DAO equity tokens. ICOs can be programmed with a single line of code with a secure, carefully audited smart contract using ZeppelinOS. The confusion behind legal regulation in various jurisdictions makes it more difficult than that sounds, but in principle, a decentralized process for investing in decentralized companies has been technologically solved.

In the rest of the chapter we explore further financial tools that are needed for the future decentralized economy, including banking, trading marketplaces, insurance and lending, and stablecoins.

https://doi.org/10.1515/9783110673937-008

Banking and ZKRollups

Blockchain transactions will always be expensive compared with other P2P transactions. Blockchain transactions are required to be stored eternally and redundantly on as many machines as possible to aid decentralization. Other P2P transactions, such as distributed hash table transactions can be forgotten, and stored temporarily on a variable number of computers based on how important or valuable the information is.

Therefore, there is a difference of efficiencies that can be exploited to earn a profit by bundling small transactions in temporary storage. Then, once the bundle becomes valuable enough, make a single permanent transaction on the blockchain, which secures all the small transactions at once.

The most obvious application is for currency transactions. This is already done to some degree, opaquely, with centralized companies, such as exchanges. But these have famously lost or stolen many billions of USD. Decentralized exchanges (referred to as DEXs) are possible between separate blockchains with some cryptographically secure tricks starting with atomic swaps, and they're becoming more complicated with the 0x protocol, MakerDAO's smart contract, Plasma on Ethereum, Lightning Network on Bitcoin, etc.

The increase in price efficiency is matched by the increase in speed. Decentralized banking helps solve a major problem with blockchains called scaling. If you double the number of participants and transactions, the linear nature of the blockchain makes the production of blocks slow down by half. To scale up to a global network like the Visa credit card company would make Bitcoin grind to a halt. As of writing, Loopring offers an open source algorithm, which creates a relatively decentralized DEX for cross chain transactions starting on Ethereum. It securely bundles transactions using ZK proofs. This makes the scheme trustless, meaning it doesn't matter whether you trust the bundlers or not, they can't steal your data. The worst that can happen – if some malicious middleman breaks the protocol – is that your transaction doesn't go through and you would need to resend it.

The techie term for this cryptographically secure bundling process is a ZKRollup. A ZKRollup starts on the blockchain (Layer 1) and uses ZK proofs to bundle transactions anonymously using more efficient nonblockchain P2P distributed hash table architectures (Layer 2). Then the ZKRollup distills the extremely complicated bundle and makes a simpler transaction on the blockchain (Layer 1). The Layer 2 calculations are fast (more bandwidth and less latency) but insecure and transient. The Layer 1 transaction secures the transactions making them permanent.

Loopring claims to scale from Ethereum's native 15 transactions per second (TPS) to 160,000 TPS. The Visa network handles 24,000 TPS. However, this is merely the volume of transactions that can happen at this average rate. The bandwidth is 160,000 TPS. The dual concept of latency is the more important measure for user experience.

Latency refers to how long you must wait for your transaction to finalize after you initially transmit the request to the network. These theoretical estimates of 160,000 TPS come with a current theoretical latency of 20 minutes or longer with a claim of theoretical latency of 1 minute if other updates work as promised.

The application that banking most improves, however, is not currency tokens, but reputation tokens. Reputation transactions include voting, resolving a validation pool and distributing the results, the initial minting and staking of the reputation tokens, and the reevaluation of reputation tokens through review. This is done for every single action that is meaningful for generating reputation. The amount of computation that is required is enormous, similar to how a blockchain needs to make hash function calculations for every message sent between every member in the network. In order to maintain consensus in a decentralized network, with no central authority to check in with, a reputational system needs to verify each other's votes extremely redundantly, which leads to substantial overhead costs in computation. It was not possible before the current state of information technology. But banking can make it much more efficient with randomly delegated validation pool judges.

Before such votes are recorded permanently, one or more validation pools could be completely resolved. Since reputation is reviewable, it is more secure from gaming. A few randomly selected DAO members could be entrusted to check each other to bundle reputation transactions, especially on the noncontentious validation pools, since the results should always be nearly unanimous. On contentious issues, such as debates on protocol development, the voting is loosely coupled, so there is no need to access the blockchain.

If protocols like Loopring's can be made truly decentralized, through good governance, it solves one of the major technological obstacles that has been hampering Web3. Currently, ZKRollups have only been deployed to bundle currency transactions, but cryptographers have been improving ZK proofs and can now handle much more complicated logic. The goal is to bundle general smart contracts. In the meantime, banking schemes are handling general smart contracts without cryptographically securing them, by using game theoretical incentivization to encourage people to honestly bundle general smart contracts. Incentivization boils down to a reputation mechanism, where at bottom, the bundler stakes money, which is slashed if they are proven to be dishonest. Uniswap is an example.

But liquidity has always been a problem in decentralized exchanges, as meaningful history and reputation are difficult to achieve when there is little to no governance structure, no insurance, no appeals process, and no reputable decentralized news service to help you evaluate the health of any DAO. In particular, people are used to the security that traditional central banks provide, such as fraud protection. Decentralizing these features requires new architectures for decentralized insurance, which we explore in the next section. Once such overhead processes are instituted and more complicated transactions such as bank bundling are instituted, these decentralized exchanges will become more practically (instead of just theoretically) efficient and secure.

Underwriting: Insurance and Lending

Insurance is essential for every type of business transaction, every type of property, every type of service you engage – every type of economic action is made more efficient when decisions are hedged, so we can be more confident in our investments in the future. We require the trust that the transactions will finalize satisfactorily as planned or that the contract will be made whole by the platform running the marketplace. Decentralized insurance requires networks of policy writers with individual reputations for efficient underwriting of every type of transaction.

Insurance is an essential industry for the modern economy. Like the appeals process of the law, like policing, like the effort to keep track of reputation and maintain the protocols of governance, insurance is an overhead cost that does not directly generate profit. It's a type of business cost that any efficiency-minded engineer would prefer to eliminate entirely. But since we can't predict the future, insurance is valuable. Insurance improves the efficiency of the economy by investing in the future, to guarantee the system will continue running, despite inevitable unforeseen problems. Insurance mitigates risk. Insurance helps people overcome their fear of joining a transaction because of the risk of loss. In physics jargon, insurance is a catalyst, which provides activation energy for a transaction.

It is claimed that insurance has been practiced since the foundation of civilization.[1] Evidence from Mesopotamia suggests Mediterranean sailing merchants used bottomage. An agent would take a loan to fund their voyages and would promise to return the loan with interest if successful. Bottomage is an extra amount included in the interest. The normal interest rate was limited to 20% if the borrower had collateral (such as the promise to enslave his family for three years). Without collateral, the bottomage rate was 100% with an unlimited loan time. Under bottomage, if the shipment was stolen or lost at sea, the lender promised to cancel the loan. The Code of Hammurabi, c. 1754 BC, obliquely refers to this in three laws, #103, #106, #107.

The new tools of information technology give us the opportunity to improve the efficiency and stability of underwriting through transparency and decentralization. But how do we ensure privacy in a decentralized environment? As mentioned above in Chapter 2, zero knowledge proofs allow individuals to retain privacy over their

---

1 Charles Farley Trenerry, *The Origin and Early History of Insurance: Including the Contract of Bottomry*, P.S. King and Son, Ltd., p. 6, 1926.

information while revealing some facts. For example, a DAO devoted to healthcare insurance could give members a synthesized health score from 0 to 100. The protocol for synthesizing your complex health history could be public, but your particular health history would stay private while you reveal only your final health score to the insurance DAO. For greater privacy and security, even that number could be mixed with other information, such as parts of your property that would be tokenized and insured.

Tokenization

Early Underwriting DAOs likely will be for tokenization of commodities and properties. Tokenization is the use of digital tokens to represent the ownership of physical assets. For example, you can create an Ethereum token to represent a barrel of oil. We can then engage a smart contract anonymously where a person can pay money for the token. The smart contract can be trusted to execute precisely as programmed, acting as an automated escrow service to guarantee the money is traded for the token representing the oil.

However, the basic problem of tokenization is to determine whether a token that claims to represent ownership of an asset truly does. Does the oil exist? Does the person selling the token actually own the oil? Does giving you the token mean you can actually make legal claim on the oil? Anyone can mint 100 billion tokens and put a label on them, claiming they represent property on the moon. Tokenization doesn't mean anything without something to back it up. A token's meaning must be attested by something substantial. It must be *underwritten* by someone who is putting their reputation – and ultimately their money – on the line to assert the validity of the token.

Consider the history of financial innovation when gold coins first replaced the barter economy. The use of gold to represent value led to major leaps in economic efficiency. First, you didn't need to bring your chickens directly to me to trade them for my labor. Second, the contract was much clearer – it was complete when money changed hands. Third, it allowed a separation of the business contracts – money traded for chickens was separate from money traded for labor. Fourth, contracts could be fractionalized – you couldn't trade a fraction of a chicken so easily as you could gold. Later paper money replaced gold coins, so you didn't need to carry the heavy gold or expertly assay its quality. Around 50 years ago fiat cash replaced gold-backed specie, so you didn't need the gold at all, and nations gained a new tool for regulating their economies. Then digital money replaced paper cash allowing light-speed transactions over global distances.

Now tokenization allows an increase in efficiency by digitizing commodities and properties for direct sale, while also enabling fractionalization. Further, smart contracts allow us to instantiate any imaginative legal arrangement for partial ownership and rights to properties or assets. For example, transparent public timeshares – for houses or cars or any other physical object – can stipulate any behaviors the owners or renters choose, with self-executing and self-regulating contracts. You can even tokenize your personal space, selling the right to advertise on your social media account or selling your place in line on a carnival ride.

Tokenization will be crucial for IoT applications, which requires decentralized marketplaces as neutral territory for all the various owners within the supply chain, as discussed further below.

Chit Fund Example

Another important application of underwriting is lending. An important market for decentralized underwriting is microloans and simple insurance in markets with little regulation, as is often the case in developing countries. Similar to how Web 2.0 capitalized on untapped decentralized market information, Web3 will capitalize on untapped economic potential by decentralizing marketplaces, which all will require underwriting. Craig's students, Mounvi Morthala and Sai Amulya Gandham, are developing transparent, decentralized lending schemes based on chit funds, which are common in India and have been used for centuries to provide a relatively decentralized mechanism for insurance and lending.

Chit funds are only "relatively" decentralized, because they are traditionally run with opaque centralized control from "foremen," individuals who rely on their informal personal reputation in the community and charge roughly 5% commission for managing the fund. The principles of transparent decentralized underwriting, using the scheme we present below, has the potential to make such chit fund schemes more efficient and secure.

A basic chit fund example is as follows. Suppose 100 people agree to invest $20 in the fund every month for 100 months. Each month an auction takes place, where the members can bid to receive a fraction of the current total chit fund. The lowest bid wins. Once you win an auction, you can't win another, but you are still required to add your $20 each month until the end.

The idea is that $2,000 enters each month for 100 months. For $20 entry you can withdraw almost $2,000 in the first few months, if you bid lowest. If you wait longer, the early bids will typically be lower than $2,000, so the fund will hold more than $2,000 and will continue to grow as fewer people can bid each month. Early withdrawal is like taking a loan that is repaid for 100 months with interest, later withdrawal is like a bank deposit that earns interest.

Web3 technology can greatly improve the efficiency and security of the scheme. First, smart contracts replace the foremen and their 5% commission, eliminating the risk of a foreman absconding with the fund. Officially sanctioned chit funds are run through banks, as in Kerala, India, adding overhead through regulation and audits. Further, if they implement a reputational system, honest participation can be tracked across many different chit funds, as people will earn reputation each time they pay their required monthly fee. The more often they participate honestly, the larger their reputation will grow. Then participation in larger and more complex chit funds can be dependent on reputation, which will incentivize healthy collaboration. It will come as no surprise that one of the major overheads making this scheme less efficient is members defaulting on paying the premia. It's been estimated that 35% of chit fund subscribers have defaulted at least once recently and 24% have defaulted after winning an auction.[2]

All things being equal, larger groups dilute the risk of individual default. A chit fund with a large number of people with high reputation can pay small premia for insurance. One million people investing $1 daily for 50 years allows 50 people per day to immediately begin taking an average payout of roughly $20,000. More investors investing smaller amounts in shorter increments, means more people can withdraw at any point. By monitoring and analyzing the performance of a fund, programs can suggest values that can be withdrawn at any given time. By automatically bidding when the fund rises above expected levels, the fund can be stabilized to give predictable returns – especially if multiple funds are connected.

With no initial reserve backing, this allows people to bootstrap their way to greater financial security and stability, assuming the reputation system is sufficiently strong to guarantee a low percentage of defaults. Further efficiency improving mechanisms are mentioned below when we discuss a more general architecture for underwriting.

Like other overhead costs (the appeals process, policing, etc.), insurance is cheaper when the system is running well. The more automated the decentralized economy becomes, for example, with code-is-law smart contracts, the less insurance is required. The purpose of insurance is to decentralize risk. Ideally the risk would be decentralized perfectly and then the need for ensuring individual transactions would disappear. Given that no system will ever be perfect, insurance will always be essential. But by implementing the new tools of information technology and the new architectures of P2P distributed computing, we can create more effectively decentralized organizations. Decentralizing risk makes insurance more stable and efficient, which improves the economy.

Decentralized Architecture

The following model for the Underwriting DAO[3] consists of a network of underwriters, who roughly correspond to the shareholders of an insurance company.

---

2 Preethi Rao, Sharan Buteau, "Modelling Credit and Savings Behaviour of Chit Fund Participants," *Gates Open Research*, 2(26), 2018.
3 Craig Calcaterra, Wulf A. Kaal, Vadhindran K. Rao, "Decentralized Underwriting," May 30, 2019. Available at https://papers.ssrn.com/sol3/papers.cfm?abstract_id=3396542 (retrieved 6/30/20).

These underwriters each hold a certain number of reputation tokens in the DAO, which correspond to their experience and skill as insurance agents. An agent's reputation tokens are likely to increase over time only if the agent follows sound and successful underwriting practices.

The inductive argument for building a reputation architecture gives us insights on what is necessary to create an Underwriting DAO. How do we create the proper incentives for organizing a group competing to gain money? How do we develop a legislative governance process to continuously improve standards to protect an organization from gaming and corruption and innovate in response to new market threats and opportunities? Can we do this while preventing the competitive forces from naturally centralizing the system?

Again, secure and meaningful reputation is key. Reputation needs to be grounded to be meaningful, so reputation tokens should only be minted when fees (policy premia) enter the group. Reputation should dictate power in the group. So, reputation should determine how the fees are shared, through reputation-weighted salaries. And reputation should be staked in reputation-weighted democratic validation pools to transparently establish consensus within the DAO, to police every member's contributions, to settle debates on new protocols.

Reputation tokens serve multiple purposes:

1. **Reputation determines membership.** Only token holders can participate in underwriting insurance policies. Policies may be underwritten either singly or jointly by these agents. New business is attracted by token holders' sales initiative, or else it is attracted by the fame of the DAO – in which case underwriters can be randomly assigned based on reputation weight, or members can bid on the policy, etc.

2. **Reputation-weighted salaries.** Tokens serve as claims on the future cash flows generated by the DAO. Insurance premia collected by the DAO are distributed among the token holders in proportion to their token holdings. It is worth emphasizing that the premium from a policy is not considered the revenue solely of the underwriters. Instead, premia are treated as the revenue of the entire DAO and shared among the DAO participants. Thus, the value of the tokens is a function of the expected future cash flows of the DAO.

3. **Underwriting builds reputation.** Agents who underwrite policies by staking their reputation tokens are rewarded with a certain number of newly minted reputation tokens (as discussed in chapters 4 and 6, the amount of reward depends on the current goals of the DAO). Thus, the total number of tokens grows over time. This implies that "passive" agents who hold the tokens purely to receive a share of future premia will find their proportional ownership in the DAO decrease over time. Their income may however still increase if the overall revenues of the DAO grow at a sufficiently increasing pace. Therefore, the effect of the design is to incentivize agents to play an active role by participating in

underwriting activities and thereby grow the business, while still allowing passive investors to derive income and speculate on growth.

4. **Reputation collateralized against risk.** Underwriters "stake" or "encumber" an appropriate number of tokens against each policy they underwrite. These tokens in effect serve to secure the promises of the underwriters. The number of tokens to be encumbered is based on a preset formula with the objective of ensuring that the value of the encumbered tokens is sufficient to meet any claims that may arise at any point in the life of the policy. Such encumbered tokens continue to remain under the ownership of the respective agents and entitle the owners to receive their share of future premia. In case there is no claim on the policy, the tokens are "freed up" or become "unencumbered" when the policy matures. In case the insured event was to occur during the life of the policy, the agents who underwrote the policy would lose control of their encumbered tokens, which would be sold at auction to meet the claim. If the auction does not result in sufficient currency to meet the claim, sufficient new tokens are minted and sold to satisfy the claim. All current DAO participants (especially the policy writer) as well as outsiders interested in joining the DAO may bid for the tokens in this auction.

To initiate the Underwriting DAO, to prime the pump, the first reputation tokens would be minted and distributed to members who encumbered money in a smart contract analogous to the capital holdings of an insurance company. Once the DAO is running at equilibrium, with numerous policies bringing in regular premia, the reputation tokens will gain measurable value as measured by the market, and the capital reserve holdings can be diminished or eliminated.

We would consider the need to mint more reputation tokens to meet a policy claim to be a breach. Under what circumstances would a breach occur? It would occur only if the market values the encumbered reputation tokens as less than the payout. This would happen under two broad scenarios. First, the DAO might accept a general practice allowing agents to write policies with less than full backing, to attract more profits from premia while sharing the risk. Then the whole DAO shares the risk that their reputation tokens will diminish in value because more tokens are minted. This would necessitate more strict protocols for the types of policies the Underwriting DAO writes, and careful policing of which customers were accepted. In addition, if the DAO's protocols require all policies to be fully backed, the only reason for a breach would be because the reputation tokens' initial valuation diminished before the payout. In general, our models suggest this will happen only if there is a dramatic shift in the future prospects of the DAO, such as a sharp decrease in expected future revenues or a sharp increase in expected payments on outstanding policies.

The Underwriting DAO structure can be used by traditional insurance companies as well as niche players specializing in a narrow range of specialty policies.

A blockchain-based DAO has the potential to take mutualization of risk to a whole new level of aggregation and efficiency. One may even speculate on the possibility of a nonprofit version that insures its members against various specified risks. Possible examples range from device protection for individuals to long-term-care insurance for retirees to health insurance for an entire country.

By decentralizing risk, insurers as well as consumers can enjoy the benefits of transparency, efficiency, and greater stability. An Underwriting DAO not only has the potential to lower capital requirements for insurance, but also to broaden and deepen the market for such capital as any individual or corporate entity can partici-pate in the DAO. The particular design outlined above facilitates the entry of new players to the insurance market. Such participants could buy tokens when they come up for auction, and then use these tokens to participate in underwriting, or else just hold the tokens as a passive investment. Decentralization taps into infor-mation at the edge. Individuals with more fine-grained information about their neighbors and community can make better underwriting decisions than a central-ized hierarchy can. This diversification decentralizes the market, making it more liquid, more efficient, and more profitable.

The design allows for collaboration among DAO underwriters as well as be-tween underwriters and consumers. The need to trust is minimized by appropri-ately designed economic incentives, which allows pseudonymous participation, thanks to the greater value of meaningful, auditable reputation. The governance rules of the DAO can be set up to ensure that minority token holders are appropri-ately protected. The rules can ensure that the proportion of policies written by an agent in the long run is commensurate with the proportion of the agent's token holdings.

Bad business decisions by one underwriter need not impact the other under-writers or the DAO. If a certain underwriter makes the mistake of underestimating the risk of the insured event, the losses will be suffered purely by the underwriter as long as the value of the staked or encumbered tokens covers the claim. Policing this quantity of encumbered tokens is the responsibility of the entire DAO. All members of the DAO are incentivized to develop successful protocols through good gover-nance in order to protect the value of their reputation, which is continually revalued each time a claim occurs and the market determines the price of a reputation token. As far as consumers are concerned, potential claims are fully backed or secured by the entire DAO.

In the case of traditional insurance companies, whether the company is solvent and can meet its obligations depends on the safety and soundness of its invest-ments; whereas in the case of a DAO, this depends only on the safety and sound-ness of the DAO itself. The advantage of a blockchain-based system is that the latter information would be transparently auditable by everyone.

In this decentralized system, the tokens essentially substitute for reputation. Even if the underwriters of a particular policy were to breach the contract, the auction of the encumbered tokens and the sale of additional tokens as needed, ensures that the policy holder's claim is fully met. Thus, what we are referring to as a breach on a particular insurance contract does not necessarily imply any losses for the consumer as long as the entire DAO is more valuable than the individual customer's claim. A breach leads to no losses for other members of the DAO, as long as the encumbered tokens match the payout of the claim.

The structure of incentives embedded in this design has the potential to substantially lower capital requirements and the related need for capital regulation in the insurance industry. We note that the burden of maintaining sufficient liquidity in order to meet claims is not on the DAO, but rather is distributed among the individual underwriters that make up the DAO. Each underwriter would of course need to maintain sufficient liquidity and economic capital in order to be able to reclaim tokens as and when claims occur. However, it is possible under certain conditions that the total amount of capital that these agents will collectively hold is lower under this design than if the burden of meeting the liability were to be on a traditional insurance firm, which has more centralized risk.

This result is based on the premise that the amount of capital each underwriter will hold will be based on the risk of the underwriter's overall portfolio. The overall portfolio of an individual underwriter, especially a nontraditional one, may benefit from the addition of underwriting due to diversification, as attested to some extent by the existence of insurance-linked securities such as catastrophe bonds.

As a result, the sum of the incremental VaRs (Value at Risk amounts) of the individual underwriters may be less than the VaR of an insurance firm that has underwritten the same contracts. More importantly, how much capital an underwriter holds is a matter of their personal risk preference. An underwriter who is willing to tolerate fluctuations in their token holdings need only provide for expected losses. The key point is this: from the viewpoint of consumers and regulators, the encumbered tokens (which as we know derive their value from the DAO's future cash flows) essentially serve as a substitute for capital. Financial distress or bankruptcy of an individual underwriter does not have to affect either consumers or the DAO. As mentioned previously, in case of a breach on a particular contract, the policy holder's claim can still be met by an auction of the encumbered tokens. Additional resources, if required, can be raised by minting new tokens. Barring highly adverse market conditions, the availability of "capital on tap" protects the DAO from default and bankruptcy. Thus, the design has the potential to greatly simplify and strengthen capital regulation.

In sum, the larger the network of Underwriting DAO members, the more distributed and decentralized the risk can be spread, making the system more efficient and stable. This makes the economy more predictable, efficient, and prosperous.

Trading Markets

> From the time I first understood economic principles, I was always concerned also that any system be operated on an efficient basis, which meant decentralization because knowledge is not concentrated anywhere. It's based on motivation, and so these are . . . the cautious case for capitalism, that the market system is efficient.
>
> –Kenneth Arrow, *Interview with the Federal Reserve Bank of Minneapolis*, December 1, 1995.[4]

General Principles

Decentralization and bureaucratic transparency are essential to the efficient operation of marketplaces.

The liquidity of a market depends on how quickly its assets can be sold and how much prices change when they are sold. A market's depth is how much can be bought and sold at any given moment. A market can only remain liquid under various conditions if it is also deep. The efficiency of price discovery characterizes a market's liquidity. Liquid markets are more efficient and stable. Business on a liquid market is less risky and more profitable.

All things being equal, larger, decentralized, transparent markets are more efficient. The larger the market, the deeper it is, and the more liquid it becomes. Second, the more autonomous the members of the market are, the more they will have divergent interests and desires, which improves the market's liquidity. Concentration of power (especially monopolies or trusts) decreases liquidity; decentralization of power improves liquidity. Another obvious disadvantage of a centralized market is the overhead that a central authority charges; in a decentralized market the members police themselves. Third, the more transparent the statistics of the market's transactions is, the better it is for price discovery, which improves the market's liquidity. The more liquid a market is, the more transparent it is, the more open it is, the closer it becomes to what is technically called "perfect."

Therefore, markets become more efficient, more profitable, and less risky when they achieve greater power decentralization, greater transparency, and more open membership. The foundational values of Web3 are the basic principles that improve an economy.

However, greater transparency is at odds with more open membership, because larger networks are only achieved when privacy is ensured. Privacy and power over your own personal information need to be prime values for development, but this is generally achieved at the expense of transparency and efficient price discovery. Further, anonymity is a threat to many market schemes, such as the chit fund example

---

4 https://www.minneapolisfed.org/article/1995/interview-with-kenneth-arrow (retrieved 6/23/20).

discussed above. Reputation and sophisticated ZK proof protocols can help to address this tension. Pseudonymous wallets held by private keys can encumber reputation tokens in such a way that they are staked and can be automatically slashed if violations are provably committed. Statistics on transactions can be revealed with ZK proofs without revealing information from the individual transactions.

Web3 has achieved the technology required to build liquid decentralized markets, with smart contracts and cryptography. The most primitive approach is to have a network engaging smart contracts with offers to sell at different prices and buy at different prices. Whenever there are two smart contracts that cross (buyer offering higher than the seller is demanding), the next block producer combines the contracts and completes them in the block and collects the difference. Those differences are the reward for maintaining the network, shared with everyone owning reputation tokens. These smart contracts can be active as long as required before a coincidence of wants is found. The owners can put limits on their validity, so they self-destruct after a short, set time, then update the contract as they observe the market.

The decentralized market is the most efficient mechanism for price discovery. Price discovery determines the price of an asset but also the ideal quantity the economy needs and the ideal levels and types of services the economy needs. The market finds the right equilibrium between all the industries and companies to determine how much of each work and good is required to keep civilization running efficiently.

The Basic Financial Markets

The basic financial assets are currencies (foreign exchange, or Forex), commodities, equities, securities, and derivatives.

We mentioned decentralized Forex above with DEXs (P2P decentralized cryptocurrency exchanges), such as the 0x protocol, MakerDAO's smart contract, Plasma on Ethereum, and the Lightning Network on Bitcoin. Many other protocols are competing to take part in the crypto economy. DEXs epitomize market decentralization because they allow users to interact and trade anonymously in a secure environment without the need for third party intermediation.

In a DEX, proprietary trading intermediaries, such as market makers and centralized third-party operators, cannot inject themselves in a transaction. As a result, conflicts and counterparty risks are absent in a DEX. Moreover, the fee structure in a DEX is different from a centralized cryptocurrency exchange, which typically charges a percent of the total value of the transaction. Instead, on a DEX, the users pay a fee as gas (Ethereum's fee for motivating the network's nodes to add your transaction), more akin to a per-trade fee, which is a fraction of the percentage charged per transaction on centralized cryptocurrency exchanges. Because a DEX does not centralize authority over users' assets, users can sign and start trading anonymously, that is, without identity verification. Centralized cryptocurrency exchanges struggle keeping up with know-your-customer and anti-money laundering rules. Nevertheless, most DEXs have been struggling with liquidity and price discovery.

Orders on a DEX are matched and settled through the operational rules provided by the code. Unlike central order books on centralized exchanges and the settlement back office that facilitates the finalization of a trade, on a DEX, the code facilitates the P2P exchange without the involvement of any intermediary.

Despite many of the benefits that derive from its decentralized exchange model, DEXs may not be able to ensure market integrity. Just like centralized cryptocurrency exchanges provide certain traders with benefits that may provide them with advantages at the expense of other traders, the code that creates a DEX may also allow the asymmetric distribution of trading information based on user status.[5] The code may also create new risks to market integrity because of its automation and lack of a human backstop in compliance, back office, and settlement. Wash trading, frontrunning, and insider trading are risks to market integrity that can materialize on a DEX, among other price-manipulation practices. Again, regulation and governance are crucial to the future of the decentralized economy.

The next assets to consider are commodities. To make decentralized commodities markets, the key is tokenization. This was explained above, where we argued underwriting is necessary to give tokenized commodities and properties meaning and value. Tokenization is technologically achievable on Ethereum with standard ERC-20 and ERC-721 tokens. But such tokens don't hold value without secure reputation and transparent history.

The next assets to analyze are equities. An equity is a token of ownership in a company, such as a stock. ICOs, as introduced by Ethereum, prove we have the technological tools to cheaply create and sell decentralized stocks in a company, called ERC-20[6] tokens. These tokens can give their owners more practical powers than traditional stocks. Due to their smart contract functionality, any imaginable business transaction can be programmed, with the token being used as proof of ownership.

The ICO market peaked from March 2018 to June 2018. The percentage of ICOs in relation to total fundraising of blockchain startups dropped from 80% to around 35% in August 2018 and only marginally recovered between September 2018 and February 2019 at around 40% to 50% before dropping to 20% in March 2019. From March 2017 to June 2018, ICOs were the overwhelmingly dominant fundraising tool for the blockchain industry. The demise of the ICO market turned the overall trend away from ICO funding to traditional venture funding in the blockchain industry.

---

5 Barbara Underwood, "Virtual Markets: Integrity Report," Office of the New York State Attorney General, September 18, 2018, https://virtualmarkets.ag.ny.gov/ (retrieved 6/1/20).
6 Ethereum has a primitive governance system for coordinating updates in its codebase. One element is their public ERC proposals. ERC stands for Ethereum Request for Comment, and 20 is the proposal identifier.

The emergence of the ICO market changed the market for venture funding. In the traditional venture capital model, venture capital funds invest significant amounts of money in the hope of finding the next unicorn start-up. This investment process is subject to long, complex, and time intensive processes leading up to a late liquidity event in the form of an IPO or acquisition. By contrast, ICOs provide liquidity to investors much faster and allow venture capital funds to capitalize on existing profits early. Venture capital funds which invest in crypto start-ups gain access to much earlier liquidity via ICOs by converting their cryptocurrency profits into Bitcoin or Ether through any of the cryptocurrency exchanges and can thereafter transfer into fiat currencies via online services such as Coins-Bank or Coinbase. During the ICO boom years, the venture capital market in the decentralized technology sector ground to a halt. In the aftermath of the ICO boom and collapse, traditional venture funding has become, again, the predominant model for funding blockchain startups.

Market decentralization via ICOs and other decentralized funding methods has significant disruptive effects on finance. ICOs provide lower barriers to entry for a more diverse body of investors and thus increase the diversity and the heterogeneity of start-up funding. Through borderless online sales, ICOs are directly marketed to a worldwide potential pool of investors, bypassing the typical legal, jurisdictional, and business hurdles in traditional venture capital financing. Moreover, ICOs benefit from limited accreditation standards, as well as from multiple global cryptocurrency exchanges that provide continuous access to trading. ICO promoters and their developers are not forced to sacrifice their equity in the project in exchange for the funds they raised.

The next type of financial market to consider is securities, which are other financial instruments that make some guarantee to pay off money in the future, such as bonds or annuities. Smart contracting allows us to create decentralized transparently auditable securities with extremely complex business logic.

The final type of asset is a derivative. They are called this because they are second-order contracts, such as options, which give people the right to buy (a "call") or sell (a "put") another financial asset in the future. By managing risk, futures stabilize the market, improving its liquidity and efficiency. Traditional markets hold perhaps US$1 quadrillion in derivatives. Therefore, this is a rather important target for DeFi development. There is a great multiplicity of possible traditional futures contracts that use complicated business logic, so it would seem to be the ideal application for self-executing smart contracts. However, there is not much liquidity in decentralized derivative exchanges. At three years old, and functional for much less than that, the Augur DAO is one of the older decentralized options. There are other protocols, such as Opyn on the Uniswap DEX.

At the time of writing, the market for decentralized options is extremely shallow – especially considering how turbulent the other decentralized financial asset markets are. The problem, again, is reputation. In order to guarantee liquidity, someone who wishes to sell a call option is required to actually own the asset, since there is unlimited potential for growth. In other words, the inability to trust the platform or the anonymous users currently requires these decentralized derivatives to be capitalized at least 100%, which would be impossibly onerous in traditional markets. We will discuss this problem again, below, as a major flaw in today's stablecoins, and again suggest the solution demands more sophisticated reputation and history.

Regulation

The anarchist and libertarian philosophy that informs most Web3 developers' public pronouncements has led to an antiregulation fervor that is damaging the potential for widespread adoption of decentralized P2P tools.

Securities commissions in every major market (such as the SEC in the US, the ECMS in the EU, and the CSRC in the PRC) were ostensibly created to protect investors from patterns of bad business that naturally arise when creating and trading equities and other assets. However, these centralized bureaucracies are slow to update their regulations, which means these regulations often hurt the very people they were designed to help. The average citizen is not capable of benefitting from the power of many financial derivatives, for example, because safeguards from the SEC require million-dollar outlays. But the SEC provides many systems that improve the market and protect basic consumers, which the crypto economy is currently lacking.

The charge of every securities commission in every major nation is to protect the average small investor from predatory groups, by ensuring transparency and good accounting and business practices. As such they have a duty, both professional and moral, to do everything in their power to prevent Web3 technologies, which are used for rent-seeking, insider trading, and outright digital theft. Bitcoin.com has estimated that more than US$3 billion worth of cryptocurrency was stolen in 2018 alone.[7] Much of this was never retrieved, partly because the regulatory agencies are not up to date on the new technology.

At the same time any project that matches or exceeds traditional standards for transparency in accounting and good business practices should be encouraged. Truly decentralized projects that surpass traditional regulatory standards have the potential for improving our economy and revitalizing our society. Any nation that stifles innovation that improves the status of its citizens and increases their opportunities doesn't deserve the mandate of governance it is given by its people. If it doesn't update to match the challenge of these new technologies and architectures, the SEC will no longer be deserving of its charge.

---

7 https://news.bitcoin.com/9-million-day-lost-cryptocurrency-scams/ (retrieved 7/20/20).

Standards for transparency and external audits of equities should be natural additions to the decentralized economy, and Web3 developers should welcome them. Open source protections for consumers gives individuals more power, making them more autonomous, making the network more decentralized.

It is, however, not possible to create a centralized organization, such as the SEC, for regulating the decentralized economy. Submitting to such regulatory power would place the supranational decentralized market under competing jurisdictions, which naturally have contradictory regulations. Submitting to centralized regulatory control limits the network to members from a single jurisdiction, which would limit the network effect, making the market less liquid, less efficient, and less profitable.

Dynamic standards under decentralized control are necessary. Both the SEC and Web3 need to change. Again, effective decentralized governance and a genuine bureaucratic transparency are crucial.

Stablecoins

All money is a matter of belief.

–Adam Smith

What is a stablecoin? What makes them crucial for the decentralized economy? How are they built? What is missing?

A stablecoin is a cryptocurrency token from a blockchain that is designed to maintain its value, instead of rising and falling under temporary market changes. Stablecoins distinguish themselves from other digital money, like bitcoin and ether, whose value fluctuates strongly in response to changes in market demand, switching between the need for cash or investments.

Stability is an obsession in this book. Stable motion, liquidity, is the most efficient state of the economy. A liquid market rapidly matches the "coincidences of wants" necessary to form business deals, so people can cooperate and trade to meet their needs and desires. Stability is necessary to make good predictions so that your investments in the future are more successful.

A currency that maintains a stable store of value is more efficient for an economy than one that does not. The US dollar (similar to every other national fiat currency) is managed by the U.S. Federal Reserve in order to maintain a steady and predictable value in the long run. Since 2002, their stated target is 2% annual inflation. The value of a dollar is determined by comparing what a basket of goods costs, year to year, in many different locations. The "basket of goods" are typically commodities, such as oil or minerals or grains, which have a relatively constant supply and demand.

Bitcoin and other cryptocurrencies are extremely volatile compared with almost every form of national fiat currency. This is natural, since the value of cryptocurrencies is almost entirely due to speculation on their future usefulness in the currently nonexistent decentralized economy. If bitcoin ever does become widely adopted and used, however, its price will likely not completely stabilize. The total quantity of Bitcoin is capped at 21 million tokens. This means, like gold, its value will change depending on the market demand. The demand will change whenever the trends change for people's economic behavior. More use of the currency, through more transactions, and more savings, generally increase the demand for the currency, which raises its value, due to its scarcity.

Currency with price volatility on the order of gold, is not a good choice for a currency. Without stablecoins, typical consumers should never hold their checking account in the currency. No one should ever make a long-term contract for any essential service in bitcoin. Neither the renter nor the landlord should sign a contract if its value might halve or double in any given month. Renegotiating contracts each time the value of a currency changes is inefficient, and continually punishes one of the parties. The economy should not be founded on gambling, so any future decentralized economy requires stable cryptocurrencies.

Since their inception in 2014 with Tether, stable cryptocurrencies have primarily been used as a cash equivalent for cryptocurrency portfolios. They are used as a safe harbor to weather the volatility in digital assets. By 2019, stable cryptocurrencies grew substantially in popularity as an answer to the high volatility associated with the cryptocurrency markets. Depending on their design, they can offer additional features, such as transparency, privacy, and increased decentralization. Stable cryptocurrencies can also offer lower fees and faster transaction speeds, making them rather useful for international transactions and everyday payments.

However, today's cryptocurrencies are still in their infancy, and offer very few of these features. The largest stablecoin platform is Tether (USDT), which pegs its value to the USD. As of June 2020, Tether holds 85% of the US$10 billion market share of stablecoins.

In 2014, Robert Sams introduced the first attempt at creating a stability mechanism for cryptocurrencies.[8] In 2020, the leading notable stable cryptocurrency start-ups and their respective approaches include: Tether, Coinbase, MakerDAO's DAI, and many, many others. They all naturally have flaws, but give useful tools for today's crypto speculators. We criticize their design and identify areas for improvement in this section.

---

8 Robert Sams, *A Note on Cryptocurrency Stabilisation: Seigniorage Shares*, BRAVE NEWCOIN, Apri 28, 2015, https://assets.ctfassets.net/sdlntm3tthp6/resource-assetr390/5a940afb21681d19c0b3b76 cf69259e1/58ebe9e2-1f28-4a8d-8ce1-26abef07aedf.pdf

Basic Design

Design architectures fall into two broad categories, for example, collateralized and uncollateralized mechanisms. Both are subject to downsides. Collateralized projects use either fiat currencies or cryptocurrencies as reserve backing. The function of the collateral is as follows.

Imagine a stablecoin DAO that mints a cryptocurrency token and pegs its value to the USD. The idea is that the token can be sold in a public exchange, and the value is kept at one token for $1. Whenever the price of the token goes up, the smart-contract-automated mechanism mints more of the tokens and sells them on the exchange. This brings the price down to $1. Whenever the price drops below $1, the algorithm buys tokens on the exchange and deletes ("burns") them, which raises their price back to $1, according to the Quantity Theory of Money.

Fundamental to this scheme is that the DAO needs to hold a reserve of foreign assets, collateral, such as fiat currencies (dollars, euros, yen . . .) or cryptocurrencies (bitcoin, ether . . .). This collateral is sold when the price is low and is bought with the newly minted tokens when the price of the tokens is high. When running properly, this mechanism actually makes money while maintaining the stablecoin's stability.

Unfortunately, fiat currency collateralization is expensive and inefficient, and no stablecoin can currently compete with traditional currencies and services. The basic problem is that the reserve is expensive to maintain. Because of the threat of the Soros attack, all the major cryptocurrency platforms have publicly committed to maintaining reserves, which back their coins 100%. If there are $1 billion worth of coins in the public, they promise to maintain a reserve equivalent to US$1 billion in some banks. To see why this is necessary let's discuss the basic idea behind the Soros attack[9] simplified as follows.

Imagine the Bank of England institutes a policy of maintaining a peg of one British pound artificially high, equal to $2. But the market sees the true value as $1 - per pound. The Bank of England maintains a reserve of foreign currency worth $10 billion to keep the peg at $2 to 1 pound. Under these conditions George Soros would arbitrage the system as follows:

1. Take out a loan for $10 billion in pounds.
2. Sell $10 billion of the pounds at $1.99 per pound, so that the bank of England pays George almost $10 billion to maintain the peg at $2.

---

9 The Soros Attack is named after investor George Soros because of his role in Black Wednesday, which occurred September 16, 1992. Soros believed the British pound sterling was overvalued based partly on low interest rates and high inflation and so built a large short position and initiated the attack described in this section. The British government failed to maintain its peg and was forced to withdraw from the European Exchange Rate Mechanism. The British government lost over £3.3 billion sterling, while Soros profited more than £1 billion. Matthew Tempest, "Treasury Papers Reveal Cost of Black Wednesday," *The Guardian*, London, UK, February 9, 2005.

3. Now the reserve is depleted, the Bank of England cannot defend its artificial peg, so the market drops to its genuine valuation of the pound at $1.
4. Now that the peg is broken, George repurchases the pounds at $1, which is half what he was paid for them, so he only pays $5 billion.
5. George repays the loan and pockets the $5 billion difference.

The lesson of the Soros attack is that if the value of a cryptocurrency is pegged at a value higher than its true market value, the difference must be backed 100% by a foreign reserve of collateral holdings. Otherwise financiers can make money breaking the stablecoin's peg.

As an indictment of the stablecoin developers' faith in their own product, every major stablecoin publicly claims their tokens are backed at least 100%. This means they think their coins' fundamental value is $0. We don't entirely agree. But given the instability of the cryptocurrency market, and the lack of fundamental features such as decentralized governance, we don't entirely disagree.

The maintenance of a 100% reserve is too expensive to be efficient and signals the need for more sophisticated mechanisms. All the value in the reserve that backs the cryptocurrency needs to be liquid, otherwise arbitrage opportunities, such as the Soros attack, are possible – especially with an algorithmic stablecoin. Whatever value is held liquid in the reserve, costs its users due to the loss of opportunity to invest the money. The price tag of fiat-backed tokens is, at a minimum, the interest rate of the pegged fiat currency and the cost to maintain the platform. As long as the market is so unstable, platforms can profit from the buy low, sell high mechanism mentioned above.

Cryptocurrency-backed tokens are even more expensive than fiat backed tokens, because the stability is achieved with much more unstable cryptocurrencies. Any cryptocurrency-backed token must be backed with much more than 100% of the current value of the cryptocurrency in case the basket of other crypto currencies' value drops. For example, in MakerDAO, if a token is backed by ether, and the value of ether drops by half at any moment, then the automated scheme will punish anyone who has not backed their tokens by more than 200%. Given how unstable the market is, users need to back their tokens by even more, or risk automated punishment.

Hot Money

On the contrary, we argue that a 100% reserve is not always necessary, as is the case with any currency, which has an intrinsic worth. At minimum, for example, a national currency has the intrinsic worth represented by the confidence gained from the ability to pay taxes. But the amount of value represented by the currency also contributes to its intrinsic worth. For example, the amount of money invested in company shares, annuities, insurance, and property all contribute to the value that is authentically determining the total value the currency intrinsically represents.

A cryptocurrency can be measured to have intrinsic worth if there are similar authentic business transactions that rely on its tokens. Authentic transactions are distinguished from hot money. Hot money is money that is being used on second-order investments, such as speculating on the market. It is hot, because it can immediately exit the system, for example, if it is exchanged for a foreign currency. It's easier to distinguish between authentic and hot money transactions for typical cryptocurrency transactions than traditional business, since transparency makes them more easily auditable.

Soros was not able to break the Bank of England because it wasn't fully backed with foreign reserves, but because the British pound was being pegged at a value that was inauthentic. In fact, no nation holds anything near to a 100% reserve for the obvious reason that it would be too expensive to have a large liquid reserve. The U.S. foreign reserve, for example, is less than 2% of its money. Holding any liquid reserve is a loss of opportunity cost that is a type of economic friction its users must subsidize, explicitly through transaction taxes, which transparently pay for maintenance of the peg, or implicitly through holding taxes, which bearers of the currency pay, usually through inflation.

Therefore, determining the fraction of a currency that is hot money is necessary for efficient defense of its stability. A currency that overestimates this hot money ratio will cost more to use. A currency that underestimates the ratio will be insecure. The tension between these two values of efficiency and security motivates a careful estimate of the hot money ratio. This means a sophisticated decentralized governance system is crucial for any efficient stablecoin.

Today, we estimate that a majority of all cryptocurrency is used for speculation. It's virtually all hot money. Worse, these open source platforms can be cloned and replaced by competitors within minutes. So, their fundamental value is questionable.[10] Therefore, it needs to be backed fully or risk collapse. We need a robust decentralized economy before a stablecoin can reduce its collateralization. We need an efficient and useful stablecoin before we can build a robust decentralized economy. This is another of the many chicken-and-egg problems that hamper the adoption of new systems.

---

10 On the other hand, a major source of stability of a decentralized organization comes from the autonomy of its members. This makes it extremely unlikely for them to all do one thing and exit *en masse*. This means the more decentralized the platform is, and the larger and older the platform is, the more intrinsic worth it will have, and the less it will be hot money. No stablecoin should be backed 100%. And a well-designed stablecoin should anticipate the future when it is used for more authentic economic activity and can drop the reserve to well below 100%.

Stablecoin Design Choices

Here we briefly discuss how to build a stablecoin.[11] The quantity theory of money dictates how you can stabilize the value of a token by minting new tokens to drop the price and burning tokens to raise the price. Theoretically, all things being equal (which is never accurate in practice), if the economy has twice as many tokens available, prices should be twice as high. If there are half as many tokens in an imagined mirror economy, the price of goods would be half as much.

Reserves and bonds can be used to burn tokens and raise the price. The bond mechanism is to mint and sell bonds at auction for the stablecoin; the stablecoins earned through the sale are then burned raising the price of the stablecoin; then the bonds are redeemed for newly minted stablecoins at some later date. The reserve mechanism is the same as described above with the Soros attack. Reserves should be used to defend the peg against hot money short-term fluctuations. Bonds should only be used when the larger economy is experiencing longer-term changes, when one of the Four Horsemen visits.

To maintain the network's operation, the price should be borne by transaction fees. To stabilize the value due to inefficiencies in the economy (spoilage, overhead, other frictions/corruption), holding taxes should be used. Holding taxes means the currency's inflation rate, that is, if you hold the money for a year, the inflation rate tells you how much value you lose. Inflation is controlled by dictating how the peg of value changes.

Finally, if the economy has a fundamental change, the currency should be repegged. A fundamental change may include a black swan event that makes the market reevaluate the value of the economy. Trying to maintain a peg at an artificial level prevents new members from adopting the currency and punishes members as they need to pay to maintain the artificial valuation. Maintaining the artificial valuation is the most likely way to induce a death spiral, which collapses a currency.

Most importantly, good governance principles are crucial for every aspect of instituting any long-term stablecoin due to inevitable changes in the market and the fundamental obstacle represented by the Folk Theorems of Game Theory. How does the stablecoin DAO determine when and how to adjust the parameters of the stability algorithm to react to market changes? How do we know whether a change in price is due to hot money or more fundamental factors? What type of assets should be maintained in the reserves? To address these problems, we need decentralized central banking systems. The long-term governance of the DAO requires the best expertise to keep the currency stable. To find the best people to make governance

---

11 A deeper analysis can be found in Craig Calcaterra, Wulf A. Kaal, & Vadhindran K. Rao, "Stable Cryptocurrencies: First Order Principles," *Stanford Journal of Blockchain Law & Policy*, 3(1), 2020.

decisions, requires a secure and meaningful reputation system to filter that talent. Secure means the reputation provides the right incentives and defenses to police the system and prevent gaming. Meaningful means the reputation pays the members properly for their expertise.

Summary

In the 2020s the market for DeFi has started to take off but fully decentralized DeFi solutions still have a long way to go. The fundamentals go both ways, predicting DeFi's current failure and eventual success.

First, the decentralized economy is missing the major institutions that our society relies on to conduct profitable business, especially a secure and meaningful system for evaluating reputation for anonymous supranational partners, and an effective and dynamic governance system that we can trust will guarantee justice and predictable continual improvement.

Second, in the opposite direction, these decentralized networks have grown past the tipping point and are now immortal. The only way a centralized nation can control a decentralized network within their borders is to ban it completely, like the PRC has for many blockchains. But that will pose no threat to their existence. Like the nomadic Apaches, or filesharing apps like BitTorrent, attacking them will only make the decentralized economy stronger. In countries where it is allowed, it will thrive, making them more economically efficient and competitive under global capitalism. Though the PRC has banned its people from using current cryptocurrencies, they have been developing several stablecoins for years. The global social media giant, Facebook, has been developing its own stablecoin, Libra. If successful, such initiatives could link the crypto economy with establishment institutions.

The comparison of new P2P projects with older projects, like BitTorrent, is instructive. BitTorrent has been the subject of intense legal scrutiny and regulation,[12] yet it still exists because of its decentralized nature. However, these older P2P projects did not receive anything close to the level of accredited academic support that the newer blockchain projects are receiving. The technology is improving quickly, as is public and scientific understanding. In 2018 most voices that made it to major media outlets proclaimed DeFi will vanish, that "crypto is the mother or father of all scams and bubbles."[13] In 2020 there are more peer-reviewed articles

---

12 More than 200,000 lawsuits were filed in the United States over the use of the decentralized protocol from 2010 to 2011. "BitTorrent: Copyright Lawyers' Favourite Target Reaches 200,000 Lawsuits," *The Guardian*, August 9, 2011.

13 CNBC quoting a New York university professor in a hearing with the U.S. Senate Committee on Banking, Housing and Community Affairs (October 11, 2018) https://www.cnbc.com/2018/10/11/rou bini-bitcoin-is-mother-of-all-scams.html (retrieved 7/28/20).

published each day with improvements from accredited scientists, than there are stories criticizing the technology. Academics have begun to take the technology seriously as a new tool for improving peoples' lives.

Ethereum has the most DeFi investment. It is growing, but today, it is still insignificant. Only 3% of ether tokens (market cap US$26 billion) are locked in DeFi smart contracts. The intrinsic value of cryptocurrencies will only become significant once tokenization of commodities and other authentic uses of the money are achieved.

When will DeFi take off? When the economy becomes viable – when cryptocurrency is used in authentic transactions such as insurance and equities in broad segments of industry and tokenization of commodities and properties is instituted. This will happen when people can trust the systems, which will only happen when decentralized reputation and governance are achieved. The technological problems are tantalizingly close to being solved, but so far, the inability to trust each other due to the requirements of anonymity is crippling the DeFi market. So traditional markets have a fundamental advantage. Decentralized markets are overcollateralized. To make a decentralized financial transaction, such as a loan, or buy an insurance policy or a derivative instrument, someone needs to completely back the product with 100% collateral. In the case of secondary layers, you need more, such as MakerDAO's scheme, which requires much more than 200% collateralization. This would be an unthinkable obstacle to liquidity in traditional markets. It is only being used in the crypto space because of a lack of decentralized alternatives.

However, once secure and meaningful reputation is incorporated into the Web3 environment, this imbalance will be reversed. Since reputation tokens are more meaningful than identity, and much easier to valuate, even less collateralization will be required than traditional protocols, and the decentralized economy will gain the upper hand over traditional centralized institutions. Locking your reputation tokens instead of your assets would be a strong leap in efficiency, giving a powerful economic advantage over traditional finance. This can only be achieved with a coherent system that securely tracks the value of a reputation token.

Not until the problems with decentralized governance are addressed will the decentralized economy be stable enough to invest fully, for the long term. These problems need to be solved before the decentralized economy can realize its full potential for efficiency. Once they are solved, however, the crypto economy is ready to grow explosively. The technical tools have been built. The legal and business dimensions just need to be arranged to ensure security and fairness through the proper incentives.

But even with all this, there is still another basic component missing – one more institutional overhead system that gives business the catalyst it needs. How can the average person participate in the decentralized economy? How can they know what is a good network to participate in? How can they know what to invest in? We need trustworthy open source decentralized institutions for recording and parsing history, for investigating and reporting the news, for guiding our attention to the future.

Chapter 9
Historiography

> We are not makers of history. We are made by history.
> —Martin Luther King, Jr., *Strength to Love* (1963)

Dual to cryptography, which is the process of writing secrets, historiography is the process of distilling and sharing information publicly. Historiography is the way you choose to write the past – how it's recorded, what information is stressed as important, how it is presented. Do we present history as a list of the important decisions kings and queens have made, or do we stress the social developments that provoked those decisions, or do we point to the technological innovations that fomented those social changes?

In business, your choice of historiography determines what past events are important to consider when making economic decisions. Your historiography is your perspective. To achieve liquidity, marketplaces must be trustworthy. They need momentum. It's not enough to achieve motion in any particular instance. Momentum must be observed to give trust to the marketplace. These observations need to be collected in a history to give them weight and meaning.

In decentralized organizations, governance is the key ingredient for driving effective collaboration toward a goal. Governance relies on meaningful reputation to decide who or what to focus on. The meaning of reputation is determined by its history and how that history is analyzed and presented. Information, especially through news sources, controls a decentralized organization.

How is our attention focused and organized? Which details are important? Which narrative do we follow? What is the internet search engine for the decentralized P2P environment? How do you tell the story of what the data means? How trustworthy, how efficient, how effective is any particular DAO, compared with other DAOs? To answer all these questions, you need to answer how history is recorded and disseminated.

The choice of historiography is the design choice of the architecture of higher-order information storage. The purpose of the judicial branch is to finalize information storage, to decide what is true. The architecture of history, historiography, is the architecture for judicial governance. Historiography is our method for putting the authoritative stamp on what is true. This stamp sets the stage to analyze our situation and decide what to do next (legislative governance/information processing), then to do it (executive governance/information transmission).

In this chapter we describe how to build decentralized news services for DAOs, known as oracles. Incidentally, this explains how to revitalize our failing news media, the vaunted fourth estate, and educational institutions that are essential to the functioning of the larger DAOs of our democratic societies, using the principles of decentralization.

https://doi.org/10.1515/9783110673937-009

Oracles

In the decentralized economy, trusted news sources become even more important than in the traditional economy. Business contracts are becoming more automated, reacting immediately to news events. Automated news services in P2P systems are called oracles.

Many oracles exist today that work with P2P projects, such as Provable (formerly Oraclize) and Town Crier, which are centralized (Provable uses Amazon's Web Services virtual machine and Town Crier uses Intel). These centralized oracles are recommended for any contemporary P2P project, because as of 2020, no decentralized oracle is robust enough to be trusted for valuable transactions. To make DAOs secure in the long run, however, many different types of trusted decentralized oracles need to be developed.

Why do you need a decentralized oracle? The same reason all the other institutions that business relies on need to be decentralized before a DAO can reach its full potential. Any time your DAO relies on a centralized feature, that is a centralized point of failure that is a threat to the survival of the organization. That means the system is technically centralized. In that case it would be more efficient to completely centralize around the single point of failure the DAO is automated around. The effort you're making to decentralize and give each member redundant power is wasted, because the point of failure might as well be the supreme leader.

For example, if the DAO relies on a centralized oracle, that means someone in the oracle's hierarchy has the power to decide what information to share. A DAO is automated by its smart contracts to rely on the information coming from the oracle. The DAO is automatically triggered to make monetary transactions based on that information. Eventually, the people who have the relevant power in the centralized oracle will become aware of the power they have over the DAO. Eventually there will be an opportunity to exploit that information. And from a game theory perspective, given the competitive nature of capitalism, they are right to take advantage of that power.

You can never achieve a perfectly decentralized system, any more than any organization's hierarchy can ever become perfectly centralized. There is always going to be a problem and weakness somewhere with any practical instantiation of any project. And machines don't need to be perfect in every regard to work. But if we can identify a weakness, we can address it.

Theoretically, you can make overarching centralized laws dictating such exploitation shouldn't happen. In fact, there are many laws related to this sort of insider information. But the very existence of this opportunity for arbitrage means systems will evolve around whatever rules exist to exploit the advantage. Instead of legislating, the proper response is to engineer a better system. More to the point, robust decentralized oracles would be superior.

A robust decentralized oracle would find better information. The wisdom of the crowd can be employed to discover the truth. Averaging information is typically better for any complex situation, since they're less subject to the prejudices of the individual, who has more limited information. All things being equal, the individual mistakes that overestimate some measurement are balanced by the individuals that underestimate. Decentralized oracles are more reliable. Their failures will be smaller, because they are more diluted through averaging. Centralized oracles have more singular sources of information, leading to higher variance in their mistakes.

Condorcet's Jury Theorem

A rigorous explanation of the wisdom of the crowd was first introduced in 1785 by Condorcet. The same French revolutionary genius whose paradox (Chapter 4) prevents us from finding a perfect democratic voting method also gives us this argument in favor of democracy. Condorcet's Jury Theorem says bigger democracies are better than having smaller groups in charge. Sort of. Condorcet demonstrated that larger groups of slightly intelligent people are better than smaller groups for democratically finding the truth.[1]

Here's the setup: Suppose you have a group that is going to vote on an issue. Also suppose the group is slightly intelligent, meaning the average group member is more than 51% likely to get the right answer, rather than the wrong answer. In this case, the more people you use to vote on the issue, the more likely they are to come to the truth. The bigger the network, the more efficiently it will come to the correct answer. The crowd's answers are much wiser than the average individual's answer.

Since it's a rigorous logical result, it also is balanced by the fact that larger groups of slightly stupid people are worse than smaller groups of stupid people. The idiocy of the mob is the counterbalance to the wisdom of the crowd. Stupid, here, is defined as being wrong slightly more than half the time. It's not clear whether any mortal escapes that assignation in sum – perhaps we're all slightly stupid in the larger scheme of things. But in some areas, we can train ourselves to be at least slightly competent. So, an oracle DAO needs to filter its network to guarantee the average member is correct, at least slightly more than they are incorrect. Then the larger and more decentralized the network becomes, the quicker and more certainly it will converge on the truth.

---

1 Bernard Grofman, Guillermo Owen, and Scott Feld, "Thirteen Theorems in Search of the Truth," *Theory and Decision*, 15, 1983, pp. 261–278.

SchellingCoin Protocol

One decentralized approach to generating oracle information is based on the SchellingCoin protocol, explained for Ethereum in 2014 by Vitalik Buterin. The idea is to have your Oracle DAO members stake their reputation tokens on their answer to a question a DApp is asking. Then you reward those closer to the resulting median value and punish those whose answers deviated further. The median answer is the Schelling point, a concept from game theory.

For example, suppose an insurance DAO needs to know whether to pay out to policy holders for a hurricane. The policy stipulates that it will pay out if the wind in your coastal town is higher than 100 mph. Oracle DAO members may post their estimate of the top wind speed in Virginia Beach last Thursday and encumber their reputation tokens in a smart contract. When the deadline to report the wind speed arrives, the smart contract calculates the median value of all submissions, weighted by the stakes. Then the encumbered reputation tokens are redistributed to the group, with more tokens given to members who answered closer to the median, and less for those whose answers were farther away.

There are infinitely many choices for the redistribution process. The original proposal suggested minting some amount N of new tokens and distributing them to those with answers between the 25th and 75th percentile. Incentivization can be optimized by selecting over the set of all designs. Different questions and DAO behaviors should have different reward schemes. For instance, if all members are behaving honestly, and the answers are satisfactory within a predetermined tolerance, your reputation shouldn't be arbitrarily reassigned because you were a tiny fraction of the median value further away than the majority. In that case everyone should earn a share of the new reputation.

What protocols are followed in answering any particular oracle questions should be determined by the experts on the particular subject. Giving the experts, themselves, control of their own organization is better than relying on a static centralized hierarchy. The experts know best how to game their own system, and how to prevent gaming to protect their hard-earned reputation. The experts will find the most efficient and secure methodology for providing trustworthy answers.

Assuming there is no systemic bias in the members, meaning that the group is diverse and decentralized, the median should be close to the truth, so Oracle DAO participants are incentivized to answer as honestly as they can. Fees are later distributed among the Oracle DAO members proportionate to their reputation holdings.

This approach may also serve as a forecasting device. Members would stake their reputation tokens on bets on future events, making the DAO into a more literal oracle, like those in Ancient Greece.

Though decentralization improves information discovery, it further improves when you filter out the bad sources of information. All things are not equal. Every network has biases that need to be filtered out. Reputation, governance, and review provide a stable system for filtering the bad sources of information and improving accuracy.

Unfortunately, robust decentralized oracles don't exist, yet. Proposals have been well funded by ICOs since 2017, but we have little confidence in any scheme currently being built. Chain.link has a protocol that demonstrates proof of concept – the technology exists to build a decentralized oracle. But the difference between theory and practice is often vast.

Put simply, decentralized oracles are DAOs, so they still lack the proper incentive structure and governance processes and history that all DAOs suffer from. Until the decentralized protocol is secure and robustly enacted, it is better to rely on centralized oracles, and make sure your network doesn't grow to gain such a large monetary value that an incentive arises for the centralized newsfeed to manipulate the data. A decentralized oracle is not secure until it has significant momentum and history – an oracle is not even truly decentralized until this is achieved, until it has a large network of active members.

When sophisticated DAOs that represent banking and lending and insurance finally emerge, the structure will be easy to adjust in order to properly motivate and govern oracle DAOs. Unfortunately, oracle DAOs and DeFi DAOs rely on each other for their very existence. Which will come first, the chicken or the egg? Mixing two more metaphors, the skeleton of our proposal for priming the pump is detailed at the end of Chapter 4, above. People first must prove their worth in a development period, before they become invaluable to other DAOs and can charge fees for their services.

News and Education

Centralized civic institutions always become corrupt in time. Then this corruption becomes obvious once a new technology disrupts their operation, revealing their weaknesses. Today, trust in the news media has cratered due to the corruption of the institution.

People periodically give up their power of information transmission to centralized institutions, which are more effective and efficient. These institutions become corrupt after their hierarchies centralize and ossify, then new technology allows people to bypass these centrally controlled media institutions. It used to be that a far greater percentage of people were publishers. Letter writing was relatively decentralized among anyone literate who could afford ink and paper. Then bookmaking concentrated the power of information storage throughout medieval Europe in the clergy, as teams of monks were devoted to the task. Economies of scale made it prohibitively expensive to produce a book of comparable quality without going through the Church. Europe trusted in the institution of the Christian hierarchy, which became corrupt in time and eventually stultified individual progress. With the power of information creation and storage, the Church had the power of making history, which is ultimately the power of thought, as was used famously against Bruno and Galileo. The Church's corruption was revealed when the new technology of the printing press unleashed the Protestant Reformation, under which the Catholic hierarchy collapsed and reformed.

The printing press automated bookmaking, so that a few people could do the job of hundreds of monks. Every small community of a few hundred people had competing printing presses.[2] This gave people power to make local broadsheets so that local newspapers could run local stories written by local citizens on local interests. Naturally, power eventually concentrated again, through economies of scale, until a few global corporations now primarily run global stories catering to globally powerful interests.

Throughout history, advances in technology give individuals more power to spread their information to more people, but unchecked competition accumulates power in hierarchies of more successful groups. We give our individual power to institutions, which initially serve us more effectively and more efficiently. But as these institutions age, they become more corrupt. This is revealed as new technology disrupts their operations, as the internet is currently doing.

Today, global news media institutions of all types are being revealed as weak and corrupt. Unprofessionally produced stories reveal the major professional media corporations are failing to provide unbiased and relevant information for their average consumer. These unprofessional stories are spread with the new Web 2.0 technologies, such as Twitter, YouTube, and Wikipedia, widely displaying the corruption of our older institutions.

If we don't build transparent democratic institutions to replace the corrupt institutions, new opaque centralized institutions will. Already, Facebook, YouTube, and Twitter are creating secret algorithms that control what type of story can be spread through their platforms, with absolutely no democratic power of oversight. To prevent the corruption such centralized control inevitably leads to, we must foster transparency and individual autonomy over information. Powerful decentralized media institutions need to be built, using dynamic governance design principles to keep them stable and responsive. How do we use P2P tools to achieve this?

Decentralization has always been a crucial factor in manufacturing the news. Social truth can only be discovered using diverse and decentralized sources. What is a fact? What facts are important? The ultimate answer is that valuable knowledge affects people's lives and experiences and decisions; it helps humanity. How do we best organize news collection and dissemination to create valuable knowledge?

---

2 For example, by 1550, less than a century after Gutenberg's original printing press, Geneva had more than 300 printing presses and 17,000 citizens, for an average of 1 printing press per 57 people. Elizabeth Eisenstein, *The Printing Press as an Agent of Change*, Cambridge University Press, 1979, p. 410.

Traditionally, a healthy news media, our fourth estate, relies on a variety of competing companies. Truth discovery in any market, including the marketplace of ideas, is more effective and efficient when news aggregators are more decentralized. When there are 10 newspapers reporting on a story, a more accurate historical picture emerges than when one newspaper reports on the story 10 times. "The wisdom of the crowd" is the phrase that distills the fact that this diversity improves the focus and accuracy of the information reported, and it improves as it becomes more diverse, from the level of companies all the way down to the individual. Newspapers, radio, and movies, from television to internet platforms, diversity of media company ownership contributes to diversity of viewpoint and serves more audience interests, from local to national to global audiences and between groups at each scale.

On the one hand, advances in information technology have been regularly improving our ability to disseminate news and history to the masses for centuries, increasing the quantity of stories and the number of people they reach.

On the other hand, economies of scale naturally lead media companies to merge and concentrate power in territorial monopolies and trusts. American faith in media has reliably fallen in direct correlation with the consolidation of broadcasting power, as long as active statistics have been studied. Since the 1990s with the Telecommunications Act of 1996, and especially with several decisions by the FCC in the 2000s, there has been a string of deregulation, which has allowed global companies to increase their power in local communities. In 2007 the FCC voted to eliminate media ownership rules that included a law forbidding a single company from owning both a newspaper and a television or radio station in the same city.[3] Since then, iHeartMedia (formerly Clear Channel Communications) grew to 1,200 radio stations. In 1983 the top 50 companies owned 90% of the media and entertainment industry in the United States,[4] comprising businesses that produce and distribute movies, television, commercials, streaming content, audio recordings, radio, newspapers, books, video games, and supplementary services and products. By 2012, 90% was controlled by the top six media conglomerations. As an application of Zipf's Law, the values scale roughly exponentially, with AT&T owning roughly twice as much as Comcast, which is worth twice as much as Walt Disney Corp, then Viacom, then Fox (see Figure 9.1). Without external regulating forces, this is the natural and predictable result for centralizing forces under competition.

The most obvious problem with news consolidation is that national or international centralized corporations do not devote the same degree of focus to the interests

---

3 Labaton, Stephen, "Plan Would Ease Limits on Media Owners," *New York Times*, October 18, 2007.

4 Lutz, Ashley, "These 6 Corporations Control 90% of the Media in America," *Business Insider*, June 14, 2012.

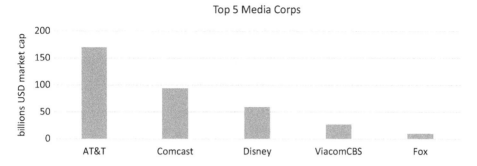

Figure 9.1: 2019 valuations of the top media corporations follow Zipf's Law.

of the local communities they serve.[5] Again, love doesn't scale. Diversity of viewpoints is diminished when power is concentrated. Editorial freedom is decreased. News corporations certainly must value accuracy and truth in their reporting; but they also must consider what news stories and perspectives will attract and maintain advertising, what positions serve their owners' interests. A mega trust conglomeration, like GE and Comcast each owning half of NBC, diminishes market liquidity with large scale static power relations, which leverage the increased internal firm efficiencies through economies of scale, leading to frictions and corruption that undermine the efficiency of the larger market.

Wide scale decentralization of power in the media will not collapse the power of centralized corporations, any more than file sharing services like Napster and BitTorrent[6] collapsed the power of the centralized music companies. These disruptive technologies merely transformed how entertainment is consumed and business is done. The entertainment industry is more powerful and pervasive in our global culture than ever before. Decentralization is more efficient for empowering individuals in every way. It doesn't take power from centralized actors; it increases everyone's power. Decentralization is only a threat to those who refuse to participate in the new collaborative networks and embrace the new tools of communication at our disposal. Musicians and record companies now have more influence in their

---

5 The Communications Act of 1934 mandated that the FCC must act in the interest of the "public convenience, interest, or necessity." The FCC argued in 2006 that consolidation would bring more focus on local news, because the larger organizations would have more resources. This argument failed in practice, as there was an average decrease exceeding 10% of local news stories within the first year of transfer of ownership. Obar, Jonathan. "Beyond Cynicism: A Review of the FCC's Reasoning for Modifying the Newspaper/Broadcast Cross-Ownership Rule." *Communication Law & Policy 14*(4), 2009, pp. 479–525.
6 Hundreds of decentralized file sharing programs and communities have evolved to avoid centralized legal restrictions. See https://en.wikipedia.org/wiki/Timeline_of_file_sharing for a list of some of the major historical developments.

fans' personal lives through social media. Decentralization creates new opportunities for collaboration at a higher level.

Simultaneous with the consolidation of traditional media outlets in the 2000s, Web 2.0 companies like Facebook, Twitter, and YouTube decentralized content creation while retaining centralized ownership and higher-order control. This centralized control had the same effect in media communication that it did in commerce with Amazon and Alibaba – users go largely unregulated until a major problem comes to the attention of the central authority. Fake news generators, trolls, fact checkers, and citizen reporters now unite into communities within hours and scatter just as quickly, thanks to platforms such as Twitter and Reddit, which leverage the new information technology to tap the talent of the masses to generate news content. Without editorial control, the content is self-evidently unreliable. People rely on unconscious algorithms that use popularity to determine what is authoritative content. But the lessons of the Folk Theorems again arise, to remind us that such algorithms can always be gamed. A more effective means of distilling what information is important is required. To handle the profusion of information created by empowering the populace with decentralized content creation, we need a decentralized solution.

A central authority is perfectly well incentivized to ignore minor problems that only partially eat into their profits, as long as they maintain ultimate control of profits. When users are given more control of their content, decentralized regulation can be more effective, with immediate policing and protocol changes. With proper reputation design, history and momentum can be built to filter the information more productively. With decentralized governance, where all members have a proper balance of power to police their platforms, regulation of these decentralized platforms can be more effective. Stories can be properly evaluated, with proportionately increased or decreased visibility according to their merit, without censoring them.

News organizations with greater power decentralization have been proposed such as WikiNews (funded by the same nonprofit Wikimedia Foundation that publishes Wikipedia), the Decentralized News Network (DNN), and Steemit (2016). All these examples appear to us to have failed to gain wide adoption due to a lack of ambition. The goal should be to empower individuals with greater ability to communicate and cooperate.

Imagine a hybrid mix of social media platforms (like Facebook or LinkedIn) with the news and entertainment media corporations (like the BBC or *The New York Times*). Instead of a paywall, newspapers should be encouraging participation. If you read many articles on a particular subject, you are more expert in that subject. If you comment productively on articles, or if you create the content, you are more expert. If your discussions stimulate more discussions and more content, you are more of an expert. If an article generates more meaningful, reputable connections, then the article is more valuable. If it doesn't, it isn't. Your expertise, your reputation, is based on whether you are helping create content or bringing attention to something that actually matters – meaning it is connected to profitable enterprises. If you create content that does not connect to something profitable, or if you promote such unproductive knowledge, especially if you are a troll, your reputation will not grow in the DAO, which values other behaviors and polices their reputation properly. Different definitions of what profitable means, will lead to different types of reputation or expertise that people strive to attain, and different measures of power in different endeavors with separate DAOs.

Major news corporations have the opportunity to rival the power of Facebook by decentralizing their institutions. People could have news accounts that keep track of how many articles they've read, how many comments they've made, on which subjects, with a Reddit style accounting system of up and downvotes[7] for how well their contributions are appreciated, by which people, who have how much and what type of reputation. How many articles have you initiated? How much do those articles contribute to further comments and articles? Each article is weighted, based on how much extra content it generates, and recursively, based on how influential that content ultimately proves to be.

Every software programmer understands how important the contributions to Stack Overflow[8] are, but these contributions are not rewarded by anything but bragging rights. If we can find a fair way to value such contributions, it would contribute to a more effective and efficient system of collaboration. Following the principles of building secure and meaningful reputation from Chapter 6, articles must have a foundational meaning in fungible currency. New reputation should only be minted when the articles are connected to profitable endeavors – advertising, paid analyses, new protocols that are relied upon for decentralized business contracts. Then other contributions gain valuable reputation if they are linked through references.

The exact process of steps 1–7 for the Software Review DAO in Chapter 4 can be cloned to build a news story review DAO. Reviewers could judge stories' veracity according to the standards the News DAO chooses. As before, reputation in the News DAO becomes valuable once News DApps steer viewership to stories based on your News DAO reviews. Then media sites will pay fees to get their stories reviewed more quickly. Reviewers will be incentivized to give honest reviews despite fees, because the reputational system rewards members mostly based on future fees. Unlike centralized platforms, like Twitter, which don't fairly share profits or power

---

7 Better yet, they would build an automated system of staking your reputation on your up or down vote using some of the methods explored in chapters 6 and 7 below.
8 Stack Overflow is a social media platform for computer science professionals that promotes good questions and answers with a gamified upvote system similar to Reddit where users can earn badges. It has become so valuable in programming circles they joke that the solution to any new software programming problem is to copy code from Stack Overflow.

with their members, policing can be properly incentivized in a DAO, to discourage reviewers who erode the integrity of the system. The success of this system, however, will depend on the effectiveness of the choice of protocols, which govern the DAO.

The purpose of news media is education. Such a system, which takes advantage of our new power in information technology, can track our attainment of expertise (or lack of attainment) more accurately than our traditional systems of professional licensures or college degrees. Tracking and aggregating our reputations in various DAOs can build a more accurate picture of our expertise and experiential gaps than our traditional educational institutions have. The expertise that has evolved in the century of public education[9] would be essential to designing effective curricula. Meaningless certification and licensure programs would be quickly revealed as the worthless pursuits they are.

Notably, the transparency and openly reviewable nature of a DAO greatly adds to the trustworthiness of the system. Being eternally open to audits and reviews from anyone on the planet greatly improves the integrity of the system. Such improvements to transparency and accountability in the institutions of media and education have the opportunity for improving many aspects of society.

Such transparency is a hallmark of the open source culture that is a pillar of the Web3 movement. Unfortunately, the open source culture makes no sense.

Open Source Culture Requires a Culture of Respect for History

The open source culture of the Web3 movement is absolutely essential to the goals of decentralizing the economy. Transparency is crucial in a decentralized network. Every function needs to be publicly auditable for people to trust it. Without a central authority to approve it, unexpected malicious behavior can be built into any opaque code. The open source culture has been extremely successful in generating useful distributed applications, which are essential to the functioning of Web 2.0. An open source environment is much more innovative.

But open source culture makes no sense from a business perspective. Whenever we've tried to explain the open source culture to a nontechnical businessperson, we've been met with incredulity. It *might* make sense in a fantasy world utopia, where we imagine no scarcity, where everyone is a saint who shares freely with no expectation of enjoying the rewards of their labor. But it certainly doesn't make sense in our capitalist business world, where the incentive structures address our essential,

---

9 The institution of education is as old as civilization, but the current system of compulsory public secondary schools started around 1910 during the Progressive Movement in the United States. The majority of the U.S. public first earned high school diplomas in 1940. Jurgen Herbst, *The Once and Future School: Three Hundred and Fifty Years of American Secondary Education,* Routledge, 1996.

base instinct of selfishness that has preserved life for more than a billion years. Open source makes no sense from an economic perspective. So why do people do it? From the game theory perspective, the current open source culture advocated in the Web3 movement is not sustainable in the long term.

Unless we marry it with a culture of respect for history.

The way to build sustainable incentives for fostering open source culture is to simultaneously foster a culture that acknowledges the contributions of the past. Academics of all stripes have lived in an open source culture for centuries, arguably for millennia. Like Web3, academia thrives on transparency and open collaboration with strangers. Periods when societies are less transparent with their ideas, less collaborative, are usually referred to as Dark Ages. Open source culture has always been the lifeblood of progress, in societies around the globe, throughout history. But to sustain that open culture, a culture of respect for the past simultaneously evolves, so resentment doesn't build. The solution to the game theory conundrum of how to incentivize a player to freely give up their intellectual property at one stage of a repeated game, is by guaranteeing a reward in a future stage, by fostering a culture of acknowledgement of past contributions. The players then seek the future rewards of fame by freely distributing their work in the present.

Some academic subjects have stronger cultures respecting history, such as philosophy and theology and especially the law, as evidenced by the density of footnote references in any paper. Some are weaker, such as science and especially mathematics, where typically a few essential references are perfunctorily tacked on at the end of their introduction.

It's not efficient to be constantly conscious of the source of our ideas. It's easier to simply state your ideas and build your arguments without referencing each idea's debt to previous thinkers. It's unnatural to have a culture of respect for history that needs to be consciously policed – it's another of the essential catalyst institutions that needs to be built into the decentralized economy.

But the new advances in information technology allow us to create a more sophisticated system of acknowledging minute past contributions than previously imagined possible, with digitally accurate, automated accounting methods.

Let's take a final brief digression into technical territory to explain how these new architectures are built.

Review Gives Momentum

Mathematical analyses of the different ways the network of references can be weighted makes it possible to design protocols for promoting the goals each particular DAO happens to value. This network of references is technically referred to as a citation graph. As indicated in Chapter 7, governance needs to be designed in harmony with the values of the group. A full example is beyond the scope of this text. However, the elements of citation graph analysis are quite basic, similar to how all of the symbolic logic involved in the most complex smart contracts boils down to understanding the NOT and AND operators.

The set of all posts and comments in a News DAO can be interpreted from an abstract perspective as a weighted directed acyclic graph (WDAG) (see Figure 9.2). This technical math jargon is the term for a relatively simple concept in graph theory, which underlies the mathematical analysis of any network.

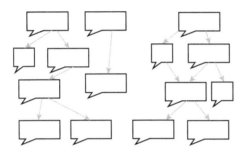

Figure 9.2: The forum as a weighted directed acyclic graph (WDAG).

A graph is a mathematical term that distills the crucial elements of a network (see Figure 9.3). A **graph** consists of two collections: a set of **vertices** (the dots, or the nodes, or the posts, or the members of the network) and a set of **edges** (connections, or references, or citations, or transmission lines in a network). If we add an arrow to an edge, indicating one post is referencing another, the graph becomes a **directed graph**. A graph has a cycle if three vertices are connected to each other in order, with vertex A connected to vertex B, which is connected to vertex C, which is connected back to vertex A. Citation graphs, or reference graphs, don't have cycles, since an older post cannot reference newer posts before they exist. We call such graphs **acyclic**. Finally, we can allow a post to indicate precisely how important its

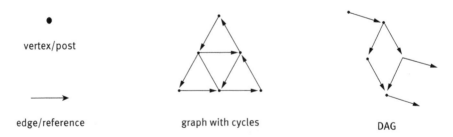

Figure 9.3: Elements of graphs.

connections are, how important the older posts are, by weighting the references. When we attach weights to the edges/references, the forum of all posts/comments becomes a **weighted directed acyclic graph** (see Figure 9.4).

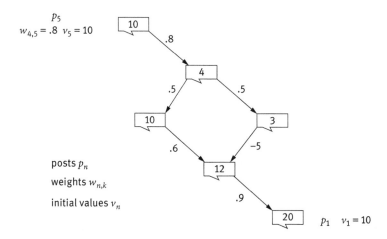

Figure 9.4: Weighting the references changes older posts' values.

The idea of the weighted references is to determine how much the new posts affect the older posts with their review. If you give a high weight, close to 100%, then the reference will affect it's value it more than a low weight, closer to 0%. A positive weight suggests that the referenced post deserves to increase in value. A negative weight suggests the older post should diminish in value – it is not contributing value to the DAO (see Figure 9.5).

Simple arithmetic will change the value of the older posts. The changes cascade through the WDAG of posts in the forum, readjusting the value of all connected contributions, continually improving previous judgments.

There are many choices that need to be made for exactly how the cascade works. How many levels deep do the references affect the value of posts? The deeper the calculations go, the more history is relevant. How much do the new posts share their value with old posts? More value-sharing with older posts will promote long-term contributions and innovations and increases stability; less value-sharing encourages new contributions and immediate work. How you design the calculation tells us whether you give more value to long-term or short-term contributions. Deeper graph theory analysis allows us to optimize design choices to incentivize behaviors, which lead to the goals that further the DAO's particular values.

Hard protocols stipulate how the algorithm automatically calculates the changes to the value of the posts. Soft protocols stipulate how the DAO requires the posters to behave. An example of a soft protocol is the requirement that whenever a poster

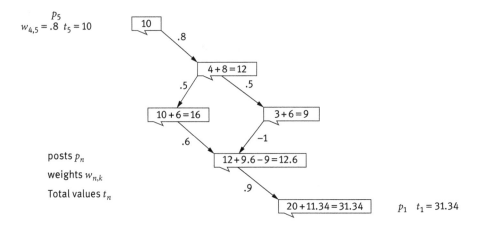

p_5
$w_{4,5} = .8$ $t_5 = 10$

10

.8

4+8=12

.5   .5

10+6=16   3+6=9

.6   −1

posts p_n

weights $w_{n,k}$ 12+9.6−9=12.6

Total values t_n .9

20+11.34=31.34 p_1 $t_1 = 31.34$

Figure 9.5: Weighted references cascade value to older posts, increasing or decreasing their value. This enables review of past behavior, rewarding long-term contributions and guarding the DAO against gaming.

discusses a new topic within a category, like local politics, they must reference the previous protocols posted, which set up the DAO's rules for discussing the politics of how to spend taxes – say 0.1%. This enables the DAO to reward older contributions, from the time when the DAO was initially being developed and not yet attracting money. If a new post doesn't reference older posts properly, according to the protocols that have been established by the DAO, then the UI of each user can follow the soft protocols and automatically punish the poster with downvotes. Again, the governance design, in this case the parameter choices, reflect the values of the DAO.

In summary, reviewing through references enables punishment and rewards in DAOs, which changes the motivations of members from a focus on immediate rewards to the future, encouraging delayed gratification and sacrifice for the good of the group. Review changes the game theoretical perspective from a single stage game, to a repeated game. This leads to more efficient cooperation instead of internal competition. This makes business sense for how the open source environment, essential to the decentralized economy, can be sustained in the long run. Review helps create a decentralized history for a DAO, which gives them momentum. History gives meaning and focus to our perceptions. History is the basis for making governance (steering) more effective. It allows members to judge whether they are properly promoting their unifying transcendental values. History brings clarity and stability.

To keep a decentralized organization stable in the long run, they need this momentum gained from a clear history. But momentum toward what purpose? If the system is not moving toward a healthy and productive goal, it will not last long. The most important aspect of a decentralized organization, the feature that ultimately determines its long-term success, is the group's set of transcendental values.

Chapter 10
Transcendental Unifying Values

> Without myth, however, every culture loses its healthy creative natural power: it is only a hori-
> zon encompassed with myth that rounds off to unity a social movement.
>
> —Friedrich Nietzsche, *The Birth of Tragedy*

This final essential institution is the most important for long-term stability, and demands eternal reevaluation. Decentralized organizations require strong unifying
values to remain coherent. Decentralized organizations live by their ideals.

The decentralized economy requires decentralized creeds for each DAO. Similar to
how the authors of the U.S. Constitution considered freedom of religion and speech as
the very first principle, the point of decentralization is to give individuals more autonomy, to give them more freedom to choose the right path in their behavior. The very
first principle of human autonomy is freedom of thought; without it, there is no autonomy. So despite the fact that we can witness a single global society emerging, where
everyone on the planet is connected in more intimate ways than a medieval city was,
there should not be a single power-centralized hierarchy to control it. Instead, the better, more efficient, more stable state of this global society is an organization that is
power decentralized, giving individuals and subgroup DAOs more autonomous power
to contribute to the health and wealth and happiness of all. Therefore, we take for
granted a multiplicity of beliefs and creeds and values in the various DAOs that form.

In order to maintain efficiency, we must understand the answer to the question,
"Efficiency in the pursuit of what goals?" Understanding our goals is effectively the
same as understanding our values. Therefore, to maintain the system, to maintain
its efficiency, we must adhere to our values. By the insights gleaned from the Folk
Theorems of Game Theory, transcendental values are necessary to maintain long-
term stability in the face of ever-present strategies for subverting any formal, explicitly specified protocol.

Integrating Polar Values

In this chapter we analyze some transcendental values that people might use to
help unify a DAO. The point of unifying people is to bring together individuals with
different perspectives. A maximally effective set of unifying values will achieve the
seemingly impossible feat of integrating opposing values.

For instance, in order to keep a car running properly, you need to harmoniously
integrate the functions of accelerating and decelerating while you steer stably toward your goal. Similarly, liberal and conservative values are both important to
keep a society running in the long run. Liberal values can be identified with the

https://doi.org/10.1515/9783110673937-010

automobile's accelerator. Conservative values are associated with the brakes. Liberal values are concerned with change and progress, improvement. Conservative principles are devoted to preservation and protection. Walls are identified with conservative values. Eradicating divisions between people, breaking down walls, is stereotypically a liberal value. Building secure walls with well-designed doors is the proper way to embody both values, integrating them harmoniously in your economic system. You need to secure your system from ruin, to build walls to protect your group from the Tragedy of the Commons and malicious threats. But you also need to build doors, to revitalize your group with fresh inputs from anyone willing and able to help. Twenty-first century Web3 doors can be programmed with dynamic rules to continually evolve to improve their function.

To keep any society stable and healthy, history reveals three polar opposite sets of fundamental values that need to be integrated:

- **Communal cooperation vs. individual freedom** (information transmission; what do we do, individually and communally) Cooperation is the basis of human wealth and safety. But it comes at the cost of individual agency. A harmonious balance between these values is necessary for survival, and so is evolutionarily built into our animal nature.

- **Bureaucratic transparency vs. personal privacy** (information storage; what do we know, individually and communally) Internet communication and information storage gives us the power to make all decision-making processes available to everyone concurrently. Cryptography allows us to keep our personal information secret, allowing us to interact anonymously in even the most sophisticated business transactions.

- **Equity of necessities vs. meritocracy for nonessentials** (information processing; what do material objects mean to us, individually and communally) Equity in economic theory is the distribution of resources with the goal of making all members equally powerful and wealthy. Meritocracy distributes power to the people who can best use it for the benefit of the individual and the community. How does society share essential and nonessential resources? How do we individually use essential and nonessential resources?

Each pair of values is in tension with its opposite. It is natural to imagine that strengthening one diminishes its opposite. But that is plainly false in any complex situation.

For example, a society that is completely equitably leveled materially, crushes its meritocratic instinct by eliminating all individual reward. Its next generation will not be able to produce as much to share because of the inefficient allocation of power to those who cannot use it well. It will then share less overall, diminishing its equitable share as the years progress. This failure was repeatedly demonstrated in numerous 20th century communist countries.

For the mirror opposite, a society that uses only meritocratic rewards will soon have an exceptionally large disenfranchised subgroup due to Price's Law (exponential differentiation of rewards, since the rich get richer). In succeeding generations, the bottom tier will not be able to afford training to compete and the separation will exacerbate until the society destabilizes and collapses. That society then obviously gives less rewards to those who deserve them, diminishing its meritocracy. This failure was exemplified in 19th century America, which had few social protections for the poor and disenfranchised. The resulting staggered economic collapses fueled the Progressive Era from the 1890s to the 1920s which led to improved regulation of industry, markets, and society. Scientific management revolutionized every aspect of society. The economy was transformed by antitrust regulation. Finance was reorganized with the Federal Reserve system. Medicine was professionalized, and education saw the first public schooling.

Throughout history, governments have recognized the need to balance these values. The goal of a healthy society requires promotion of equal opportunities by providing equity of necessities, but also strives to provide fair rewards with a meritocracy for nonessentials. The debate always erupts on the definition of the line between necessities and nonessentials. If you say nothing is essential, you are strongly favoring meritocracy. If you say everything is essential, you are strongly favoring equity. When you define your dividing line, you are signaling your personal judgment about what is valuable.

Is air essential, or water? What about education? For two centuries, most every nation has agreed a literate populace is beneficial to society and provided compulsory public grammar school for children. How far does your belief in the right to an education extend? Some believe graduate study at universities should be available to our citizenry, as a right, throughout life. Some societies force people to become professors in specific fields based on an IQ test in childhood. Do you believe society should force those successful in business to share their knowledge and secrets in public online lectures? How much education is a necessity–how much should education be controlled by the group instead of the individual?

As another example of the split, consider the goal of Web3 engineers to eliminate corruption by automating away legal regulation, policing, and insurance with smart contracts, as described in the previous chapters. By automating insurance, the economy becomes more efficient. We then have the power to maintain automated insurance for ourselves, without using middlemen insurance agents. Individuals become more autonomous and more powerful. Individuals choose the level of catalyst protection they need, as they are best able to evaluate what is optimal.

But if the larger society is going to thrive under these new choices, we must avoid a race to the bottom. It's more efficient in the short term for an individual to forego any insurance, so some will outcompete others if they are lucky enough to avoid rare tragedies. But the rare unprotected tragedies can chill the entire system. Insurance, policing, legal regulation, appeals, and news provide the overhead catalysts business needs to maintain liquidity.

The answer that makes the economy efficient, is that all of society should share the essentials, but individuals should be free to chase after their own desires for nonessentials however they see fit. There are two types of business: government business and private business. Government business should oversee essentials. Private business should be free to pursue nonessentials.

Overhead institutions, like insurance or policing, provide the catalyst activation energy to guarantee liquidity in business – both government and private. The catalyst overcomes friction; it fights corruption. Overhead institutions to protect or promote essentials should be governed and borne by the group, protecting and promoting non-essentials should be governed and borne privately. Each DAO must decide what is essential to its function; protection of those assets is governed democratically according to their particular system. Each DAO has different goals and concerns. But to illustrate the point with an overhead institution everyone is familiar with, consider healthcare. Every country has determined a different level of healthcare as essential. How much the society bears the cost of healthcare tells us how essential it is to them. Some societies might care so much about healthcare, they would believe continual elective cosmetic surgery is a human right for all. At the other end of the spectrum, some societies might have no respect for medicine or individual health and provide absolutely no legally protected medical support – for example, even life-or-death emergency services would not be given unless the individuals provide for themselves ahead of time. The choice of dividing line between essentials and nonessentials is the line between government and business.

Individuals need to be responsible for choosing their own level of protection for nonessentials. Individuals choose to regulate their own choice of overhead investment to promote their pursuit of nonessentials based on their momentary personal tolerance for risk. For example, do you choose to pay to insure your smartwatch for 10 years or none? Do you hedge your personal investments with derivatives or not?

The network must identify the difference between essentials and nonessentials. This means the network must identify its values. Importantly, the decision of what is essential versus nonessential will change depending on the market. The system must have a dynamic governance process for constantly reinterpreting our values in the face of changing circumstances.

If the society values knowledge as a human right, to promote the development of the individual, the society will provide advice on the options for overhead coverage available to individuals for the protection of their nonessential pursuits. This requires that society recognizes the need to educate individuals about the functions of the middlemen and their value. In this case the networks need a well-functioning history generator – good news sources and information repositories. These analyses need to be dynamic, because the market continually changes. If the system is running well and everyone is profiting, there is less need for insurance. When the profits decrease and the system becomes more competitive, cheating becomes more attractive, and more insurance and reputation policing is needed. All this hinges on the determination of what products are essential and what are nonessential. What is social property, what is individual property? The answer depends on your particular values, and you should participate in the network that works to promote those values.

Similarly, the other two dimensions divide along a single definition. In the distinction between bureaucratic transparency and personal privacy we define the difference between public and personal information. Where is the dividing line between what the individual has a right to keep secret and what the society/network needs to know to maintain security? Does society need to know what chemicals you are experimenting with in your basement? Does society need to know your genetic information so it can determine what type of preventative medical care you should be given? Does society need to know your personal thoughts to determine whether you are a criminal risk? These are all extremely contentious issues. This dividing line is the distinction between the government and private media.

What does government keep secret or make public? What technology does the government use to make public information available? Should all congressional deliberations be made public? Should every conversation a representative has regarding public policy be recorded and made easily available to their constituents? Should all police wear body cameras with continuous footage made available immediately to the public? Should all government-funded weapons research be made public? Most draw the line at less than complete and full transparency in every governmental action, but a perfectly democratic society requires complete transparency. This is an abstraction, but a DAO should clearly specify where their values lie, and where they would draw the line between bureaucratic transparency and secrecy.

America tends to push the distinction toward personal privacy much further than China does. America has decided the quantity and type of weapons in my basement is none of my neighbor's business, and the government should not be involved. In Germany, governmental officials periodically inspect houses to count the number of TVs to ensure German households pay their proper public fees for TV licenses. In mainland China, the PRC decides who your best friend will be for the rest of your life when they decide who your roommate is, what university you will attend, and what major you will study. The line between what is public information and private information is a function of a society's values.

In the distinction between communal cooperation and individual freedom, we are defining the difference between governmental rights and personal freedom. What choices can you make – what can you do? In a healthy democracy, this dividing line separates the power of government over peoples' lives, versus the freedom we have in our social lives.

In a healthy society, whether democratic or not, these dividing lines are a faithful reflection of that group's values.

We can categorize every society, past and present, according to how they have favored one value or its polar opposite (see Figure 10.1). Failing to maintain a

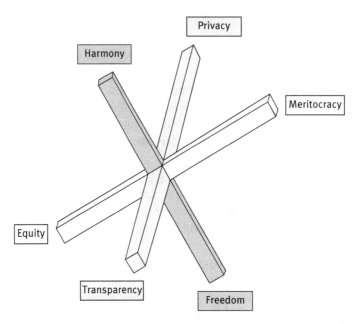

Figure 10.1: The three axes of values: 1) communal cooperation vs. individual freedom, 2) bureaucratic transparency vs. personal privacy (information storage; what do we know, individually and communally), and 3) equity of necessities vs. meritocracy for nonessentials.

healthy balance – one which faithfully reflects its peoples' values – is what topples empires and leads to social catastrophe.

Finding a healthy balance between opposite values is an eternal challenge. Not least because the definitions of the lines between the axes of these values should change under different circumstances. When a society is at war, values change from when it is at peace. But remember the goal is always to maximize both polar opposites in each dimension.

At the same time that these transcendental values are crucial for maintaining group coherence, they need to remain transcendental. Once they are formalized too rigorously, they become more manipulable. For example, once the definition of necessity versus nonessential is specified clearly, it becomes a focal point for competition, instead of a unifying principle to maximize both equitable distribution of necessities and meritocratic distribution of nonessentials.

This idea is illustrated by the tripartite motto, which was popular in 18th century revolutionary democracies (especially in France), "Freedom, Equality, and Good Will toward Men"[1] (*Liberté, Egalité. Fraternité*). Individual freedom and social equality are

---

[1] "True patriotism springs from a belief in the dignity of the individual, freedom and equality not only for Americans but for all people on earth, universal brotherhood and good will, and a constant

at odds with each other. But both qualities should be maximized. If we were to make a clear distinction between where our individual rights stop and social responsibilities start, then that formal line becomes a focal point for competition, which makes the system brittle and unstable. Instead the line between the two values must remain vague. The values need to be integrated with a third transcendental value, "Good Will towards Men," whatever that means technically – it's not a logical prescription. You know it when you see it. You can't clearly define it, but it's important. Be good to each other. Individuals, help your society; and society, help your individuals. Once you clearly define the boundaries of that power, the focal point for competition leads to some gaining outsized power, corrupting the system, then things fall apart.

These three dimensions of values each split along the definition of what is individual, and what is social. Beyond any Folk Theorem justification for stability, the ultimate reason we should not impose a clear distinction between the two is that there is no clear distinction in nature. For instance, consider how babies are not viable individuals, they depend on their caregivers for everything. Before they are six months old, they are not in control of their limbs and they must whine in order to (unintentionally) manipulate their caregivers to give them food, instead of using their hands to put the food in their mouths. When an individual grows up their material reliance on society never ends. Thanks to our dependence on technology, no one can survive long without depending on the complex tools that society provides. The distinction between the individual and society is never clear cut, and the values of a network need to reflect this vagueness. Every organization, especially every DAO, needs to value both the individual and the group.

Throughout the book, we've argued that giving individuals more autonomy through a decentralized architecture is more efficient. This needs to be balanced by the need to unite as a group. Cooperation is more efficient than individual autonomy. The network effect is only achieved when individuals subsume their freedom to act in concert with the group. Again, both individual autonomy and group cohesion need to be balanced to increase both qualities. Diminishing one diminishes the other.

Identifying the values of your network, or your society, or your DAO, is not some meaningless academic exercise. Your network's values determine your goals, which determine how your rewards and punishments are set up, which determine your network's future and whether it will survive. As explored in Chapter 7, you need to match your governance design choices to your values, or else the reward structure will dictate the true goals, which will determine what the network ultimately values.

A long-term successful network requires a dynamic and responsive system of governance to keep the organization in the decentralized, democratic realm, and

---

striving toward the principles and ideals on which this country was founded."–Eleanor Roosevelt's, *Book of Common Sense Etiquette*, 1962.

prevents it from moving to the next natural stage of centralized governance with a static hierarchy. In other words, we must protect the group from falling into static power relationships. The temptation is universal, because of the efficiency of centralization, but it is provably flawed. (We explored these arguments, Condorcet's Paradox, Arrow's Impossibility Theorem, and the Folk Theories of Game Theory with reputation in Chapter 4.)

At the same time, as we develop these new systems of governance, with these newfound technological powers, we can't abandon the crucial cultural achievements that have brought each of our nations to this point in history. Ten thousand years of civilization have given us a deep collection of theories on how to govern ourselves and create a fair and just world. We ignore this collective wisdom at our peril. There are many essential institutions to be rescued from the corruption of our past political regimes.

Our new tools for designing and implementing centralized hierarchies are far more sophisticated than ever before imagined. Our automated computer processing, information storage, and light-speed globally networked communication infrastructure are capable of achieving centralized organization that is more pervasive and powerful than had been previously imagined in fiction. These tools can monitor and guide the behaviors of every person, animal, and machine on the planet through a single, centralized bureaucracy.

If we commit too completely to this global, centralized, manmade hierarchy, if we allow our bureaucracy to become too rigid and impersonal, the predictable fall could be the final collapse. At this moment, and for the first time in history, we are building a structure and organization that is encompassing the entire planet. We would do well to heed the collective wisdom of history from such folk tales. The descent into chaos and collapse from centralized hierarchies is a common theme across cultures throughout history. The stories are there to warn us, so we can avoid such stumbling stones. The collapse of a hierarchy can come in many ways, not all of them catastrophic. We must understand the step that follows any centralized organization and be attentive to its signs and warnings. Why does a centralized hierarchy collapse? When is it best to give power to centralized organizations, and when is it best to invest in decentralized organizations?

A centralized hierarchy becomes too rigid when those policing the rules gain more power than the members who are honoring the transcendental value that originally founded the organization. The spirit of the law should always reign above the letter of the law. As an organization loses touch with its transcendental values, members use the rules to jockey for position in the hierarchy, and corruption erodes the effectiveness of the organization.

Giving away personal individual power to structures with rigid rules is always enticing, because it is often more efficient to follow the rules and not question them. A moral justification is that the rules apply equally to all. And people have been habituated for untold millennia to trust that cooperating with others is a better choice than causing strife in the group by resisting the flow.

Our success over other animals is often attributed to our opposable thumbs, our upright posture, ability to form complex speech, or our big brains' outsized capacity to process information. But from an organizational point of view, humanity's unique strength is its ability to cooperate on a massive scale, which really kicked in around 50,000 years ago. This derives from our ability to copy each other's behaviors by holding a mental model of other humans in our mind. We can go further than other animals in this ability as we can make models of what we imagine the other humans have in their minds. We can visualize how Alice thinks about what Bob thinks about what Carlos thinks about Eve. Supposedly, this modeling process goes six or seven levels deep in humans.[2] This ability to learn from others' behaviors gives us enormous capacity to unleash the efficiency of cooperation. But it also gives us untold power to trick other people as we imagine manipulating others to corrupt the organization for our individual benefit at the expense of the group.

These same information-processing tools that can lead to centralized cooperation are also capable of empowering individuals and guarding against the abuses of a corrupt hierarchy. The tools of internet communication allow individuals to connect with anyone on the planet to foster new opportunities for inventing collaboration. The transistor revolution is putting a supercomputer in every person's pocket. Each individual has access to a personal information repository with the capacity of all the books in the U.S. Library of Congress.[3] Never in any previous generation of history has any emperor had the personal power over information that the average person has today.

The goal of this book has been to explain the new social structures that are evolving, which can give individuals more power while also giving groups more social cohesion. More robust decentralized systems can provide greater bureaucratic transparency *and* more personal privacy. We have new technologies that can be employed to make the economy more efficient, productive, and sustainable by enabling a fair meritocracy *and* a more responsive regulatory environment, which promotes equity. These decentralized organizations can provide the level playing field that allow local centralized groups to flourish, while preventing the degeneration naturally resulting from competition, which leads to a rigid and brittle globally dominating centralized organization.

---

2 Crows can make at least two levels of mental models, since they can watch another crow experiment and learn to solve a puzzle opening a box for a food reward. The crow who watched will immediately solve the puzzle when faced with the challenge for the first time individually. A pigeon, on the other hand, will watch another learn to solve a puzzle, then display no learning once they are personally faced with the same challenge.

3 There are around 16 terabytes of data (not including pictures) in the 16 million books, which costs less than US$300 commercially in 2020.

To enact this vision, we need universal transcendental values, which can unify all of humanity. Do such ideals exist? If not, can we construct them?

Universal Values from Science and Poetry

Most scientists take for granted that nature, even the entire universe, is a decentralized organization, a DAO. They are looking for the rules behind it all, the protocols, the code that keeps it running autonomously in an organized manner. Most scientists, if they profess a faith, claim to be atheists; unlike the religious faithful they don't believe in a centralized universe, a single hierarchy that governs all existence. But most scientists also aren't nihilists. They believe the cosmos has order. They don't believe there is nothing but empty, meaningless chaos, because they devote their lives to finding patterns in nature. Why do they believe such a position, that there are rules behind the jiggling of atoms in the void? Why do scientists bother to seek rules at all? Why should they expect order to arise from behind their investigations if there isn't a God to put it there in the first place, to make meaning from the chaos?

Darwin created the first successful scientific model that posits the possibility of sustained complex order arising from chaos, without the intervention of any intelligent, organizing ruler. Life is a local contravention of the Second Law of Thermodynamics from physics, which posits that all organized systems move toward chaos and away from order when seen from a wide enough perspective. Thanks to the Sun pumping vast energy into our system, flooding Earth with light, life forms can utilize some small part of the energy the sun is dissipating to scrap together order – persistent patterns – from the muck. The Theory of Darwinian Evolution is an extremely simple law for explaining the profusion of natural forms, from biological organisms to global ecosystems: Through the rather wasteful destruction of trillions of lives, successful biological forms are naturally selected from unsuccessful mutant variations simply because they survive and reproduce. More complex variations occasionally outcompete simpler life forms, and so complexity emerges.

From a wider perspective, if we imagine the universe eternally chaotically jiggling its energy in the void of space, we can imagine all possible patterns revealing themselves eventually. The anthropocentric position puts forth the proposition that we are here in this little vicinity of order because the universe waited unfathomably long periods of time, perhaps through many universes' births and deaths, before the patterns became suitably complex for organized life to witness it. We're seeing order, because of an extremely rare random shift in circumstance generated the unlikely coincidence that allowed partly ordered beings to witness it. Then we're doomed to degenerate back into chaos for most of the rest of time. Perhaps even simpler, from a probabilistic perspective, among all the patterns that ever emerge, the patterns that repeat themselves will be observed more often. So, it should be no surprise statistically that we exist to witness such a state.

As Darwin predicted (and Nietzsche before him), the revelation that nature doesn't need a personalized God to explain its complex existence led (and still leads) many people to renounce their religious faith. Darwin feared the consequences to society when they lose the prime justification for their transcendental values – the values by which society can justify overcoming their selfishness in order to cooperate harmoniously.

Still, while abandoning a religious fundamentalist vision of any personalized God, by their very occupation of seeking theories, scientists believe in a simple, meaningful order behind the confusing illusion of chaos that confronts us personally on a daily basis. Scientists search for fundamental order that our tiny speck of a brain can comprehend to explain the infinite cosmos. Why would it be possible for a tiny fraction of the universe to be able to form a complete map of the whole? That could only happen if there are simple laws that govern the whole universe, if there is meaning that organizes being, if there is such a thing as truth. If there is a universal truth, then there is at least a hierarchy of human understanding, a ranking of better and worse perspectives and ideas. A universal set of laws, fundamental truth, predicates the existence of a centralized organizing force to the universe. A centralized organizing principle that touches every person's life, in an intimate way through palpable forces, each moment of every day. That truth, itself, is the God that scientists worship. The ultimate Truth is the God they seek. Even the scientists who rigorously discipline themselves to erase all evidence of a benevolent deity from their thoughts and beliefs, find themselves enthralled to a fundamental urge to see the universe as ultimately hospitable to life and truth.[4]

Science distinguishes itself from every other spiritual network by measuring its success in carving out pieces of their ultimate truth with mundane, reproduceable demonstrations of its laws. Compared with the miraculous and larger social question that religions attempt to explain, science has therefore necessarily focused on more basic, trivial phenomena, such as the motion of a rolling ball

---

4 We're not aware of the precise philosophical term for this argument that science is effectively a religion with Truth as its God, but it is by no means a novel concept. Indeed, this idea spawned several sects and cults shortly after the success of Darwin's work on evolution. For example, in William James, *The Varieties of Religious Experience*, 1917, he writes on p. 76, "Science, and our so-called 'Civilization' as these things are now organized and admiringly believed in, form the more genuine religions of our time" referring to J. R. Seeley, *Natural Religion, 3d edition*, Boston, 1886, pp. 91, 122. See also pp. 90, 138 where he uses the term "naturalism" to refer to this idea of science as religion, and p. 483. One of the many definitions of "scientism" is close to this argument. See Thomas M. Lessl, "Naturalizing Science: Two Episodes in the Evolution of a Rhetoric of Scientism," *Western Journal of Communication*, 60(4), 1996, pp. 379–396. Related ideas include deism, the Cult of Reason, the Cult of the Supreme Being, Religion of Humanity, transcendentalism, rationalism, materialism, positivism, empiricism, and energeticism. C. Hakfoort, "Science Deified: Wilhelm Osstwald's Energeticist World-View and the History of Scientism," *Annals of Science*, 49(6), 1992, pp. 525–544. Notice that none of these movements have endured long.

(gravity), or the sparks discharged by rubbing sheepskin on glass (electricity), or pollen jiggling in a vat of beer (atomic forces). The discovery of the laws behind these three palpable forces has led to every modern technological advance on the market. Scientists measure their success by how much they contribute to the goal of revealing these universal rules which govern the universe; their status in their particular quasi-religious hierarchy is notably more measurable and objective than other religions.

Science as a globally open discipline is extremely decentralized politically. No person, university, institution, or nation has monopoly control over whether any theory becomes established scientific fact. But this global science DAO is very protocol centralized around objective universal Truth.

Most scientists take for granted the universe itself is a decentralized organization, a DAO. They are looking for the rules behind it all, the protocols, the code that keeps it running autonomously in the organized manner we predictably witness. We personalize or anthropomorphize these rules when we make the leap to a religious perspective, by asking what values this universal protocol reflects. What is the goal of the universal DAO? Most atheist scientists reject such questions as unnecessary, even unearned and contraindicated, from the collection of truths that science has managed so far to assemble.

But scientists have not earned the right to make such a judgment, and they never can. Science's focus on the mundane has created remarkable advances in mundane technology. Their obsessive myopic focus on mundane forces limits their area of expertise to mundane physical arenas. Our understanding of psychology and sociology has made profound advances. But we are still far from definitively addressing how to solve personal conundrums in any way approaching the authoritative solutions science provides in answering how to put a rocket on the moon. Freud promised a scientific answer to such personal and social problems more than a century ago, but we are further than ever from that goal. Our scientific understanding of consciousness is superficial, despite the resources we've expended in the investigation. Scientists do not deserve to rule on the question of whether we should ask what the meaning is behind the rules guiding the universe, or the values they might reflect. They have less authority on this subject than someone who studies spirituality or theology or morality or poetry.

The Folk Theorems and other impossibility results illustrate the need for transcendental values for unifying people in harmonious cooperation. Transcendental values cannot be stated formally and explicitly, unlike scientific laws. People who are in touch with transcendental beauty, true poets, need to be the authors of our transcendental values. But these poets need to be grounded. They need to have concrete contact with the universe. They need to understand it – to comprehend the universe and its laws – to make meaningful goals.

Decentralization requires every member to participate in the construction of those values. A decentralized network is only as strong as its members and the environment it exists in. The strength of a decentralized organization is measured by summing the power of each member in their individual autonomy, but this is modified by the ability of the group to organize and effect its goals in the larger society. How well can members cooperate? The power of a DAO is its power to unite in service to the goal of shared values. In a decentralized organization, which doesn't coerce its members like centralized organizations do, its power is determined by how devoted its members are to its values. In constructing and following these values, every member needs to be a poet and a historian, a monk and a scientist, linking the talents of writing transcendental values and evaluating grounded mundane facts.

Decentralized organizations demand more from their members and return more, in autonomous power and profit. Centralized organizations shelter their members within a niche in a hierarchy. Centralized organizations limit the power of their members, stultifying them, in exchange for the security of knowing they will have a place to belong, as long as they fulfill their role as a cog in the very powerful machine, as long as the group survives. Decentralized organizations are ultimately more efficient and versatile, more stable socially and individually generative. They're as stable as their autonomous members' adherence to their ideals. But their very autonomy requires the members to construct the unifying ideals for themselves. They are individually responsible for nourishing and revitalizing those unifying ideals, continually. No book can contain those transcendental values. Our goal in this chapter is not even to make a failed attempt. We only wish to point to the necessity for such individually generated, socially unifying ideals, and offer a gauge with which to analyze them and measure their success.

Conclusion

Throughout this book we critique the existing state of P2P technology of blockchain tools. It should be clear that the developments being engineered are progressing at an astonishing pace. The power of these tools is terrifying and wondrous. The people who understand these new tools will be instrumental in choosing the pathways to the future.

Technological development has been noticeably accelerating for decades. The consequence is unprecedented cultural transformation in our times.[1] We are at the very beginning of a technological revolution that is reshaping society into a globally unified, supranational economic system.

Innovation in information technology is fueling these rapid changes: digital information storage, light-speed computer transistor information processing, and globally networked information transmission. Memory, computation, and communication. These new tools will unite humanity with unanticipated opportunities for communion, and at the same time they will demark new battle lines for competition. They will free us with new powers and bind us with new rules.

The exponentially growing rate of these technological developments is changing our personal abilities. Smartphones give us access to knowledge today that would have seemed like near omniscience a mere generation ago. Our maps react dynamically, filtering traffic information as we travel, telling us the most efficient routes to the best food, entertainment, and shopping. Drop us in the middle of any new location and we have more detailed understanding of a neighborhood's current commerce than the most savvy native could have dreamed two decades ago. Social media gives us better insight into the inner thoughts and opinions of our acquaintances than their parents have. We have new platforms for revealing the previously opaque inner workings of government and police (Twitter, WikiLeaks, YouTube, Facebook Live, Electronic Frontier Foundation, Sunlight Foundation, etc.).

Apocalypse means uncovering, or revelation. It shares meaning with the word discovery. Our information technology is revealing the inadequacies of the institutions governing our society. Our democracies were built on the notion of slowly filtering the best ideas through representatives, who would personally share and monitor social decision-making power. These old processes were built under the assumptions of 18th century modes of communication, under 18th century patterns of social relationships. With modern globally networked telecommunication, every person's opinion can be reliably polled, recorded, and tallied, every second. But our governmental institutions do not interface with this information in any formal

---

1 https://en.wikipedia.org/wiki/Great_Acceleration The result of this change is visible in the geological record, and geologists have labeled this change as a new epoch, the Anthropocene, due to the obvious impact mankind has had on the planet.

https://doi.org/10.1515/9783110673937-011

way. Our commerce and entertainment companies, however, are utilizing this instantaneous information. The new media of YouTube, Facebook, and Twitter is broadcasting this rolling apocalypse. The awareness of divisions between people that social networks are uncovering is made plain. This information technology revolution is accurately compared to the invention of the printing press in Europe. The resulting public dissemination of bibles to the public, led to the Protestant Reformation and transformation of European society at every level. Similarly, our governmental organizations currently stand revealed as obviously inadequate to the task of modulating this revolution and guiding society harmoniously into the future.

From many quarters, people are even calling for an end to government. This is especially alarming when it comes from powerful technocrats who are building tools that could plausibly replace our established governmental institutions.

Bitcoin cryptocurrency is a theoretically credible alternative to national fiat currencies. Bitcoin is not able to compete with the US dollar as the world's reserve currency, at least not at this moment. But weaknesses that have been recently revealed, particularly in U.S. political governance and its Federal Reserve's economic governance, have spotlighted the need for a neutral, global alternative to the USD. With no serious candidate available to fill the void, a decentralized solution is becoming a compelling argument.

As our legal systems' corruption, its stagnation, becomes ever more apparent, the need for transparency and efficiency in transactional execution and regulation is glaring. The Ethereum blockchain is offering a decentralized platform for programmatic business contracts that self-execute and self-regulate. They are bypassing institutions built on millennia of hard-earned business wisdom.

Like Bitcoin, the Ethereum network is not ready to replace our legal and business infrastructure, at least not today. There are serious technological challenges to implementing a level playing field on a global scale. The radical democratic principle of decentralization demands every user in the network have equal power over information visibility, processing, and dissemination. The goal is to leverage the enormous computing power, information storage, and P2P networking ability of each laptop and smartphone, to make every person on the planet technologically equal. We have built proof-of-concept networks that are currently running. Currently, they are too slow to replace our infrastructure for contemporary global commerce. However, scientific engineering is always progressing, increasing efficiency in speed and volume (latency and bandwidth). Our laptops currently support secure blockchain networks available to anyone on the planet who is connected to the internet. These blockchains demonstrate proof-of-concept for maintaining secure decentralized money and escrow services for business contracts, the two most fundamental ingredients for business. The rate of development of technology makes it easy to anticipate a time in the near future when these networks are *not* too slow to meet our commercial needs.

Bitcoin and Ethereum and many other P2P technologies are developing quickly. Most likely, the engineering problems will soon be solved, which provide the tools for decentralized money and business contracts. But will people use these solutions? Will we adopt these tools in our day-to-day business?

There is a lot more to business than money and contracts. Ten thousand years of civilization has led to cultural advances that most of us take for granted. Uniformitarianism is the fallacy that assumes the world has always been the way it is now. That our social harmony in the state that we enjoy today, has always been this way. That people have always been able to cooperate this way. That we've always shared our current moral values. The average person in a developed country has experienced peace for their entire life. The fallacy of uniformitarianism leads us to assume this peace is natural, but it is actually unique in human history.

This unprecedented peace is built on cultural developments that were earned by the blood of millions, in revolutions through the millennia. The institutions built on these cultures are artificial, not natural. If we abandon our traditions, according to the naive demands of the software developers who are engineering these decentralized networks, the natural state we will revert to is not peace and universal prosperity, but chaos and violence. As we dismantle the cultural institutions that support our business, as we dismantle our legal systems and our political government, we need to be certain they are replaced by something better.

This approach to solving problems, bypassing institutions haphazardly, is both naive and extremely dangerous. The systems we have in place are extremely complex and sophisticated, evolved throughout history. The theory involved in designing a modern environment for commerce is so deep and extensive that no single person has any more than a slight fraction of the understanding and wisdom necessary for the job. Plainly put, you are both naive and ignorant. And so is everyone else. The key to improving our extremely complex contemporary systems is collaboration on a scale far larger than the Manhattan Project.[2]

Yet nobody has the authority to initiate such a supranational project. Not only are national representatives incapable of comprehending the urgency of shoring up our failing legal and governmental systems, the international groups have no power to push such solutions. Throughout history great leaders have risen to the challenge of being figureheads for movements, which transformed society at critical moments. In recent history, with the increased scrutiny that our new technology has put people under, we have not seen any unifying leader able to meet the challenges of our times. Perhaps this is because our society is no longer morally united behind universally held ideals, so no one can rise to the top of such a society and remain the champion of varied and contradictory values, which are impermanent.

---

2 The Manhattan Project leveraged talent and resources across America, Britain, and Canada in 1942 to build the first nuclear bomb.

Or perhaps it is not possible for anyone to be worthy of being the leader of such a large group. But it has become increasingly obvious that a popularity contest to pick one person to put in charge of the hierarchy of a nation, much less the world, is not sustainable under exponentially growing complexity.

The ultimate crisis for humanity is looming. The word crisis comes from the Greek for decision. The advances in information technology make a global society inevitable. Our critical moment is to decide between consciously creating decentralized structures to protect our individual autonomy, or letting the natural progression of competition evolve a rigid and unstable centralized global power hierarchy. Democracy or dictatorship? We fear this will be *the* crisis, because once this decision is made, it could well be the last important choice we make collectively. The grips of this organization may be too strong to ever change and the power of a global society may conceivably have too much inertia to ever resist.

The coming crisis becomes more obvious as the societies under centralized nations break down. Democratic nations are not using the new tools of information technology at the governmental level. Corporations are, however, which makes the absence of these tools conspicuous in the public arena. As democratic governments and justice systems continue to refuse to incorporate contemporary information technology, our public institutions become irrelevant and lose their power to regulate our societies. We are witnessing their breakdown as people sidestep our public institutions, relying instead on centralized corporations. That breakdown can be an opportunity, if we are aware of it, as it naturally leaves space for us to reorganize. Will we have a society controlled by an opaque centralized bureaucracy with a PRC-style social credit system, or will we use these new tools to govern democratically and transparently?

This is obviously a terrifying moment in history, hearing about disruption in business, watching our institutions being overturned.[3] It is our responsibility and obligation to make wise decisions about how this new global society will be arranged, how power will be distributed. Our best chance is to understand the choice before us, deeply and thoroughly.

Centralized organizations are optimally efficient for making decisions at a group level, so they naturally emerge in response to large scale conflict. Strong centralization gives temporary social harmony, since the role of each person is clear in the hierarchy and there is no opportunity within the system for conflict. But a centralized organization tends to become ever more rigid and static, which leads to instability. As the hierarchy fails to adapt to changes, people tend to rely more on the hierarchy making it more rigid and eventually brittle. Human history is a record of the cycles of revolution that attend the emergence and inevitable fall of centralized Tower of Babel hierarchies.

---

3 Catastrophe (n.) from the Greek word *katastrophe*, "to overturn."

Decentralized organizations are more stable. They give people autonomy and equality. This leads to more permanent social harmony. This is the wiser choice for our emerging globally networked world of rapidly changing commerce. We need to take immediate steps toward this democratic approach while we still have the peace and resources that allow it. Otherwise, in a moment of chaos, the temporarily more effective option of centralized dictatorship will be forced upon us.

More centralized control is the less engaged choice, or the desperate choice in chaotic times. But it is not the wise choice. No single individual could ever deserve or wisely wield global decision-making power. A centralized global hierarchy is not the right design for the governance of society. The solution is giving more power to those who can wisely use it for the benefit of the group. Such delegatory power must be nimble and secure, to prevent corruption and react efficiently to the dynamic social and market changes our new technological power has unleashed. A well-designed incentive structure determines its long-term success.

We must use the very technological tools that are generating this global crisis to solve it. Decentralized governance can be achieved with the tools of global communication, secure decentralized information storage and processing, cryptographic information security, and the new designs of distributed computing architecture.

The only solution imaginable is to use the power of decentralized networking itself to access the talent and information at the edge to engage a new Manhattan Project. One that can build a new infrastructure for legal and governmental processes using the new information technology tools at our disposal to address the new global problems at hand. Strangely, the tool we wish to build is the very tool required to build it. We must carry ourselves into the future by our own bootstraps.

Fully decentralizing our current business, legal, and political institutions requires more than just solving the technological problems of decentralized currency and smart contracting. It includes creating a robust governance process that empowers every individual, not a process for eliminating government or regulation altogether. But the outdated and corrupt legal system and government need to be revitalized. They need to be reorganized dramatically, to formally interface with these new information tools of secure, distributed information storage, processing, and global communication. It starts by committing more fully to the ideals of establishing bureaucratic transparency and protecting personal privacy, of nurturing communal cooperation and protecting individual freedom, providing equity of necessities while encouraging a meritocracy for nonessentials.

Diagnosis

Continuing the categorization of reality into the information technology qualities of transmission, storage, and processing, we can split human society into the categories of business, media, and social life. Business is identified with data transmission, including whatever people do physically, travel and trade—what we do materially as a community. Media is identified with information storage, including history and news—the knowledge of the community. Social life consists of what we think, believe, and how we behave as a community—the process of arriving at meaning as a society.

From this perspective, the three branches of government are seen as the overhead institutions, which provide the catalyst for more sophisticated interactions of business, media, and social life. Executive-branch governance (which abstractly is policing in one form or another) provides the catalyst for business. Judicial governance grounds media. Legislative governance depends on social life to function and bounds social life with norms of behavior and rules for rewards and punishments.

When you see a breakdown in any area, you can trace the problem to its associated higher or lower-level counterparts. Since each branch affects all the others, deficits or excesses in one are reflected in the other branches.

The most obvious branch to diagnose as problematic is our social life—how we think, believe, and behave together as a community. The institutions of science, religion, and entertainment have evolved around these divisions. For centuries, these institutions have not been in harmony. Entertainment is play is education is communication, between science and religion to humanity. In information technology terms, entertainment is social information transmission; science is information processing; religion is information storage.[4] The schism between religion and science has been obvious and persistent for centuries. The schism between science

---

4 This repeated division of areas of analysis is not mystic numerology. Splitting any subject into three parts makes sense from a mathematical modeling perspective. The only way to achieve complex behavior is to label at least three variables in a dynamical system. Two or less variables have qualitatively simpler possible dynamics – such models cannot produce mathematical chaos, for example.

The process of analysis then proceeds by distilling the most important parts of the categories, identifying them, and describing their qualities. (The Greek word *analysis* can be etymologically traced to mean loosen, separate, or divide.) Throughout this book, the triumvirates were mere conveniences, following "the rule of threes" of storytelling.

We use this pattern from the lowest to the highest abstract perspectives. The animal experience of moving through its environment is split into the realms of perception, thought, and action. Information technology – starting with human speech and bringing us to the internet age – is information storage, processing, and transmission. Government is split into judicial, legislative, and executive branches. Civil society is divided into business, media, and social life. If these divisions seem arbitrary, that's because they are, and the intellectual game can be profitably repeated, endlessly. For example, information technology is not always split into the three categories of processing, storage, and transmission. Sometimes a fourth category is added: information retrieval. In this book we've considered retrieval mostly a part of transmission, though it obviously depends also on storage and processing. This primitive analysis is necessary, because there are no successful, coherent scientific syntheses of individual and social behavior available on the level of global economics.

and entertainment has also been evident for the last hundred years—the average person can't understand the basics of science, they certainly can't participate in its creation. Science has gone too far. Technology alienates us and estranges us from one another.

Our global society is at once too interconnected and too distant for anyone to feel deep belonging. The six degrees of separation of everyone on the planet means each person should be familiar with every community—with their culture and customs and values. More importantly, the interconnectedness of global society means you participate in these alien communities, in meaningful and measurable ways, despite your profound ignorance—your choices affect them, and they affect you.

Finally, the schism between entertainment and religion has emerged in the past few decades, evidenced by people abandoning their faiths in greater numbers with each new generation. Because science, entertainment, and religion are not working harmoniously together, social life is also breaking down. Without effective means for updating our information storage, our religions lose relevance to society. Without the ability to access meaningful communal information on our values, our science loses relevance as the information processor for society. Without access to science, our entertainment industries—media—becomes increasingly disconnected with reality and irrelevant for improving society with scientifically accurate information reflecting our morals and spiritual values.

This diagnosis is not, however, unique to our age. In fact, it is the natural state of human society. These complaints have been true since the inception of civilization. The gap between the state of the art of science and the average person was evident when the first caveman became a specialized toolmaker, knowing better than others how to harden pitch to fasten a rock to a stick, making a superior spear. One of the first stories in the Jewish Torah is about the first full human, Cain, being cursed and exiled. Cain's progeny invented cities and weapons of war, evoking the separation we feel from our technology and science.

Even before villages took over from family groups, people who weren't closely acquainted were still negotiating trades. Ancient people felt the danger of relying on foreign people with differing values for their economic survival, certainly more palpably than we experience today.

Some of the first messages in cuneiform decry the loss of faith of the younger generations, 5,000 years ago. It's part of the pattern of history that older generations judge the young as inferior in their appreciation for what's truly important.

Social life is breaking down. It is always breaking down. Such disintegration is necessary—the soil must be tilled—before new patterns of social behavior can emerge.

The prescription for improving society has always been the same. The divisions in society that naturally arise as our institutions centralize their power, require people and ideas and institutions capable of bridging those schisms. We need people, all people, to improve their competence in the areas of science and spiritual values and entertainment, to improve our communities' social lives. We need people who understand the technologies behind the supply chain, the moral and legal aspects of trade, and the details of the world to improve business. And we need people to be experts in history and current events, skilled in the theories for analyzing these facts and synthesizing meaning from them to improve our media.

The average person needs to improve themselves, just as our social structures need maintenance and upgrades. Embracing decentralization, means building institutions and organizations that strengthen individual autonomy in order to improve civilization—business, media, and social life. Our new tools and insights for governance must be consciously engaged to construct the nurturing environment that allows us to flourish. By encouraging the natural diversity of thought and behavior from the profusion of diverse natural talents of individuals across humanity, decentralized markets are strengthened.

Without deliberate interference, the natural evolution of human networks moves from chaos to decentralized organization, which then centralizes, then becomes brittle and collapses back to chaos. Consciously using the tools of decentralization, we can make stable improvements to our businesses and society, to defend our decentralized democratic institutions from the natural concentration of power that occurs in any competitive environment, or we can transition from unstable centralized institutions to decentralized organizations without the need to fall all the way back to chaos before new order emerges. The wisdom of the crowd and information at the edge improve the efficiency of society in the long run. Flatter markets with more diverse interests and talents are more effective and efficient at achieving truth discovery, such as price discovery and the identification of ideal solutions to arbitrary new problems that arise. Decentralization promotes that diversity by improving its members' autonomy and freedom, nurturing their natural development.

Network consensus through proper incentive design using secure and meaningful reputation keeps a decentralized organization stable by encouraging cooperation. Reputation inhibits the centralizing forces that attend the concentration of power from competition in the zero-sum, single-stage game when money is the primary goal. A focus on valuable reputation motivates members to strive for future rewards by building a history of profitable collaboration. Like love, reputation is not a limited resource suitable for competition—you can build reputation from nothing simply by behaving well. The more reputation a network has, the more power it accumulates. Reputation scales to networks of arbitrary size, distance, and time, as was employed in the Maghribi trading coalition.

Let us briefly encapsulate the essential requirements for building a DAO in one dense paragraph. Blockchain-based reputation tokens allow groups to use P2P digital ledger technology to securely track and maintain a global reputational system without appealing to any central authority. To be meaningful, the reputation tokens must be grounded with a connection to future money and power in the organization—all profits are shared in proportion to your reputation. To exploit the network effects of a modern global network, the reputational system should establish an open network, allowing anonymous participation by as many people as possible who can contribute, anywhere on the planet. Anonymity is protected with public-key cryptography and further advances in ZK proof technology. To further build the network, open source culture promotes interoperability. To guarantee harmony and security with such diverse members, the reputation must be for specific talents that further the specific goals of the particular DAO, so there must be many incompatible domain-specific reputation token types. Domain-specific reputation tokens also promote justice and efficient matching of talent to job, preventing the DAO from devolving to the corruption of inappropriate distributions of power. To secure the token against sock-puppet attacks and to promote fair rewards and meritocracy, the DAO must be governed by a weighted democracy according to reputational holdings—more reputation means more power and more rewards. Governance according to reputation includes protocol upgrades (legislation) and policing. With the proper governance incentive design, the DAO can promote its values, including maintaining its decentralization by rewarding diverse inputs instead of concentrating power within a few positions in the organization. With secure and meaningful reputation, the members have the power to protect their reputation and the integrity of the group through self-governance without relying on any form of centralized autocratic rule. Bureaucratic transparency is necessary in any decentralized organization as the rules and behavior of the organization must be auditable by every member. Transparency further grounds the reputation tokens with historical inertia. Finally, to further promote cooperation with future-oriented incentives, review is built into these decentralized reputational systems to reconsider past actions to properly valuate all contributions fairly. This secures the tokens against many arbitrage schemes and allows an economically justifiable open source culture reward design, as the system can properly reward protocol development after it is revealed—assuming the governance process has a tradition of fairly accounting and rewarding development after the fact.

This book is about decentralization, so it may appear that we are biased against centralized organizations. On the contrary, they can be superior structures to decentralized groups in many situations. Ideal centralized organizations are more efficient for the specific tasks they are designed for, because their structure eliminates all redundancies. Centralized organizations are not inherently evil or corrupt. But centralization is unstable. Without disciplined maintenance, centralization naturally leads to internal corruption; it can be easily conquered from the outside by taking control of the central authority. It is not adaptable to big changes in goals, because the hierarchy resists reorganizing to promote new talents. Centralized organizations eventually fail. Centralization is a good solution for subgroups with a specific temporary goal. Decentralization is the ideal choice for broader, long-term movements. Decentralized organizations are immortal. They never die. They morph into other organizations as their values and goals drift, often turning into central-ized organizations.

Perfectly flat decentralized organizations are not competitive with centralized organizations on well-defined limited tasks. Centralized organizations can set up static hierarchies with clearly defined roles and control while eliminating redun-dancies. A centralized organization can copy the DAO open source technology, im-prove on some aspect, and beat the slow DAO to market in a short period. For such temporary tasks, a DAO can adopt a temporary substructure with centralized orga-nization. Following the lessons of modern democracies, the DAO can protect their overall power decentralization—their members' autonomy—using dynamic gover-nance with a cyclic architecture of checks and balances with elected or randomly selected office holders weighted according to reputation to protect against concen-tration of power. With the advantages of contemporary information technology, the DAOs can further protect against concentration of power and rent-seeking by fairly accounting for all contributions, building pervasive microdemocracies, which scale from the smallest automated tasks which reward the network for automated partici-pation to the most abstract consciously manipulated decisions, such as protocol development.

The new tools of information technology are leading to algorithmically auto-mated social and business networks of ever-increasing sophistication, enabled by hardware improvements in the areas of information storage, processing and trans-mission. Software improvements include advances in mathematical theory (hash functions and ZK proof cryptography, incentive design with game theory and im-possibility results teach us how to build secure and meaningful reputation) and P2P architecture (blockchains and distributed hash tables). Decentralized organizations with open source cultures foster interoperability and API development, providing a neutral platform that can host the machine-oriented IoT supply chain while promot-ing human-oriented microdemocracies. Decentralized platforms build stable com-munities, and can provide the nurturing environment that gives members greater power and autonomy, while providing the incentives for human participation and collaboration toward the group's goals, helping to express and promote its human values in this age of rapidly accelerating technological automation.

Bibliography

Antonopolous, A. (June 17, 2017). Ethereum, ICOs, and Rocket Science [Video]. YouTube. https://www.youtube.com/watch?v=OWI5-Avndgk.

Antonopolous, A. & Wood, G. (2018). *Mastering Ethereum*. O'Reilly Media.

Apache Software Foundation (July 29, 2020). The Apache® Software Foundation Announces Annual Report for 2020 Fiscal Year. The Apache Software Foundation Blog, https://blogs.apache.org/foundation/entry/the-apache-software-foundation-announces67

Apache Software Foundation (June 10, 2020). Trillions and Trillions Served [Video]. YouTube. https://www.youtube.com/watch?v=JUt2nb0mgwg&feature=youtu.be

Apache Software Foundation, http://apache.org/

Apple Newsroom. (April 10, 2020). Apple and Google Partner on COVID-19 Contact Tracing Technology. https://www.apple.com/newsroom/2020/04/apple-and-google-partner-on-covid-19-contact-tracing-technology/

Aragon. (n.d.). Aragon Network [White paper]. https://github.com/aragon/whitepaper

Aristotle. (n.d.). Politics: A Treatise on Government. *Project Gutenberg*, https://www.gutenberg.org/ebooks/6762

Attiya, H. & Ellen, F. (2014). *Impossibility Results for Distributed Computing*. Morgan and Claypool Publishers.

Baier, C. & Katoen, J-P. (2006). *Principles of Model Checking*. The MIT Press.

Ballotpedia (n.d.). Local Government Responses to the Sharing Economy (ridesharing/homesharing). https://ballotpedia.org/Local_government_responses_to_the_sharing_economy_(ridesharing/homesharing)

Bano, S., Sonnino, A., Chursin, A., Perelman, D., & Calibra, D.M. (April 22, 2020). Twins: White-Glove Approach for BFT Testing [Unpublished article]. https://arxiv.org/pdf/2004.10617.pdf

Barbrook, R. (1998 with 2005 update). The High-Tech Gift Economy. *First Monday, 13* (12), https://firstmonday.org/ojs/index.php/fm/article/view/631/552

Bartlett, R.C. & Collins, S.D. (2011). *Nicomachean Ethics*. University of Chicago Press.

Bech, M.L. & Garratt, R. (September 2017). Central Bank Cryptocurrencies. *BIS Quarterly Review*, https://www.bis.org/publ/qtrpdf/r_qt1709f.htm

Berensten, Al & Schar, F. (2018). The Case for Central Bank Electronic Money and the Non-Case for Central Bank Cryptocurrencies. *Federal Reserve Bank of St. Louis Review*, 100(2), 97–106.

Big. (n.d.) In thesaurus.com https://www.thesaurus.com/browse/big/14 (retrieved 8/15/20).

Billner, A. (October 26, 2018). *Now There Are Plans for 'e-Krona' in Cash-Shy Sweden*. Bloomberg: Economics, https://www.bloomberg.com/news/articles/2018-10-26/riksbank-to-develop-pilot-electronic-currency-amid-cash-decline

Brafman, O. & Beckstrom, R.A. (2008). *The Starfish and the Spider: The Unstoppable Power of Leaderless Organizations*. Portfolio.

Brosnan, S.F. & de Waal, F.B.M. (2014). Evolution of Responses to (Un)fairness. *Science, 346*(6207). https://doi.org/10.1126/science.1251776

Brugge, J., Denecker, O., Jawaid, H., Kovacs, A., & Shami, I. (August 2018). *Attacking the Cost of Cash*. McKinsey & Company, https://www.mckinsey.com/industries/financial-services/our-insights/attacking-the-cost-of-cash#

Buck, J. (October 1, 2017). Dubai Will Issue First Ever State cryptocurrency. Cointelegraph, https://cointelegraph.com/news/dubai-will-issue-first-ever-state-cryptocurrency

Bush v. Gore, 531 U.S. 98 (2000).

Buterin, V. (February 6, 2017). The Meaning of Decentralization. Medium.com https://medium.com/@VitalikButerin/the-meaning-of-decentralization-a0c92b76a274 (retrieved 5/10/20).

Calcaterra, C. (2018). On-Chain Governance of Decentralized Autonomous Organizations [Unpublished article]. https://ssrn.com/abstract=318837

Calcaterra, C., Kaal, W., & Andrei, V. (February 18, 2018). Blockchain Infrastructure for Measuring Domain Specific Reputation in Autonomous Decentralized and Anonymous systems [University of St. Thomas Legal Studies Research Paper No. 18–11].

Calcaterra, C., Kaal, W.A., & Rao, V.K. (2019). Decentralized Underwriting [Unpublished paper]. https://papers.ssrn.com/sol3/papers.cfm?abstract_id=3396542

Calcaterra, C., Kaal, W.A., & Rao, V.K. (2020). Stable Cryptocurrencies: First Order Principles. *Stanford Journal of Blockchain & Policy*, *3*(1), 62–82.

Cap, C. & Leiding, B. (2018). Ensuring Resource Trust and Integrity in Web Browsers Using Blockchain Technology [Presentation]. Advanced Information Systems Engineering Workshops – CAiSE 2018 International Workshops, Tallinn, Estonia.

Century of Humiliation. (September 5, 2020). In Wikipedia. https://en.wikipedia.org/wiki/Paramount_leader

Chapman, L., Eidelson, J., Cutler, J.E., & Bloomberg. (September 11, 2019). New Labor Bill Passed by California Senate Would Transform the Gig Economy–and Could Cost Uber $500 Million a Year. Fortune: Tech, https://fortune.com/2019/09/11/gig-economy-california-senate-uber-law-labor-rights-union/

Chen, J. (2008). *Chinese Law: Context and Transformation*. Martinus Nijhoff.

Cheung, S. (n.d.). Baojia System. In *Encyclopedia of Modern China, 1*, 136–137.

Chohan, U.W. (February 7, 2018). Cryptocurrencies as Asset-Backed Instruments: The Venezuelan Petro [unpublished paper]. https://papers.ssrn.com/sol3/papers.cfm?abstract_id=3119606

Confucius. (1979). *The Analects*. D.C. Lau (translator). Penguin Classics.

Conklin, J. (2006). *Dialogue Mapping: Building Shared Understanding of Wicked Problems*. Wiley Publishing.

Constitution of the People. (September 13, 2020). In Wikipedia. https://en.wikipedia.org/w/index.php?title=Constitution_of_the_People%27s_Republic_of_China&action=history

Contract Killing. (September 12, 2020). In Wikipedia. https://en.wikipedia.org/w/index.php?title=Contract_killing&action=history

Cooper, J.S. (1986). *Clay Cones La 9.1 Presargonic Inscriptions*. The American Oriental Society.

Creech, W.L. (1995). *The Five Pillars of TQM*. Plume.

Cristianini, N., & Scantamburlo, T. (2019). *On Social Machines for Algorithmic Regulation*. AI & Soc.

D'Errico, F. (2003). The Invisible Frontier: A Multiple Species Model for the Origin of Behavioral Modernity. *Evolutionary Anthropology*, *12*(4), 188–202. https://doi.org/10.1002/evan.10113

Das, S. (November 26, 2016). Senegal Will Introduce a Block-Chain-Based National Digital Currency. CCN, https://www.ccn.com/senegal-will-introduce-blockchain-based-national-digital-currency/

de Barry, W.T. & Bloom, I. (1999). *Sources of Chinese Tradition from Earliest Times to 1600* (2nd ed.). Columbia University Press.

de Cleyre, V. (1890). The Economic Tendency of Freethought. *Liberty, XI*, Article 25.

Democracy Index. (September 24, 2020). In Wikipedia, https://en.wikipedia.org/w/index.php?title=Democracy_Index&action=history

Drexel University (October 12, 2016). Just Give Me Some Privacy: Anonymous Wikipedia Editors Explain Why They Don't Want You to Know Who They Are. Phys.org, https://phys.org/news/2016-10-privacy-anonymous-wikipedia-editors-dont.html

Dwoskin, E. (August 21, 2018). Facebook Is Rating the Trustworthiness of its Users on a Scale from Zero to 1. *The Washington Post*. https://www.washingtonpost.com/technology/2018/08/21/facebook-is-rating-trustworthiness-its-users-scale-zero-one/

Ebrey, P.B., Walthall, A., & Palais, J.B. (2006). *East Asia: A Cultural, Social, and Political History*. Houghton Mifflin.

Edelman. (January 21, 2018). 2018 Edelman Trust Barometer: Global Report. https://www.edelman.com/research/2018-edelman-trust-barometer

Eisenstein, E. (1979). *The Printing Press as an Agent of Change*. Cambridge University Press.

ETH Staking. (n.d.). Correct by Construction (CBC) Casper. Guide to Ethereum Proof of Stake and Casper, https://ethstaking.io/correct-by-construction-cbc-casper/

Ethereum Studio, https://studio.ethereum.org/

Evans Hughes, C. (2019). *Conditions of Progress in Democratic Government*. Forgotten Books.

Evans, D. (2011). The Internet of Things: How the Next Evolution of the Internet Is Changing everything [White Paper]. Cisco. https://www.cisco.com/c/dam/en_us/about/ac79/docs/innov/IoT_IBSG_0411FINAL.pdf

Farmer, F.R. & Glass, B. (2010). *Building Web Reputation Systems*. O'Reilly Media.

Federal Reserve Bank of Minneapolis. (December 1, 1995). Interview with Kenneth Arrow. https://www.minneapolisfed.org/article/1995/interview-with-kenneth-arrow

Fernández Cara, E. & Zuazua Iriondo, E. (2003). Control Theory: History, Mathematical Achievements and Perspectives. *Boletin de la Sociedad Espanola de Matematica Aplicada*, *26*, 79–140.

Forsyth, D. (2006). *Group Dynamics* (5th ed.). Cengage Learning, 388–389.

Forte, A., Andalibi, N., Greenstadt, R. (2017). Privacy, Anonymity, and Perceived Risk in Open Collaboration: A Study of Tor Users and Wikipedians. Proceedings of the 2017 ACM Conference on Computer-Supported Cooperative Work and Social Computing, Portland, OR, 1800–1811, https://dl.acm.org/doi/10.1145/2998181.2998273

Gates, T. (director), MacFarlane, S. (writer). (October 26, 2017). Majority Rule (Season 1, Episode 7), in Braga, B., Clark, J., Goodman, D.A., Heldens, L., MacFarlane, S., & Wild, W (Executive Producers), *The Orville*. Fuzzy Door Productions; 20th Century Fox Television.

Gehrlein, W. (2002). Condorcet's Paradox and the Likelihood of its Occurrence: Different Perspectives on Balanced Preferences. *Theory and Decision*, *52*(2), 171–199.

Girondin Constitutional Project. (June 14, 2019). In Wikipedia, https://en.wikipedia.org/wiki/Girondin_constitutional_project

Global Surveillance Disclosures (2013–present). (July 19, 2020). In Wikipedia, https://en.wikipedia.org/wiki/Global_surveillance_disclosures_(2013%E2%80%93present)

Goertzel, B. (August 8, 2020). Decentralized Tech Will be Ready for Humanity's Next Crisis. Coindesk, https://www.coindesk.com/decentralized-tech-will-be-ready-for-humanitys-next-crisis

Goodin, D. (May 1, 2012). Skype Replaces P2P Supernodes with Linux Boxes Hosted by Microsoft (updated). ArsTechnica, https://arstechnica.com/information-technology/2012/05/skype-replaces-p2p-supernodes-with-linux-boxes-hosted-by-microsoft/

Government by Algorithm. (July 28, 2020). In Wikipedia, https://en.wikipedia.org/wiki/Government_by_algorithm

Great Acceleration. (September 23, 2020). In Wikipedia, https://en.wikipedia.org/wiki/Great_Acceleration

Greenwald, G., Ackerman, Sp., Poitras, L., MacAskill, E., & Rushe, D. (2013, July 12). How Microsoft Handed the NSA Access to Encrypted Messages. *The Guardian*, https://www.theguardian.com/world/2013/jul/11/microsoft-nsa-collaboration-user-da-ta#:~:text=Microsoft%20has%20collaborated%20closely%20with,documents%20obtained%20by%20the%20Guardian

Greif, A. (1989). Reputation and Coalitions in Medieval Trade: Evidence on the Maghribi Traders. *Journal of Economic History*, *49*(4), 857–882.

Greif, A. (2006). *Institutions and the Path to the Modern Economy: Lessons from Medieval Trade*. Cambridge University Press, 428–452.

Greif, A. & Tabellini, G. (2017). The Clan and the Corporation: Sustaining Cooperation in China and Europe. *Journal of Comparative Economics*, *45*(1), 1–35.

Grofman, B., Owen, G., & Feld, S. (1983). Thirteen Theorems in Search of the Truth. *Theory and Decision*, *15*, 261–278.

Hakfoort. C. (1992). Science Deified: Wilhelm Osstwald's Energeticist Worldview and the History of Scientism. *Annals of Science*, *49*(6), 525–544.

Hamilton, A. or Madison, J. (February 5, 1788). Federalist No. 49. *The New York Packet.* Available at https://guides.loc.gov/federalist-papers/text-41-50#s-lg-box-wrapper-25493416

Herbst, J. (1996). *The Once and Future School: Three Hundred and Fifty Years of American Secondary Education.* Routledge.

Hileman, G. & Rauchs, M. (2017). Global Cryptocurrency Benchmarking Study. Cambridge Centre for Alternative Finance, https://www.jbs.cam.ac.uk/fileadmin/user_upload/research/centres/alternative-finance/downloads/2017-04-20-global-cryptocurrency-benchmarking-study.pdf

Hirschfeld, D., Popper, J., & Popper, N. (2018, March 20). White House Bans Venezuela's Digital Currency and Imposes Further Sanctions. *New York Times*, A1.

Hofstadter, D. (1985). The Prisoner's Dilemma: Computer Tournaments and the Evolution of Cooperation. In *Metamagical Themas*. Bandam Dell Publishing Group.

Hu, S. & Yuan, Z. (2015). Erratum: Commentary: Large-Scale Psychological Differences within China Explained by Rice vs. Wheat Agriculture. *Frontiers in Psychology*, *6*, 489. https://doi.org/10.3389/fpsyg.2015.00489

Human Action. (July 2, 2020). In Wikipedia, https://en.wikipedia.org/wiki/Human_Action

Hunt, G. (Ed.) (1910). *The Writings of James Madison: 1819–1836.* G.P. Putnam's Sons, 361.

Ignatieff, M. (2018). *Open Society.* Central European University Press.

Intellipedia. (June 6, 2020). In Wikipedia, https://en.wikipedia.org/wiki/Intellipedia

Introduction to Logic, http://intrologic.stanford.edu/public/home.php

James, W. (1902). *The Varieties of Religious Experience: A Study in Human Nature, Being the Gifford Lectures on Natural Religion Delivered at Edinburgh in 1901–1902.* Longmans, Green & Co.

Jee, C. (July 10, 2020). 8 Million People, 14 Alerts: Why Some COVID-19 Apps Are Staying Silent. *MIT Technology Review*, https://www.technologyreview.com/2020/07/10/1005027/8-million-people-14-alerts-why-some-covid-19-apps-are-staying-silent/

Kahneman, D., Fredrickson, B.L., Schreiber, C.A., & Redelmeier, D.A. (1993). When More Pain Is Preferred to Less: Adding a Better End. *Psychological Science*, *4*(6), 401–405.

Kastelein, R. (December 28, 2015). Tunisia to Replace its National Digital Currency, eDinar, with Blockchain-Driven Monetas Currency. Blockchain News, https://www.the-blockchain.com/2015/12/28/tunisia-to-replace-its-national-digital-currency-edinar-with-blockchain-driven-monetas-currency/

Kharpal, A. (September 27, 2017). Japanese Banks Are Thinking of Making Their Own Cryptocurrency Called the J-Coin. CNBC: Tech Transformers, https://www.cnbc.com/2017/09/27/japanese-banks-cryptocurrency-j-coin.html

King James Bible, 1769/2017, Matthew 25:29.

Kiss, J. (August 9, 2011). BitTorrent: Copyright Lawyers' Favourite Target Reaches 200,000 Lawsuits. *The Guardian*, https://www.theguardian.com/technology/pda/2011/aug/09/bittorrent-piracy

Kolonin, A., Goertzel, B., Duong, D., & Ikle, M. (n.d.). A Reputation System for Artificial Societies [Unpublished article]. https://arxiv.org/ftp/arxiv/papers/1806/1806.07342.pdf

Koning, J.P. (November 15, 2016). Fedcoin: A Central Bank-Issued Cryptocurrency. R3, https://www.r3.com/wp-content/uploads/2017/06/fedcoin_central-bank_R3.pdf

Korjus, K. (December 18, 2017). We're Planning to Launch Estcoin – and That's Only the Start. Medium, https://medium.com/e-residency-blog/were-planning-to-launch-estcoin-and-that-s-only-the-start-310aba7f3790

Labaton, S. (October 18, 2007). Plan Would Ease Limits on Media Owners. *New York Times*, https://www.nytimes.com/2007/10/18/business/media/18broadcast.html.

Lalley, S. & Weyl, G. (2018). Quadratic Voting: How Mechanism Design Can Radicalize Democracy. *American Economic As-sociation Papers and Proceedings, 1*(1).

Larson, R. (2020). *Bit Tyrants: The Political Economy of Silicon Valley*. Haymarket Books.

Last Universal Common Ancestor. (September 19, 2020). In Wikipedia. https://en.wikipedia.org/wiki/Last_universal_common_ancestor

Lessl, T.M. (1996). Naturalizing Science: Two Episodes in the Evolution of a Rhetoric of Scientism. *Western Journal of Communication, 60*(4), 379–396.

Levine, Y. (July 16, 2014). Almost Everyone Involved in Developing Tor Was (Or Is) Funded by the US Government. *Pando Daily*, https://pando.com/2014/07/16/tor-spooks/

Liao, S. (April 5, 2018). Major Blockchain Group Says Europe Should Exempt Bitcoin from New Data Privacy Rule. *The Verge*, https://www.theverge.com/2018/4/5/17199210/blockchain-coin-center-gdpr-europe-bitcoin-data-privacy

List of Last Stands. (September 19, 2020). In Wikipedia. https://en.wikipedia.org/wiki/List_of_last_stands

Lloyd, W.F. (1833). *Two Lectures on the Checks to Population*. Oxford University.

Locke, J. (1690). *Two Treatises of Government*. London: Printed for Awnsham Churchill.

Luther King, Jr., M. (1963). *Strength to Love*. Beacon Press.

Lutz, A. (June 14, 2012). These 6 Corporations Control 90% of the Media in America. *Business Insider*, https://www.businessinsider.com/these-6-corporations-control-90-of-the-media-in-america-2012-6

Machiavelli, N. (1513). *The Prince*. W.K. Marriott (translator). Project Gutenberg, https://www.gutenberg.org/files/1232/1232-h/1232-h.htm

Macroprudential Surveillance Department (November 2017). *Financial Stability Review*. Monetary Authority of Singapore, https://www.mas.gov.sg/-/media/MAS/resource/publications/fsr/FSR-2017.pdf

Madison, J. (February 1, 1788). Federalist No. 47. *The New York Packet*. Available at https://guides.loc.gov/federalist-papers/text-41-50#s-lg-box-wrapper-25493412.

Madison, J. or Hamilton, A. (February 8, 1788). Federalist No. 51. *The New York Packet*. Available at https://guides.loc.gov/federalist-papers/text-51-60#s-lg-box-wrapper-25493427

Mailath, G.J. & Samuelson, L. (2006). *Repeated Games and Reputations: Long-Run Relationships*. Oxford University press.

Mausoleum of the First Qin Emperor (August 8, 2020). In Wikipedia. https://en.wikipedia.org/wiki/Mausoleum_of_the_First_Qin_Emperor

McLuhan, H.M. (1966). Address at Vision 65. *The American Scholar, 35*(2), 196–205.

Meaning, J., Dyson, B., Barker, J., & Clayton, E. (May 18, 2018). Broadening Narrow Money: Monetary Policy with a Central Bank Digital Currency [Staff working paper no. 724]. Bank of England. https://www.bankofengland.co.uk/working-paper/2018/broadening-narrow-money-monetary-policy-with-a-central-bank-digital-currency

Mellen, R.P. (2013). Modern Arab Uprisings and Social Media: An Historical Perspective on Media and Revolution. *Explorations in Media Ecology, 11*(2), 115.

Mencius. (1988). *Mencius*. D.C. Lau (translator). Penguin Classics.

Merkle, R. (May 31, 2016). DAOs, Democracy and Governance [Version 1.9]. Merkle, http://merkle.com/papers/DAOdemocracyDraft.pdf

Mersch, Y. (July 24, 2017). Central Banking in Times of Technological Progress [Conference presentation]. Central Bank of Malaysia Monetary Policy Conference, Kuala Lumpur. https://www.bis.org/review/r170807c.htm

Metcalfe's Law (August 12, 2020). In Wikipedia, https://en.wikipedia.org/wiki/Metcalfe%27s_law

Mistreanu, S. (2018, April 3). Life Inside China's Social Credit Laboratory. *Foreign Policy*, https://docs.house.gov/meetings/FA/FA18/20180711/108531/HHRG-115-FA18-20180711-SD001.pdf

MIT Media Lab, Digital Currency Initiative, https://dci.mit.edu

Motamedi, S. (2014, July 21). Will Bitcoins Ever Become Money? A Path to Decentralized Central Banking. TannuTuva.org,https://tannutuva.org/2014/will-bitcoins-ever-become-money-a-path-to-decentralized-central-banking

Mozur, P., Zhong, R., & Krolik, A. (March 1, 2020). In Corona-Virus Fight, China Gives Citizens a Color Code, with Red Flags. *New York Times*. https://www.nytimes.com/2020/03/01/business/china-coronavirus-surveillance.html

Murphy, C. (January/February 2020). Our Predictions about the Internet Are Probably Wrong. *The Atlantic*, https://www.theatlantic.com/magazine/archive/2020/01/before-zuckerberg-gutenberg/603034/

Murphy, R.P. (2002). *Chaos Theory* [Self-published].

Netcraft (April 15, 2010). April 2010 Web Server Survey, https://news.netcraft.com/archives/2010/04/15/april_2010_web_server_survey.html. (For an external audit and more recent claims see Apache Software Foundation (2020, July 29). The Apache® Software Foundation announces annual report for 2020 fiscal year. The Apache Software Foundation Blog, https://blogs.apache.org/foundation/entry/the-apache-software-foundation-announces67

Neumann, E. (1954). *The Origins and History of Consciousness*. Princeton University Press.

Nevins, T.J. (2004). Introduction. In H. Ingstad, *The Apache Indians: In Search of the Missing Tribe* (p. xxiv). University of Nebraska Press.

Nietzche, F. (2011). *The Birth of Tragedy*. Maestro Reprints.

Nussbaum, J.L. (1984). Apple Computer Inc. v. Franklin Computer Corporation Puts the Byte Back into Copyright Protection for Computer Programs. *Golden Gate University Law Review*, 14(2), Article 3.

O'Dea, S. (August 17, 2020). Mobile Operating Systems' Market Share Worldwide from January 2012 to July 2020. *Statista*. https://www.statista.com/statistics/272698/global-market-share-held-by-mobile-operating-systems-since-2009/#:~:text=Android%20maintained%20its%20position%20as,of%20the%20global%20market%20share

O'Reilly, T. (2013). Open Data and Algorithmic Regulation. In B. Goldstein (Ed.), *Beyond Transparency* (pp. 289–300). Code for America Press.

Obar, J. (2009). Beyond Cynicism: A Review of the FCC's Reasoning for Modifying the Newspaper/Broadcast Cross-Ownership Rule. *Communication Law & Policy*, 14(4), 479–525.

OpenBazaar, https://openbazaar.org/

Ostrom, E. (1990). *Governing the Commons*. Cambridge University Press.

Paramount Leader. (September 21, 2020). In Wikipedia. https://en.wikipedia.org/wiki/Paramount_leader

Peters, S. & Ruff, N. (n.d.). Participating in Open Source Communities. *The Linux Foundation*, https://www.linuxfoundation.org/resources/open-source-guides/participating-open-source-communities/

Pines, Y. (Winter 2018). Legalism in Chinese Philosophy. *The Stanford Encyclopedia of Philosophy*, Edward N. Zalta (ed.).

Popper, K. (1945). *The Open Society and its Enemies, Vol. I: The Spell of Plato*. Routledge.

Popper, K.R. (1994). *The Myth of the Framework: In Defence of Science and Rationality*. Routledge.

Post-Quantum Cryptography. (August 22, 2020). In Wikipedia, https://en.wikipedia.org/wiki/Post-quantum_cryptography

Powell, A., Shennan, S., & Thomas, M.G. (2009). Late Pleistocene Demography and the Appearance of Modern Human Behavior. *Science*, 324, 1298–1301. https://doi.org/10.1126/science.1170165

Pratchett, T. (2001). *Thief of Time*. HarperTorch.

Prichard, J. V., baron de Montesquieu, C. d. S., Nugent, T. (1900). *The Spirit of the Laws*. D. Appleton.

Putnam, R.D., Leonardi, R., & Nanetti, R. (1993). *Making Democracy Work: Civic Traditions in Modern Italy*. Princeton University Press.

Rao, R. & Buteau. (2018). Modelling Credit and Savings Behaviour of Chit Fund Participants. *Gates Open Research*, 2(26).

Rawls, J. (1999). *A Theory of Justice* [Revised ed.]. Belknap Press.

Raymond, E.S. (1999). *The Cathedral and the Bazaar: Musings on Linux and Open Source by an Accidental Revolutionary*. O'Reilly Media.

Reinsel, D., Gantz, J., & Rydning, J. (2018). The Digitization of the World: From Edge to Core [White paper]. IDC. https://www.seagate.com/files/www-content/our-story/trends/files/idc-seagate-dataage-whitepaper.pdf

Rogoff, K.S. (2016). *The Curse of Cash*. Princeton University Press.

Rooney, K. (October 12, 2018). Bitcoin Is the "Mother of All Scams" and Blockchain Is Most Hyped Tech Ever, Roubini tells Congress. CNBC.com, https://www.cnbc.com/2018/10/11/roubini-bitcoin-is-mother-of-all-scams.html

Roosevelt, E. (December 16, 1941). *The Eleanor Roosevelt Papers*. United Feature Signature, Inc.

Roosevelt, E. (1962). *Book of Common Sense Etiquette*. Macmillan Company.

Rosenfeld, E. (February 9, 2015). Ecuador Becomes the First Country to Roll Out its Own Digital Cash. CNBC.com, https://www.cnbc.com/2015/02/06/ecuador-becomes-the-first-country-to-roll-out-its-own-digital-durrency.html

Rosenhead, J. (2013). Problem Structuring M. In *Encyclopedia of Operations Research and Management Science* (3rd ed.). Springer Verlag, 1162–1172.

SACA. (August 15, 2019). Neverending Story: ISP Market Consolidation. SACA's Blog, https://www.sacatech.com/2019/08/15/neverending-story-isp-market-consolidation/

Sams, R. (April 28, 2015). A Note on Crytpocurrency Stabilisation: Seigniorage Shares. Brave Newcoin, https://bravenewcoin.com/insights/a-note-on-cryptocurrency-stabilisation—seigniorage-shares

Schrab, R. (director), Harmon, D. (writer), Blum, J. (writer). (March 6, 2014). App Development and Condiments (Season 5, Episode 8). In Harmon, D., Kienlen, P., McKenna, C., & Shapeero, T. (Executive Producers), Community, Paramount Productions.

Sedgwick, K. (May 2, 2018). $9 Million a Day Is Lost in Crytocurrency Scams. Bitcoin.com,https://news.bitcoin.com/9-million-day-lost-cryptocurrency-scams/

Shapiro, C. & Varian, H. (1999). *Information Rules*. Harvard Business School Press.

Share Barcelona, https://share.barcelona/

Shlieffer, A. & Vishny, R.W. (1997). A survey of corporate governance. *Journal of Finance*, 52(2),737–783. https://doi.org

Smil, V. (2017). *Energy and civilization: A history*. MIT Press.

Social Cedit System (August 7, 2020). In Wikipedia, https://en.wikipedia.org/wiki/Social_Credit_System

Sosis, R. (2000). Religion and Intragroup Cooperation: Preliminary Results of a Comparative Analysis of Utopian Communities. *Cross-Cultural Research*, 34(1),70–87. https://doi.org/10.1177/106939710003400105

South by Southwest (March 12, 2012). Social Media in Arab Spring [Video]. YouTube, https://www.youtube.com/watch?v=1bSj4f9f8Eg&desktop_uri=%2Fwatch%3Fv%3D1bSj4f9f8Eg

Speake, G. (2002). *Mount Athos: Renewal in Paradise*. Yale University Press.

Stack, M. & Gartland, M. (2003). Path Creation, Path Dependency, and Alternative Theories of the Firm. *Journal of Economic Issues, 37*(2), 487.

State Council (October 18, 2016). State Council Guiding Opinions Concerning Establishing and Perfecting Incentives for Promise-Keeping and Joint Punishment Systems for Trust-Breaking, and Accelerating the Construction of Social Sincerity [GF No. (2016)33]. China Copyright and Media. https://chinacopyrightandmedia.wordpress.com/2016/05/30/state-council-guiding-opinions-concerning-establishing-and-perfecting-incentives-for-promise-keeping-and-joint-punishment-systems-for-trust-breaking-and-accelerating-the-construction-of-social-sincer/

Statista. (2020). Most Popular Social Networks Worldwide as of July 2020, Ranked by Number of Active Users. https://www.statista.com/statistics/272014/global-social-networks-ranked-by-number-of-users/

Steinwender, C. (2018). Real Effects of Information Frictions: When the States and the Kingdom Became United. *American Economic Review, 108*(3), 657–696.

Steward, K.J. & Gosain, S. (2006). The Impact of Ideology on Effectiveness in Open Source Software Development Teams. *MIS Quarterly, 30*(2), 291–314.

Syrus, P. (85–43 BC). Maxim 108. Sententiae, http://quoternity.com/quotations/Publilius_Syrus

Tekisalp, E. (August 29, 20018). Understanding web 3 – A user controlled internet [Blog]. Coinbase. https://blog.coinbase.com/understanding-web-3-a-user-controlled-internet-a39c21cf83f3

Tempest, M. (February 9, 2005). Treasury papers reveal cost of Black Wednesday. *The Guardian*, https://www.theguardian.com/politics/2005/feb/09/freedomofinformation.uk1

Thomson Reuters. (October 25, 2017). Cryptocurrencies by Country. Thomsom Reuters Blog, https://blogs.thomsonreuters.com/answerson/world-cryptocurrencies-country/

Tiemann, M. (October 1, 2002). History of the OSI. Open Source Initiative. (retrieved 7/31/20).

Timeling of File Sharing. (August 17, 2020). In Wikipedia, https://en.wikipedia.org/wiki/Timeline_of_file_sharing

Towers of Bologna (September 15, 2020). In Wikipedia, https://en.wikipedia.org/wiki/Towers_of_Bologna

Treib, O., Bahr, H., & Falkner, G. (November 17, 2005). Modes of Governance: A Note Towards Conceptual Clarification. European Governance Papers, No. N-05-02, https://www.ihs.ac.at/publications/lib/ep6.pdf

Trenerry, Ch.F. (1926). *The Origin and Early History of Insurance: Including the Contract of Bottomry*. P.S. King and Song, Ltd.

Tribune Wire Reports. (August 21, 2015). Experts: Deleted Online Information Never Actually Goes Away. *The Chicago Tribune*. https://www.chicagotribune.com/business/blue-sky/chi-deleted-online-information-never-goes-away-20150821-story.html

Tron, V., Fischer, A., Nagy, D., Felfoldi, Z., & Johnson, N. (2016). Swap, Swear and Swindle: Incentive System for Swarm [Orange paper]. Ethersphere. https://ethersphere.github.io/swarm-home/ethersphere/orange-papers/1/sw%5E3.pdf

U.N. Charter art. 2, para.4.

Underwood, B. (September 18, 2018). Virtual Markets: Integrity Report. Office of the New York State Attorney General. https://virtualmarkets.ag.ny.gov/

Ungerleider, N. (August 25, 2014). How Fast Food Chains Pick Their Next Location. *Fast Company*, https://www.fastcompany.com/3034792/how-fast-food-chains-pick-their-next-location

von Mises, L. (1949). *Human Action*. Yale University Press.

Wardle, J. & Bassett, J. (April 18, 2017). Looking Back at r/Place. Reddit Blog, https://redditblog.com/2017/04/18/place-part-two/

Watson, B. (translator and editor). (1967). *Basic Writings of Mo Tzu, Hsun Tzu, and Han Fei Tzu*. Columbia University Press.

Weber, S. (2004). *The Success of Open Source*. Harvard University Press, pp. 38–44. (More details on most of the history in this section is reviewed in History of free and open source software. [July 31, 2020]. In Wikipedia, https://en.wikipedia.org/wiki/History_of_free_and_open-source_software).

Williams, D. (2014). *Condorcet and Modernity*. Cambridge University.

Williams, S. (2002). *Free as in Freedom: Richard Stallman's Crusade for Free Software*. O'Reilly Media.

Wright, J. (director), Schur, M. (writer), & Jones, R. (writer). (2016, October 21). Nosedive (Season 3, Episode 1). In Brooker, C. & Jones, A (Executive Producers), *Black Mirror*. Netflix.

Xiangming, Z. (2002). On Two Ancient Chinese Administrative Ideas: Rule of Virtue and Rule by Law. *Culture Mandala: The Bulletin of the Centre for East-West Cultural and Economic Studies, 5* (1), Article 7.

Yakowicz, W. (September 20, 2013). Cash Costs U.S. Businesses $40 Billion a Year. Inc., https://www.inc.com/will-yakowicz/dealing-with-cash-costs-american-businesses-55-billion.html

Zagaris, B. (2018). U.S. Bans Venezuela's New Cryptocurrency and Adds 3 Officials to Sanctions List. *International Enforcement Law Reporter, 34*(3), 157–161.

Zamfir. V. (March 10, 2018). Governance 101 [Conference presentation]. Ethereum Community Conference, Paris, France. https://youtu.be/w8DjFbCTjus

Index

https://doi.org/10.1515/9783110673937-013

Printed in the USA
CPSIA information can be obtained
at www.ICGtesting.com
CBHW061245021223
2267CB00008B/31